T0244202

A QUIET COMPANY
OF DANGEROUS MEN

A QUIET COMPANY OF DANGEROUS MEN

The Forgotten British Special Operations Soldiers of World War II

SHANNON MONAGHAN

VIKING

VIKING
An imprint of Penguin Random House LLC
penguinrandomhouse.com

Grateful acknowledgment is made for permission to print the following:

Excerpts and photos from the papers of Julian Amery,
Churchill Centre Archives, used with permission of Leo Amery.

Excerpts from the private papers of Peter Kemp at the
Imperial War Museums used with permission of Ian Kemp.

Excerpts from the private papers of Billy McLean at the
Imperial War Museums used with permission of Marina Cobbold.

Excerpts and photos from the private papers of David Smiley
used with permission of Xan Smiley.

Photos on insert pages 1, top left and bottom; 2, top and middle; 3, middle and bottom;
4, top, middle, and bottom; and 5, middle, from the papers of Julian Amery,
Churchill Archives Centre. All other insert photos from the private papers of David Smiley.

Maps by Jeffrey L. Ward

LIBRARY OF CONGRESS CATALOGING-IN-PUBLICATION DATA
Names: Monaghan, Shannon, author.
Title: A quiet company of dangerous men: the forgotten British Special
Operations soldiers of World War II / Shannon Monaghan.
Other titles: Forgotten British Special Operations soldiers of World War II
Description: New York: Viking, [2024] | Includes bibliographical references and index.
Identifiers: LCCN 2024011748 (print) | LCCN 2024011749 (ebook) |
ISBN 9780593491225 (hardcover) | ISBN 9780593491232 (ebook)
Subjects: LCSH: Great Britain. Special Operations Executive—Biography. |
World War, 1939–1945—Secret service—Great Britain. | Kemp, Peter, 1915-1993. |
Smiley, David, 1916-2009. | Amery, Julian, 1919–1996. |
McLean, Billy, 1918–1986. | Cold War. | Spies—Great Britain—Biography. |
Spies—Great Britain—History—20th century.
Classification: LCC D810.S7 M5383 2024 (print) | LCC D810.S7 (ebook) |
DDC 940.54/8641—dc23/eng/20240328
LC record available at https://lccn.loc.gov/2024011748
LC ebook record available at https://lccn.loc.gov/2024011749

Printed in the United States of America
1st Printing

Book design by Daniel Lagin

For Imogen

All men dream: but not equally. Those who dream by night in the dusty recesses of their minds wake in the day to find that it was vanity: but the dreamers of the day are dangerous men, for they may act their dream with open eyes, to make it possible. This I did.

—T. E. Lawrence, *Seven Pillars of Wisdom*

CONTENTS

•

A NOTE ON SPELLING

The men in this book ranged in their rich lives across places that have since seen changes in borders, governance, and even language. As such, the spellings and even choices of names are not necessarily obvious. In all things, I have aimed for both familiarity and clarity. I have given preference to spellings contemporaneous with the times to avoid aggressive intervention in the original source material. But the making of such choices is an imperfect science, and as Edward Gibbon wrote of the same conundrum, "In these, and in a thousand examples, the shades of distinction are often minute; and I can feel, where I cannot explain, the motives of my choice."

CAST OF CHARACTERS

Julian Amery: An SOE officer, Amery was dropped into Albania in 1944 with Billy McLean (a former Eton classmate of his) and David Smiley.

Peter Kemp: A Spanish Civil War veteran, Kemp served in the Commandos and in SOE.

Billy McLean: Originally an officer in the Royal Scots Greys and later in SOE, McLean served in Abyssinia and led the "Concensus" missions into Albania.

David Smiley: An officer in the Royal Horse Guards, Smiley served in North Africa and the Middle East before dropping into Albania with SOE.

In Albania and Yugoslavia

Josip "Tito" Broz: The leader of the Communist Partisans in Yugoslavia, he became that country's dictator.

Edmund "Trotsky" Davies: A career officer with experience on the North-West Frontier, Davies was dropped to McLean and Smiley to oversee the expanding missions in Albania.

Alan Hare: A cavalry officer serving in SOE, Hare was dropped into Albania with Davies.

John Hibberdine: Peter Kemp's partner in Kosovo, Hibberdine was an SOE officer who also served on the Kra Isthmus with Billy Moss.

Enver Hoxha: Leader of the Albanian Communist Party, he later became dictator of Albania until his death in 1985.

Mehmet Hoxha: Of no relation to Enver, he was head of the Kosovar Communists, a group known as the Kosmet.

Bill Hudson: An SOE officer whom Amery delivered to Montenegro by submarine. He was also Peter Kemp's companion in Berane and leader of their mission in Poland.

Abas Kupi: The Albanian warlord of the Mati, Kupi was the leader of the Zogists, those supporting the exiled King Zog.

Frederick Nosi: A committed Communist and Enver Hoxha's spy inside McLean's camp in Albania.

George Seymour: A cavalry officer, he jumped into Albania just ahead of Kemp, with whom he later shared a tent.

Mehmet Shehu: The military mind behind the Albanian Communists, Shehu was Enver Hoxha's second-in-command. Like Kemp, he was a veteran of the Spanish Civil War but from the opposite side.

King Zog: The wily, self-made king of the Albanians was exiled as a result of the Italian invasion in 1939.

At the SOE Staff Office

Basil Davidson: A journalist by training, he was also an SOE officer and an associate of James Klugmann's.

Margaret "Fanny" Hasluck: An expert on Albania, she joined SOE early and was Amery's partner in establishing intelligence networks within the country.

Cleveland Mervyn "Bolo" Keble: A disgraced military intelligence officer, he became head of SOE Cairo.

James Klugmann: A member of SOE's Cairo and Bari staff offices, Klugmann was a committed Communist and worked to shift British policy toward exclusive support of the Communists in the Balkans.

Philip Leake: A former schoolmaster in his forties, Leake was head of SOE's Albanian Country Section.

Eliot Watrous: Philip Leake's very young and inexperienced successor as head of SOE's Albanian Country Section.

In Thailand

Aaron Bank: An American OSS officer dropped into Thailand in 1945; he actively supported the Viet Minh against the French.

Edith Fournier: François Klotz's wireless operator, Fournier was a French officer who served in both France and Thailand.

John Hedley: The "Mad Major" and intelligence officer extraordinaire was an old Burma hand who fought with the Chindits and helped Smiley disarm the Japanese in Thailand.

François Klotz: A French officer in an SOE-like unit, he was Peter Kemp's partner in Thailand.

Pridi Phanomyong ("Ruth"): Sometimes also referred to by his conferred title, Luang Pradit Manutham, he was the officially collaborative regent of Thailand and the head of the resistance in that country.

Rowland Winn: Winn served with SOE in Albania and Thailand; he won an MC in the Korean War.

In Yemen and Oman

Muhammad al-Badr: He was the last imam of Yemen, and it was his government that McLean, Amery, and Smiley helped support in the 1960s.

Talib bin Ali: An insurgent military leader in Oman, he was Smiley's enemy during the assault on the Jebel Akhdar in 1958.

Others

Catherine Amery: Daughter of former prime minister Harold Macmillan, wife of Julian Amery, and mother of four children.

Simon Courtauld: A barrister by training, he accompanied McLean on his raid to spring an Algerian dissident from jail in the 1960s.

Xan Fielding: One of Smiley's closest friends, he was also an SOE officer, serving in Crete and France. He later joined MI6.

Peter Fleming: Older brother to Ian Fleming, author of the James Bond series of spy novels, Peter ran the D Division's deception operations in Asia.

Sandy Glen: A naval intelligence attaché to SOE, Glen was Amery's friend (and recruiter). He served in the Arctic and in the Balkans.

Cynthia Kemp: Peter Kemp's second wife, she was a kind and lovely woman who enjoyed gardening. She divorced Kemp after twelve years of marriage.

Patrick "Paddy" Leigh Fermor: SOE officer and cofounder of the original Tara, he planned a mission in Crete to capture a German general with Billy Moss.

Daška McLean: Known as "the Pearl of Dubrovnik," she was Billy McLean's wife. Previously married, she had four children with her first husband.

Billy Moss: Leigh Fermor's right-hand man during the Crete raid. He was McLean and Smiley's conducting officer in Cairo, and he invited them to live at Tara.

Harold "Perks" Perkins: Head of SOE's Polish Country Section, he sent Peter Kemp into Poland. After the war, he joined MI6 and was involved in the 1949 Albanian operation, among others.

Kim Philby: The most infamous member of the Cambridge Five spy ring, he was a long-standing mole who nearly made it to the very top of MI6.

Hilda Elizabeth "Lizzie" Phillips: Peter Kemp's first wife, who divorced him in order to marry George Seymour.

Moy Smiley: David Smiley's wife, she was a formidable woman who served as a cipher clerk during the war. She reprised that role during the 1949 Albanian operation. She had two children from her first marriage and two with Smiley.

Sophie Tarnowska: The beautiful Polish countess of Tara who had flirtations with both David Smiley and Xan Fielding but ultimately chose to marry Billy Moss.

MISSIONS IN ALBANIA, 1943–44

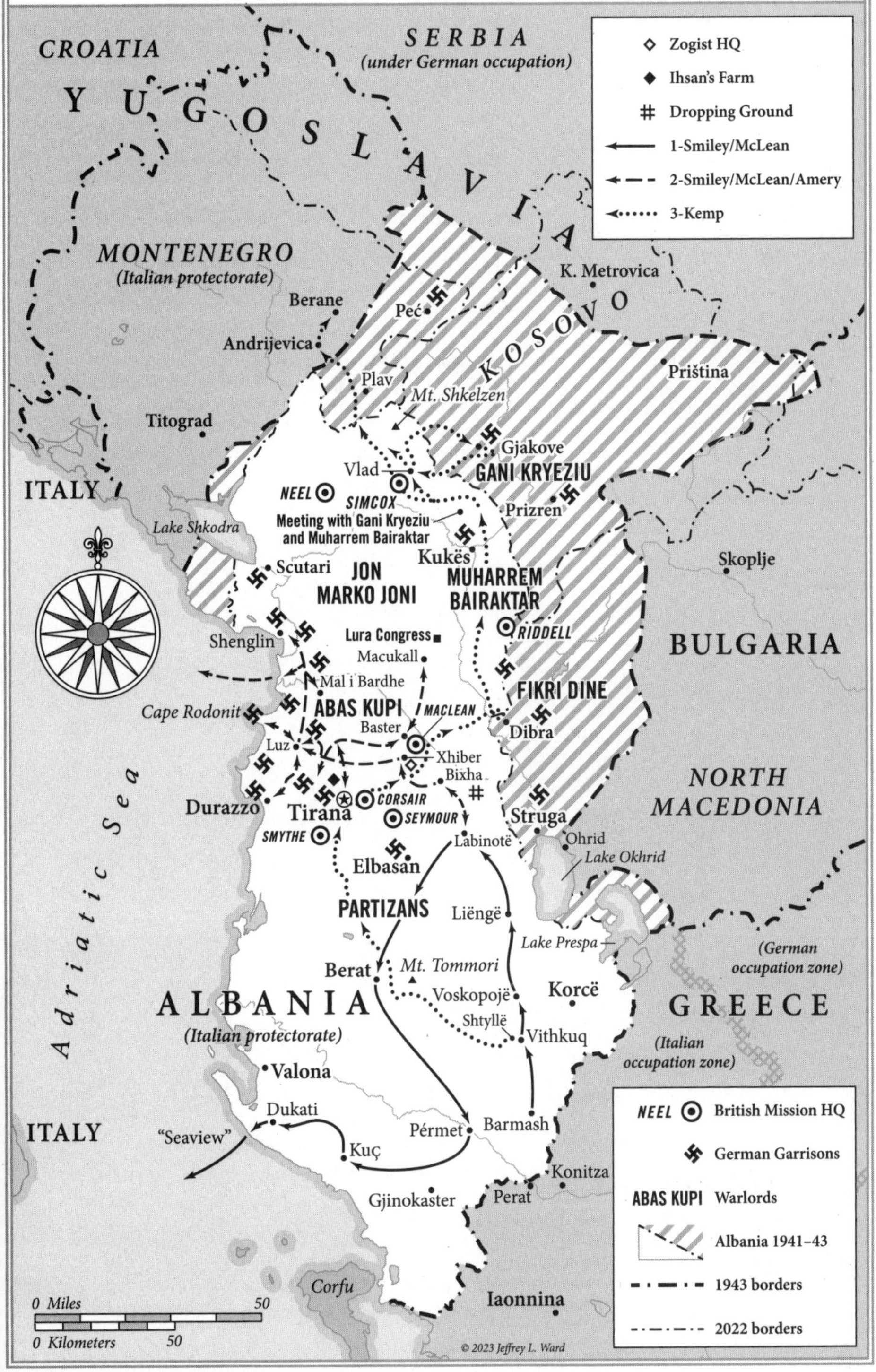
CROATIA
SERBIA
(under German occupation)
YUGOSLAVIA
MONTENEGRO
(Italian protectorate)
KOSOVO
Zogist HQ
Ihsan's Farm
Dropping Ground
1-Smiley/McLean
2-Smiley/McLean/Amery
3-Kemp
K. Metrovica
Berane
Peć
Andrijevica
Plav
Mt. Shkelzen
Priština
Titograd
Gjakove
Vlad
GANI KRYEZIU
ITALY
NEEL
SIMCOX
Meeting with Gani Kryeziu
and Muharrem Bairaktar
Prizren
Lake Shkodra
Kukës
Skoplje
Scutari
JON
MARKO JONI
MUHARREM
BAIRAKTAR
RIDDELL
BULGARIA
Lura Congress
Shenglin
Macukall
Mal i Bardhe
FIKRI DINE
Cape Rodonit
ABAS KUPI
MACLEAN
Baster
Dibra
Luz
Xhiber
Bixha
NORTH
MACEDONIA
Durazzo
Tirana
CORSAIR
SEYMOUR
Struga
SMYTHE
Labinotë
Ohrid
Lake Okhrid
Adriatic Sea
Elbasan
PARTIZANS
Liëngë
Lake Prespa
(German
occupation zone)
Berat
Mt. Tommori
Korcë
Voskopojë
ALBANIA
(Italian protectorate)
Shtyllë
GREECE
Vithkuq
(Italian
occupation zone)
Valona
Dukati
ITALY
"Seaview"
Pérmet
Barmash
NEEL British Mission HQ
German Garrisons
Kuç
Konitza
ABAS KUPI Warlords
Gjinokaster
Perat
Albania 1941–43
Corfu
1943 borders
Iaonnina
0 Miles 50
0 Kilometers 50
2022 borders
© 2023 Jeffrey L. Ward

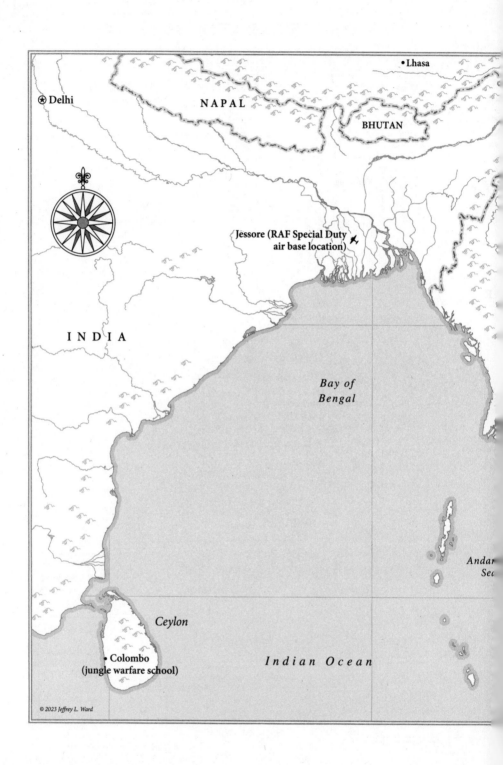

Lhasa

Delhi

NAPAL

BHUTAN

Jessore (RAF Special Duty
air base location)

INDIA

Bay of
Bengal

Andar
Sea

Ceylon

Colombo
(jungle warfare school)

Indian Ocean

© 2023 Jeffrey L. Ward

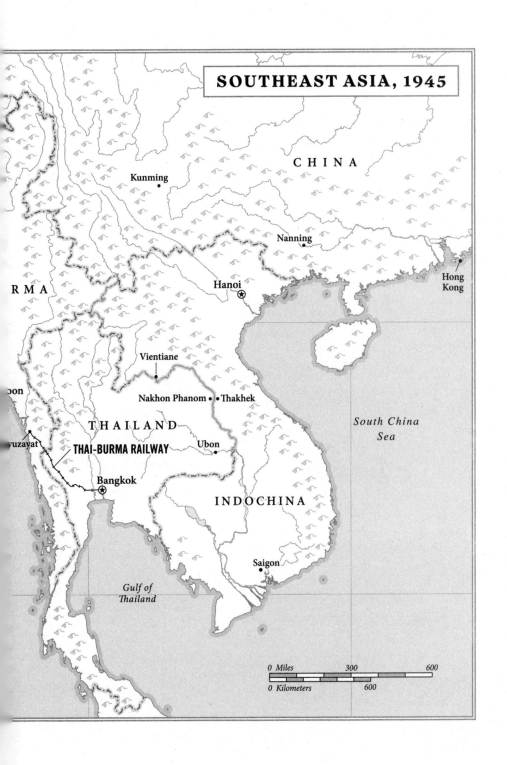

SOUTHEAST ASIA, 1945

CHINA

Kunming

Nanning

Hanoi

Hong Kong

R M A

Vientiane

Nakhon Phanom • • Thakhek

THAILAND

on

uzayat

THAI-BURMA RAILWAY

Ubon

South China
Sea

Bangkok

INDOCHINA

Saigon

Gulf of
Thailand

0 Miles   300   600

0 Kilometers   600

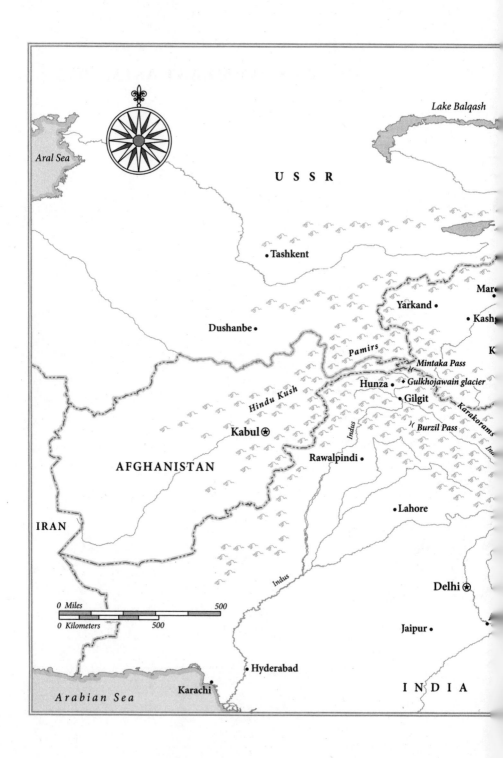

Lake Balqash

Aral Sea

U S S R

Tashkent

Mar

Yarkand

Kash

Dushanbe

Pamirs

Mintaka Pass

K

Hunza   Gulkhojawain glacier

Gilgit

Hindu Kush

Karakorams

Burzil Pass

Indus

Kabul

AFGHANISTAN

Rawalpindi

Lahore

IRAN

0 Miles   500

0 Kilometers   500

Indus

Delhi

Jaipur

Hyderabad

Arabian Sea

Karachi

I N D I A

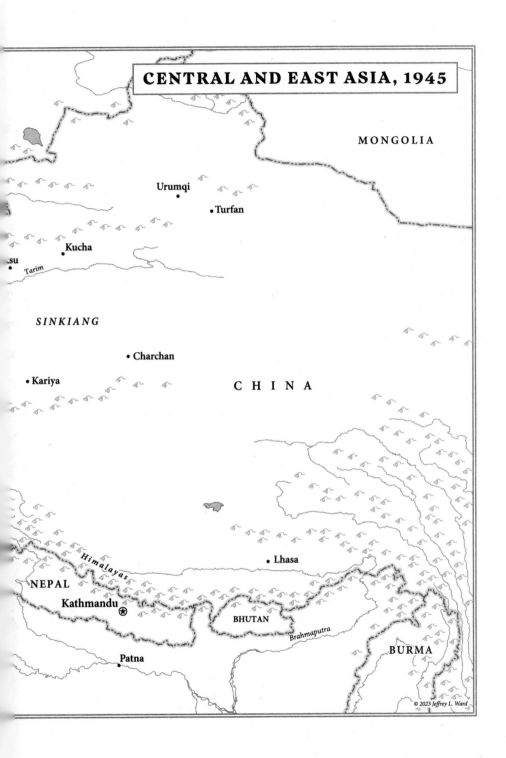

CENTRAL AND EAST ASIA, 1945

MONGOLIA

Urumqi

Turfan

Kucha

.su

Tarim

SINKIANG

Charchan

Kariya

CHINA

Himalayas

Lhasa

NEPAL

Kathmandu ⊛

BHUTAN

Brahmaputra

BURMA

Patna

© 2023 Jeffrey L. Ward

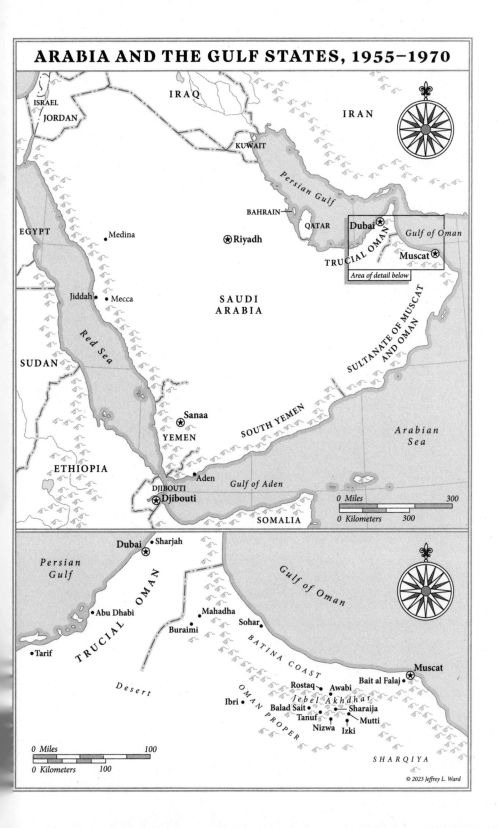

ARABIA AND THE GULF STATES, 1955–1970

ISRAEL
JORDAN
IRAQ
IRAN

KUWAIT

Persian Gulf

EGYPT

Medina

BAHRAIN
QATAR
Dubai
Gulf of Oman

Riyadh

TRUCIAL OMAN
Muscat

Area of detail below

Jiddah • Mecca

SAUDI
ARABIA

Red Sea

SULTANATE OF MUSCAT
AND OMAN

SUDAN

Sanaa

YEMEN

SOUTH YEMEN

*Arabian
Sea*

ETHIOPIA

Aden

DJIBOUTI
Djibouti

Gulf of Aden

SOMALIA

0 Miles 300
0 Kilometers 300

---

*Persian
Gulf*

Dubai • Sharjah

TRUCIAL OMAN

Gulf of Oman

• Abu Dhabi

Mahadha
Sohar

Buraimi

BATINA COAST

• Tarif

Desert

Rostaq
Awabi
Bait al Falaj •
Muscat

Ibri

Jebel Akhdhar

OMAN PROPER

Balad Sait • Sharaija
Tanuf • Mutti
Nizwa Izki

SHARQIYA

0 Miles 100
0 Kilometers 100

© 2023 Jeffrey L. Ward

INTRODUCTION

At a private dinner with family and friends in the midst of the Blitz in 1941, Winston Churchill was asked how British forces were going to get back into Europe. They were alone. Dunkirk had been evacuated, France had fallen, the Luftwaffe was overhead, and the Americans were nowhere to be seen.

The prime minister picked up an orange from the table. He said that if he were a worm and wanted to get into the piece of fruit, he would bide his time and go on walking around it. He might have to wait until a rotted hole appeared, but he would get in somehow, if he did not starve first.

It was an apt metaphor for the year in which Britain stood alone, a desperate time with no clear end in sight. It is also an apt metaphor for the story of this book: the story of four men—one of whom was at that dinner with Churchill—who fought together behind enemy lines throughout the Second World War in North Africa, Europe, and Asia and then together continued to serve, officially and unofficially, for decades after. Often, they found themselves in the hot parts of the Cold War. They were a real British "Band of Brothers," operating in settings whose complexity rivaled that of a John le Carré spy novel yet were nevertheless true. Theirs is the story of the twentieth century—one of determination and daring, betrayal and loss, friendship and loyalty—in the most personal of terms.

Their story has all the heroism and courage expected of a great World War II tale, but it has fallen by the wayside until now, despite a cast of characters that includes Nazis, Churchill himself, the Viet Minh, Soviet moles, MI6, and Ian Fleming's older brother (to name just a few). Our heroes—the Spanish Civil War veteran Peter Kemp, the demolitions expert David Smiley, the born guerrilla leader Billy McLean, and the political natural Julian Amery—joined one of Britain's earliest and most exciting special-operations units: the Special Operations Executive, or SOE. The unit's job was, in Churchill's words, to "set Europe ablaze": to foment local revolt, gather intelligence, blow up bridges, organize active resistance, and do anything that could help disrupt the Axis cause. Think Lawrence of Arabia but with countless missions across multiple continents. These men conducted their work through persuasion and by bribery. They traded in the only currencies that mattered: solid-gold sovereigns and deliveries of weapons, parachuted in from the heavens.

In 1943, these four men were dropped behind enemy lines into Nazi-occupied Albania with the mission of organizing, training, and leading resistance forces. Albania may be small, but its value to the Allies during the war was outsize: the Germans had thirty divisions in the Balkans. A small group of highly trained men could help tie down significant portions of nearly half a million soldiers, crucial reinforcements that Hitler was trying to move back into Europe to fight the Red Army. Their job was to punch above their weight.

Kemp, Smiley, McLean, and Amery overlapped and worked with some of the most elite special-operations units of their time. At the beginning of the war, Peter Kemp trained David Stirling, the man who in 1941 founded the Special Air Service, or the SAS. Kemp had served in Spain with men who joined what may be the most effective special-operations unit in history: the Long Range Desert Group. Smiley and

Kemp both served in the Commandos; McLean, in Orde Wingate's
Gideon Force. Amery started on the intelligence side early, joining a
precursor to SOE. During a period of leave in London, Smiley briefed
American Jedburgh teams. In Thailand, Smiley and Kemp worked with
the American Office of Strategic Services (OSS), the forerunner to both
the Green Berets and the CIA. They were supplied with special tools
from a place called the Museum, the real-life inspiration behind Q's
gadget shop, which cooked up an exploding pen and tricked-out Aston
Martin in the James Bond franchise. (Smiley was given a briefcase bomb.
It was supposed to burn papers; it blew up in his face.)

In Albania, they found plenty of Germans. They also found Albanian nationalist resisters and Communist partisans, the latter of whom
were often more interested in attacking the former than in attacking the
Axis. In the middle of the Second World War, they saw the makings of
the Cold War taking shape right before their eyes. Kemp saw more in-
klings of the next conflict when he served in Poland at the end of the
European war; Amery and McLean saw yet other signs in different parts
of China. The problem followed Kemp and Smiley to Thailand, where
they tried to liberate POWs from the Japanese in 1945 as a civil war raged
around them, complicated by the arrival of the Viet Minh.

After the war, Smiley stayed in the army. Amery and McLean became MPs in the British Parliament. Kemp officially worked as a life-
insurance salesman. But unlike most of the men of their generation who
came home in 1945, they kept fighting. In 1949, they were involved in an
attempt to pull a Bay of Pigs–style invasion of Albania (more than a decade before the actual Bay of Pigs). They took on various intelligence
and military roles in Poland, Hungary, Oman, and Yemen. There were
excursions to Congo during its early decolonization crises; to Southeast
Asia; to South America; to the Middle East. All told, they had a hand in
some of the biggest events of the twentieth century—the fight against
Hitler and Stalin, obviously, but also the Hungarian Revolution, the Algerian Revolution, the Suez Crisis, the Vietnam War, decolonization in

Africa and the Middle East, and even, at the very end, the Soviet invasion of Afghanistan.

Their story embodies the old saying of truth being stranger than
fiction. For all the seeming absurdities (solid-gold coins, exploding
briefcases), they were serious people. They were always volunteers. Their
experiences of the Second World War affirm many of our common
assumptions—the bravery of exceptional men in the face of incompre-
hensible danger—but also challenge our lazy beliefs about the nature of
the conflict. In what is so often pitched as a simple war against good and
evil, these men often found themselves behind enemy lines in complex
situations, where the locals were threatened by multiple enemies and
the Second World War revealed itself to be more accurately described
as several different wars. Not for nothing, many of the places where they
risked their necks are still in the news today as sites of political tension,
if not outright war: Xinjiang, the Balkans, the Tigray and Amhara regions of what is now Ethiopia, and even Poland and the former satellites
of the old Soviet Union, now staring down renewed threats from the imperialist Russian menace.

And that menace was real, even during the war, when the Soviets
were nominally allies of the West. The SOE team was hindered by a Soviet mole in its own staff office and by a host of fellow travelers whose
wishful thinking blinded them to the true nature of their Communist
ally. There were bad parachutes, mysterious deaths, and information
that went straight to the headquarters of one of Stalin's Balkan minions.

Like everyone else, Smiley, McLean, Kemp, and Amery knew that
they had signed up to fight a big war. But like few others, they sensed the
next conflict brewing under their noses—what would become the Cold
War, while the fight against Hitler was still in its earlier stages. They suffered at the hands of others' deluded hopes about the intentions and ambitions of the Russians, a sad handicap that would continue to burden
the West in the decades to come, and that arguably still does today.

———

IT IS OFTEN LAZILY SAID THAT IT WAS STALIN WHO BEAT HITLER, BUT in 1940, Stalin was still Hitler's ally. The Second World War was long, and the ultimate results hinged just as much on the beginning as on the end. In 1941, when Churchill picked up that orange, Stalin stood with Hitler. Britain resisted alone: bearing the Blitz, enraging the Führer, and buying time for the rest of the world to come to its senses. For much of the Cold War, these men struggled similarly, fighting against the obvious enemy, as well as the sad examples of traitors on their own side. They fought an uphill battle against an enemy who had once been their ally but had turned on them even before the war was over. (Kemp was imprisoned in Poland by the NKVD in 1945; in 1944, the future Communist dictator of Albania attempted to imprison McLean and Smiley and try them in what he called a "Partisan military court.")

Kemp, Smiley, McLean, and Amery fought against totalitarianism for nearly half a century. Theirs was not an easy journey. They lost brothers, friends, and comrades. Old souls to begin with, they grew old before their time. They had their own children, but they also raised those of other men. They became their own family. They stood as best men at each other's weddings. And, in the end, they gave the eulogies at each other's funerals.

Pericles said that "famous men have the whole earth as their memorial." These men were not famous. The nature of their secretive work ensured it. But they fought for a better world, to which we are grateful heirs. For both their actions and their example, we owe them more than we realize. This is their story.

A QUIET COMPANY

OF DANGEROUS MEN

CHAPTER 1

A RUGGED NURSE
OF SAVAGE MEN

———————————————————————

His feet dangling through the hole in the floor of the British Hali-
fax bomber, David Smiley was enchanted by the twinkling lights
of the villages below, and by the snow on the mountaintops. The blacked-
out windows of the bomber had prevented any previous glimpse of the
ground. The scene distracted him from his fear. It was April 17, 1943. Two
thousand feet below him was Nazi-occupied Greece, close to the border
with Albania.

Now a captain, Smiley had started his military career in the Royal
Horse Guards, known as "the Blues," which remained his official army
unit. That had been an elegant, but mostly ceremonial, posting. In
peacetime, half the year was spent at Buckingham Palace, the other "on
foreign service across the Serpentine" at Windsor Castle. The Blues
looked formidable, but they expected to fire all of eighteen shots a year
in practice.

Smiley had first deployed to the Middle East with the Blues but had
then joined a newly raised Commando unit famous for its silently lethal
knuckleduster-handled knives. With them, he'd fought in the Abyssinian campaign against the Italians, in present-day Ethiopia, where the
League of Nations had failed to stop Mussolini's 1935 invasion.

In Abyssinia, the No. 52 Middle East Commando in which Smiley served had traveled through Sudan, encountering on the way rhinos, leopards, bush and water bucks, chimpanzees and baboons (the latter of which caused no end of trouble for anyone on guard duty), and crocodiles. There were also parakeets and—as Smiley couldn't help but notice—plenty of game birds, such as guinea fowl, sandgrouse, and francolins. Smiley and the company sergeant major went out one morning with a shotgun and brought back enough guinea fowl to treat the whole commando to breakfast.

In the Abyssinian campaign, the enemy was called the Banda Torelli, part of the guerrilla forces of Italian East Africa commanded by the wily Amedeo Guillet, whom the British called "the Devil Commander," and not only for his razor-sharp mustache. A dashing Italian nobleman, he was a cavalryman to the core, partial to a sword, a pistol, and a white horse. Fighting often took the form of tracking and ambushes, with both regular and unusual weapons. The wildlife, and the six-foot-tall elephant grass, added a foreboding feel to the landscape. A patrol could be quietly moving along one moment and completely lit up the next. That strange noise could simply be a bird never heard before. It could also be a sniper in a tree, as once happened on one of Smiley's patrols.

When that sniper dropped out of the branches, Smiley's commando quickly realized that it had come into contact with a significant force. Bullets whizzed overhead, the men threw grenades, and Smiley gave two orders: one directing the man bearing the Bren, a light machine gun, to spray the elephant grass ahead of them, through which they could see nothing, and another asking all of his men to execute a right hook, which would prevent encirclement.

The grass went up in flames. Whether it was from the grenades, the firing, or arson, no one knew. The Italian force had fled; one of Smiley's officers said he had seen them retreating, about fifty Abyssinian troops in all, commanded by an Italian officer on a white horse—possibly Guillet himself. Smiley had fired his pistol but hadn't connected.

His Bren gunner had. A wounded Abyssinian fighter lay on the ground, in agony from the burst that had caught him in the stomach. He was making terrible noises and had no hope of survival. The commando had no medic and no means of evacuation. (Orders in those days were to leave even their own wounded behind, so as not to slow down the unit.) The brush fire was now getting serious. To leave the wounded man would be to consign him to either death by suffocation or death by being burned alive.

A debate ensued, but the decision came down to the captain. Smiley gave permission to one of his sergeants to "finish him off." As he later put it, "A shot through the head put an end to his suffering, but it was a horrible decision for me to make. In retrospect I feel I did the right thing." It had been his very first fight.

YEARS LATER, HIGH IN THE SKIES ABOVE NAZI-OCCUPIED GREECE, DA-vid Smiley was about to descend into another fight. The V-shaped signal fires that the Greek guerrilla fighters had lit for the British planes came into view. The pilot switched on the red warning light for action stations. It was half an hour to midnight when the light switched to green and the dispatcher shouted, "Go!" The dispatcher slapped the back of the officer in front of Smiley: the signal to drop.

This was Billy McLean. He was a major, in command of the small group of men on the airplane. In addition to Smiley, this consisted of a lieutenant and a few NCOs, including the wireless operator. Hand-picked from the elite regiments of the British military, these men were now all on loan to the Special Operations Executive, known as SOE, a new outfit operating outside the Army's traditional chain of command.

Smiley and McLean had met on a sweltering troopship (cabin temperatures had reached a balmy 123 degrees) in 1940, when both were trying to join the Somaliland Camel Corps, which they thought would get them into the fight as quickly as possible. A genteel Scot and fellow graduate of the Royal Military Academy Sandhurst who, like Smiley, had until lately been an officer in one of His Majesty's most prestigious old regiments, McLean was an officer in the Royal Scots Greys, still best known for their charge at the Battle of Waterloo.

McLean was tall and calm, and very few who ever met him failed to add the descriptor "languid." Raised as a quintessential English gentleman, he was actually the child of a wealthy and quite long-standing Scottish family with impressive and far-flung martial antecedents. It was said that he was related to the man who had once served as the commander of the armies of the sultan of Morocco. McLean was adventurous, charming, and far less contained than he looked. He cut an impressive physical figure, not just because of his height but because of an enviable widow's peak that added both dash and a look of wisdom to his twenty-four years.

He bore, in talent if not in material appearance, a sharp resemblance to another British officer whom he, and all his companions, held in the highest regard: T. E. Lawrence, better known as Lawrence of Arabia. Lawrence had helped organize the Arab Revolt behind enemy lines during the First World War and perfected the guerrilla tactics of blowing up railroad tracks and ambushing the crucial train lines that supplied the Arabian Peninsula. Lawrence was also a gifted Arabist and archaeologist with fluency in his operational language and a well-honed ability to tease his British superiors.

McLean possessed experience unlike that of most men in the British army: he had led guerrilla operations staffed by locally recruited troops. Like Smiley, McLean had also fought in Abyssinia. (Neither had managed to serve with the Camel Corps.) McLean had joined Orde Wingate's Gideon Force. He had already begun learning Arabic during his first deployment, which sent him to Palestine. When he arrived in Abyssinia, he began to work on Amharic. (His tutor, somehow a Czech, was "unintelligible in fourteen languages other than English.") Not only did this allow McLean to chat up locals who could provide information that would make his troops' mortar fire more accurate, but it also meant that he was good at collecting native soldiers who were deserting from the Italians.

After the successful British capture of the city of Debra Tabor in Abyssinia, McLean was made into a temporary captain in command of 950 men, including his own British troops but mostly local former Italian colonials. They called the unit McLean's 79th Foot. With these troops, he was part of the final assaults of the East African campaign on the ancient city of Gondar in Amhara, close to the borders of the province of Tigray. On November 27, 1941, the day before his twenty-third birthday, he and his local shock force were among the first to break into the city. A newsreel from the time cracked that Gondar had added "Italian relics in the form of prisoners" to its cultural collections.

A fellow officer who bumped into McLean after the fall of Gondar and had not seen him since the beginning of the campaign wrote: "He now looked twice his size and twice his age, with a great yellow beard and hair falling to his neck—the reincarnation on the wet Amhara hills of some Gaelic chieftain of the Atlantic isles." As the brigadier who recommended him to SOE had put it, "This officer is a born leader of 'irregulars' and should not be left to cool his heels in the Middle East, if there are similar jobs to be done."

THERE HAVE ALWAYS BEEN SPECIAL WARRIORS; ACHILLES AND HIS MYR-midons are the obvious classical examples. What we now think of as "special operations," however, were born in the Second World War. That conflict saw the development of the Special Air Service (SAS), the Special Boat Service (SBS), the Long Range Desert Group (LRDG), the Commandos, and the Chindits—and those are just among the British. In the United States, it produced the 101st Airborne, the 82nd Airborne, Merrill's Marauders, and the OSS. Special operations *are* special, but more for the people than for the missions. They are almost always small teams operating in extreme conditions. Current military jargon calls them "force multipliers." They are more than the sum of their parts.

One British brigadier once suggested, in jest but not without cause, that the man who founded the SAS should have a Distinguished Flying Cross, an award given to fighter pilots, because his men had destroyed more enemy airplanes than anyone else. The most valuable intelligence concerning the war in the desert came from the LRDG, which kept up a small watch on the only road that the Axis could use to move men and material. The Commandos did impossible raids in the English Channel and on the French coast; the Chindits harried the Japanese in Burma.

SOE was formed in 1940 to expand Britain's capacity in the department of unequal combat; there simply wasn't enough capacity at that moment to fight the Germans head-on in the traditional way. To these new operatives went the jobs of intelligence collection and sabotage, of setting ambushes in occupied countries, and of the organization, training, and arming of resistance groups to fight the Axis. With a small number of determined fighters, they could hold down whole divisions, force the Germans to hunt them, move warily, and distrust their safety in their own rear. They could build fifth columns, ready to spring during the future Allied invasion of Europe. It was an effective use of manpower for a relatively small island still under siege and standing alone.

SOE went by many names in its brief life, among them MO4 and Section D. It would have more, including Force 136, used during the war in Asia. It was born in extremis, of scattered parts. One element came from a propaganda wing of the Secret Intelligence Service (SIS), better known as MI6. When told to figure out a way to change public opinion and run secret offensives in enemy countries, the British Army officer who was brought on to run it reflected that "one felt as if one had been told to move the Pyramids with a pin." More than a few fighting tactics were borrowed from the IRA. Two of SOE's early leaders had learned from the frustrating experience of trying to catch Michael Collins and his plainclothes guerrillas, who prosecuted Ireland's war for independence against the British.

The first man tasked with overseeing SOE as a whole was an academic economist whose public title was the Minister for Economic Warfare. He received Churchill's command, when the unit was first established, to "set Europe ablaze." In short, the British Empire was about to create two of the things that it had struggled against for so long: saboteurs and guerrillas. At its height, SOE employed thirteen thousand people across the globe, not including the local manpower needed for packing, transport, and the like. As with most military units, the majority of those people provided support to the men (and some women) in the field, who likely numbered in the low thousands.

These SOE operatives traveled light but had unusual uniforms, which included gear for escape, evasion, bribery, and ambush. Once they landed, they would be navigating on foot. They concealed compasses in their buttons. If those failed, they carried pencil clips that, when balanced on the point of the pencil, would point north. They had files, maps, and money sewn into their clothes. Though they had none of the scientific American K rations, they carried gold in thousand-sovereign bags. Their even more convincing possessions were supplies dropped by air, which included arms and ammunition for anyone willing to fight the Axis.

SOE "liaison officers," as they were called, were borrowed from many storied units, such as McLean's and Smiley's rarefied cavalry regiments. It was an officer-heavy system, and a top-heavy one at that. Each team was assigned a few NCOs and occasionally even a private; these men served as paramilitary experts and as wireless operators. In SOE, the officers got their hands dirty. Smiley liked to shape his own gelignite charges when blowing up bridges, even at the rank of major. In a traditional unit, a major would command a company.

Their training was extensive. Pistol training was done with a British captain who could literally hit an ace of spades at thirty yards with his pearl-handled Colts. They also received demolitions training and parachuting practice. By way of a broadly described "dirty tricks course," the men had been treated to a very special school in escaping, taught by none other than the famous British magician Jasper Maskelyne, then performing for the British Army as a captain. They learned how to identify and operate enemy arms, the assumption being that they would capture some, though hopefully not as a desperate measure of resupply. In the field, they had discretion and independence; they also required a strong dose of self-reliance. When they were dropped in, they had no idea when they would be coming out, or how.

London was the central hub. The day-to-day operations were run out of different "country section" offices, which were located as close as possible to the theaters they were meant to be overseeing. The office in Cairo, which eventually moved to Bari, Italy, after the Allied successes there, oversaw the Balkans. SOE Cairo included country sections for Greece, Yugoslavia, and Albania—the site of McLean and Smiley's assignment in 1943, when the war's tide was just starting to turn.

IF AFGHANISTAN WAS KNOWN AS THE GRAVEYARD OF EMPIRES, ALBANIA should have been known as their football. It is a small country, lying on the sparkling Adriatic almost directly across the Strait of Otranto from the base of the heel of the Italian boot. To the north are the fishermen of Montenegro; to the east, the Macedonians. The Greeks lie to the south. To the northeast is much-contested Kosovo and beyond that the angry irredentists of the region: the Serbs, dominating what was then still Yugoslavia.

Unlike the Serbs, the Albanians are not Slavs. Unlike the Greeks, they are not majority Orthodox. The Romans called them the Illyrians, a name breathed with fear. Nevertheless, they were conquered and absorbed into the Roman Empire. Next came the Byzantines, stepping into Rome's still-warm shoes. The Ottomans arrived afterward, bringing Islam. The Austro-Hungarians took their turn. The Albanians lay ancestral claim to Alexander the Great and Mustafa Kemal Atatürk, dozens of Ottoman pashas and grand viziers, rulers of Egypt and generals of various states and empires, but in two thousand years, only two Albanians have ever ruled Albania.

The country created warriors and intriguers but not statesmen. From the air, Albania looks as though a small, angry child had balled up a piece of stiff felt and thrown it down on the floor, a landscape that the word *craggy* might have been invented to describe. There are plains, but the mountains dominate. This gave its conquering empires headaches. Even Alexander had difficulty with the Albanian terrain. The locals found that the landscape posed no fewer challenges to their own attempts at centralizing control.

Theirs was a tribal society, driven to be so by geography. The mountains of Albania were difficult to access; in a poor country, this meant that it was nearly impossible for the central authority (no matter the era) to project state power into the mountainous regions. Without state power, there was little policing outside the valley cities. That Albania and its people had been the political football of so many invading empires did nothing to cultivate a habit of trust in the central authority. Without policing, problems were settled as they were in the days of the American Wild West and the Hatfields and McCoys: by physical violence.

Even during the Second World War, Albanians recognized little formal law but carefully regulated their relations with a well-respected honor culture. They lived with a level of freedom almost unknown in a modern state. But any violation of the rules of the honor code sparked blood feuds, a violent but effective mechanism in regions where policing (and prisons) held little sway. One Albanian historian noted that a man was not considered a man unless he had taken revenge on anyone who had wronged him; he was, until then, an outcast, with "no dignity, no place amongst decent people." As a British observer put it, the

Albanians understood both power and politics instinctively. Proud, brave, and immensely difficult to organize, they matched their dignity with violence, died "with reluctance rather than regret," and wielded the weapons of realpolitik with a skill that would have impressed Bismarck.

Albania packed a minefield of competing tribal, religious, and political tensions into a small space. There were two main tribes in Albania at the beginning of the twentieth century: the Ghegs, who inhabited the north of the country, and the Tosks, who inhabited the south. In the north, there was a sizable contingent of Roman Catholics; in the south, Eastern Orthodox followers formed most of what was still called the peasantry, though the landlords were usually Muslim, a holdover from the days of Ottoman domination. The center of the country was mostly Muslim, a category complicated by the fact that across Albania there was also the mystical Sufi sect of the Bektashis.

Since 1925, Albania had been ruled by a man who called himself King Zog, a skillful politician in the old Ottoman mold. He was born under Ottoman rule to an influential Gheg family in the country's northern Mati region. Zog volunteered for the Austrians in the First World War, took part in the Albanian independence movement, and joined parliamentary politics. By 1925, he was president. Three years later, he turned Albania into a monarchy and made himself king.

Zog soon found that his weak economy needed a sponsor, and he found one in the Italians. This brought him into Mussolini's imperial orbit, and the Italians tried to turn Albania into a client state. Zog resisted. On Good Friday in 1939, Italy invaded. The invaders timed their arrival to align with the birth of Zog's first child, hoping to catch the new father alongside his incapacitated queen. The royal family escaped, first to Cairo and eventually to London, thanks to a heroic stand in the city of Durazzo led by another Gheg warlord, Zog's second-in-command, a man named Abas Kupi.

As in so many other places throughout Europe, the resistance that sprang up to fight the Axis had its own competing power centers. There were the Zogists, royalist nationalist supporters of the exiled king, led by Kupi. There were the republican nationalists behind the Balli Kombëtar, men who disliked Zog almost as much as they disliked the occupiers. And then there were the Communist Partisans.

This last group was known as the National Liberation Council, abbreviated from the Albanian as the LNÇ. It claimed to be independent and democratic, but the Soviet Communist Party was in control behind the scenes, though the British wouldn't realize that until later in the war. Josip "Tito" Broz's much stronger Communist headquarters in neighboring Yugoslavia overshadowed Albania's Communist movement, though this, too, was not yet understood by the officers working in the field. Through Tito, the lines of control ran to Moscow.

Tito had elevated a man named Enver Hoxha to head the Communist Partisan movement in Albania. Hoxha, in his mid-thirties, had a wide and attractive face with generous lips. He also, as Smiley could not help but note when they met, had an excess of flesh and a poor handshake. Bold and clever, he was diplomatic enough to hide his loathing of the British, though he later admitted in one of his own books that he considered McLean's eyes to be "savage." He insisted on being called Professor, despite having failed to complete a degree with the scholarships he had won to university in France. Later, he would bestow upon himself the grander title of Colonel General.

His second-in-command was Mehmet Shehu, thirty years old, small and dark. Shehu was the military man between the two of them, having fought with fellow Communists in the Spanish Civil War. Impatient, he shared Hoxha's ferocity and Party allegiance.

Albania's tribalism overlaid the political distinctions among the resistance. Historically the more dominant force, the Ghegs, who had fought for Albania's independence against Austrians and Italians alike, sided with the nationalist resistance forces. The Tosks were more likely to turn to Communism. Officially, SOE didn't care whom they supported, so long as they fought the Axis.

IN THE SPRING OF 1943, TINY ALBANIA WAS VALUABLE TO THE ALLIES FOR a host of reasons. Britain no longer stood alone. General Montgomery, better known as Monty, had halted the drive of Field Marshal Erwin Rommel in the Western Desert at El Alamein in Egypt, which had saved the city of Cairo, the Allies' position in Africa and the Mediterranean, and the crucial Suez Canal. The Americans had entered the war, landing in North Africa for Operation Torch. Hitler had destroyed his own Sixth Army at Stalingrad in February 1943, having dragged Stalin into the war by invading the Soviet Union in 1941. The Red Army was now advancing from the east. The Germans were on the defensive.

Albania, with its Adriatic coast, was a potential landing zone for what Churchill called the "soft underbelly" of Europe, a place for the Allies to invade. Even if that option were bypassed, as it would turn out to be, Albania had other charms. The Germans and Italians were occupying the Balkans with thirty divisions, or nearly half a million men. Hitler needed more men to stop the Soviet steamroller, now about to bear down on him from the east. Those men had to come from somewhere, and the geographically logical place from which to take them was the Balkans. If the team commanded by McLean could organize, train, and expand the Albanian resistance, pinning down valuable troops that Hitler desperately needed, its men would more than punch above their weight.

SOE'S BEST INFORMATION ON ALBANIA CAME FROM EARLIER INTELLI-gence work conducted in the region by an elderly woman whom David Smiley later described as having the look of an "old-fashioned English

nanny." Her name was Margaret "Fanny" Hasluck. The widow of a famous archaeologist, she was herself a respected authority on Albanian
folk traditions. Fluent in the language, she was enamored with the complicated, feuding people of Albania. She had lived there for twenty years
but was forced to flee to Istanbul upon the invasion of the Italians, who
suspected her of being a British spy. They were wrong; she hadn't yet offered her aid to British intelligence. She briefed McLean's team and tried
to teach the men a smattering of Albanian to help them get by.

The network of Albanian resistance that Hasluck and the rest of the
intelligence team had developed was busted by the German invasion in
1943. (The Italians, there since 1939, had caused fewer problems.) This
was why McLean and Smiley had to drop into Greece and make their
way to the Albanian border on foot: there were no friendlies available
to receive them. They did not know if there were any friendlies at all.

Smiley followed McLean out of the airplane, slipping through the
hole in the floor. He reminded himself not to lean too far forward on
the way. He knew that many men did so, compensating for either their
eagerness or their nerves. The result was a broken nose.

Smiley dropped. His chute opened easily, and he swayed in the
wind. At one point, he came alarmingly close to McLean, to whom he
shouted a warning. He landed in a rocky creek bottom, tearing a leg
muscle in the process. The pilot had lived up to his excellent reputation:
Smiley landed only five yards from one of the signal fires.

He could hear the gentle jingling of livestock bells on sheep and
goats kept by the local Epirote farmers. Out of the darkness, a bear of
a man appeared. In battle gear and sporting an enormous beard, the
Greek guerrilla swooped down upon the wriggling Smiley, who was still
struggling his way out of the parachute harness. The bear kissed him on
both cheeks, offering a welcome that Smiley admitted was "indeed
Greek to me." Handed a flask of what he assumed to be water, Smiley
took a swig. It was, in fact, ouzo, the Greek spirit. He nodded politely as
it burned its way down.

All the men landed safely. The only casualties were the wireless set, whose chute had failed to open, and a single case of ammunition, likely squirreled away by the locals. They signaled their successful drop to the plane as it made a low pass to review their signal lights. Then the aircraft flew off, and the last direct link to their world was gone.

AFTER BEING WELCOMED BY THE GREEK GUERRILLAS, SMILEY AND McLean collected their gear and headed toward Albania. Smiley made sure to retain his parachute. In those days, chutes were still made of real silk and came in a variety of colors. Later in the war, they would be issued in the standard camouflage green, and the silk would be saved for paratroopers only. (Supplies, like the wireless set, got cotton chutes.) Smiley's parachute turned out to be a lovely pale shade of blue. It was all he could do to keep the locals, whom he described as occasionally "light-fingered," from relieving him of it, as they had that case of ammunition from the initial drop. Later, the industrious teenage daughter of one of their Greek hosts would make him several shirts and a set of pajamas from the material.

Following a frustrating wait after crossing the border, Smiley and McLean met with an Albanian Partisan leader. These Partisans, with their red-starred hats, were characteristic of the Communists in the area. Hungry for power, and armed, they were jealous of their position and deeply concerned by anything that offered a whiff of competition, such as other resistance groups, especially since those groups were not Communist. They believed that their enemies lurked around every corner, and on their list of adversaries, the Germans and Italians ranked low. There was also an age-old border problem in this area, with Greece and Albania claiming the other's territory. Ultimately, the Albanian Communists sent Smiley and McLean back across the border to Greece while they awaited orders from Partisan superior officers. The return trip took a full nine hours of hiking.

A few days passed before Smiley and McLean developed an alter-native plan: they would split up. To improve their chances, Smiley of-fered to cross the border in another sector and attempt to make contact with the Communist Partisan representatives there. His goal was the border town of Koritza, from which he could send a message of intro-duction to the Partisans. He set off on foot, accompanied by two pack mules and two frequently lost guides.

After successfully making contact with a different Partisan leader, Smiley was invited to observe a Communist attack on a local Italian out-post. Yet along the way there were concerning signs. First, he was as-signed two "bodyguards." Then he was assigned two more. When they passed through another Albanian village, his hosts insisted that he cover his uniform. He made the journey swaddled in an old Italian Army raincoat, pulled over his own gear and topped off with a red-starred hat. His arm obligingly gave the Communist salute when prompted.

In the village, his hosts showed him to a room in a hilltop house, relieved him of the Colt .45 in the holster attached to his right thigh (along with the smaller .25 tucked into a second holster at his waist), and detained him there for a week. He had nothing with him to read but the Bible. It was, he discovered, more impressive than he had ever quite found it before.

His jailers worried that, despite Smiley's lack of facility with Greek, he just might be a Greek spy. The village where they were was held by the Balli Kombëtar, and the Communist Partisans were jealous of the attentions of the British officer (assuming he really was a British officer, not a Greek spy). They were worried that he would provide weapons, ammunition, tactics, support, and funds to a rival resistance group. The Communists' fears were not unfounded. British orders were to help or-ganize, train, and arm anyone who would fight the Axis, regardless of their political affiliation. If the British officers could develop good rela-tionships with members of the Balli Kombëtar, they would help them as well. The Communists aimed to prevent this.

After a week, a Communist officer arrived to interview Smiley. It went well, and Smiley earned both his release and the Communists' trust.

AFTER HIS RELEASE, SMILEY CONTACTED MCLEAN, AND THE COMMANDER came across the border with the rest of his team. Smiley's work with the Communist officer who had released him formed the basis of the relationship that allowed McLean to raise SOE's First Partisan Brigade, which was composed of Albanian Communists and overseen by the British. Training this new army would occupy the next six months of their mission. It would also bring them into direct contact with the true power player in Albania: Enver Hoxha, head of the local Communist Party.

This new ragtag army needed guns, ammunition, and food. These were supplied to them by air. This came with its own complications. Once, an Italian bomber spotted their signal fires, tailgated their plane, and bombed their drop zone. The men waiting there were saved by only Smiley's sharp ears, which identified the Italian plane in the dark. Those Italians crashed on their way back to base, thwarting their ability to report the British position. McLean's Mission, as the British called it (its official and misspelled name was Concensus), also needed a support structure. McLean hired mules, muleteers, cooks, and armorers for their camp near the village of Shtyllë. Smiley called them the local "camp followers."

McLean was quickly immersed in the power struggles of the different resistance groups. No one trusted anyone else, which was normal. The Communists sometimes seemed more interested in eliminating their rivals than in fighting the Germans; a few of their rivals sometimes seemed quite willing to consider the Nazis allies if it would protect them from the others.

This was not Smiley's department. He preferred more fighting and less talking. McLean, however, was a people person who delighted in politics. In Abyssinia, he had learned how to navigate between two powerful but competitive warlords, one of whom was officially the minister of war and the other of whom, with no official position, actually controlled the larger and more impressive fighting force. This could not be so different.

But in Abyssinia, McLean had only been fighting the Italians. For him, this new opportunity to fight the Germans was very personal. His younger and only brother, Gillian, had been at Dunkirk. A lieutenant of only nineteen in the Cameron Highlanders, he had been wounded as the British retreated toward the Channel. His wound, presumably either from a shell fragment or to a difficult area like the chest or stomach, had been deemed undressable. By necessity, he had been left exposed for six hours due to heavy shelling, then survived five days on a truck as he was slowly evacuated to the coast. He was shunted between three different ships, which were each in turn bombed, during the heroic sea evacuation; the last of the three vessels was meant to transport cattle. Gillian made it across the Channel, but he died two hours after arriving at a British hospital. McLean was already in the Middle East. Gillian was cremated. All that would await his older brother in England was a cold piece of stone at Bristol's Arnos Vale. McLean now had the chance to exact his own vengeance.

CHAPTER 2

AN OFFICER AND
A GENTLEMAN

The details of the work McLean's team was doing in Albania piqued the interests of senior SOE staff officers in London. To gather more intelligence that could help their officers behind enemy lines, they sent a junior officer to speak to the exiled Albanian monarch, King Zog, now living in a comfortable suburb of the British capital.

The junior officer happened to be an old friend of McLean's from Eton, a brilliant young man named Julian Amery. Amery was the younger son of the political giant and Conservative politician Leo Amery, who had his hands in nearly every overseas British involvement of his lifetime. Leo had served as Colonial Secretary and First Lord of the Admiralty in the 1920s, and during the Second World War, he was serving as the Secretary of State for India and Burma.

Julian Amery had quite the pedigree: he had been kissed on both cheeks by King Feisal of Iraq, coddled by David Lloyd George, and mock-wrestled with Lawrence of Arabia, all by the time he went to kindergarten. He also had a precocious mind. As he later recounted, when faced with an exasperated father inquiring as to whether his bilingual child knew the French word for "chatterbox," he stopped the Cabinet member short with his response: "I replied gravely that it would be *bavard* or *loquace* but that if the chatterbox was repetitive, it should be *radoteur.* This reply silenced the Secretary of State, and I retired to my nursery satisfied that I had got the better of that particular debate."

Amery could have coasted into a simple and safe position during the war. He had, however, other ideas. Only twenty years old at the start of the war, he was younger than both McLean and Smiley. In the summer of 1939, he was on the Dalmatian coast, considering his looming exams and desperately attempting to cram into his head all "the work that I had left undone in my first two years at Oxford." As a member of the cadet corps of the Royal Air Force Reserves, he wanted to get to Poland, but SOE would have other plans for him.

One day, the assistant naval attaché, a man named Sandy Glen, asked him to write up a report on Albania, which the intelligence office knew nothing about. The only problem was that Amery knew nothing about it either. At a loss for material but rich in connections, even in the backwaters of the Balkans, he rang up an old contact from his days covering the Spanish Civil War (an endeavor he had undertaken while still a student, which at least partially explains the dereliction of his studies). The local correspondent for *The Times* fielded this call from British intelligence as if it were a common thing to happen on a Tuesday, which it may well have been. He offered to collect a few contacts who knew something about the place and told Amery to come around to his flat for drinks at six o'clock in the evening.

Upon arrival, Amery was introduced as a journalist. For an hour, he spoke with the only two Albanians he had yet met, after which he returned to his desk and wrote the solicited memo. At Glen's order, he presented this to "the Chief" at dinner. A few days later, a request arrived at his office on behalf of the said Chief: "Our staff in Belgrade would be greatly strengthened by the co-option of Julian Amery, whose expert knowledge of Albanian affairs would be an invaluable asset to the organisation." And so Amery, "journalist," college student, woefully untrained RAF cadet, and neophyte on the world of Albania, joined Section "D," one of the forerunners of SOE in 1940.

AMERY HAD HELD VARIOUS POSITIONS IN INTELLIGENCE AND STAFF circles since his recruitment by Sandy Glen in Belgrade. Despite his own Tory credentials, Amery had been an early proponent of backing both traditional royalist resistance forces and Communist Partisans throughout the Balkans, and he had a series of connections with the nationalist and royalist forces in Yugoslavia as well. At one point, he had been involved in a plot to assassinate Hitler via a terminally ill Macedonian terrorist named Vilmar; the man actually managed to get himself to what was essentially the right place in Vienna, but gave himself away the night before while drinking at a nightclub with too many pretty girls. Amery had spent time working with an intelligence network in the Middle East, and he had once been briefly detained by the Vichy French, who nearly turned him over to the Germans. While in Palestine, he helped make a few connections between colleagues who had been developing sabotage operations; one of the men whom Amery helped supply lost an eye in a successful raid. That man turned out to be Moshe Dayan, the future Chief of Staff of the IDF and later the Defense Minister of Israel.

In 1941, Amery believed that it was crucial to get contacts into Yugoslavia; the British had been chased out by the German invasion there. His attempts to land a British liaison officer were stonewalled by bureaucratic infighting at the office. Amery felt no compunction about floating this idea to his Cabinet-sitting father, who mentioned it to Churchill, who mentioned it to the ultimate SOE boss. It was an efficacious process that was nevertheless unlikely to make him any friends below the Cabinet level. The idea was a good one, and with Churchill's support, Amery's program moved forward. He personally accompanied the submarine that delivered an SOE officer named Bill Hudson, along with three Yugoslavs, to the coast of Montenegro.

Amery itched to get back into the Balkans himself in a more active capacity. In March 1943, before Smiley and McLean had left for Albania, one of Amery's previous bosses had requested that Amery join his staff on a mission in Yugoslavia. Permission was denied.

AMERY'S WAR HAD BEEN COMPLICATED BY EARLY MISSTEPS RESULTING from the impolitic combination of a strong personality backed more by youthful confidence than by earned experience. His error was in having the temerity to be junior, bold, and correct all at once. While still working in Belgrade before the German invasion (at the time, for both Section D and the Foreign Office), Amery had accurately diagnosed the impending Nazi collaboration with the dynastic rulers of Yugoslavia and Bulgaria, and he had argued to the highest reaches of Section D for doing something about it. He then began making inquiries on the intelligence side himself. The traditionalist Foreign Office was not pleased to be proved wrong in its initial support for the crowned heads when the resistance showed itself to have the greater fighters. Nor could Foreign Office bigwigs forgive the fact that Amery had gone both behind their backs and above their heads to pursue his goals. Amery had, as one biographer put it, earned himself (albeit temporarily) a "black mark" from the powerful Foreign Office. Life at the staff office in Cairo, where he usually worked rather than in the more senior London office, was complicated as well.

The role of the staff office is to not only give orders but also handle all the elements of a military operation that the men in the field can't handle themselves. The staff office is like a quartermaster, politician, spymaster, and general all rolled into one. This is where the supplies (and for McLean's team, gold sovereigns) are organized and from where they are delivered. It is where the military equivalent of human re-sources sits; where signals are decrypted and from where communica-tions are sent; where intelligence is turned over, collated, investigated, and redistributed; where strategic (rather than tactical) decisions are made; and where junior officers toil and provide analysis to more senior officers, who make the decisions that have life-or-death consequences for the men serving in the field. Staff work is inglorious, but no unit can survive for long in the field, especially behind enemy lines, without a good staff office supplying it with materials and intelligence.

SOE's Cairo staff office, which handled missions in the Balkans, was not a good staff office. It was instead prone to a level of bureaucratic in-fighting that was borderline obscene. This was exacerbated by rivalries with the other offices with which they were meant to be working pro-ductively. The Foreign Office was jealous of any potential challenge to its imperial policy supremacy. The British Army's General Headquar-ters Middle East was concerned about resources being diverted from the conventional war effort. There were personality and political conflicts between the office of SOE London (the more senior staff office, which oversaw all SOE missions) and that of SOE Cairo. As one staff officer later put it, "Nobody who did not experience it can possibly imagine the atmosphere of jealousy, suspicion, and intrigue" that percolated through the staff office in Cairo. There was also a Communist mole, un-beknownst to everyone but the man himself, with a straight line to the NKVD.

The staff office was run by a man almost universally described as "formidable," though a more candid description might have included "tyrannical." His name was Cleveland Mervyn Keble, though with his squat, square frame and enormous head mounted on massive shoulders, the drawing-room names were a poor fit. Anyone who was allowed to address him by something other than his rank called him Bolo. (The women in the office, meanwhile, called him Tim—for "touch I must.")

He was, in the words of one of the officers who served in Crete, "a globe-shaped little militarist" who did "his best to conceal his natural and professional shortcomings by a show of bloodthirsty activity and total disregard for agents in the field."

Keble had come to SOE Cairo through that most insalubrious of channels: getting kicked upstairs. In December 1941, Keble was the assistant to the head of military intelligence in the Middle East. One of the tasks of his office was to study the matériel and armor (specifically, tanks) available to the German Field Marshal Erwin Rommel, dubbed the Desert Fox, as he attempted to break the British lines.

Keble had access to not only the Top Secret ULTRA decrypts of German signals from Bletchley Park but also some of the finest human intelligence available from the LRDG's Road Watch. Now reports from the Road Watch were coming in, informing Keble that there were twenty-two new Mark III and IV tanks rolling into Cyrenaica (modern-day Libya). This information was backed up by the brigadier commanding the 4th Indian Division.

For some reason, Keble denied it. Insisting that the Germans did not control shipping capable of unloading such heavy tanks, he convinced his boss that both the LRDG and the brigadier were seeing things. The ship that had delivered the tanks, the *Ankara*, had originally been designed to transport locomotives to South America. She was built to unload items even heavier than tanks, and she did.

Rommel used those tanks to break through the British lines in Cyrenaica, in a prelude to his storming march across the desert, which very nearly ended with the capture of Cairo. The British managed to hold the line only at El Alamein.

Keble's boss was sacked not long thereafter. Unable to axe Keble outright, the higher powers still felt the need to find another place to park him. Traditional military types looked down on SOE at the time; to the generals, it seemed a good place of banishment for Keble. He arrived at SOE Cairo's staff office in the summer of 1942, elevated to brigadier.

The inauspicious beginning never mellowed into a functional reign. It is unclear if Keble's behavior was driven by an attempt to rehabilitate himself or by the same blind assumption of his own superiority that drove him to discount the eyewitness reports regarding two easily identifiable German tank models. Most likely, Keble was the kind of underperformer who is just intelligent and self-aware enough to realize that he doesn't stack up, and narcissistic enough to insist that he deserves better anyway. He was belligerent, unable to take criticism, single-minded to a fault, and hypocritical when he wasn't also being underhanded.

The trumped-up brigadier saw in SOE an opportunity to make his star shine: he would discover a new place and means of breakthrough, a trick to win the war. Keble thought he saw this in, of all places, Yugoslavia, Albania's eastern neighbor. Keble had retained his Top Secret ULTRA access, and he heard about a group of Communist Partisans led by Tito, the Stalin-backed operative. Tito, in turn, was backing Enver Hoxha, McLean's contact in Albania.

Keble staked his ambitions on Tito, who he hoped could tie down German divisions. It might have worked, with good judgment and good information. What Keble had instead was a Communist mole in the form of a trumped-up, drafted private turned accidental officer, a man just shy of thirty who already had an NKVD code name (Mayor), something usually bestowed upon foreign agents. Keble thought him smart, deferential, and hardworking, and saw him as a valued ally as he set about burnishing his own tarnished résumé. The officer's name was James Klugmann.

Klugmann was a repressed homosexual and an atheist Jew in an era when casual anti semitism was not only acceptable but also, to a certain extent, socially fashionable (and when same-sex activity was technically illegal). He had been recruited by the brilliant Soviet agent Arnold Deutsch. Deutsch seemed to specialize in finding privileged men with just enough of an excuse to feel themselves oppressed by bourgeois society: the flamboyant Guy Burgess; the bisexual Donald Maclean; the "sexual athlete" with father issues, Kim Philby; the gay Anthony Blunt; and John Cairncross, the working-class man in a sea of elites whom Klugmann helped recruit. These made up the Cambridge Five, Deutsch's most successful spies. Since the 1930s, Klugmann had acted as a Soviet talent spotter.

By the time Klugmann arrived in Cairo in 1941, while Smiley and McLean were fighting in Abyssinia, he had managed to subvert dozens of troops on his transport ship. He had been sent to the labor corps and then became a clerk. (Despite Klugmann's declared affinity for the working man, actual work did not hold much appeal for Klugmann.) A colonel, surprised to see a talented Cambridge graduate who spoke fluent Arabic dressed as a private, realized that they had attended the same prep school. He set out to get Klugmann a new job. Every office turned him down but the last, and that last was the staff office of SOE Cairo.

KLUGMANN WAS A GIFTED OPERATOR, CHARISMATIC AND SLICK. EVEN Smiley later had to admit that he was entertaining company, as did others who found Klugmann's actions odious but his manners charming. Klugmann's undercover role was to increase affinity, even if covert, for Communist policy in the staff office. His big goal was to switch British support in the Balkans exclusively to Communist groups, such as Tito's and Hoxha's respective Partisan movements. Coincidentally, this was just what Keble thought *he* was doing, and the brigadier was none the wiser.

After the war, Klugmann was recorded by MI5, the British version of the FBI, in a conversation with someone he trusted, explaining how he made sure that only left-leaning fellow travelers approved by himself and the group he was developing would go to the Yugoslav Partisans, because they would naturally send reports back to Cairo that were supportive of the Communists. Klugmann meant to keep those whom he considered "the really bad types," people who weren't fellow travelers, either away from the Partisans or out of Yugoslavia, so as not to hamper his plans. Explaining it later, one clever and perhaps belatedly embarrassed associate would split these hairs even further, insisting that Klugmann was harmless while simultaneously referring to the group in the office as "we 'partisans.'"

At the staff office in Cairo and later in the Italian port city of Bari, where the office moved after the Allied invasion of Italy (the latter all the more convenient for being farther from bustling Cairo, where there were more people watching), Klugmann had developed "a group of about ten people—how can I say—sympathetic to Communism, and even to the Party, without going further than that, but thoroughly pro-Partisan. And we were able to act as a sieve; all information coming out of the country had to go through one of our other departments and to see that what got back was satisfactory." He queered the pitch in Yugoslavia. As he put it: "as a result of mass recruiting of a rather nefarious character, the Yugo-Slav mission was nearly all—was 90% pro-Partisan and friendly, and was almost organised." Operating parallel to these programs was a consistent and repeatedly documented habit of harassing officers in the field who did not conform to Klugmann's own preferences. Years later, MI5 would consider this a "betrayal of information," a "most unforgivable offence," and "very nearly a Party cell established on the traditional basis, and engaged on a Party task."

With the characteristic flexibility of a good Party member, Klugmann embraced the decadence of wartime Cairo, though always with an eye toward his clandestine activities. He lived in a large flat in the center of Cairo, and his friends recalled him hosting endless parties, ones whose guests moved slowly through the fog of smoke and bodies to behold the bespectacled Klugmann, perpetually lighting another cigarette between his tobacco-stained fingers, grandiosely holding forth on his favorite subject.

Despite his outspoken Communist sympathies, Klugmann had always managed to stay just a few steps ahead of an overburdened security service. They had lost his initial files in a fire, thanks to a German raid during the Blitz. He quickly got himself put in charge of intelligence in the Yugoslav Country Section of SOE Cairo's staff office.

Security eventually got wind of him, and Klugmann was interrogated in 1941, but he skillfully avoided self-incrimination. Klugmann had a wonderful knack for finding powerful protectors, and Keble, despite his very different politics, had been one of them. Keble, as already noted, did not take criticism well. He also saw personal slights where none were even meant. Enraged by anyone who dared suggest that there was a mole among his officers, Keble reacted vociferously to accusations that Klugmann might be a problem.

Klugmann was "thoroughly reliable, most painstaking, hardworking, absolutely trustworthy, loyal, and secure. I can say little more," exclaimed Keble during Klugmann's 1941 investigation. "I should be very sorry indeed if I ever had to lose Klugmann, as he would be hard to replace," insisted Keble, who had in the meantime bundled Klugmann into an office toilet stall and conspiratorially promised the junior officer his protection. "Furthermore, I should be extraordinarily surprised if I ever had to eat any of the above words," huffed the man who had been rewarded with his current job by dismissing equally strong evidence in his last one.

JULIAN AMERY SOON HAD HIS OWN EXPERIENCES WITH KLUGMANN, though he didn't appreciate the depth of them at the time. One of the officers for whom Amery had previously worked sent a new recruit to him at the SOE Cairo office. This man was a former Yugoslav officer with strong radio transmission skills. He was also a former Communist who had fought in Spain. Repulsed by what he had seen the Soviets do during their purges there, he had renounced the party and moved to the United States. Later, he had been recruited to the Chetniks, the royalist resistance forces in Yugoslavia.

Amery himself was overburdened, and he asked that the operative, whom he called Robertson, be tended to by someone who spoke Serbo-Croatian. One person in the office who spoke Serbo-Croatian was James Klugmann.

Strange things started to happen to Robertson. He was assaulted on a street in Cairo. SOE minders who arrived as the attack ended claimed his attackers were right-wing Yugoslavs, but Robertson recognized them as Communists. He insisted that he had been tracked and outed by a mole on the British side. As Amery later put it, "Following a natural British prejudice, we preferred not to believe him, foolishly as it proved."

It took several attempts to drop Robertson into Yugoslavia, several of which appeared, in retrospect, to have been sabotaged. He was attached to the conservative Chetnik forces but made contact with Communist Partisans soon after his arrival. Then he wound up murdered. No one in the office realized at the time that Robertson had been correct in his initial hunch about a mole among the ranks, and that the same issue had cost him his life. It was soon to plague the team in Albania as well.

CHAPTER 3

THE ALFÉREZ

On the night of August 10, 1943, after more than three months in Albania, Smiley and McLean received a prize drop. Their staff office in Cairo had decided to send more officers so that McLean could oversee a wider mission. That evening, four arrived. One was a well-respected mountaineer. He climbed the local peaks each morning for exercise, giving great pains to his reluctant Partisan guards, under orders to never let him out of their sight. He was accompanied in the first airplane by another officer who got sick on the way out and had the unusual distinction of descending faster than his vomit. In the second plane was a cavalryman named George Seymour, universally recalled by his compatriots as having a mustache of nineteenth-century style. The final officer was Peter Kemp.

The first three were all regular officers who had been serving in the British Army since before the war. Like many others who served in the conflict, Kemp held a wartime commission only; he was not a graduate of one of the military academies. Kemp was thus not what was called a "regular officer," nor, as Smiley put it, "was he ever likely to be taken for one, being both unconventional and eccentric." Still, as Smiley noted, "in spite of this he had probably been involved in more active fighting than his three companions put together." One of those companions had been wounded at the battle of El Alamein.

"I hate being shot at," Kemp wrote, but he kept being drawn to circumstances in which exactly that happened. A 1936 graduate of Cambridge, he was one of the few Brits who had fought on the Nationalist side in the Spanish Civil War. Kemp was a romantic, not a politician. He had joined for the duration well before the future dictator General Franco became the undisputed leader of the Nationalist side. Derided for his choice, Kemp pointed out that no one ever seemed to accuse his former enemies of having fought for Stalin. He explained for the rest of his life that he had joined the Nationalists as an anti-Communist, and that he had a well-demonstrated distaste for both Fascism and totalitarianism of any sort. His anti-Communism was a long-standing habit. While a schoolboy, he had managed to get himself an MI5 file for posing under a false name and attempting to procure information from the local Communist Party, with the aim of passing it on to the British government. ("This is really very amusing," wrote one of the investigators.)

He had slipped into Spain with a journalist's cover and enlisted as a private. Speaking no Spanish on arrival, he earned both fluency and an officer's commission as an *alférez*, or lieutenant, though he never managed to reach his own high standards. Leaving his pistol's safety on too long while clearing a trench, he thought to himself, *If ever a man deserved to die, you do now!* Later, he would transfer from his royalist unit to the Spanish Foreign Legion, the best fighting unit in Spain. It was as a Foreign Legion officer that he met then Oxford student Julian Amery, visiting as a journalist, while sheltering from shelling in a ditch.

The Foreign Legion was almost entirely Spanish. Its motto was "Viva la Muerte!" (Long Live Death!), and its men were known for their fearlessness and their aggressiveness. Foreign Legion officers led from the front. Their men had been known to make miserable overnight postings in the rain more manageable by neatly spreading out on the ground the dead bodies of their opponents and sleeping like babies atop them.

In Spain, Kemp experienced street fighting (only two weeks of it, he later told an interviewer, but "I can assure you, two weeks of street fighting is enough"), was nearly overrun not once but twice, and narrowly escaped being blown up by a clever opponent who had tunneled under his unit's position. He commanded infantry and machine-gun platoons. He had lost his own men by the droves. Ordered to hold a position with his machine-gun team at all costs, he was injured and nearly killed after returning to the front line despite a bullet wound to the throat and an invitation to go to the hospital. "I had not the face to follow up this suggestion," Kemp later said.

In 1938, Kemp was in a shallow trench network outside the city of Seròs when the enemy began mortaring his position. He was speaking to his captain when one of the rounds burst directly beside him. The bomb exploded just to his left, and his jaw caught the worst of it. The back of his throat was severely burned, probably from the white-hot shrapnel of the round. The metal embedded itself into his skin, his mouth, his throat. His jaw was shattered. It hung loose from the rest of his skull, disconnected and broken. The feeling in the back of his mouth was of pebbles floating in a scalding bath. He realized one shocked second later that these were his teeth, afloat in his own blood. He was terrified. His mind nearly separated from his body, and he expected to die.

Transferred out on a stretcher, he heard one of his medics say to another that there was no point in evacuating him. He somehow rolled himself up onto his elbow and looked at them. They smiled and put him in the next ambulance, just to placate him. Years later, after the war, he met that medic again, who said, "When I sent you off in that ambulance from Seròs, I never thought you would live."

He never lost consciousness. He submitted to multiple operations, all without anesthetic. One Spanish surgeon was so frustrated by the state of Kemp's throat that he "asked how he could possibly be expected to operate on someone whose throat was so badly burnt." Kemp brought a bottle of brandy to his operation, never complained, and never thought that he had quite lived up to the better example of others: "I was quite proud of myself until I remembered that this was the manner in which operations were usually performed before the last century." He was left with false teeth, little hearing in his left ear, and facial scarring that his fellow officers were too polite to mention.

When the Second World War started in 1939, Kemp found himself relegated by his wounds to a role in the Postal Censorship Department. Irrepressible, he made his way into SOE. In the interim, he had served in the Commandos. Kemp was the man you sent when you wanted to try to land a raiding party in Norway by submarine, or when you needed to descend upon a German outpost in Brittany and get your men so close to the sentries that they could hear their breathing, and their mundane conversation, before killing them.

Kemp had a gentleman's soul and peppered his memoirs with references to Kipling, Shakespeare, and Horace. He combined the manners of a prince with the combat instincts of a pirate. Having suffered so much on account of his fighting in Spain, he was no jingoist. Recalling how he felt at the outbreak of the Second World War, Kemp wrote, "I knew enough of war to feel no elation at the prospect; I was conscious only of a grave anxiety at the strength of the forces matched against us, a grim realization of what defeat would mean, and the hope that the experience I had acquired in the face of much disapproval and ridicule might not prove entirely useless to my country."

IF KEMP WAS SOMETHING OF A NOBLE KNIGHT-ERRANT, HE WAS ALSO prone to accident. His first parachute jump at Ringway in England ended with him being dragged across the pavement. He never would have an uneventful drop. When on his way to join Smiley and McLean in Albania in 1943, he was dropped off target. Landing halfway up a mountain, or so it seemed, he smacked his head.

With little memory of the actual event, Kemp felt as though he were simply and suddenly standing upright on a rock, peering down at a small, bewhiskered man who he thought looked suspiciously like a satyr in the dark. Chattering excitedly, the satyr welcomed him to Albania. "Albania," said Kemp, "Albania." "Albania, yes!" said the satyr, who filled him in on the details and then mimed Kemp's headbanging arrival, with sound effects. "Poum!" exclaimed the satyr, whose name was Stefan.

Collected by his fellow parachutist, the cheerful, mustachioed George Seymour, and loaded onto a mule, Kemp still struggled to come to his senses. As they approached the camp, he saw a tall, fair, handsome figure striding toward them. Wearing jodhpurs, an open-necked shirt with major's crowns attached, his ever-present crimson cummerbund, and a charming smile, it was Billy McLean.

KEMP'S FIRST JOB WAS TO SLEEP FOR THIRTY-SIX HOURS, WORKING OFF what must have been a concussion from his unceremonious arrival. Once Kemp was awake, McLean took him on a walk. He gave him a briefing—and a warning. In the camp, there was at least one known spy for a local resistance group: Frederick Nosi, a bright young man who was a die-hard Communist. Nosi's loyalty was to the International Communist Party and its local commander, Enver Hoxha. He had managed to get himself a posting as an interpreter on McLean's team, and Hoxha was adamant that he keep it. McLean, who needed to preserve the good terms of his relationship with Hoxha in order to convince the Communists to fight the Axis, was forced to let Nosi stay. "Few were the messages we sent to Cairo or to each other," Kemp noted, "that Frederick Nosi did not do his best to read."

IN ALBANIA, A CIVIL WAR WAS BREWING UNDER MCLEAN'S NOSE. HE brought the former Spanish lieutenant Kemp up to speed on the tensions

between Hoxha's desires for Communist domination, the various nationalist groups' desires to prevent them, and the German and Italian
threat to both. The Communist Partisans claimed that the republican
nationalists of the Balli Kombëtar were not fighting the Germans. The
Balli, which the British were now also trying to help, complained that
the Communist Partisans intentionally engaged the Germans near its
villages—the Partisans held few of their own but did better in urban areas or in Tosk territory—in order to instigate reprisals. For the Partisans, this was a two-for-one deal. They could claim to be fighting the
Germans, while in reality they got the Germans to wipe out their local
competition.

"How much truth is there in the Balli excuses?" Kemp asked.

"A good deal in what they say about reprisals," McLean replied.

Reprisals were a nasty and common German tactic. In Oradour-
sur-Glane, in central France, the Germans destroyed an entire village,
burning down buildings with the locals locked inside as a reprisal for
the death of a single German soldier. The French still keep the village
in ruins, as a reminder.

"There's one little boy of seven in Shtyllë now," McLean continued.
"Both his parents were burned alive in Borovë, and he was twice driven
back into the fire before he found a way to crawl out, badly burnt. No
wonder the villagers are fed up!" McLean confessed that it was increasingly difficult to follow the Mission's orders to help aid the resistance
groups at the same time.

"What are you going to do about it?" Kemp asked gloomily. This was
a situation he had been trying to avoid. Like McLean and Smiley, he,
too, had initially been slated to drop into the larger and even more strategic Yugoslavia. Like McLean's and Smiley's, his tentative orders for that
country had never materialized. Klugmann had likely kept them out.

By the time Kemp had arrived for dispatch, a few months after Smiley and McLean, a civil war had broken out in Yugoslavia between the

Communists and non-Communists. When he arrived at the staff office to do predeparture paperwork, Kemp had been appalled when one of Klugmann's group tried to force him to sign a declaration stating that SOE London had tried to indoctrinate him into supporting the royalist, anti-Communist leader in Yugoslavia. He had refused and opted for Albania instead.

McLean gave Kemp a few more practical details, including background on both the Albanian Communist Partisans' Enver Hoxha, the political leader, and Mehmet Shehu, the general. And then he gave an additional word of warning: "Remember, Peter, be very careful what you say in front of Frederick Nosi. Every word gets back to Enver. Above all, no mention, please, of your part in the Spanish Civil War!"

IT WAS NOT THE FIRST TIME THAT KEMP HAD HEARD THIS REFRAIN. THE conflict, which had given him more valuable experience than possessed by many officers who had been fighting in the current war, could be an albatross. Just as the Second World War had started, Kemp was reminiscing with his uncle, who had been chased out of his retirement on the Italian Riviera by the emergence of hostilities. "Of course they must let you wear your Spanish Civil War medals," boomed a voice that Kemp assumed "generations of Indian Army subalterns had learnt not to contradict." He was never granted permission to wear those decorations, several of which were for bravery. It had initially been difficult for Kemp to get into the British Army at all. By the time he landed in Albania, after his missions with the Commandos, the war against the Germans had become as personal for Kemp as it was for McLean.

Like McLean, Kemp had one sibling: Neil, whom he idolized. The brothers were functional orphans, having been sent to boarding school in England from the age of four while their parents served in India. Five years older, Neil was the golden child, their father's favorite, and Peter's model for what their father wanted him to be. He felt this acutely. Of his father, he said, "'Manliness' and a serious attitude to work were the qualities he looked for, and sadly failed to find, in his younger son; he considered me feckless, indolent and feeble." When Kemp got into a car accident just before his Cambridge graduation, his father's response was withering: "Sometimes I think that God must have made you for a bet."

Neil was a pilot. In January 1941, the aircraft carrier *Illustrious*, on which Neil was based, was attacked off the coast of Sardinia. The news was a hammer blow: Neil was gone. Kemp's mother sent word by telegram. He wrote: "I couldn't believe that a crumpled piece of buff-coloured paper could contain so much human misery."

What Kemp didn't mention were the awful details. German Stukas had bombed the ship. Neil was standing in the hangar, talking to his squadron's commander. Theoretically reinforced, the hangar could not withstand the bombardment. Neil was decapitated immediately: the commander found himself staring at a standing headless body as all hell broke loose. As a fellow pilot wrote, "Even in death Neil refused to lie down."

The attack was retaliation for Neil and his fellow pilots' air assault in the Battle of Taranto, during which they sank the Italian fleet. (The Japanese paid attention: it would inform their later attack on Pearl Harbor.) They flew wood-and-fabric biplanes whose maximum speed was eighty knots. The navigators gave directions on paper from the open back seats. The Royal Navy expected 50 percent casualties at Taranto. The pilots dodged twenty-three thousand rounds of ammunition slung back at them from the shore-based antiaircraft guns alone; the gunners on the ships fired even more. The British pilots who were dropping flares didn't even release all of them because the sky was lit up with so many enemy tracers and explosions that there was no need for more illumination. They lost only two planes. Neil hit his target, a large Italian battleship.

Two months later, the Stukas had seemingly come out of nowhere, and Neil was gone. He would have no grave but the sea.

Kemp, then in the Commandos, quickly went to see his sister-in-law, Diana. She was a lovely woman, but he barely knew her. When she had married Neil, her head crowned in orange blossoms and crystals, surrounded by bridesmaids in turquoise-blue chiffon along with a little boy who served as trainbearer and wore a sailor suit to match the honor guard of naval officers, Kemp had not been there.

He was instead in Spain, at a hospital, where he lay in substantial pain between two major (and anesthesia-free) surgeries to repair his wounds from the mortar. One of Neil's fellow officers stood in his place as best man. Now Diana had only her six-month-old son, Ian. Neil had never met him.

KEMP, STILL RECOVERING FROM HIS ABRUPT INTRODUCTION TO ALBA-nian soil, was beginning to nod off over dinner the next evening when there was a commotion outside. Into the room strode an annoyed but satisfied David Smiley. If Smiley admired Kemp, the feeling was mutual. "Reserved in manner, economical in speech, he had a shrewd insight and quiet self-confidence which enabled him to make up his mind quickly and speak it with a directness that compelled attention without giving offence," Kemp later wrote of his impression of Smiley, though the last trait, by Smiley's own admission, was not necessarily always true in Albania. Above all, "in the most dangerous situations, he appeared phlegmatic to the point of indifference, not because he lacked the intelligence to feel fear but because he possessed the priceless self-discipline that can conceal and suppress it." In "American," as Smiley would have put it, this was what was known as having brass balls.

Smiley was returning from his first attempt at an ambush with one of the non-Communist resistance groups. This one was a Balli Kombëtar *çeta*, or militia band.

"It was quite successful, but not half as good as it might have been," Smiley said.

He and the Ballist officer had taken the *çeta* to do a daylight reconnaissance of the spot on a local road, near the village of Barmash, where
they intended to ambush the Germans. There they found that they had
also been under observation—by a group of Communist Partisans led
by a man who insisted that he was going to lay an ambush in the same
place. "Of course this was just to bitch the Balli," Smiley huffed as he explained.

Exasperated over what he believed was an obvious attempt by the
Communists (acting, most likely, on information from the spy Frederick Nosi) to prevent a good military relationship between the Ballists
and the British, Smiley had told the Partisans to shove off.

"If you do an ambush here tonight," Smiley had threatened, entirely
without authority, "I promise you that the LNÇ [Communist Partisans]
will receive no more arms or money from the British Mission, and we
will give all we get to the Balli Kombëtar." This threat worked, and they
set up for the ambush.

Smiley mined the road with ten of the Ballist troops, but they were
green and easily frightened away by sounds in the distance. "My men
have not had much training," their captain apologized. Smiley and the
crew ambushed a German convoy towing a substantial 88-millimeter
gun. The explosion as a half-track and the lorries behind it hit the mines
was huge. Smiley was pleased to snap a photo with his camera just as
the mines went off. As members of the *çeta* fired their rifles, Smiley shot
the 20-millimeter Breda cannon and "was delighted to see several of my
shots score direct hits."

The Albanians finished off the raid and brought out identifications
for the eighteen dead Germans, all from the elite First Alpine Division.
Another convoy came down the road. Many of the men had assumed
the job was done, and melted away. The remainder stayed alongside
Smiley and nearly finished off the second convoy, with Smiley again using the Breda to light up several lorries before retreating into the mountains. The regrouped Germans were now "too close to be healthy."

The British continued their delicate dance, trying to tamp down internecine tensions while working with all the resistance forces. The next day was to be the inauguration ceremony for the First Partisan Brigade, which Smiley and McLean had been training since their establishment of ties with the Communist Partisans. Then would come the big test: a significant ambush led by Partisans under British observation. The Partisans spoke boldly of their big attacks on the Germans. Those attacks were real, as were the complaints by nationalist villagers about reprisals from the Germans over Partisan harassment. But the British officers never received proof of the size or scope of the Partisans' attacks, such as through identification badges like those that Smiley had sent the Ballists to fetch from their victims.

The Partisans were very clever, as the Germans were known to enact disproportionately brutal reprisals. A small oppositional action by the Partisans, with little risk to themselves (and little expenditure of ammunition), could still get the Germans to punish their rivals. The only sticking point was the inevitable absence of captured badges, or proof of sizable numbers of dead Germans—in other words, the very thing that the British were giving them guns and money to produce.

For the informal and scrappy guerrillas, the inauguration was a grand ceremony: eight hundred Partisans lined up for a parade, a march-past, and speeches delivered by the leadership, from Enver Hoxha to Mehmet Shehu to Billy McLean. The whole thing took several hours. Kemp, recovering the next day, remembered the raki and the songs, one of which had a "stirring, haunting rhythm." Smiley, exasperated, declared that the event had included "the longest and most boring speeches it has ever been my fate to listen to." McLean's was best because it was shortest, Smiley decided, though he also wished that the Italian pilots had done a flyover and scattered the whole bunch, "but no such luck."

While other British officers set out to different parts of Albanian territory to continue the work of contacting resistance groups, McLean, Smiley, and Kemp went with the Partisan commander Mehmet Shehu and the freshly minted First Partisan Brigade to conduct the ambush. Kemp remembered to forget that he and Shehu had fought on opposite sides in Spain. They marched for ten hours.

Kemp, perched astride a mule he had bought on the advice of McLean (Smiley already had his own, a beloved creature named Fanny, after Mrs. Hasluck), rode behind the two cavalrymen and could hear snippets of their conversation as they rehearsed a scene from another world: full-dress drill for the mounting guard. "You do that, Billy, and you go straight back to riding school for the next six months!" Kemp heard Smiley declare to McLean. (This had once been Smiley's own fate after parading on horseback down London's Mall with stirrups that were too long.) Kemp "admired their detachment before an operation that meant so much to them both."

Settling in for the night before the planned dawn ambush, Kemp was "disagreeably startled by the sound of machine-gun fire." Soon an angry Shehu appeared, declaring that he had called off the ambush because they had run into some Germans on a hilltop post.

"We must withdraw. There is nothing we can do here," the Albanian Partisans' top military mind said.

The British officers were astounded. Smiley and McLean insisted that Shehu eliminate the hilltop post and proceed with the ambush. Shehu in turn insisted that "my first action must be 100 percent successful" and that action was therefore impossible. How many Germans are up there? asked the British. Perhaps twenty, came the reply.

"Do you mean to tell me that eight hundred Partisans cannot attack and wipe out a post of twenty Germans?" McLean exploded.

Shehu turned and walked away, accompanied by what Kemp called "some plainly audible comments from Smiley," disgusted at the idea that so much training and effort had come to naught. It turned out to be only eighteen Germans, not twenty.

Demoralized, the British stayed in place overnight after the Partisans had left. McLean wasn't giving up so easily: "I'm damned if I'm leaving here without having a crack at something," he declared.

Smiley needed to return to camp to oversee the latest supply drop, but McLean invited Kemp on what he called a "Boy Scout operation": the two of them would ambush a German staff car out of what Kemp later admitted was "sheer exasperation." An interpreter named Stiljan volunteered as well. One of the mulemen kept their mules and supplies hidden off the road. A lone German staff car began to round the bend. McLean, in command, waited for the right moment to fire, and then: "All right, let 'em have it."

They poured fire into the car, which shuddered to a halt. Kemp's gun, a new British-designed submachine gun prototype called the Welgun, jammed. He pulled out his .45 pistol instead. To Kemp's horror, McLean leaped down to finish off the staff officers and retrieve any useful materials.

"Give me covering fire, boys! I'm going down," he shouted.

Kemp desperately directed his inexperienced interpreter's fire as McLean danced around the bullets snapping near his feet, then retreated along with Kemp and Stiljan.

Kemp was anxious to get the mules going. McLean took out a tortoiseshell comb for his hair. "Don't be so damned windy, Peter," McLean teased, combing. A crack of machine-gun fire struck the rocks beside them. McLean's smile froze and then morphed into what Kemp identified as a sheepish grin. "On our way, boys!"

Smiley, seeing them upon their return, confessed himself "very jealous."

TOWARD THE END OF AUGUST, SMILEY AND MCLEAN WERE SITTING AT a table inside when an Italian shell landed nearby, shattering the windows and dropping the plaster from the ceiling. Kemp was sleeping in, having stayed up late to work on the signal traffic. Smiley stuck his head in the room as Kemp jerked awake and pronounced, "We're being attacked, but never mind." Kemp, not exactly a slave to timeliness (one review from a superior officer in his parachute course had noted, "Not once, nor twice, but three times have I seen this officer punctual"), dressed with rapidity. Both their camp and the adjacent village of Shtyllë were being bombarded. Smiley took a few shots at the offending bomber flying over them but missed low and behind; their 20-millimeter cannon was not mounted for antiaircraft fire.

"Pack it in, David, and let's get weaving!" McLean shouted as they ran to the hideout Smiley had prepared in the woods, a mile or so north.

The villagers abandoned their homes. "If I had been entranced before I came to Albania by the romance and glamour of guerrilla warfare," Kemp recalled of watching them flee, "this was a sobering reminder of its squalor and injustice." There were wounded among the civilians. An old man with a leg injury died that afternoon. A teenage boy had his stomach laced with shell splinters. He begged for water, but Smiley, following his training to never give fluids to anyone with a stomach wound, refused. All the same, Smiley was so berated by the Albanians that he finally gave in and produced a glass of water. "He seemed greatly relieved—and so was I," snapped a frustrated Smiley, "for within five minutes he was dead."

By evening, it was clear that the Italians were making a push toward the next town of Vithkuq. Mehmet Shehu sent messages of confirmation and promised to hold the town for the Partisans. Kemp was sent ahead by McLean to find Shehu and observe the Partisan fighting, while McLean took Frederick Nosi to sound out Vithkuq and Smiley organized the camp.

What all the British officers found was the same: the Partisans would not hold under sustained shelling. One commander, whom Kemp tried to encourage by pointing out his excellent position, insisted that his men would not stand up to bombardment.

Working his way back to camp, Kemp found Smiley and McLean again despondent over the lack of results they had gotten out of the Partisans after so much training. The Italians in Albania were not the most formidable of opponents, but the Partisans would not withstand them. Kemp demurred: no monthlong training could teach green troops the discipline needed to stand up to such an assault.

During the Spanish Civil War, Kemp had once been bombarded on a bare mountainside, with his entire platoon holding a host of mules. Those troops were some of the hardest and most disciplined men in Spain; their officers dealt with insubordination immediately, summarily, and with a pistol. (Kemp was once berated by his own superior officer for not shooting on the spot a soldier who had cursed at a warrant officer.) What Kemp had seen then was a "nightmare abattoir," complete with screaming men and mules; when it became clear that the bombers above them were making a second pass, even those soldiers "began to run wildly in all directions, up the flanks of the mountain, in a mad, useless and suicidal rush to escape."

The Partisans were not nearly as well trained, or well disciplined, as those men. Smiley was exasperated to find himself beside one Albanian commissar who "kept throwing himself flat on the ground every time after a shell had fallen, and I could not persuade him this was the wrong way to do it." Smiley decided this behavior was "windy."

All three agreed that the Partisans needed to focus on more mobile, ambush- and guerrilla-style tactics rather than on "brigade actions." This was good advice but with a significant flaw: it assumed that the intention of the Partisans was to fight the Axis.

CHAPTER 4

WITH FRIENDS
LIKE THESE

The Italians surrendered to the Allies at the beginning of September, 1943. In Albania, it was a moment of change and expectation. One thing that everyone agreed on, from the nationalists to the Communists to the Germans, was that the Allies would make a massive landing in the Balkans. Anticipation over a new power joining the fray destabilized the existing order. For the British officers, tensions rose with the Communist Partisans, who were trying to dominate their rivals before large Allied forces arrived. German offensives picked up.

And there were the Italians. David Smiley was sent up the road ("having smartened myself up as much as possible, to look like a British officer") with an Albanian man he cheekily referred to as his "American-speaking" interpreter, who only went by the name Tom, in order to accept the surrender of a local garrison. It was a surreal experience, with local women pressing so many flowers into Smiley's hands that he couldn't carry them. The Italian commander had as little idea about his orders as Smiley did, though Smiley did manage to convince the Italians to destroy their 75-millimeter gun so as to keep it out of the hands of both the Germans and the Partisans, the latter of whom frequently mistreated Italians who did not directly surrender to them.

The Italians had been enemies but not aggressive ones. As Peter Kemp noted, they were gentlemanly in their attacks; they liked to shell you for a day or so first. The Germans appeared, murderously business-like, before dawn and with no warning at all. Accordingly, Smiley tried to limit the Germans' movements in their direction. He blew up the road from Elbasan to Pogradec with several muleloads of explosives, leaving thirty yards of a nice drive overlooking a completely impassable lake. He also started destroying bridges, a specialty that he would hone with great pleasure during his time in Albania.

The first bridge he chose, over the Shkumbin River, was close to a series of German fortifications and valuable to their movement and re-supply. Smiley set two charges using SOE's time pencils as detonators. These were a relatively new addition to the British "dirty tricks" arse-nal. They were not like the more familiar plunger-style detonators. The "pencil"-like mechanism of each device held within it an acid-filled vial that was attached to a fuse. When the pencil was squeezed, the vial would break, and the acid would then be released to eat into a wire. Once the acid ate through that wire, it would release a striker, which would in turn set off the fuse and thus the explosives. The amount of "time" in the pencil was meant to be correlated with the thickness of the wire through which the acid had to eat, but this was an inexact science.

To his horror, Smiley found that there were two compounding mis-takes. The first was his own: setting off a time pencil at the end of the bridge that he wanted to exit from first. The second was one of manu-facture. Just a few moments later, as he was setting the second time pencil—both were supposed to give him a ten-minute "fuse"—the first one went off, not only producing a very sizable hole in the bridge, along with flying debris, but also leaving him stranded on the wrong side of the river. Beating a rapid retreat in case the timing of the second pencil proved as inaccurate as the first, he found himself both swimming the swiftly flowing Shkumbin and being swept toward the detonating bridge. He hauled himself across just before the second charge went off,

prodded in his haste by the sound of German rifle shots from the opposite bank.

Smiley thought it an excellent start to their explosives operations
against the Germans. Enver Hoxha and the *Shtab*, the Partisans' self-
appointed General Staff, did not. Hoxha stormed into camp demanding
to know who had given Smiley permission to do such a thing. Smiley
took no orders from the *Shtab* and told Hoxha so. As he confided to his
diary, the Communists were getting more difficult to deal with the more
the British gave them arms and money. "A pity there is little to show for
it," Smiley noted acidly.

The Communists' actions against the Germans had been less and
less impressive since Mehmet Shehu had aborted the attack of his eight-
hundred-strong brigade on a platoon of eighteen Germans. They had set
up a roadblock at which they managed to kill three German soldiers in
a car. Smiley was told by one of the participants how four more were
taken prisoner and led into the woods to be shot. Told to remove their
boots, they threw rocks at their captors, whose shooting was so bad that
the Germans did some damage, and one even escaped for some time.
And as per usual, the Partisans failed to produce identification that
would prove their claims. It fell to Smiley, days later, to recover the relevant badges from the dead bodies. "The smell was awful," he complained. "I suppose the Partisan told you that to show you how brave he
was to go on shooting at the Germans while they were throwing stones,"
said Billy McLean when he and Kemp heard the story.

One day, a Ballist leader arrived to make a present of three German
prisoners to Smiley, who received them with dismay. Prisoners were a
burden in guerrilla warfare. Frequently, no one took them, as there was
simply no way to keep them. The "gift" was not gracious. The British could
not keep the prisoners. The Partisans pleaded to have them shot on the
spot, but Smiley wasn't going to be party to a war crime. He patched them
up, interrogated them in what he called his "halting German," and deposited them on a road where he could observe their successful repatriation.

The whole place was becoming more of an armed camp than it had been before. Smiley and McLean were one day invited to be the godparents of two local infants. The priest took his Sten submachine gun, placed it on the pulpit (under what Smiley deemed his "wonderful robes," he wore both battle dress and bandoliers), immersed the naked infants in holy water, and then tapped them "smartly" on the head with a bit of parachute cord.

KEMP HAD ALREADY SET OFF NORTHWEST TOWARD THE CENTRAL AL-banian city of Berat, where he would be the local liaison for both the Communist Partisans and the area's Balli Kombëtar leader. Kemp's ultimate goal was to go to what was then called *the* Kosovo to report on and organize the local resistance there, but his orders had not yet come through from the SOE office in Cairo. Both Smiley and McLean wanted to keep him for themselves. "He is such good value," as Smiley put it, contriving excuses.

Kemp reconnected with the man who had landed with him in Albania, the mustachioed George Seymour, whose radio he needed to borrow; his was giving his wireless operator trouble. While Seymour dealt with his own version of the Italian surrender, a disgraceful affair in which the local Italian commander deceived Seymour and went over to the Germans, Kemp was left to deal with the local Communist group.

The task was more difficult than Kemp had expected. Under McLean's tutelage, he had become accustomed to meetings with the Communists in Shtyllë. To Kemp's understanding, these proceeded in predictable stages: First, there were demands for money, followed by indignant howls when the Communists' more "outrageous" figures, in Kemp's opinion, were challenged, despite the lack of receipts or other solid proof. Then followed the stage of sulking or enraged outbursts, the latter of which were a specialty of Enver Hoxha. Then came requests for arms, which were passed on to Cairo. Then came the theater interlude, in which the

Partisans regaled the officers with accounts of German or Italian soldiers killed or wounded and presented "imposing figures" that had nary a shred of evidence to back them up. Complaints were the real heart of the endeavor. "These were divided into complaints against the Balli Kombëtar and complaints against the British Mission," Kemp said. "The one usually led on to the other, with little variation in the form of either."

It took hours. Kemp had found his previous meetings aggravating but not unendurable. Now, robbed of the unruffled McLean's protection, the tide changed. Kemp's relations with the Communist Partisans became "exacting, dull and uncongenial." He found that he was regarded by the Partisans "almost as their servant," and one whom they treated quite callously at that: opening British letters, skipping meetings, taking up hours with petty complaints, and staying steadfast in their refusal to allow either Kemp or Seymour to observe their claimed operations, leading both men to conclude that "they did not welcome any check on the accuracy of their reports."

AT SOE's STAFF OFFICE IN CAIRO, LEADERSHIP DECIDED THAT THE NUMber of missions in Albania was expanding at such a rapid clip that McLean's efforts should be overseen by someone even more senior than him. He was a decorated officer with experience in Palestine and what was then the North-West Frontier of India, now the still-precarious Pakistan-Afghanistan border in the Pashtun areas.

Brigadier Edmund Davies, of the Royal Ulster Rifles, was known to all as "Trotsky." A nickname given to him in his earlier years, it reflected not his politics but slang that signaled a youthful vituperativeness toward the higher powers. Davies himself chose to keep the name in his signals, oblivious to its local connotations. Purges against perceived "Trotskyites" had raged in the Soviet Union (and Spain) throughout the 1930s. Some of the Communist Partisans were to find his sobriquet sinister.

Davies's deployment was a decision made by that "globe-shaped

little militarist," SOE Cairo's chief of staff, Brigadier Keble. While there
is no hard proof, rumors have flown ever since that Keble's desire to send
a brigadier to Albania was based on the informal concept of the "rule of
three." This held that any officer commanding three officers of a given
rank should himself hold at least one rank above theirs. In this case, Keble's sending of additional brigadiers to the Balkans (Yugoslavia had its
own contingent) would have meant a promotion for himself to major
general. This would not have been uncharacteristic of Keble's careerism.

TROTSKY DAVIES KNEW NOTHING OF THE STAFF OFFICE DRAMA AND AR-
rived as ready to work as anyone. He did, however, bring more luggage
than the younger officers had expected. Experienced in guerrilla warfare, he had been, as Kemp put it, "on the receiving end," not the prac-
titioner's end, in his previous efforts. He arrived with a staff, including
his assistants, Lieutenant Colonel Arthur Nicholls and Captain Alan
Hare. What Smiley proclaimed himself "flabbergasted" over was all the
gear, including camp furniture and two containers of stationery, plus a
typewriter and an NCO clerk to go with it.

Trotsky was probably flabbergasted at what he found as well. By
their own admission, both McLean's and Smiley's attire had become
"individualistic," including McLean's ever-present crimson cummerbund and any piece of headgear that sported the silver eagle of the Royal
Scots Greys, as well as Smiley's preferred studded climbing sandals, issued by the Italian Alpini, and white Albanian fez. They once heard,
through the thin walls of their huts, the kind but formal Nicholls ad-
monishing the more junior Hare for his dress: "You're getting as untidy
as those fellows McLean and Smiley, and they've gone completely native."

It was poor Nicholls who tried to bring a bit of tidiness to the camp.
Smiley and McLean had given up on trying to correct the local habit of
littering, but Nicholls suffered from no such exhaustion. Rounding up

a collection of Vlach mulemen, Italian deserters, and Albanian Partisans, he marched them across the camp to pick up detritus. Reaching the far end, Smiley recalled, Nicholls "expressed his pleasure and told them to fall out, whereupon to a man they threw on the ground everything they had collected. Nicholls's comments were unprintable." Nicholls thought he was cleaning up the camp; the participants thought they were humoring a mad Englishman. Only Nicholls was disappointed.

Despite Davies's insistence that he "never understood why a soldier need look like a brigand when he is on special operations," he was eager to learn the complexities of the situation from McLean. "In Cairo I had been told to back any political party which would fight the Italians or Germans, and it had sounded very simple," said Davies. "In Albania I was to find the whole matter very complex and difficult."

DAVIES DECIDED TO SEND MCLEAN AND SMILEY BACK TO LONDON VIA Cairo. This would give them leave after seven months behind enemy lines, as well as an opportunity to give briefings and detailed reports to the SOE staff in both offices. Not knowing when they would return made it a bittersweet parting. "Our Albanian bodyguards, mulemen, and Italians looked very sad as we said goodbye," Smiley recalled. "Some even wept."

For Smiley, the hardest parting was with his mule, Fanny, who had carried him for these long months, never giving him any cause for concern, even among the precipitous mountains. Abrupt as he could sometimes be with humans, when it came to Fanny, Smiley was tenderness itself. Kemp noticed how devoted Smiley was to his mule, and how "whenever he felt depressed or particularly disgusted, he would stalk out of the mess and over to the mule-lines, where he would be found with his arm round Fanny's neck, whispering into her ear." Someone took a picture of Smiley as he said farewell to Fanny. Her head was held

near his, obscuring the side of his face. Taken from a ways off, the image shows Smiley holding Fanny's head in both hands, near her muzzle,
the two of them cheek to cheek.

McLean and Smiley had a journey of nearly one hundred miles as
the crow flies. It was probably double the way they would traverse it. It
would be the only time in Albania that they would move, if very briefly,
by car. Most of the journey would be on foot. Smiley was riding a borrowed horse along one of the mountain tracks toward the coast when
the poor beast stumbled and lost its footing. Smiley whipped his feet out
of the stirrups and dove off the horse just as the unfortunate animal
tipped over the side of the precipice and fell to its death. He vowed never
to ride a horse in the mountains again.

Their route led them multiple times through both Ballist and Partisan territory. The Partisans took their passage as an opportunity to
impress their demands upon McLean one last time. Smiley was more
grateful than usual for McLean's aplomb in dealing with their partners.
Politicking was never Smiley's favorite ("bored stiff" was how he described its effect), and his mood was not improved by their declining
health or the scarcity of food during parts of their journey.

Smiley's frustration with the Communist Partisans was born of politics, personalities, and a generalized annoyance with their military in-
effectiveness and increasingly obvious duplicity. This extended beyond
the issue of the Partisans' reluctance to seriously engage the Germans
despite British support. The Partisans would insist that their organization was not Communist but democratic. Once, while showing Smiley
a map of how the world would inevitably turn out, literally colored Communist red all over, Hoxha asked him how he would like to see the world.
Unable to resist, Smiley, who admitted that he became more "capitalist
and imperialist" to tease Hoxha the more the latter prattled his propaganda, replied, "I too would like to see this map painted red all over, but
not the sort of red you mean." Hoxha, who prided himself on being a

well-educated intellectual, missed the reference to the iconic red in which the British Empire was often rendered on world maps.

Smiley and McLean passed into part of the territory overseen by the local Balli Kombëtar leader. There the nationalist commander offered them a piece of paper. It was a captured Communist document, and Smiley felt confident that it was "definitely an original." It made sense of Mehmet Shehu's refusal to attack that platoon of Germans with his eight hundred well-armed Partisans. Shehu was no physical coward, and his reluctance to attack was not a question of military effectiveness or bravery; rather, it was about preservation of military might for future attacks against the non-Communist forces in Albania.

The document was a clear order to preserve the Partisans' arms for the coming civil war. This meant evading conflict with the Axis forces in favor of fighting the non-Communist forces instead. The Communist Partisans had a habit of writing down things that others would have avoided committing to paper. Hoxha was not above signing assassination orders with his own name. The Communist Partisans were not unwilling to fight; they were just picking their battles. Now they had plenty of British arms and training to turn on their real enemies.

Smiley and McLean soon passed through a Communist town, its walls plastered with hammers and sickles and its good hotels open only to Party commissars. As Smiley observed, "It is just like a comic opera, and to make things more amusing, the Germans are waiting on the outskirts, but have not yet come in. I am glad I am not staying here any longer."

THE PAIR HURRIED TOWARD THEIR EXTRACTION ZONE, WHICH HAPpened to be the new territory of the British officer who had descended faster than his vomit upon dropping in. Here their frustrations with their mercurial staff office increased, as food ran seriously short and excuses for delays in the promised boat's arrival kept popping up. Smiley was reduced to collecting water from puddles with his sponge. In the meantime, the pair received advice on how to treat the worms they had contracted. The first step, as the signal from Cairo read, was to "starve for twenty-four hours." Smiley later retorted, "By my reckoning, we had already complied with this part of the treatment!"

During the two nights before the Royal Navy finally arrived, Smiley sat on the shore beaming the letter *K* in Morse code with a flashlight. This served as their recognition signal. There was no other ship-to-shore communication available, and they had no idea when the ship, which turned out to be a motor torpedo boat, or MTB, might arrive. A small dinghy was sent from the MTB in the harbor to a landing zone that the British officers had dubbed Seaview. As the dinghy pulled up to the beach, two men jumped out. One was a Polish officer of the Royal Naval Reserve. The other was a naval intelligence officer named Sandy Glen.

Glen was small and Scottish, and while not actually fat, he was somehow rounded in all of his aspects, from his prematurely balding head (he was at this point in his early thirties) to his toes. No slouch, Glen had been, before the war, a member of two serious expeditions to the Arctic. At the beginning of the war, his expertise had been crucial to British operations in that zone. He had evacuated a series of Russian and Norwegian miners from Spitsbergen and had set up commando-like posts in the Arctic to prevent the Germans from gaining strategically valuable operating spaces there. He was wise, good-humored, and remarkably energetic, and if ever a woman were asked to choose the perfect combination of the voices of Jeremy Irons and Sean Connery, it would sound exactly like Sandy Glen.

After his Arctic adventures, Glen had been sent to the Balkans in 1940. This was where he had recruited Julian Amery into being both his flatmate and his partner in crime in the then-nascent Section D, a forerunner to SOE. As Amery later said of Glen's activities, "It was soon clear to me that they had little to do with the Navy, and were by no means as blamelessly 'diplomatic' as my own."

Glen surveyed the scene. The dinghy in which he had arrived from the MTB, and on which Smiley and McLean were meant to be extracted, had a hole in it. Glen bailed on approach. As the two strandees seized the dinghy, Glen protested, "You can't go in that goddamned thing. It's got a hole in its bottom."

"Oh yes we can," Smiley replied. "Anything to get out of this god-forsaken country."

Smiley and McLean had no actual luggage, but they did each have a briefcase full of sensitive documents and other important items to deliver to Cairo. Smiley rowed as hard as he possibly could while McLean bailed out water with equal vigor. Still, they were sinking fast, though nearing the MTB. Just as it sank completely, the two briefly swam one-handed, holding the briefcases aloft and tossing them to the sailors on the ship before being dragged out themselves. Glen, watching the scene from shore, thought their departure "rather like Christ walking on the water."

PETER KEMP, ENSCONCED WITH THE MUSTACHIOED GEORGE SEYMOUR near Berat and still suffering the attentions of the Partisans' Central Committee while recovering from a viciously high fever, received a summons from Brigadier Trotsky Davies back at the main camp.

"George!" Kemp called into their shared tent. "The Brigadier wants to see me right away. From the wording of this signal it looks as though I may be going to Kossovo [sic]."

"Good show, old boy!" came Seymour's reply.

Kemp left both his wireless operator and wireless set with Seymour and set off the next morning. When he arrived back at the main camp in Bixha, he found to his chagrin that he had missed Smiley and

McLean by just thirty-six hours. Though separated from them, Kemp was nonetheless starting to discover the same things they had about the Partisans' long-term plans, which the nationalist commander had revealed on paper to his compatriots.

While Kemp was at camp, preparing to leave for Kosovo, Davies was holding a series of meetings with Hoxha and the Central Council, along with the Balli Kombëtar and Abas Kupi, a nationalist resister and supporter of King Zog. Kupi and the Balli had both agreed to work together with the other factions against the Axis. So had Hoxha, though he did not yet know of the others' agreement. When Davies moved to bind all three parties to the agreement by having the declaration broadcast by the BBC, Hoxha exploded.

Shouting and enraged, he commanded Davies to suppress the report of the agreement before it went to the press. Hoxha had not expected the non-Communist elements to agree to work together and was furious that they had done so. He had wanted the denial to be on their side. Hoxha's acquiescence had only been for show. He had no intention of working with the non-Communist forces, whom he planned to dominate, and never had. Davies was appalled.

As the brigadier put it, "The whole affair had been bungled by Enver; he had not come out of it very well; had broken a promise, had been outwitted by the Balli, and he was in a thorough temper. I spoke quite plainly: if he did enter civil war, I would cut off all supplies from the LNÇ [Communist Partisan] Mission. I was only empowered to back him if he fought the Boche, and in my opinion, he could not do both." Expressing dismay, Davies added, "The only result would be that he would attack the Balli as soon as he felt strong enough, and go on attacking them until they were finished. There would be little fighting against the Germans."

Hoxha was undeterred. He ordered his Communist Partisan units to attack the Balli. Kupi and his Zogists he would leave for later. The Civil War was on.

CHAPTER 5

A STATELY
PLEASURE-DOME

Billy McLean and David Smiley returned to SOE's headquarters in Cairo to report. They arrived after a stop in Bari on the Italian coast. There they had been "deloused" in a bath of what Smiley called a strong carbolic, and Smiley had lost his special battle dress—magnetic buttons and all, including silk maps of the Balkans sewn into the waist belt, a six-inch hacksaw in one seam, and two gold sovereigns in the trouser cuffs—to the incinerator, which was standard procedure when dealing with pests.

Cairo was in decline from its glory days early in the war. Then the city had seemed like a place out of time. As the Blitz raged in London, officers could be barred from the dining room of one of Cairo's most popular hotels for the sin of wearing shorts. When one officer, a recent arrival from London, protested, he was informed by more senior officers that "captains had no right to an opinion on the matter." Cairo boasted a spectacular social calendar, riches beyond description, a kaleidoscopic population that included kings (throned and exiled), pashas, British officers, local Egyptians, fleshpots of every description, and a glamour rivaled only by the Raj at its height.

The position of the British in Egypt was odd. So was the position of the Egyptians. As one writer put it, an Egyptian "did not have to be a passionate nationalist to reach the conclusion that [Egypt] was being run for, and by, foreigners." This had been the case for centuries and was by no means limited to British imperialism. First had come the Ottomans, in the sixteenth century. Since the nineteenth century, a succession of Western European powers, first the French and then the British, had gotten their turn, eager to control the Suez Canal in particular. They held the country in an unofficial protectorate that everyone was careful not to label as such. As a result, most of Egypt's elite society was certainly elite but by no means Egyptian. King Fuad, ruling at the turn of the twentieth century, was embarrassed that he spoke French, Turkish, and Italian but no Arabic. During the war, the country was ruled by Fuad's chubby and immature but fully grown son, Farouk, and a parliament, but it was in all practical ways run by the British ambassador, Sir Miles Lampson.

During the Second World War, Egypt remained the great crossroads of the Middle East, North Africa, and the Mediterranean. It also boasted a partially Levantine culture, especially in the north, that reached back to the Ptolemaic dynasty, which ended with Cleopatra. (The Greek traders stayed on.) Cairo had street urchins who would eviscerate someone's car if they were not paid their customary tips; sprawling villas; and a massive sporting complex, the Gezira Club, featuring golf, racing, and the very smartest dining terrace, unrivaled within the very heart of almost any major city then or since. In the late nineteenth century, Cairo had been rebuilt, much like Paris, in the Haussmann style of wide boulevards. Also as in Paris, the language of upper-class society was French.

Sparing Cairo from aerial bombardments and rockets, which drove the people of London underground night after night, the war initially gave Cairo an excuse for even more parties. Not a weekend went by without some charity ball or another. One diplomat wrote home, describing a Christmas party hosted by one of the local aristocrats. The grand villa's garden was enclosed in a tent, dressed to look like a giant hall with a pool at the center, surrounded by professional musicians, low tables, cushions, belly dancers, and whisky (labeled as "about the only drinkable fluid left in Cairo"). The diplomat said it was "like something out of the Arabian Nights." After listing his titled and prestigious dance partners, the gentleman caught himself and explained, "I'm afraid this reads rather like a gossip column, but Cairo is like that, and the great thing is to treat it as rather a joke and not let it impress you ... For good- ness' sake, please keep this description very quiet, because I think peo- ple at home would be horrified if they knew how unaustere Cairo is." Cairo was unaustere. By the time McLean and Smiley had arrived in the fall of 1943, it was on a downswing from its former heyday. But for McLean and Smiley, this posed no major impediment: Cairo, as they found it, was an intoxicating respite from the wilds of Albania.

They were assigned to an extremely tall, blond, and almost inde- cently good-looking young officer named Billy Moss. He had graduated from Charterhouse just before the war broke out, when he was nineteen. In 1939, he had been brushing up on his language skills in Latvia (his mother was a White Russian) when he returned to take a commission in the Coldstream Guards. After his unit had been nearly destroyed in the Western Desert, he had arrived in time to serve as one of the replace- ments, chasing westward after Erwin Rommel following the breakout at El Alamein. He had made his way to SOE but was still waiting for an overseas assignment.

Moss was charged with being McLean and Smiley's "conducting of- ficer." In the whirl of briefings and meetings that McLean and Smiley were meant to attend, it was Moss's job to get them there and to get them there on time. But what Moss offered was even better than a taxi ser- vice. Along with his somewhat older friend and fellow SOE officer Pat- rick "Paddy" Leigh Fermor—the gifted travel writer who had set out to walk from London to Istanbul at the age of eighteen in 1933—he had found a grand villa for rent in the upscale district of Zamalek. It was filled with parquet floors and spacious rooms. They called it Tara. Whether the place was named after the seat of the ancient high kings of Ireland or after Scarlett O'Hara's manse was unknown. Moss invited McLean and Smiley, who had otherwise expected to reside in the barracks known as Hangover Hall, to live with them. There would be no fewer hangovers: Tara was the informal party capital of the young and adventurous set.

Leigh Fermor—who, in addition to being an inveterate traveler, was a European cosmopolitan and gifted linguist who would eventually get himself name-dropped in a commentary on voodoo in Ian Fleming's *Live and Let Die*—was the elder statesman of the house. Chased out of his posting to military intelligence in Greece during the German invasion of that country, he was evacuated first to Crete and then off Crete after the German airborne invasion of the island in 1941.

While Leigh Fermor and Moss had found better housing than the barracks could provide, they had also realized that paying rent for the entire house while deployed was going to be foolish. They tried to recruit several women to share the house, and the costs, with them. Initially, there were three, but two dropped out, leaving only a woman named Sophie Tarnowska. She agreed to come so long as, to preserve her honor, she was accompanied by a fictitious and frequently ill tenant named Madame Khayatt.

Tarnowska was the heart of the house. She was by birth a Polish countess, and like that of so many of her countrymen, her family's experience was tragic. Married young to an equally aristocratic second cousin with whom she had fallen in love on a wolf hunt at the age of seventeen, she lost her first son on the day that her second was born in 1939. In a dramatic gesture, she burned her passport, intending to stay in Poland even as the region descended into war. But soon she and her family, including her brother and his wife, fled by way of Belgrade and the Levant. They carried with them a Polish national treasure in the form of the personal standard of King Gustavus Adolphus of Sweden, which had been captured at her family's home during a battle in the seventeenth century. In Belgrade, she lost the second child. Soon after, her husband, who had been close friends with one of Smiley's older brothers at Oxford, informed her that he was in fact in love with his sister-in-law, her brother's wife. By the time they all arrived in Cairo, she and her husband had separated.

Barely in her mid-twenties, having lost two children, a husband, and her ravaged country, she moved into Tara with a swimsuit, an evening dress, and two pet mongooses. She was tall, elegant, and glamorous. She also bore an aura of damage that some men found irresistible. The fight for the hand of Tarnowska, then technically still married, was to prove an indelible feature of life at Tara. While he was working on staff at SOE Cairo, Julian Amery once arrived in the middle of the morning to find half a dozen young officers breakfasting around Tarnowska's bed while she reclined on her pillows and brandished a cavalry sword to ensure that their distance was properly kept.

As Amery put it, "Life at Tara was luxurious rather than comfortable. Sometimes there were lavish dinners. Sometimes there was only bread and cheese. In principle, there were hot baths for all. But sometimes there were no baths at all because Vodka was being made in them. There were two kinds of Tara Vodka: Vodka and Old Vodka. Vodka took twenty-four hours to make; Old Vodka, three days."

Tarnowska came up with the idea of putting fruits, such as apricots or plums, into the vodka to make liqueurs, as had been done at her father's estates. But proper alcohol takes time, and the results after three days were not what they should have been given the three weeks' maturation time required. At one point, two people passed out after consuming the mixture. Whether the fault rested more with the premature development or more with the volume consumed has not been indicated.

Given the parties that the house hosted, a certain volume of alcohol was simply required. A wandering and exhausted set of Polish partisans once shot out all the lights in the house but also left behind an

honest-to-goodness dancing bear trained by Gypsies. Egypt's King Farouk, who enjoyed the parties, brought both a crate of champagne and
a set of policemen to take the bear for its daily walks. Tarnowska was
known to release one of the mongooses when "the conversation became
tedious or the guests outstayed their welcome." There was also a story
that involved King Farouk defending the royal ankles from said mongoose with his fork and napkin from a standing perch atop a dining-
room chair. Presumably, he had offered the police escort for the bear
sometime before.

One day, the mongoose got loose and nearly killed the pet parrot of
the next-door neighbor, Lady Keown-Boyd, whose rich husband was
crucially involved in the Middle East Supply Centre. SOE's dyspeptic
chief of staff, Brigadier Keble, chose to dress down McLean and Smiley
over the incident. When the parrot failed to survive a repeat attack, Lady
Keown-Boyd insisted that both mongooses be shot.

Smiley, who happened to possess what he called "a rather good silencer," was appointed executioner: "I got behind the poor brutes and
blew their brains out." McLean did not make friends by retelling the
story, with emphasis on the heartlessness of the demanded execution,
at dinner one night to a guest who turned out to be Lady Keown-Boyd
herself.

Tara was also home to an Alsatian puppy inaptly named Pixie. The
problem child of two captured Gestapo dogs, he once chased a water
buffalo out of the Nile, after which the besieged beast crashed down a
flight of steps and into the apartment of a nice French family. Not long
thereafter, he pantsed a young taxi boy, who had him temporarily locked
up in jail.

A year later, Moss and Leigh Fermor would provide an entirely new
kind of sparkle to the Cairene social set: in early May of 1944, after a short
disappearance, they would return to Cairo with one General Heinrich
Kreipe in tow. A veteran of the Battle of Verdun in World War I and a
former commander on the Eastern Front, he had not one but two Iron

Crosses. Alas, he was not the general they had wanted. (That man, General Friedrich-Wilhelm Müller, known as "the Butcher of Crete," was a nasty piece of work whose repression of the island's civilians was notable even given the Wehrmacht's well-known habit of reprisals.) Kreipe was Müller's replacement as head of German operations on the island. Moss and Leigh Fermor had kidnapped him right off Crete, in a mission dreamed up and planned by Leigh Fermor, with a small hand from Smiley and McLean, who briefed the would-be kidnappers on ambush techniques as Leigh Fermor drew crude practice maps of the potential target areas on Tara's steamed bathroom walls. Moss later tried to publish his own book on the adventure as early as 1945, though the authorities sensibly prevented a wartime release. Known as *Ill Met by Moonlight*, it eventually birthed a film with the same name, starring Dirk Bogarde.

BUT THESE ADVENTURES WERE STILL IN THE FUTURE; FOR THE TIME BEing, in the late fall of 1943, Smiley and McLean were the most glamorous swashbucklers at Tara. Their current task involved a volume of paperwork and report writing that was not amenable to either one of them (or to, as Moss remembered it, the "sulky-faced typist" assigned to help them). Leigh Fermor observed that the two were "definitely mightier with the sword than the pen." They had at their willing disposal someone who was well versed in staff-office paperwork, the specific political machinations of the offices of both SOE Cairo and SOE London, and the wider political picture of the war: McLean's old school friend, Julian Amery.

Amery was still trying to land an active role in the Balkans but was stuck at SOE Cairo's staff office. He had been forbidden from taking a job on staff with the new, young, and decidedly non-collaborationist King of Yugoslavia, Peter II; an attempt to join a brigadier in Greece was canceled. In the fall of 1943, just as McLean and Smiley appeared in Cairo on their return from Albania, Amery was beginning to lose hope: "The winter of 1943/44 remains in my memory as a period of deep depression verging at times on despair."

His exclusion from service in the field was intentional on the part of the higher authorities. "All organisations tend to develop cliques within them," Amery later wrote, "and this is particularly true of Secret Services where security can always be invoked to stifle criticism." This was one of Brigadier Keble's favorite tactics; he had once ordered an engineer to monitor personal calls on the phone lines, only for that engineer to find a gentleman named Keble making assignations with said engineer's own secretary. Amery maintained that, on both personal and political grounds, the group then in control of SOE Cairo did not like some of the men with whom he had worked early on in the war, "and they did not like me." They had barred him from any sort of active deployment to the Balkans, where they likely feared his outsize influence. He had, after all, already been not only so attentive as to be prescient but also highly effective in marshaling his not-insignificant personal network.

But by the fall of 1943, Keble had overstepped his mark in the SOE staff office. Still planning to revive his career by "discovering" the Yugoslav Communist Tito, Keble was incensed to find that Churchill, himself frustrated with the slow progress in the Balkans, planned to send his own man into Yugoslavia. Fitzroy Maclean was an intelligent, energetic, newly minted brigadier in his early thirties. Not to be confused with Billy McLean and hereafter referred to as simply Fitzroy, he was a former Foreign Office diplomat who had traveled extensively throughout Central Asia while treating his dismayed NKVD babysitters as a travel agency. He also sat through the entire show trials of some of Stalin's most senior henchmen during the purges of the 1930s.

This was not the sort of man whom James Klugmann, the Communist spy in Keble's office, would have wanted anywhere near Yugoslavia. Like everyone else, Klugmann would later be surprised by Fitzroy's support of Tito, with whom the brigadier remained very close for decades. As someone who would be supplied by SOE but not under its control, and who would have a direct line to Churchill, Fitzroy was the very last sort of person Keble wanted anywhere near the prize on which he intended to stake his career.

Keble had now graduated from misreading information to simply making it up. He faked a signal from the British General "Jumbo" Wilson to Churchill decrying Fitzroy's appointment and later enlisted a senior officer to spread malicious rumors about Fitzroy, including that he was "a hopeless drunk [and] an active homosexual" and had shown himself "consistently cowardly and unreliable." Unbeknownst to Keble, Fitzroy and Wilson were personal friends. Wilson rapidly uncovered the ruse.

Thus, by late fall, Keble was on the way out. This opened up opportunities for Amery, and perils for James Klugmann. As Keble's power waned, the mole Klugmann came under suspicion once more. Two other Communist agents in SOE London's staff office had recently been caught and tried, which again raised questions. Klugmann was put through further security interrogation as the security services tried to uncover his links to the Communist Party, and through those ties to the Soviets.

Klugmann's interrogation in 1943 lasted for four hours, but he kept his nerve. He admitted to his student participation in Communism but insisted that he simply wanted to win the war and "did not approve of contact with outside bodies." Moreover, he claimed, "I'd do what I was told to do until the war was ended, and I wouldn't have any political life outside the Army until the war was ended." This was a curious statement for someone who, throughout his posting at the SOE staff office, not only explicitly sought to change British policy on Yugoslavia in order to support the Communist Partisans but also passed classified information to the Partisans; advised the Partisans on how to manipulate Churchill's personal and uncontrollable envoy, Fitzroy Maclean; manipulated which British officers went to the Partisans versus non-Communist groups; filtered and massaged information from the field before he passed it on to his superiors; and saw to it that the British officers with the Partisans were well supplied, while those with non-Communists were frequently ignored. British security procedures, which in good liberal tradition were designed to protect an individual's rights, required a smoking gun. Thanks to Klugmann's missing records and willingness to lie, his interrogators couldn't quite find one. He was cleared.

USING KLUGMANN-ESQUE LANGUAGE, KEBLE HAD PERSONALLY PLAYED a role in keeping Amery out of the Balkans. In a letter to his father, Amery recalled how, that fall, Keble had tried to send him off to India. When reminded that Amery's heart was really in the Balkans, Keble produced twenty minutes of rambling discussion, the gist of which was that Amery was "not the right sort of person for the job." With Keble's removal, Amery had reason to hope for a brighter future.

Amery helped McLean and Smiley finish their report on their time in Albania and did them another favor: just before Christmas, he wrote to introduce McLean, his "very good friend" from Eton, to his father. McLean and Smiley were off to London to brief even more senior members of the government. McLean, Amery wrote, would be "grateful for any advice" that Amery père could give. McLean was no mean political hand. It would have been very clear to him, from his experiences in Albania and in the staff office, that his work was going to involve politics of both a high (international) and a low (internecine bureaucratic infighting) order. Leo Amery, with his decades of experience, would make an excellent mentor.

Following Julian Amery's introduction, McLean and Smiley found themselves invited to the Amery household for lunch, which included their second, and blissfully unofficial, meeting with King Zog and his wife, the very beautiful Queen Geraldine. (The first had taken place during one of the briefings they'd been sent to London to conduct.) When not lunching with royalty, they gave more briefings, lectures, and

presentations to various officials, including Anthony Eden, in the Foreign Office. It fell to McLean to give the lectures on Albanian politics
and personalities. Smiley covered the technical aspects. This eventually
put him in touch with the American-led Jedburgh teams, who orches-
trated an unorthodox swap: his information on modern guerrilla warfare in Europe in exchange for a new .30 semiautomatic carbine. This
was to become—in combination with that "Colt" .45, which the Partisans had temporarily relieved him of during his brief imprisonment
when he first arrived in Albania—Smiley's favorite weapon for special
operations.

Above all, Smiley stressed a more efficient supply chain in the field
and a brutally streamlined personal kit: "Take nothing with you that
you value, and treat everything that you take as certain to be lost." In
Albania, the winter was becoming desperate. On top of pressure from
the Germans, Mother Nature was uncooperative. Smiley had sent a
message asking after Fanny, his beloved mule, whom he had entrusted
to Alan Hare, Brigadier Davies's staff officer. Hare's succinct response
left a sad but understanding Smiley teasing until the end of his days that
Hare could not have been a true cavalryman: "Have eaten Fanny."

CHAPTER 6

THE BATTLE FOR KOSOVO

Peter Kemp was dreaming that he had been made a Dame of the British Empire for services to agriculture when he was shaken awake by the youngest son of the nationalist Albanian warlord in whose home he was staying. He had arrived at this house after being chased out of his scouting mission to the city of Dibra, Albania, en route to Kosovo, by a German assault. As per usual, moments before had come the standard Partisan reassurances—"There's no need for alarm" and "We shall get at least two hours' warning of an attack"—followed immediately by German machine-gun fire splattering into the walls next to them. Kemp's own paramilitary expert had been separated from him in the fray. The NCO arrived at the house later with only the clothes on his back, having been hounded by the Germans and having had to abandon all of their gear, including Kemp's experimental submachine gun. All Kemp had left was his .45 pistol and one magazine.

Kemp was still being shaken from sleep. "Your binoculars, please, Mr. Major. There are some men coming over the hill."

And there were—German men. Kemp thought the child was joking, but then bullets struck the outside wall. Kemp leaped up, concluding that the only option, given their newfound inability to defend the place, was "headlong flight." Kemp shouted for Tomaso, his Italian interpreter, but was hurried out of the house by one of the warlord's older sons. His group followed their NCOs through a small escape door in the court-yard wall.

The Germans were already there. One of the Albanian warlord's older sons took running shots from the hip while Kemp, still trying to conserve his one magazine of ammunition, fired carefully with his pistol. One British wireless operator, heroically trying to carry his heavy radio, soon tripped and smashed the thing, which he heaved into a bush. Somehow they made it through the gauntlet and down into a ravine, finally gathering together in a patch of dead ground from which they were not visible to enemy gunners.

The warlord's son was bound by the Albanian code of honor to protect his guests, for allowing harm to come to a guest was considered the gravest of offenses. He herded them into the mountains. From their perch, they could see his home burning. They had heard gunfire as they fled, signaling that his father and brothers had tried, for some time at least, to fight it out. Tears streamed down the young man's face, as he feared the worst. But by midday, they had regrouped. The family was alive, though the father had taken bullets in his shoulder and wrist, which would be stuffed, in local fashion, with a poultice made of goat cheese. But Kemp's Italian interpreter, Tomaso, was dead, shot straight through the heart as he tried to break past the German cordon.

The Germans took out their frustration on the local population. In the nearest village, they rounded up men, women, and children, lined them up against the wall of the schoolhouse, and used machine guns to massacre them all. Looking down on the smoke hanging over the burning village homes in the cold light of that rain- and lightning-stricken November day, Kemp felt that he was "staring at a nightmare canvas of El Greco."

THE FIGHT FOR THE NEARBY CITY OF DIBRA WAS LOST. NOW KEMP'S EF-
forts would best be directed against trying to understand the opportunity for a revolt in nearby Kosovo, in order to pressure the Germans
from that direction. Then as now, Kosovo was one of the most combus-
tible parts of the Balkans. Technically, the name belonged to the plain
on which the Battle of Kosovo was fought, and lost, by the Serbs in 1389.
It was after this battle that they lost their independence to the Ottomans
for nearly six hundred years. Used in common parlance, the term included the region around the plain and the cities and villages within.
Which country it belonged to would come to haunt Kemp, as it would
so many others in the twentieth century.

Kosovo was claimed by the Orthodox Serbs with a ferocity that, had
they displayed it on the plain in 1389, might well have won them the day
against their Turkish rivals. Kosovo was theirs by tradition, by right, by
history, went the argument. On the opposing side was the fact that the
population of the area was, by most counts, nearly 90 percent Albanian
(and Muslim). It was also Albania's natural granary. The Serbs, who,
Kemp later noted, "enjoy—and *enjoy* is the word—bad relations with
their neighbours," insisted that the Albanians were newcomers, immigrants, Turk-appeasing thieves of rightfully Serbian land.

In both a literal and metaphorical sense, neither side spoke the other's
language. Kosovo had been included within the borders of Yugoslavia
during the creation of the Serb-dominated monarchic confederation after the end of the First World War. It was, like so many other things resulting from President Wilson's careless use of the phrase "national
self-determination," a creation that would end in massacre.

The Germans, who were no fools, and who had their own frustrations with many borders instituted by the peace conference, knew a
good opportunity for divide and rule when they saw one. They and their

Italian allies, who had invaded Albania in 1939, made Kosovo part of
Albania. This exacerbated tensions between Serbs and Kosovars. Language of unification may have made Yugoslavia palatable to the liberal
allies after the First World War, but it had obscured the reality of an imperialist, pan-Serbian movement. With the new war, that movement
degenerated into violence. Kemp would stay in the house of a family
whose patriarch's brother had been executed in front of his entire family by Serb soldiers. Albanian victims gave as good as they got. As Kemp
put it, "In their turn they reacted savagely against their former oppressors, under the benevolent protection of their new German and Italian
masters."

   Kemp's orders were to raise Kosovar support for the Allies and gen-
erate resistance against the Germans. But the Germans were giving the
Kosovars what they wanted above everything else: independence from
what they saw as a pan-Serb, pan-Slav menace, most of which included
the Communist Partisans.

   With help from the regional warlord—Muharrem Bajraktar, the
Gheg chieftain of Luma—Kemp traveled the dangerous route (one guide
insisted they never let it be known that they carried gold) to the city of
Deg, where he met a man whose family was a crucial player in many
forms of Albanian resistance. His name was Hasan Beg Kryeziu. Hasan
warned Kemp that without a good response to the question of whether
the Allies would allow a plebiscite in Kosovo (which, by population,
could only mean Albanian retention of the territory), the Allies would
not get very far. Kemp's orders made no such promises.

   Kemp was warned, again, about the unpopularity of the Partisans
in Kosovo. Associated with the Yugoslav Communist Tito's forces, they
were considered an element of "Pan-Slav Imperialism." This was not
purely a knee-jerk reaction of anti-Communism. Albanians like the
Gheg chieftain Muharrem Bajraktar had been equally unable to come
to an agreement with the royalist Yugoslav leader, General Dragoljub

"Draga" Mihailović, over the issue of Kosovo. But Mihailović had little power in Kosovo and none at all in Albania. Mihailović's opponent, the Communist Tito, by contrast, was making inroads in a very clever way.

Serbs were not popular in Kosovo, but Tito was not a Serb—he was a Croat, and smart enough to realize that to consolidate his personal power in Yugoslavia, he would have to back the right causes. The return of Kosovo to Yugoslavia was one of them. He knew that the local Communist group, known as the Kosmet, was not very popular. But Tito did not plan to win control of Kosovo from within Kosovo. He was going to win it from within Albania.

What the British officers in the field did not realize, though they were coming to suspect it, was that the Partisan movement in Albania was overshadowed by Tito. Kemp had already seen the effects of this directly. Before he left for Kosovo, while he was working with George Seymour, two of their NCOs had been visited by two English-speaking members of Enver Hoxha's Central Committee. One of them was a rare Serb Kosovar who also happened to be one of Tito's two envoys to Enver Hoxha. When the British NCOs were not looking, the Communists read through their papers, interfered with the wireless traffic, demanded information about frequencies and other technicalities of the British wireless transmissions, tried to get the NCOs to give them summaries of the reports the officers were sending to Cairo, and finally tried to convert them to Communism.

Tito was the power behind Hoxha. Without Tito, Hoxha never would have been invited to the initial founding meetings of the Albanian Communist Party, much less have become its leader. Hoxha made sure never to challenge Tito over Kosovo. Even in 1945, when Yugoslav soldiers engaged in ethnic cleansing of a group of Albanian Kosovars who had been conscripted into their army, an event known as the Bar Massacre, Hoxha did not protest. Kosovo was part of the price for his power.

KEMP MADE HIS WAY TO THE CAMP OF ANOTHER BRITISH OFFICER TO use his wireless set and replenish what stores might be available. He was not happy to learn that the Partisans and local nationalist chiefs were on the brink of a shooting war. Nor was Kemp pleased with the news that he himself was apparently dead.

The signal had come in from Cairo the night before, claiming that Kemp had been killed during street fighting in Peshkopijë, a village near the Albanian warlord's burned-down home, from which Kemp had barely escaped. Kemp rapidly signaled back: "Still alive please refrain from wishful thinking."

A year later, he finally heard the details from Alan Hare, who had been at the main SOE camp in Bixha serving under Brigadier Davies. The story had come from a wounded Partisan who had wandered into the camp. He swore to have seen it with his own eyes: Kemp had been creeping along a street in Peshkopijë when he happened upon a German soldier. Like in the movies, they saw each other at the same time and fired at once. Both then fell dead.

Hare told Kemp he had never bought it. "The others were suitably impressed and sad. I alone knew the story couldn't be true: for one thing, you would never have been wide enough awake to fire at the same time as a German, and for another, your Welgun would certainly have jammed."

The details matched up to almost nothing that had happened. The dates, it is true, aligned: Kemp's fabricated demise had taken place at the same time as the attack on the house from which he (but not his poor interpreter, Tomaso) had escaped. But Kemp had never been creeping along a street in Peshkopijë at all, and much less had he encountered a German there. Why the Germans, who were explicitly hunting the British officers, might have wanted to play mind games was one thing. They later showed one British prisoner photos of three dead bodies in British battle dress, claiming the captured to be Kemp and two other officers. But just who had staged the photos for this patently false story, and why—and how the Germans ended up with not only the images but also the names—were questions that no one ever managed to answer.

The wounded Partisan was not passing on a rumor; rather, he swore to have seen the sorry sight with his own eyes. He had intentionally gone to Davies's camp to tell it. The Partisans, under pressure from Tito, did not want Kemp in Kosovo. If the British thought Kemp already dead (he had no radio of his own), they would not look for him if he actually disappeared. You can't kill a dead man twice.

OPERATING WITHOUT KNOWLEDGE OF WHY THE PARTISANS WANTED him dead, or at least fake dead, Kemp called his next decision "the greatest mistake I ever made": telling Mehmet Hoxha (of no relation to Enver), the leader of the Kosovar Communists, his plans for travel and reconnaissance. Kemp did not want to be accused of trying to operate behind their backs, nor were lies of omission his style. But despite Mehmet's agreement, Kemp soon found himself waylaid on the road by a group of Partisans as he set out for the city of Gjakove.

The Partisans demanded that Kemp wait for Tito's representative to the local Communists. In what Kemp described as a "most truculent manner," they also insisted that he take only one of their interpreters, that he see only people approved by them, and that their men be able to attend all of his meetings. In what was probably one of his less diplomatic encounters, Kemp informed them that "I took orders from the Allied High Command, not the Kosmet, and went on my journey." The Communists could, in other words, do what they liked about it. As he was soon to learn, what they did was send word to the Germans divulging his location.

Kemp and his men snuck into Gjakove under cover of darkness. He called it a "musical comedy routine": As they prepared to dash across the cobbled streets from cover to cover, Kemp glanced over at his Albanian guide, crouched cartoonishly over his rifle, and was struck by the observation that he looked "more like a guerrilla than a guerrilla has a right to look. I wondered fearfully whether we were in greater danger of arrest as bandits or as lunatics." Even their mule, constantly hushed, began to hang its head in shame.

When they arrived at Hasan Beg Kryeziu's house, the warlord was alarmed to hear of Kemp's confrontation with the Kosmet and warned him that, with such tensions, he would have to curtail some parts of his planned tour and introductions within Kosovo. Kemp was mortified, especially given how much personal risk Hasan was taking just to shelter him at all. Hasan's old servant just laughed and teased: "If you want to play at politics, Hasan Beg, you must be brave!"

Immersed in meetings with nationalists and irredentists (men hoping to retain Kosovo for Albania permanently), Kemp kept running into the problem of Kosovo's place after the war. If the problem of Albanian resistance in general was complicated by the fact that the Communist and non-Communist resistance groups feared each other far more than they feared their temporary German occupiers, in Kosovo that problem was compounded by the question of Albania versus Yugoslavia. Some irredentists were all too happy to work with the Germans. This wasn't Kemp's first experience with that: on his way from Albania to Kosovo, Kemp had been accosted on the road by a local robber baron who had joined the Germans during the attack on Dibra.

The benefit of hindsight means that most people today have a difficult time understanding why anyone would see the murderous and genocidal Nazis as decent allies in the midst of the Second World War. It was a challenge for the British officers in Albania as well. It was even more difficult for the staff officers, safely tucked away in Cairo, to comprehend: Why wouldn't those ordinary Albanians do more to fight the Germans? (The language was sometimes high-handed; one staff officer referred to one resistance leader's men as "hordes.")

But was the poor local who had refused to shelter Kemp and McLean after their attack on the German staff car a collaborator, a fascist, or a reactionary? Or was he just frightened and so poor that it would have been catastrophic for his family if the Germans had burned down his house in retribution for an assault he had not participated in? Did it make you a Nazi to warn the Germans about either rumors of, or plans for, an impending attack in an attempt to save your village, even if you knew that these men machine-gunned women and children and shoved little boys back into burning buildings? If you were attacked by Partisans because you owned a small farm, did it make you evil to retreat to German-occupied territory, where the Communists couldn't get to you? And what about the tempting tactic of setting up an ambush on a road near the village of your local rival, or your blood-feud enemy, hoping to see him wiped out in a German reprisal? Should you help the Allies fight the Germans if you suspected that doing so would also consolidate the power of a group that would persecute you after the war was over? What was an appropriate level of "sacrifice"—and what should you sacrifice *for*?

Many people in Europe lived in places so violent that Hitler was, incredible as it may seem, the lesser of many unavoidable evils. In such places, there was no such thing as a single Second World War, as there were a multitude of wars going on at the same time. The Albanians and Kosovars, stuck in a landscape of clashing tribes, religions, families, ideologies, and borders, lived many of them. To the Allies, the Nazis were the enemy. To the Albanians, the Nazis were but one part of a wider and much longer struggle, one enemy among many. To prize one's own Devil over another's is simply to make the mistake of prizing one's God over another's, albeit in reverse.

Today, in the aftermath of the ethnic cleansing that followed the breakup of Yugoslavia after the end of the Cold War, we still carelessly speak of the "ancient hatreds" of the Balkans, as though they were somehow a problem located in geography instead of in any human heart. Yet human competition and functional tribalism recognize the boundaries of neither maps nor bloodlines. The people of Albania, and of Kosovo, happened to find themselves facing some of man's most basic instincts for self-preservation in a very small space.

Alternately victims and persecutors during centuries-long waves of invaders, local warlords, and competitive neighbors, these people knew full well what would happen when the tide turned and the powerless became the powerful—or when the formerly powerful felt their supremacy begin to wane. Kosovo had been part of Yugoslavia. The Axis had bought local goodwill by making it part of Albania. The Kosovars knew the retribution they would face from the Serbs if they were handed back.

The Kosovar irredentists had no desire to stick their necks out just because a foreign power asked nicely, especially if that foreign power would not offer them the thing they believed could protect them from slaughter: in this case, the continued separation of postwar Kosovo from Serb-dominated Yugoslavia. Kemp, hobbled by the Allies' refusal to promise even a plebiscite to the majority Albanian Kosovars, made little headway. Meanwhile, he had learned of the Kosmet's treachery. The Germans would be onto him very soon.

Just before Christmas in 1943, Kemp was joined by a new young officer named John Hibberdine, who made a wonderful partner. ("That such stimulus was needed became apparent to me from the frequency with which I found myself losing my temper over trifles," Kemp said.) Dispiritingly, Kemp found his way forward blocked. The irredentists insisted that the German road controls in Kosovo were becoming so effective that they could no longer ensure his safety, especially since they had learned of the Kosmet's treachery in betraying his presence to the Wehrmacht.

NEWS CAME OF A BRITISH DISASTER: EARLY IN THE NEW YEAR, BRIGAdier Davies's camp had been overrun by the Germans, along with some of their Albanian quislings. Davies and two of his staff officers were wounded and captured. Arthur Nicholls and Alan Hare escaped. Nicholls, who suffered severe frostbite and exposure, died three weeks later.

This, too, was a suspicious tale, but for other reasons. It had been a miserably harsh winter, and conditions were difficult. The Partisans dealt with this by subsisting on meager rations and by living off the land. (How voluntary this was on the part of the people supporting them was unclear.) For Davies and his staff, which at one point had included a mule train of over one hundred animals, this pushed the limits of endurance.

Trying to keep up with Enver Hoxha, constantly on the move and under pressure from a German advance, was challenging for Davies's camp. On top of that, Hoxha repeatedly tried to separate himself from Davies, worrying the brigadier.

After Davies's camp was attacked, Hoxha left them in a town house with his spy Frederick Nosi. They were nearly overrun. They reconnected with Hoxha and his staff and found shared refuge in a sheepfold. Hoxha then tried to separate himself from Davies once more.

As Davies remembered it,

Enver was full of charm and good spirits. "My General, I have heard of a possible way out. I am taking the Council two days' march away, to a hide. From there we will be able to make arrangements more easily and quickly. By splitting our party in two halves, feeding will be easier. As soon as we are ready, I will send for you to join us. I am leaving Baba Faja and our defence platoon to protect you."

His smile was full of persuasion, but I did not like the thought of being parted from the Council, without warning. I could give no reason, but I was just thoroughly uneasy. I had a foreboding that if we parted now, it would be for the last time.

Hoxha installed Davies in another village, but there were rumors of Germans nearby. Davies, concerned about another raid, was assured to the contrary by one of the Partisans: "It is impossible, my General, we have spies in every village, every track is watched, we are bound to get at least two hours' warning. I have heard nothing."

This statement was followed by machine-gun fire from the Germans, joined by a Ballist faction who had made a decision similar to that of the Kosovar irredentists. Davies was shot three times, twice in the stomach. Nicholls and Hare were forced to abandon him as they tried to rush through the snow. Davies and two other officers were taken captive. By the dint of his own character, the brigadier got himself and the British officers and NCOs who were with him transferred out of the Mauthausen concentration camp, and they spent the rest of the war in prison at Colditz.

Davies was a prisoner of the Germans while Enver Hoxha had escaped. Had the failure of the Partisan guards reflected the standard Partisan lack of professionalism, or was it something more? Davies suspected that the Germans had found him the same way they had found information on Kemp in Kosovo: through Communist-planted intelligence. After the war, Davies asked a British officer who had been close with Hoxha if the Partisan leader had betrayed Davies. The officer denied it. But Davies still felt the need to ask the question. He also felt the need to publish it in his memoirs.

In London, Smiley and McLean were recalled. A second iteration of their mission, this time named (and still misspelled) Concensus II, was approved at the highest levels. McLean was by now a lieutenant colonel; Smiley, a major. (Kemp, in the meantime, had been promoted to major as well.) McLean and Smiley were to drop back into Albania and organize resistance among the nationalist and royalist tribes in the north, including the supporters of King Zog, the Zogists, led by the warlord Abas Kupi. They were ordered to stem the tide of Hoxha's civil war while turning the fire of Communists, nationalists, irredentists, and anyone else against the Germans. Anthony Eden, the Foreign Secretary, told both men to contact him directly if they had any problems.

They would bring a new team member: McLean had made a personal request for Julian Amery. The younger man had been hopeful. Before Christmas, when Amery had written to his father, he had suggested that with Keble now finally gone, a "genuine attempt" might be made to get him back to the Balkans, in reward for his persistence after so many previous assignments had been denied. "I have grown inured to disappointment, but for the present I am definitely optimistic," he wrote. This time, his deployment was approved. Returning from a trip to Saudi Arabia, Amery found a sealed package in his flat. Upon opening three inner envelopes successively marked "Personal," "Secret," and "For Amery Only," he held in his hands a note from Philip Leake, the new head of SOE's Albanian Country Section. Leake was a kindly, respected, and sensible former schoolmaster in his forties who had already worked with some of Peter Kemp's former Commando colleagues elsewhere in Africa. "Please call at my office as soon as you are back," read Leake's message.

Leake briefed Amery on Davies's capture and McLean's request for his services. To Amery, "it seemed fitting that I should end my contribution to the European war in Albania. It was there, after all, that I had begun it in 1940. Besides, there could be no better companions for such a tiger shoot than McLean and Smiley."

KEMP WAS STILL TRYING TO WORK HIS WAY THROUGH KOSOVO, DODGing Germans and angry Kosmet Partisans as he went. The former were getting ever closer to him. He was once saved by only the good graces of a local police chief, who had received warning of an impending German raid and bought Kemp time to escape. The staff office in Cairo was not much help. In January, Kemp and his partner, John Hibberdine, signaled that they had received no mail or personal items since October. They suggested that their mission, Stepmother, be rechristened Stepchild.

The Kosmet Partisans executed one of Kemp's former hosts, who had also sheltered Partisans, as a warning to others "of the consequences of befriending" the British. In the meantime, Hasan Beg Kryeziu had introduced Kemp to his younger brothers, Gani and Said, who had recently returned to Albania. They were the first Albanians whom Amery had ever met, on the night when he had rung up a British journalist in an attempt to talk to some Albanians. Their conversation had resulted in the report that had landed Amery in SOE in the first place. They were coming full circle.

Since meeting Amery in Belgrade, the brothers had infiltrated themselves back into Albania and had been captured and interned in Italy. They had escaped and made their way back to their home country. Gani could be described as little other than gung ho. He was willing to set aside political differences with the Kosmet in order to fight the Germans. Kemp and Hibberdine doubted the ease of that proposal but welcomed his intentions. As Kemp put it, "Gani convinced me—as he later demonstrated—that he meant to put all his energy and talent into the struggle."

THE COMMUNIST PARTISANS, HOWEVER, WERE NOT PLEASED WITH Kemp's success. Kemp learned that another British officer had nearly been captured by the Germans. He had been operating nearby, but the Germans had come from the direction of the town of Kukës, a journey of over twelve hours on narrow mountain tracks. Kemp found it "particularly disturbing" that they could get so far with only fifty men toting little more than tommy guns—unless the path had been made clear for them. The Communist Partisans raised no alarm. The British officer was saved by only his good personal relationship with a local, who gave him an hour's warning, allowing him to get out just in time.

Mehmet Hoxha was also very angry with Peter Kemp, still alive and successful despite the Kosmet's best efforts. Kemp had, according to the

Kosmet, been acting with "defiance" and interacting with "reactionaries." If he continued, the Kosmet would report him "to Marshal Tito and to the LNÇ [Hoxha's Communists] in Albania"—a telling combination. Gani Kryeziu attempted to reassure Kemp by setting his own guards on the roads.

Mehmet was not bluffing. As Kemp put it, the signal that came next from Cairo "shattered all my hopes. . . . Its opening words are fixed forever in my memory: 'Kemp to break tactfully all contact with Kryezius and Irredentists.'" The reason aligned with the Kosmet's threat, the importance of Yugoslavia, and the role of the mole Klugmann: "Our relations with Jugoslav Partisans are of overriding importance." The timing was odd. Only just that morning, Kemp had sent the staff office a signal with the good news of Gani's impending plans for an attack on the Germans.

Kemp and Hibberdine were horrified. "I thought 'tactfully' was good," Kemp wrote in a report penned after his deployment. "Only staff officers," he and Hibberdine privately commented, "would suppose that we could 'tactfully' abandon men who had risked their lives to help us; moreover, to desert the Kryezius at the very moment when, exhorted by Cairo and ourselves, they had taken up arms for the Allies was not only base but foolish."

Kemp was certain that this could not be the work of his colleague Philip Leake, the Albanian Country Section head and former schoolmaster who was about to send in Amery with McLean and Smiley. It was not. Mehmet Hoxha had complained to Tito; Tito had passed Mehmet's protest to a British officer assigned to him. The protest had gone to Klugmann's Yugoslav Country Section, which outranked the Albanian one.

Kemp begged to at least be able to continue contact with Gani Kryeziu, who was now actively fighting the Germans. The staff office refused. There was no work left for Kemp in Kosovo; he would have to come out to report. But how? The flooded rivers meant that he could not move south for a coastal evacuation, as Smiley and McLean had done. His only option was to move northward into Montenegro, where Tito's Partisans held an evacuation field in the city of Berane. Other British officers were waiting for evacuation there.

First, though, he would have to convince the Kosmet's Mehmet Hoxha to give him safe passage. Mehmet, delighted to be rid of the man he had been trying to dispose of for so long, gave his assent. The passage was dangerous, and Kemp could never quite bring himself to believe that Mehmet had not laid a trap for him somewhere. (Another officer had, after all, warned him that Mehmet had threatened to take "measures" against him.) It was only with the help of a very young guide that he made it through that February's snow- and German-filled forests into Montenegro. Before he left, Kemp had written a letter, passed by a trusted interpreter, to the Kryeziu brothers: "I tried to explain 'tactfully' that I had been recalled suddenly to Cairo for consultation, that I would never forget their kindness, and that I would do all in my power to supply them British arms and supplies in support of their operations. I felt too deeply ashamed to write more."

As Kemp and his guides came to the crest of a beech-covered mountain in the snow, he saw before them a small cairn marking the Montenegrin frontier. "I looked back over the moonlit mountains and dark, deep valleys of Albania, so beautiful in that clear February night that all the fears and disappointments I had suffered there vanished from my mind; in that moment of rapture, I felt a futile longing to return."

IN BERANE, THE DOOR TO WHAT KEMP LABELED A "DISMAL TWO-storeyed building" was opened by a tall man wearing a British uniform. It was Bill Hudson, the man whom Julian Amery had deposited on the coast of Montenegro by way of submarine in 1941 during Operation Bullseye. He had undergone an exciting and appalling set of adventures with both sides of the Yugoslav resistance in the three years since. Introducing Kemp to several others, including an American colonel, Hudson said, "Have some raki. Do you play bridge?"

Bridge was a way to handle the nerves of being stuck in Berane. There was no need for Kemp to have rushed. Evacuation flights were infrequent. In the meantime, they were at the mercy of the local Partisans, who seemed to enjoy their experience of power by harassing the Allied officers. One altercation led to Hudson and their American housemate, the OSS colonel, disarming an insolent guard who tried to prevent the children who did their grocery shopping from bringing the goods into the house.

"You wait," Hudson, who had plenty of experience with the Partisans, warned in the aftermath of the kerfuffle with the guard. "The next thing they'll do is try to collar our wireless set. They know that as long as we have a wireless link with Cairo, there are limits to what they can get away with. So they'll find some excuse to get it from us. Then they can treat us like dirt."

On the afternoon of March 25, the wireless operator brought a decoded message from Cairo: "In view of misunderstanding between Partisans and yourselves reported by Hunter [the liaison officer at headquarters] which may endanger British relations with Partisans in Montenegro, you are instructed to hand your wireless set to [the local commander] within twenty-four hours of receiving this."

Peter Kemp was not a man unaccustomed to severe discipline. In the Spanish Foreign Legion, he had once been forced to oversee the execution of a British deserter from the International Brigades simply because his commander knew that he was morally opposed to such things; the commander sent two legionnaires to shoot Kemp if he failed to comply. But even Kemp was amazed at the callousness of this order from Cairo, which effectively abandoned them to an obviously dangerous fate: "We could not feel that 'British relations with Partisans in Montenegro' were as important as our lives."

Hudson drafted a rocket back. It was long, bitter, and to the point:

"At least refrain from treachery to your officers in the field. Such con-duct is unworthy of prostitutes let alone S.O.E. Staff Officers." Kemp ad-mitted that the furious Hudson at least had the good sense to reject his own editorial suggestion, by which the final line would have acerbi-cally read "Such conduct is unworthy of prostitutes or even S.O.E. Staff Officers."

The office climbed down in what Kemp described as "the most ab-ject apology I have ever seen from any headquarters." Perhaps Hudson's retort had landed on the desk of a higher power or someone other than the initial creator of the order. Either way, the apology came with a "sting in the tail," albeit a welcome one: they were going home. As Kemp remembered: "We said goodbye to the Brigade Commander and the Commissar—one of the happiest partings of my life."

CHAPTER 7

THE SUBURBS
OF ARMAGEDDON

As they approached the American Dakota that would fly them back
to Albania, an American-accented pilot informed the group of
four men that their very own Peter Kemp would be serving as dispatcher
for the drop.

"No, he damned well isn't!" declared McLean, Smiley, and Amery
all at once. As much as he admired Kemp, Smiley thought the man "was
inclined to be vague." Visions of an unattached static line and a swift
plunge to earth danced before him. The Americans found someone
more qualified.

Kemp had found the trio soon after he was evacuated from Berane
to Bari. He was permitted to join them on the drop flight as a morale
booster, though his attempt to return to Albania with them had been
thwarted by Philip Leake. Apparently, men recently returned from the
field should take leave.

For eight runs lasting almost two hours, they circled over two different drop zones, one for supplies and one for men. Outside the plane,
the searchlights of Tirana backlit the flak bursting around them.

"Are you quite all right, old boy?" Kemp asked Smiley every time
the plane shook violently from an explosion. It was hard to know who

had the worse position: the men planning to get out of the bombarded plane in short order or the one expected to ride in it all the way back to Italy. For the exasperated Smiley, Kemp's concern "made us all feel much more frightened than we already were!" Nevertheless, it was a thought he kept to himself. Kemp, concealing a secret case of claustrophobia, passed around a bottle of grappa. The flak grew too heavy. The pilot called off the rest of the drop, and the disappointed team returned to Italy.

All four men were invited to dinner by a local Italian count. The count had invited other guests who turned out to be the Dukes of Spoleto and Aosta—the latter of whom technically held claim to the crown of Croatia under the Nazis' short-lived puppet kingdom. Amery noted that "as is sometimes the way of royalty," the conversation turned to their respective families, for which the men, operating under assumed names for security purposes, enjoyed concocting ever wilder and more entertaining branches of fictitious family trees. As Smiley said, "We were very relieved when [the duke] turned the conversation to underwater fishing and women."

For Smiley and McLean, the dinner was more bizarre still. The Duke of Aosta was the brother of the commander against whom both had fought, albeit in different places, in Abyssinia. Only in a war so big could the dinner table be so small.

THE NEXT PILOT ACCIDENTALLY DROPPED THEM IN A BEECH FOREST. Smiley cracked his back against a tree on the way down. The snow, covered in black ash from an eruption of Mount Vesuvius across the Adriatic, cushioned their falls. As they repacked their parachutes, McLean and Amery were furious to realize that theirs were made of cotton and not silk. Cotton parachutes were supposed to be used for supplies only, as they often failed to open.

Smiley "felt one-up because mine was the correct type for para-

chutists—made of green artificial silk or nylon—but it was a disgraceful blunder by the packers." It was a "small comfort" to discover that
those packers had been some of Tito's Communist Partisans, evacuated to their "Yugoslav base" near the SOE staff office's new location
in Bari.

Amery holstered his Colt pistol for the journey. The original grips
had been replaced, a personalization gifted to him by monks of the Bektashi order, a sect of mystic Islam popular in Albania, outside Cairo.
Made of ivory or bone, the new grips were gorgeously cream-colored
and engraved with verses from the pre-Islamic poets, a reminder and
a warning: "For the ways are many, but death is one. Wherefore then
should you be afraid?"

Setting out for their new camp, they ran into Frederick Nosi. For
his part, Nosi could not have been pleased to see Amery. The son of a
Cabinet minister would have implied significant support for men Nosi
considered enemies. "We were not unkind enough to tax him as to what
had happened to the partisan çeta which had been responsible for
guarding Trotsky's [Davies's] HQ when he was captured, though we
were tempted to do so," Smiley said. Nosi left, undoubtedly to give warning to Hoxha. In camp, Smiley was delighted to see their paramilitary
expert NCOs, C. C. Jones and George Jenkins. In addition to being
tough fighters, they happened to be best friends from the same street in
Liverpool, as well as some of Smiley's favorite people in the unit. "They
looked and acted as they always had," Smiley recalled. "No hardships
or Germans would ever worry them. Though Jenkins had suffered badly
from pneumonia during the winter, he showed no ill effects from it."

Abas Kupi, leader of the Zogists, the resisting supporters of King
Zog, arrived next. Kupi, then in his forties, bore much resemblance to
Napoleon Bonaparte. Like Napoleon, he was not a large man. A chieftain of the northern Gheg clans, son of a Bektashi priest—Amery had
once asked him if his father was religious, and he had replied, "No,
he was a Bektashi"—Kupi had lived more lives than decades. An ardent

nationalist, he had rebelled against the Ottoman Empire as a teenager, then fought as a guerrilla against the Austro-Hungarian Empire in the First World War. In the turbulent years between the wars, he had been a brigand fighting against King Zog. Finally, fulfilling Zog's hope that "the poacher might turn gamekeeper," he became one of the king's staunchest supporters.

He had fought the Italians and covered Zog's retreat in 1939, then escaped to Belgrade before smuggling himself back into the country with another British officer in 1941. He had been rallying the tribes of the north ever since. He had excellent manners, boasted a stocky build, and wore a white Albanian fez. Wary, he expressed no personal emotion. He carried no outward weapon, but Smiley noted a bulge in his pocket that indicated the presence of a pistol. He was illiterate, and spoke only Albanian, both characteristics that provided him with handicaps on the road to power that he somehow seemed to have navigated with ease. Men liked to follow him. As Smiley put it, "Each time I met him, I liked him more." The feeling appeared to be mutual: Kupi, sizing up the British officers, eyed McLean and Amery, then Smiley, and said, "Three majors: two for politics and one for fighting."

Kupi was a warlord of the dominant tribe of a tiny country wedged along the coast of a part of Europe that far greater powers had used as a sandbox for centuries. The Third Reich was the third invading empire that Kupi had fought. Like the Kosovars, he had a primary duty to his people and their land, here known as the Mati, after the river of the same name. For Kupi, as for the Kosovars, the questions looked deceptively simple: Which enemy was greater, and which evil was lesser? He owed a debt of honor to the British, who had been his allies in his darkest days in 1939 and 1940, and who were his allies still. But he owed protection to his people, from whose support he derived the power that the British wanted him to deploy. They were subject to German reprisals, and they were also about to be subject to Communist Partisan attacks. As Brigadier Davies had discovered just after the end of Smiley and McLean's last mission, Enver Hoxha had already broken an agreement with the nationalist Balli Kombëtar and had vowed to fight all other resistance groups for supremacy. Kupi was next on his list.

With the United States now engaged in the war effort, it was clear that Germany would eventually lose the war in Europe. Germany had no long-term designs on a country that could offer it so little in reward but so much pain in pacification. The Communists very much meant to stay. The southern Tosk Communists were the most pressing military threat to Kupi's power, and to the basic peace and security of his northern Gheg tribespeople. This was an old rivalry in new clothes.

Official British policy complicated McLean's task of persuasion. It promised British support to anyone who took up arms against the Germans. But British arms would arrive only *after* the resisters had attacked the Germans with their own arms and ammunition. From a British policymaker's perspective, this would show proof of will before distribution of funds and weapons.

From the perspective of Kupi and men like him, it was potential suicide. The British were also arming the Communists, who were supposed to fight the Nazis, but there was nothing to prevent them from using British arms against the Zogists instead. How could Kupi risk lives and ammunition with a well-armed enemy on the doorstep?

"We Albanians are few and poor, but in proportion to our strength we have made great efforts and great sacrifices in the common cause. So far we have received no encouragement nor recognition from the great Allies; but I still put my trust in Great Britain as I did in 1940. I have fought and I will continue to fight, but you must send me arms and make some gesture that you have our country's interest at heart, for we are Albanian patriots and not British agents," he said.

Kupi was no fool. His Albanian tribesmen were not political neophytes. Kemp had already seen the complications in Kosovo, but Kosovo was of the plains, dotted with towns and cities and the vestiges of structured and organized civilization. In the mountains, where Kupi was from, strongmen ruled. But it would be remiss to assume that the lack of formal state structures, such as police and mayors, meant there was a power vacuum. Power was not absent; it was simply raw—and it was everything. Kupi needed to look, and remain, strong.

KUPI MADE A SIMPLE REQUEST: COULD LONDON SEND HIM A MESSAGE from King Zog, whom he could not contact directly, in which the monarch indicated that fighting as the British asked was indeed his will? "Let the King send a message through your Mission, and if he tells me to fight with my bare hands, I will," Kupi said. But London prevaricated. In what Smiley called a "typical F.O. message," McLean was told to "keep the pot boiling." It was a response that suggested, as an exasperated Amery observed, "an operation which [. . .] leads in politics, as in physics, to the evaporation of the contents." Likewise, a previous suggestion that Kupi had made to meet and negotiate with Enver Hoxha had gone nowhere at Partisan HQ.

McLean pulled together the local Zogist leaders and made his pitch: The time for action was now. If they simply proved their mettle against the Germans, the British would back them.

But the chieftains of the north had not survived as long as they had for nothing. What about their Partisan attackers? If the British could not even deliver a letter from King Zog, how could they be trusted to deliver arms?

An unexpected, uninvited guest wandered up to their meeting, set outdoors in a mountainside clearing. He was elderly, unkempt, and frenetic. Shouting and waving his arms, he clearly had a message to get across. He was also clearly mentally disturbed.

Amery, intrigued, asked what the man was saying. One of the Zogists replied, "He wants us to fight the Germans, but of course he's mad!"

From the fringes, Smiley impatiently snapped, "I wish he'd bite a few of the people here!"

McLean turned to Amery. "David seems to be getting restless again; we must find him something to blow up."

This Kupi could appreciate. "Very well; you shall have action," the warlord said. "Let Major Smiley come to me tomorrow, and I will choose him a bridge. If he will bring the dynamite, I will provide the men. Then you can tell your Headquarters that Abas Kupi is fighting again."

After treating Amery to a few pretend drops of his explosive "toys," Smiley, his favorite NCO Jenkins, and Kupi's handpicked men set off. Dressed in civilian clothes—the better to escape detection but also the easier to be shot as spies if caught—they walked nonchalantly down the road, passing by a series of German lorries whose occupants had no idea that the bridge to which they were headed would soon be put quite dramatically out of commission. Smiley took the measurements and studied the demolition chambers on the bridge. Moving down to the piers, easily accessible given the trickle that the river had become during that time of year, he noted how the Germans, in typically efficient fashion, had already marked the demolition chambers with their own calculations for the required amount of explosives, presumably in defensive and precautionary anticipation of a hasty retreat.

Smiley was pleased to see that his numbers agreed with those of the Germans. Unfortunately, he also realized that he had not packed nearly enough explosives onto the mules for a bridge of this size. For three days, he and Kupi's çeta waited for the mule party to return with more, in the meanwhile occupying their time at a nearby farm. With Jenkins, Smiley shaped the gelignite charges and did the reconnaissance.

A local tried to scare them off by warning of an imminent German attack. Smiley diagnosed fear of reprisal rather than concrete information. He sent the man straight to Kupi, who ordered the farmer to give Smiley "every assistance and to defend him if he should be attacked to the last man and the last round." The interlude was interrupted by shooting. It turned out to be Germans firing off Very lights in reaction to gunfire from the settling of a local blood feud. The Germans, thought Smiley, were getting nervous.

Smiley and his men crept to the bridge that night and packed in the explosives. At one point, and much to Smiley's irritation, a German staff car "was tiresome enough to have a puncture on the bridge." In addition to prolonging the time of the operation by half an hour, the Germans' changing of a tire on the bridge also meant that Smiley and several of his çeta were trapped beneath it for fear of being seen. "One German reminded us of his presence by urinating over the side, but luckily he did not score a direct hit," Smiley sniffed.

By three o'clock in the morning, they were nearly ready. On top of the bridge itself, they laid one more surprise: SOE's tiny tire-burster mines, designed to look like mule droppings. They hoped to trap a few German lorries on the bridge before it blew. Then they settled down a safe distance away to watch.

Within five minutes, two German vehicles had blown their tires on the "mule droppings." Within ten minutes, nothing else had happened. Another ten minutes went by. Smiley went to investigate; from the grinning Jenkins came a jocular warning: "Be careful, sir." The tire-changing Germans forced Smiley's pace to a literal crawl. The bridge, the Germans, their trucks, and the remaining mines masquerading as mule droppings went up in a flash when he was about halfway there.

The ground shook. Concrete debris flew everywhere. Three spans of the bridge had collapsed, and it was completely destroyed. The explosion was so large that one of Kupi's local allies, who lived nearby, had his windows blown out. It took the German engineers six weeks to replace the bridge with something temporary. In the meantime, all of the traffic between Tirana and Durazzo had to crawl along an extra ten miles of unpaved track, impassable in heavy rain. Smiley returned with Kupi's delighted men, and went to bed with a recurrence of malaria.

———

LESS THAN THREE WEEKS LATER, IN EARLY JULY, ENVER HOXHA DE-
clared war on the royalist Zogists and the British officers with them. The
First Partisan Brigade, which McLean and Smiley had trained, attacked
Kupi. Hoxha refused to meet with Kupi to discuss terms. He attacked
McLean and his team as well. Their camp was overrun, and Alan Hare
(who had already survived a German attack on the original SOE camp)
was arrested and evacuated to the coast. Smiley, separated from the others, declared to his diary, "I am bitched."

McLean woke Amery early one morning. Calmly, despite the
sounds of machine guns and mortars in the near distance, he said, "Tell
me what you make of this: it sounds like trouble for someone." They fled
and regrouped but were attacked again and again. Dressed in civilian
clothes or Albanian gendarmes' uniforms, Smiley went on repeated
scouting missions to find evacuation routes and ambush sites for attacking the Germans. His misadventures and close calls included being
smuggled in lorries full of German soldiers, mumbling in his best Albanian when faced with a German officer who demanded his nonexis-
tent papers before pulling a pistol on him, and narrowly avoiding being
bombed by his own air force.

The Communist Partisans who attacked them were well armed and
well supplied by their own SOE staff office. The Partisans tortured one
of McLean's captured mulemen to uncover the location of their camp
once again. A literal militant priest who had attended the Zogist meeting was seized and tortured to extract similar information; his fingers
were broken, and he was flogged and branded with irons. He ended with
a slit throat. Over and over, McLean's team found themselves close to
capture. When Smiley returned from one of his scouting trips on a day
wet with rain, Amery glumly confessed to his diary, "there is no way out
that way."

It was "essential," their staff office insisted, that Kupi be persuaded to neither mobilize his men nor "attack or resist" the assaulting Partisans. Kupi had started to fight the Germans, but the staff office did not send the promised supplies. It was Kupi's nightmare scenario. As a fellow Zogist put it, "I knew my house would be burnt, but I hoped it would be by Germans I intended to attack and not by Albanians who attacked me."

Smiley was frustrated by the civil war that hampered their fight against the Axis. The Germans were about to retreat. It was imperative that the British prevent this and hold down divisions that Hitler wanted to use not only for the fight in Eastern Europe but also for the defense of Germany itself. The civil war could not have come at a worse time. But of Kupi, Smiley confessed to his diary, "I feel very sorry for him, as he is a real patriot and genuinely pro-British, and it makes me sick seeing him thrown over for a lot of very anti-British communists."

Even Hoxha's favorite British officers could not convince him to stop attacking Kupi. Hoxha insisted, without evidence, that Kupi was a Nazi collaborator and that the civil war was Kupi's fault. Hoxha had a long-running habit of lying about Kupi. The year before, he had come to Kemp to complain that Kupi had left the Partisans to do the fighting during a German attack. Eyewitness testimony from a British officer at the scene indicated that Kupi had "fought like a lion" with his men while the Partisans had barely fought at all.

NEVERTHELESS, HOXHA'S NARRATIVE WAS STARTING TO BECOME MORE convincing in a staff office recently robbed of adult supervision. Philip Leake, head of SOE's Albanian Country Section, had been killed nearly two months before, in June. His position in the office had become difficult; Fanny Hasluck, disgusted by the obvious preference among the office's Klugmann elements for the Communist Partisans, had quit. Klugmann's Yugoslav Country Section continued to dominate Leake's smaller Albanian Country Section.

Leake had dropped in to try to stop the civil war. In Italy, Kemp had tried to discourage the forty-year-old former schoolmaster from going. "Why do you have to go yourself?" Kemp asked, especially since Leake was keeping him out. "After all, you're the only experienced Staff Officer we have in the Section."

"Peter," said Leake, "for a year now I've been sitting on my bottom, sending the people into the field. Now I feel that I must go in myself— and apologize."

He had lasted six weeks, detained much of that time by an enraged Enver Hoxha, who wanted him to withdraw McLean's team with Kupi. Soon after he returned to his own camp, Leake became the victim of a vanishingly rare Luftwaffe raid. How the Germans gained intelligence about the camp's location was never discovered. It was, Kemp later said, "a most fortune accident for the Communists."

The staff officer who succeeded Leake as head of the Albanian Country Section was named Eliot Watrous. Barely in his twenties, he struggled to understand the complex situation on the ground. Despite, or perhaps because of, his complete lack of experience operating in the field, he was prone to bold statements and decisions. Writing to one of the sympathetic British officers attached to Hoxha, Watrous promised to "obtain authority to hold a pistol at Kupi's head." Gossipy letters flew back and forth between that pair. Out in the field, hunted by Germans and Partisans, McLean received no such correspondence. The staff office pressed McLean to get Kupi to fight. But at the same time, policy in the office was beginning to change. Initially, the strategy had been to promise arms to anyone fighting the Germans, as Brigadier Davies so clearly remembered being briefed on when he had dropped in.

Now the staff officers were considering picking a side in Albania's civil war. The staff office was trying to keep McLean in the dark. Only to the SOE officer stationed with Hoxha did Watrous promise updates: "I will, naturally, keep you informed of developments."

Hoxha declared that McLean and Smiley were "collaborators" and "agents of foreign reactionaries," and that they would be tried by a Partisan military court if captured. In his diary, Smiley recorded the only thing he could think of in response: "bloody cheek!" For their part, the staff officers professed mystification. Had McLean done anything to provoke Hoxha's outburst? they inquired. The team started to grow suspicious.

MCLEAN'S TEAM NEVERTHELESS MANAGED A RECRUITING COUP AS TENsions with the staff office increased. The Germans had been using an unusual set of soldiers in addition to their elite Mountain Division troops. These additional units were known as the Turkestan Legion. Made up of men from Soviet Central Asia, the Turkestan Legion included Kazakhs, Tajiks, Uzbeks, and more. Nearly all Muslim, they had been conscripted by the Red Army and used in human-wave attacks at some of the worst battles of the early Eastern Front campaigns. Many had been captured in 1942 at the Second Battle of Kharkov, where their Red Army unit was encircled and then mowed down by both machine-gun fire and aerial bombardment. To the Central Asians, the Wehrmacht had seemed the lesser of two evils.

Now they disliked their treatment again. An unofficial scout made contact with the British, and McLean soon found himself in command of thirty new men. The number would eventually rise to nearly seventy. To Amery and McLean, raised on stories of the romance of the steppes and the prowess of Genghis Khan, it was a bizarre dream come true.

The Central Asians arrived well armed. They claimed to have killed their Soviet officers in order to defect to the Germans. This was unverifiable but seemed believable. Now they had murdered their German officers to come over to the British. (One group did provide proof of this, neatly wrapped in a green handkerchief: six ears.) "Disregarding the fate of their previous officers," quipped Smiley, "we decided to employ them."

Their staff office was still encouraging Kupi to fight. McLean now had his own full-strength strike force. Between the Central Asians and the Zogists, he had more than a company's worth of men at his disposal. Before him lay the possibility of repeating his brilliant success in Abyssinia, just in time to delay the crucial German retreat from Albania.

Their first assault was planned for the next night. In the meantime, they were privy to what Smiley called an "interesting insight into the discipline of our new allies." One of them had accused their "Mareschal" (a lance corporal or a sergeant major, depending on who was asked) of being either defeatist, pro-German, or both. The Central Asians appealed to the British to settle the dispute; McLean told them to elect their own leaders. The troops had a different understanding of "election" than the British. The quiet was suddenly broken by a shot, followed by singing, dancing, and shouts of "Ka Vedk!" (Literally: He has death!) The Mareschal was dead at the hands of the young and beautiful Achmet, who in Amery's eyes looked as though he had stepped out of a piece of Persian artwork. Amery saw the Liverpudlian sergeants Jones and Jenkins exchange a meaningful look.

Anxiously pondering the distinction between repetition and habit, Amery became the mutineers' new officer for the assault against a nearby German position. Smiley took command of a machine-gun unit on the heights, which would provide covering fire and pin down the enemy in the camp. McLean, with Kupi's son Petrit and one hundred Zogists, would attack from one side while Amery and the thirty Central Asians struck from the other.

It was Amery's first experience of both combat and leadership, one made more complicated by the fact that he could not communicate with his men. He recalled a conversation with a friend who commanded an Indian Army unit: "What matters is what you do. March in front of them and they'll do whatever you do; and, if you don't run away, they'll be as good as the Guards." This advice would have to do.

A German machine gunner spotted them through the trees as Amery led the way over a stone wall. Rounds burst around them. Amery fell. He thought he had slipped, but a machine-gun round had caught him under the chin, splitting the skin but doing no other damage. His men, seeing their officer shot in the face by automatic fire, fell back. The clearing went silent. Everyone assumed that Amery was dead.

It was early. The attack was not supposed to have started yet. Infantrymen have few advantages in the face of emplaced machine guns, but Amery had one: the gunner. He was panicky, facing an unknown number of foreign-looking troops, and he didn't know that Amery was still alive. Machine gunner before him and mutinous troops behind, there was only one way out. Amery rose from the dead and charged. Putting his astrakhan cap on the muzzle of his submachine gun, he leaped forward and shouted, "Hurrah!" His troops followed with bloodcurdling yells.

The machine gunners fled in horror, and Amery and his men surged down the hill toward the camp. On the opposite side, Petrit Kupi killed the first German. Amery faced a young German, naked to the waist, blue-eyed and towheaded, holding a Schmeisser pistol. Briefly, they stared at each other. Before Amery could move to shoot, the German doubled over. Achmet—equally young but far better at killing—danced past, grinning. One of his countrymen was soon stripping the Wellington boots from the dying German.

Textbook it was not, but brutally effective it had been. They had killed ten Germans and captured twelve Italians from the labor corps. As Amery put it, "A Zogist officer with a Tajik lay among the dead to show the Germans who had been their enemies." They burned the German camp and returned to their own to tell the staff office the good news.

MCLEAN WAS ASTONISHED WHEN HE RECEIVED THE STAFF OFFICE'S reply to his signal. Smiley called it a "lunatic message": he and McLean had been ordered to evacuate Albania at once. Amery was to remain behind as a "neutral observer," in which role he should neither encourage

Kupi to fight nor promise him arms if he did. Priorities in the office were changing.

McLean had been harassed by the men in the safe, comfortable staff office before. They had harangued him over a request to promote Amery and had once accused him of mishandling classified paperwork. (To this, McLean, observing that all the papers were dated after his arrival in Albania and bore the code name of the officer serving with Hoxha, noted: "I [. . .] cannot imagine how you supposed these papers could be mine.") He also probably could not imagine that the new, young head of the Albanian Country Section, Eliot Watrous, was writing to the British officer stationed with Enver Hoxha at the same time, declaring that the "McLean crisis" had come to a head and that the decision to withdraw McLean's team had been made. That decision had come after Watrous briefed the decision-making committee with some liberally interpreted information.

McLean's problems with the office began to multiply. Soon the accounting section would refuse to send more gold to pay the team's ongoing expenses, implying that they must have been wasteful. The funds could have been wasted in Bari, where the staff office now sat. That beautifully intact city (the Allies, intending to preserve it for their headquarters, had refrained from bombarding it) boasted concerts, hotels, art shows, an opera house, rivers of alcohol, and a liberal assortment of prostitutes. It was, however, not as grand, flashy, or warm as Cairo, something that some of the staff grumbled about.

In Albania, by contrast, most houses that the men stayed in, if they stayed in houses at all, featured toilets that were simply small holes in the floor. These evacuated their contents to the space below, where the chickens were kept, in order to feed the birds most efficiently. The men saw women so rarely that when they did, it generated commentary born first of surprise and then of sadness over how they were treated as little more than beasts of burden, not so different from the mules. The fleshpot of Bari it was not. The men's gold went to pay interpreters, to buy food in the villages, to pay for rent, and to pay for silence, the last of which rarely gave receipts. In the end, they had to borrow the money from Kupi.

The staff office also insisted that Smiley and McLean hand themselves over to Enver Hoxha to be "escorted" to the coast. As Smiley put it, "We knew that this meant being treated as prisoners, if not shot on the spot." Another British officer with the Partisans soon reported that the real reason why Hoxha insisted upon "escorting" Smiley and McLean to the coast was so he could parade them through the country as prisoners to show the people the extent of his power. But would it really be nothing more than a humiliating parade? Smiley feared it would be all too easy for Hoxha to claim that he and McLean had been "'shot while resisting arrest,' or 'shot trying to escape.'" There had already been those dangerous cotton parachutes, packed by Tito's Partisans. They had been warned by their captured muleman that Hoxha had given orders to shoot them on the spot as "rebel English."

What McLean's team—and others targeted by Hoxha, such as Kupi and their interpreters—needed was a Partisan- and German-free evacuation from Albania. They also needed time. Amery bought some for them with a signal labeled "Personal." It was a note to his father, the Secretary of State for India, then in Italy on government business. "Wound no worse than bad shaving cut and has not impeded work at all," Amery assured. "Office can no doubt give you further details of action."

A staff office that had suggested that British officers hand themselves over to men who had already vowed to kill them was not the sort of place where it would have been convenient to have Amery's father, a close friend of Churchill's since boyhood, looking over shoulders and asking for his younger son's mission details. The message would also act as a temporary bulwark against any convenient Partisan fictions, such as false rumors that the team had been wounded or even killed, as had been sown about the demise of Peter Kemp in Kosovo.

Whatever was going on in the staff office, the team on the ground was now racing against time. If McLean and Amery were going to be pulled out of Albania, they wanted to do more damage to the Germans first. Their supplies were limited, but they decided to expend them on as many efficient attacks against the German retreat as possible. They now had seventy Central Asians, plus several Russian deserters, the captured Italians, their NCOs and wireless operator, and two very helpful American airmen who had been rescued after bailing out on a mission to bomb the crucial oil fields at Ploieşti in Romania. This was enough for two assault teams. Working in tandem with the Zogists, they unleashed hell for two weeks in a country that was practically made for guerrilla warfare.

One team, including a very lucky downed American airman, went with a Zogist çeta to attack the main road. They destroyed fifteen vehicles, killed more than twice that many Germans, and hauled away crucial material. Smiley's favorite NCO, Jenkins, went out again. Mining the road, he took down three vehicles. Smiley led a Zogist çeta and thirty Central Asians to destroy another bridge.

Amery and McLean followed Kupi and another Zogist leader to an ambush. Set up along an S-bend in the road, they waited for the Germans. Cartridges sliding into chambers produced their telling metallic click. The men watched for the headlights. Kupi, seeing a convoy of nine trucks, waited to give the attack signal until all the trucks were within the bracket of fire. Then the Zogists opened fire on the leading truck. Capsizing, it blocked those behind. Fire poured into the unarmored vehicles. Within fifteen minutes, all was silent. A surviving Austrian lieutenant, too wounded to move, was left on the road to tell the tale to any passing Germans. The company cleaned out the convoy and set it on fire. Even the hard-bitten Jenkins said, "It's just bloody murder."

The next night, Smiley had his turn again. With a Zogist çeta, he mined a road for an ambush. They eliminated one German lorry and killed the three soldiers inside it. The arrival of an armored car and another lorry as backup begat more shooting. But then suddenly it seemed as if Smiley and his men were surrounded, and Smiley gave the order to withdraw. The people shooting at him from behind were not Germans coming to rescue their fellows but Partisans who had somehow gotten word of the British attack. In the chaos, Smiley was separated from the çeta and wound up alone for two days as he tried to find the camp. The only local who would help him was a twelve-year-old boy; the others were too afraid—not of the Germans but of the Communists.

The team also managed to capture from the Germans an entire "bag," or package of official documents, that was in transit from divisional headquarters in Scutari to the corps commander in Tirana. This provided evidence that Kupi had never been a German collaborator. (In fact, the Germans had called him one of their "most inveterate enemies.") None of this swayed the staff office. It still insisted that the men hand themselves over to Hoxha, despite mounting evidence that the Partisans were no longer friendly to the British. Another British officer in the north was attacked by the Partisans, his tent torn down around him. The Partisans seized both him and a former Albanian Communist they found at the camp. That man, a British ally, was laid out on the ground and beaten— some said flayed—within an inch of his life. Then he was shot. But the orders from the staff office were repeated: *Hand yourselves over to Hoxha.*

SOE'S STAFF OFFICERS KNEW HOW TO RUN EXTRACTIONS FROM ALBANIA. Not long beforehand, they had picked up 150 wounded Partisans for Hoxha and taken them to a hospital in Italy. But for weeks the office claimed that it was not possible to evacuate McLean's team from the north. The Royal Navy either could not or would not come, said the office; they needed to move south, through territory entirely in Partisan hands, to be evacuated by either sea or air.

The staff officers, now led by Eliot Watrous, had indeed been playing for time. As McLean and his team had begun to suspect, they were developing, or pressing their superiors for, a new policy. That spring, British policy in Yugoslavia had switched from supporting all those fighting the Germans to supporting the Communist Tito exclusively. That had been the goal of James Klugmann, and he was succeeding. Staff officers were pushing for a similar switch in Albania.

Heavily influenced by Klugmann, the Yugoslav Country Section was far larger and more powerful than the Albanian one. Overshadowed, the Albanian Country Section was also very accessible. The office was set up in a requisitioned house, with open doors that allowed someone like Klugmann to walk into any office whenever he wished.

McLean had needed to go around Klugmann's influence to even get into Albania in the first place. He'd had a friend—a woman who worked in the office and who could, as Smiley noted, twist Keble "round her finger"—put the alternative Albania idea to the brigadier himself. She later paid a price for her success. Philip Leake had been her fiancé.

Watrous, Leake's successor, was nearly ten years younger than the charismatic Klugmann, who was so gifted at developing unwitting fellow travelers. Watrous had no experience in the field. This may have been why he later admitted to Smiley that he had insisted the team hand itself over to the Partisans "in order to test Enver Hoxha's good faith," which Smiley translated as "to see if they would shoot us or not"—not generally a choice that someone who had ever been in danger of being shot at would have made.

Watrous was born in South Africa to a New Zealander mother and an American father who worked for a Texas oil company. A child of wealth, he was nevertheless not part of the English society to which Klugmann belonged. His was a liminal experience of power, which would have been a very different experience for someone accustomed to the treatment afforded to white, wealthy men in the Johannesburg of his time. Perhaps Watrous was simply young, inexperienced, and so desirous to fit in that he did not realize that some of the material he was seeing was filtered. Perhaps, like Keble, he was ambitious, as other officers around him seemed to think. If so, it would not have been illogical if he had chosen to attach himself to the obvious power center in the office, as his chummy letters to the British officer assigned to Enver Hoxha ("I will, naturally, keep you informed of developments") seemed to indicate.

RESIGNED TO LEAVING ALBANIA, MCLEAN PRESSED SOE'S STAFF OFFICE to at least evacuate Kupi. The office played coy. Any Albanian who had ever confronted Enver Hoxha harbored no illusions about their fate should they remain in a country soon to be dominated by a dictator well supplied with Allied weapons. Before their headlong flight to the coast, the British officers, along with Kupi and his crew, climbed Mount Vela. A photograph shows Kupi and his men sitting at the summit. Several young men, all armed, stand around the warlord. Some sit near him. In the distance, the craggy mountain ranges fill the background until they fade at the horizon. In the image, Kupi sits parallel to the edge of the summit. The other men look over it, perpendicular to Kupi, to the mountains beyond. He was already looking away.

Chased by Germans and Partisans, McLean, Smiley, Amery, and their various allies crossed the swollen Mati River and made their way toward the coast. By sunrise, they had marched for fourteen hours, through the coastal fens, forest, and marsh, until they finally descended to the plains. Resting a two hours' march from the sea, they were comfortably but precariously placed. As Smiley, in charge of so many reconnaissance missions, put it: "Once the Partisans knew where we were, we should have little chance of escape." The staff office had now promised to evacuate all of them, but the staff office had reneged on its promises before. Now they were between the devil and the deep blue sea.

The staff office changed the parameters again. Kupi could not come, nor could their interpreters. McLean, in a last-ditch effort, sent a message to Anthony Eden requesting Kupi's evacuation. Eden, the Foreign Secretary, was in Italy. In London, he had told them to contact him directly if they found themselves in need. There was no response. McLean and Kupi's allies raced to find a separate boat to evacuate the warlord and some of his supporters.

Soon the orders came for the British. One boat—complete with an officer whose sole job was to ensure that no "improper" persons were evacuated—arrived and took Smiley and some of the NCOs. Then it was McLean and Amery's turn, along with two Central Asians and a few British officers from other non-Communist missions.

Informed of the orders over a game of chess, Kupi graciously said, "Inshallah! We shall play the next round in Italy!" On the beach, they said goodbye to their French-speaking interpreters, Shaqir and Halit. In his diary, Amery recorded his last words to them: "Vous étiez le plus brave." (You were the most brave.) David Smiley, later reflecting bitterly on their abandonment of men whom they fully expected to be viciously killed, wrote, "Their chief motive was to serve the best interests of their country, and they were far greater patriots than the men who accused them."

On arrival in Italy, Smiley acquired a car and drove as quickly as he could from Brindisi to Bari, a journey of nearly seventy miles. There a secretary confessed to him the fate of the emergency message that McLean had sent to Foreign Secretary Anthony Eden in an attempt to save Kupi. It went not to Eden but into the wastepaper basket, discarded by an officer who was determined to maintain the best possible relations with Enver Hoxha.

The staff officer's own secretary revealed the officer's actions because she had suffered the abuses of the office as well. Her boss had made a very unwanted pass at her, something not uncommon in 1945 and very common in SOE's staff office, where the women on staff, as earlier noted, had a name for Brigadier Keble: Tim, short for "touch I must." Smiley said she was a "very nice girl," but when she had turned this staff officer down, he "was quite bloody to her, and so there is not much she did not tell me."

Because of British libel laws, Smiley would not publicly name the officer during his lifetime. But in his wartime diary, he recorded the name of the secretary's handsy boss: Eliot Watrous. The officer who destroyed the message worked for Watrous. His name was John Eyre. A member of the Communist Party, he was later sent home from his post in the Pacific theater for attempting to suborn the troops. He stood for the Communist Party in the British national elections of 1949 and 1950.

If the reception of Smiley and McLean's team in the Bari staff office was not openly hostile, it was quite cool. Smiley heard one of Klugmann's followers call them "Fascists." Even the languid McLean was convinced that there was a plot against them. He sent another message to Eden. The Foreign Secretary responded quickly and in the affirmative, but the subject of Kupi's rescue was an issue for the Supreme Allied Command. A few days later, McLean got a meeting with General Wilson in Caserta, on the other side of the boot of Italy, near Naples. Amery followed.

"Yes, I agree with you," said Wilson, nicknamed Jumbo. "The fellow's been our friend and we must get him out. We'll do it quite openly, and we'll tell Hoxha too, but not until your man's safe in Italy." The general grinned.

There was no return flight to Bari that evening, so McLean and Amery passed the afternoon among the ruins of Pompeii. Back in their quarters, they received a telephone call from Smiley. Kupi had landed in Italy.

The private boat had finally arrived at the evacuation point. Into it went Kupi, one of Kupi's sons, and a few other allies. Kupi's wife and seven other children remained in Albania. The engine broke down, and they drifted for seven nights and six days. Finally, a British minesweeper towed them to Brindisi. Hoxha, outraged, already knew. He signaled to the staff office and demanded that Kupi be returned to stand trial. This time, though, the orders of the Supreme Allied Command were firm: Kupi would not be repatriated. Nor would he ever see Albania again. For his part, Hoxha succeeded in eliminating the rest of his rivals, including two of Kemp's contacts, the Kryeziu brothers Gani and Hasan.

WHEN MCLEAN AND AMERY LANDED IN ITALY, THEY HAD BEEN FORCED to hand over to Security the two Central Asian soldiers who had been extracted with them. On the grounds of an agreement that the Allies had made with Stalin, all Soviet citizens were required to be repatriated to the mother country. There they would be shot, or sent to the gulag.

Too much exposure to the outside world—it mattered not if it was to enemy or ally—would not be allowed in the postwar Soviet Union. When asked about the average Russian's exposure to non-Soviet life during the war, one Soviet officer replied, "Average? There is no such person. But we consider there are three categories. The first are those who enjoy and forget: they are no problem. The second are impressed but can be reeducated, and that may take a few months or years. The third category remember and draw conclusions. They will never see Russia again." The Soviets were taking no chances with the inhabitants of their restive Central Asian provinces, from which they had for decades barred any foreign visitors.

Julian Amery called at the detention center. He asked to take his two former Central Asian soldiers to lunch. Amery took them away from the camp and into the city, where they indulged in Negronis and Castel del Monte wine. He handed them cash from his own personal stash. And then he turned them loose. Years later, he was still receiving an annual Christmas card from the one who settled in Italy.

CHAPTER 8

GO EAST

I n early 1945, David Smiley found himself at lunch with Peter Kemp
in Cairo. They had last seen each other the previous fall, when Smiley, McLean, and Amery came limping out of Albania. Kemp was then
waiting for a flight to German-occupied Poland, where he and a team
that included Bill Hudson were tasked with a liaison role to the resisters
who formed the gallant Home Army, the main Polish resistance movement against the occupying Nazis.

Smiley had spent several weeks writing up his report on Albania
before getting some much-deserved leave at home in London for Christmas. He and Billy McLean had spent much of it together over oysters at
McLean's favorite haunt, Claridge's. Julian Amery had already headed
out to China. Smiley and McLean were soon to follow him east, to other
theaters of the war in Asia, and Smiley was determined to convince
Kemp to come with them.

Kemp was just out of prison. His captors had been their Soviet allies, who had not wanted an SOE unit anywhere near Poland. The leadership of SOE's Poland unit was, however, much more effective than that
of the staff office governing the Balkans. It was led by the competent and
highly experienced engineer Colonel Harold Perkins. Once Perkins got

wind of what became known as the Warsaw Uprising, he was determined to send a crew in to help. This was Kemp's team.

It was a dangerous mission. They would have improved firepower
(American .30 carbines like the one that had been gifted to Smiley by
the early Jedburgh teams). They would also, for the first time in Kemp's
experience, have cyanide capsules, known as "L tablets." (They somehow accidentally mixed these up with their aspirin supply and had to
dump the whole lot.)

The Soviets tried to block the mission, but Perkins, known as
"Perks," prevailed upon his superiors in London. London prevailed
upon Moscow. Moscow prevaricated. Eventually, Perks decided to send
the team in without permission. By then, months had passed. The Soviets had threatened to shoot down any planes that overflew their territory, and so the team instead had to fly from Brindisi, in southern Italy.
The weather going over the Carpathian Mountains was bad; on one
flight, the mystified pilot came back and said, "It's just like flying through
milk. I can't even see our wingtips."

Eventually, they made it, though much to Kemp's dismay, the Polish pilot of their aircraft accidentally dropped them from just two
hundred feet, giving their parachutes barely enough time to open and
making for a rough touchdown. Kemp wrenched his knee upon landing on the frozen ground. For several days, he would be transported
by cart.

Poland was an improvement on Albania in one crucial aspect. As
Kemp put it, "It is well known, although it can bear repetition, that Poland alone among the countries occupied by Germany produced no
Quisling." There was also no civil war. There were factions to the resistance, but for the most part, they fought the Germans, not each other,
and even the relations between the Home Army and its Communist
counterpart were, in Kemp's words, "cold but correct; there was no
fighting between them, and they gave each other warning of enemy at-

tacks." Kemp was delighted to "have the opportunity of helping these gallant people who had done so much to help themselves."

What was no help was the terrain. Albania, with its mountains, thick forests, and gorges, was a guerrilla's paradise. Poland, with its more open terrain, was a challenge. The Polish forests belonged to the area's substantial and long-running timber industry. They were large but thinned: there was no underbrush, no scrub in which to hide. They were also outfitted with "rides," or paths that bisected large swaths of forest and were used for hauling away timber. Anyone trying to hide in there for long would eventually be subject to a German effort to surround them and flush them out.

The mission of the SOE team in Poland was expressly to liaise and report. The British government needed direct information that was not compromised by its Soviet allies. But the secrecy of the mission didn't last long: both the Germans and the Soviets were aware of the SOE team as soon as its men had touched ground. Kemp resumed his habit of evading German assaults, frequently at close quarters. Often chased from place to place and driven to hide in different parts of the forest by day—one time, the team was secreted in an attic while German troops prowled the first floor, and another time, it was nearly overrun by a company of Wehrmacht infantry along with four tanks, the officers calling orders in that "half-bellow, half-scream which in their army was the voice of command," as Kemp put it—they were nevertheless well protected by the Home Army, several of whose members died in the process.

Then the Russians crossed the Vistula. Stalin had already arranged for the destruction of much of the Polish resistance during the Warsaw Uprising, when the brave Poles revolted against the occupying Germans and the Russians halted just five miles away, letting the Germans slaughter them instead. Now the Poles faced the inevitable: the partition, again, of the country they had fought so hard to defend.

The team was given orders to turn itself over to the Soviets, as had been the plan going in. The Soviets remained allies, and this was Russian operational territory. As Kemp said, "Sorrowfully we took our leave of these men who had hazarded their lives for so many years to uphold the imperishable honour of their country."

The Russians to whom they handed themselves over refused to treat them as allies and called them spies. For several weeks, they were locked in a prison that the NKVD had commandeered from the Gestapo two days earlier ("with all fittings," Kemp noted). As the door clanged shut behind them, one team member cracked wise: "Well, boys, this is it. There's only one question now: which is it to be—Siberia, or the firing squad? Personally, I'm not sure I wouldn't choose the firing squad." Between what Kemp briskly described in his notes as rounds of "starvation, no sleep, interrogations," they occupied their time with seemingly endless rubbers of bridge. ("Poker was impossible because we did not even have matches for chips; somebody suggested using lice, but that proved impracticable because they would never stay put.")

The team's leader was Bill Hudson, with whom Kemp had escaped Berane. Hudson refused to be bullied by the NKVD. He insisted that, as a uniformed colonel, he would speak to no one below that rank. (That he spoke enough Russian also helped.) Every time the Soviets felt like questioning Hudson, they would have to find a colonel to do it—or, at the very least, someone dressed up like a colonel. It was a game, and the British knew it, but it was a game they nevertheless had to play.

They were eventually shipped to Moscow. Their car pulled up outside the dreaded Lubyanka, a notorious secret prison of the NKVD. An officer stepped out of the vehicle, handed something to the guard at the gatehouse, and then got back in. They were driven on to the British Military Mission, where they were handed over to their own countrymen. It had been the Soviets' idea of a joke.

Their imprisonment, Kemp learned, had coincided with the Yalta Conference. Stalin had wanted no independent information to be sent to Churchill during the negotiation of Poland's postwar borders. After a more comfortable detainment in Moscow, Kemp flew slowly back to British-controlled territory via the required stages of the day: Moscow to Baku, Baku to Tehran over the massive Elburz range (which required flying at twenty-two thousand feet with no supplemental oxygen), and Tehran to Cairo.

THAT WAS HOW KEMP HAD ENDED UP AT LUNCH WITH SMILEY IN A small Arab restaurant, pondering freedom and his next role in the war. Smiley was resolved to go to Asia. By early 1945, it was clear that the war in Europe was coming to a close. That was not the case in Asia, where the Allies' Fourteenth Army—including the Indian Army, the largest volunteer army in the world, made up of dozens of races and ethnicities—had beaten the Japanese back from the gates of India at Imphal. And there was also China, where Amery already was.

Smiley had other reasons for wanting to leave. Cairo had lost its sheen. After he had flown in with Billy McLean and Alan Hare, the old crew had gone straight to their former lodgings at Tara, where they banged on the door. When there was no answer, they forced it open. The alluring Polish countess Sophie Tarnowska and the troublesome Alsatian dog Pixie were asleep.

Smiley had been among the many men who had vied for Sophie's hand. He and Xan Fielding, another Tara resident with whom he was close, had once taken Sophie to see Luxor together. On his own, Smiley had taken her to Alexandria, but there she had spent her time chasing Gavin Astor, heir to a vast real estate fortune. After what Smiley called "various changes of heart," Paddy Leigh Fermor had moved out of the house, and Sophie had finally decided that she would marry Billy Moss, Leigh Fermor's younger and ridiculously good-looking partner.

It was not as easy as it sounded. Sophie was still technically married to her first husband, who had left her for her brother's wife after they had escaped Poland together. As they had received a papal dispensation to marry (they were cousins), the Roman Catholic Church did not wish to issue an annulment. Sophie promptly converted and received one from the Greek Orthodox Church instead. Her wedding to Billy Moss was attended by Prince Peter and Princess Irene of Greece, and the reception was hosted by one of the princesses of the Egyptian royal family.

She and Moss would go on to have three children together, but the second, a son named Sebastian, died in infancy; he was the third son she had lost. By 1957, their marriage was over. Moss, who had moved to Jamaica with a girlfriend named Twinkle, would die at the age of only forty-four as a result of the excesses of his lifestyle.

In Cairo, Smiley also ran into an old acquaintance from back in England who happened to be a member of the Siamese royal family. His name was Prince Subha Svasti, known to all as Chin, and he wanted Smiley to join the resistance in Siam. Smiley brought him to lunch at Tara. Moss, for his part, found Chin "a delightful person, brimful of good humour and a broad intelligence."

Siam, which had recently been renamed Thailand (Smiley decided that he would stop "short of extending the change to cats or twins"), had a curious role in the war. The country, overrun by Japan, had technically cooperated with its occupier and declared war on Britain. But the Thai resistance was vast, and it was headed by the regent himself, a man named Pridi Phanomyong, also referred to by his conferred title, Luang Pradit Manutham, and known to British operatives by his code name, Ruth. There was plenty of work for SOE operatives, and Smiley wanted Kemp to come along: "I could not have wanted a better companion. My only reservation was the knowledge that wherever Kemp went, there was sure to be trouble."

FOR KEMP IT WAS NOT A HARD DECISION. HE, TOO, HAD PERSONAL PROBlems. His wife had told him that she was filing for divorce.

Kemp, as he was liable to do, blamed himself: "Looking back from time's distance, I wonder how I could have been so foolish, complacent, and blind to my own character as to ask any girl, at my age and at such a time, to marry me; it is scarcely less remarkable, I suppose, that any girl who knew me well—and this one did—should have considered me a suitable husband."

They had been having drinks in her mother's parlor and listening to the radio when Britain declared war on September 3, 1939. She was two years his junior, the privileged child of a wealthy South African diamond family. Her father had died when she was young, from the delayed consequences of wounds received in World War I. Her mother, by all accounts not the most robust or sensible of individuals, married another wealthy man and raised her three children in style.

It was her mother who breathlessly expressed to Kemp at the outbreak of war, "Oh, I don't mind for myself. But it does seem so hard that these children should have their lives blighted a second time." Kemp had just lost his brother to the German Stuka bombers in the Mediterranean. Romance and the seriousness of marriage may have been part of his recovery.

Her family circumstances were very different from his. Kemp came from the not-quite-gentry section of English society, the one with connections and education but not much in the way of capital. As Kemp had framed it, his father's (dashed) hopes for him had been that he train as a barrister and then serve in either the Indian or Sudan Civil Service, as "we were far from rich, so there was no question of my practising at the Bar in England." Money for her family, on the other hand, was no object.

In October 1941, in between a clandestine mission to Spain and Commando raids on occupied France and the Channel Islands, they were married at St. George's in Hanover Square. It was a smart address, the parish church for Mayfair. The bride wore a dress of white moiré embroidered with pearls. A Russian headdress bedecked in pearls sat above her tulle veil; in her hands rested a bouquet of white roses and gardenias. The reception was hosted at a grand private house opposite Hyde Park. One hardly would have known that the Blitz had ended just months before.

To his wife, Kemp must have looked a brave and romantic veteran, which he was. Perhaps to him, she looked like she needed saving, which he could hardly resist. But theirs was evidently a stormy relationship. This might have been a reflection of the fact that Kemp's lifestyle could not possibly match her own, though he was too polite to say so. Or it might have been an early indicator of the volume of his drinking, which was how he managed the lingering pain from the severe mortar injury to his jaw that had nearly killed him in Spain in 1938. She was also either forgetful, impulsive, or prone to acts of passive aggression, having once left her wedding rings in a hotel bathroom after they had checked out during their last summer together, after he had returned from Albania. Kemp had also chosen to continue fighting instead of trying for a position on staff in London. His insistence upon joining the Polish mission might have been a bridge too far. Or perhaps, as he would later have reason to suspect, there was someone else. Whatever the cause of the breakdown of his marriage, and despite his later attempts at nonchalance, the experience hurt Kemp badly. He would never, in any of his memoirs or essays, mention her name: Hilda Elizabeth Phillips, known as Lizzie.

Kemp had nothing to keep him in England and was not due for demobilization anyway. "There were plenty of married men in our Far Eastern forces who had not seen their families for years; what conceivable justification could I have for staying at home?" He called in at SOE's Baker Street offices and put in his request: he was going to follow Smiley to Thailand.

SMILEY FLEW TO INDIA, WHERE SOE RAN ITS ASIAN OPERATIONS, WITH McLean and Hare. Their first flight was meant to take them from Cairo to Baghdad, but they were forced to turn around when one of their engines failed over the deserts of Sinai. Smiley thought the forced return "was a nuisance, but there was some compensation in seeing the expression on McLean's face when we arrived back; he had slept for the entire journey and was still half asleep on getting out at what he thought was Baghdad."

On the next flight east, Smiley was treated to an aerial tour of a journey that he had made the much harder way back in 1941. Rejoining his Household Cavalry unit after his sojourn with the Commandos in Abyssinia, he had found the regiment at Habbaniya, next to the massive lake of the same name about fifty miles east of Baghdad. The Iraqi government was pro-British, and the British had generously trained and armed the Iraqi Army (even supplying the Iraqis with Bren guns and mortars that their own troops, including Smiley, were quite sore to be going without).

Then an outfit called the Golden Square instigated a coup, seized the capital at Baghdad, and attacked the RAF base at Habbaniya using a plan for airfield seizure that had been designed, and taught, by the coupists' erstwhile British allies. The base was held by good leadership and the ferocity of the Assyrian Levies who were employed as guards by the RAF. Ethnic minorities, they were much abused and sometimes slaughtered because of their status as Christians. As one officer put it, "In their most earnest prayers, the Assyrians could never ask for anything better than a chance to get at the Arabs who had systematically massacred them for so long."

From there, Smiley's unit had pressed east with their 15-cwt trucks, taking the northern track on a mission to cut the Mosul–Baghdad railway while a southern group pushed through difficult fighting at Fallujah on the way to the capital. Smiley's men blew the railway but found themselves pinned down, without artillery support, as they attempted to take the station at Al Kadhimain in central Baghdad. But the job was done, and Smiley's men were assigned to take another station farther north, this time in conjunction with a few of Colonel Glubb Pasha's Arab Legion troops. They found an enormous quantity of egg crates. These fed the regiment for a full week, cooked on the scalding hoods of their trucks.

Smiley's flight path was too far south for him to see the lands of Kurdistan, where he and his men had passed through the ancient city of Erbil on their way to challenge the Vichy French in Syria after their sojourn in Baghdad. It did, however, take them close to Tehran, where Smiley had arrived after his missions in Iraq. He had been too late to see any of the skirmishes there himself, but the presence of the regiment was meant to discourage anyone else from succumbing to temptations. He had found other ways to contribute. With a few other officers, and under the influence of vodka supplied by the Russians who had come south to occupy Tehran as well, he had helped to burgle the German Embassy. Out with Smiley and his coconspirators came a few pictures of Hitler, a Nazi flag, and a bronze bust of the Führer himself. This last one was promptly delivered to the mess of the regiment's NCOs, where it was installed in the urinal.

THERE WERE NO SURPRISES FOR SMILEY, MCLEAN, AND HARE UPON AR-rival in Delhi; for a change, their plane had arrived as scheduled. The heat (though not the humidity) was familiar from their combined previous experiences in desert warfare.

Smiley and Kemp had discussed Thailand, but McLean was dead set on China. He kept after Smiley, trying to convince him to head farther north. While they awaited their orders and transport in Delhi, Smiley ran into an old friend with a valuable perspective.

His name was Peter Fleming. Born into a Scottish family with a penchant for adventure, Fleming had traveled all over the world on various different assignments: sometimes for expeditions, sometimes for newspapers, sometimes for his own very successful travel writing. He had been to the deepest jungles of Brazil, to the Japanese puppet state of Manchuria, to Tokyo, and all over China, including on a dramatic seven-month journey, made with the Swiss traveler Ella "Kini" Maillart, that took him from Beijing through forbidden Chinese Turkestan, known then as Sinkiang, and over the Himalayas to India.

Fleming was clever, genial, and, by means of his considerable charm and personality, more adept than almost anyone else at working his way through obstinacy, hostility, and what would otherwise seem like sheer impossibility. A brave and creative man, he had at one point been stationed with the first Chindit expedition in Burma, but after the Japanese had chased British forces nearly back to India, his services had been put to even better use. Peter Fleming headed the Asia operations of what was then known as D Division (not to be confused with Section D, a forerunner of SOE). The D stood for "deception."

His schemes seemed nearly endless. Of those recalled by a single RAF Special Duty pilot, who was involved in carrying them out, they included dropping an Indian soldier pretending to be a double agent on the basis of (fake) anticolonial politics; dropping a map case stuffed full of false British battle plans and personal items cadged from a willing brigadier in exchange for six bottles of Scotch; dropping a haversack with falsified documents and associated aircraft parts meant to look like the remains of a plane crash; dropping a dead carrier pigeon with mock messages on the Sittang valley road; dropping a haversack alongside a parachute to simulate an accidentally discarded bag during an airdrop; and, the most elaborate, inventing procedures in order to fake a failed parachute jump so that Fleming could drop a dead body that had been planted with false documents (known to all of the pilots as "the corpse job"). Recalling what he thought was his unit's final task for Fleming, the pilot said, "But if any pilot from Jessore were to tell me now that he had subsequently had a visit one day from a charming colonel who had asked them to drop a dead goat wearing a collar with a regimental badge, I could well believe him. Contact with D Division could permanently unsettle a skeptical nature."

When Peter Fleming's younger brother Ian invented the character of James Bond, his elder sibling was one of the models for the dashing secret agent. Fleming, who had his fingers in various informational pies and knew enough Chinese to be dangerous, waved Smiley off the China track and toward the jungles of Southeast Asia.

CHAPTER 9

THE SILK ROAD

Smiley was waiting in Calcutta for transport to the RAF Special Duty Station in Jessore when Julian Amery arrived from China, tucked onto an American troop transport plane. Amery had beaten everyone to the Far Eastern theater. Upon returning to London after his evacuation from Albania, he had gone to see Lord Selborne, the head of all SOE operations. Convinced that Europe was nearly done but that the war in Asia would drag on, Amery proposed to Selborne that he go to China and scout the possibilities for similar SOE operations there.

For SOE, China posed challenges similar to those of Albania. It had been invaded in 1937 by Imperial Japan, which created the puppet state of Manchukuo in northern Manchuria, overran significant portions of mainland China, and committed atrocities such as the Rape of Nanking. China was also riven by its own internal difficulties.

The Qing dynasty, last of the ancient imperial Chinese dynasties, had fallen in 1911. What followed were decades of civil war and disorder known as the Warlord Era, in which dozens of warlord "cliques," as they became known, fought for control of the country. It was as if the Italian city-state warfare of the early modern period had merged with old-school mafia tactics, but farther east and on a far larger, and industrialized, scale. The warlords amassed power (both military and economic), fought each other, carved up the country, and further ruined the lives of the already miserable ordinary people of the country.

Out of this emerged two main rival factions, though to say that they were the only two powers would be to oversimplify the picture. One was the Kuomintang, or the KMT, often referred to as the Chinese Nationalist Party, which was led by Chiang Kai-shek. He was the successor of the reformer and liberalizer Sun Yat-sen, who had died in 1925. Chiang was married to Soong Mei-ling, the American-educated older sister of Sun's wife; in her role as the power behind the "throne," Soong Mei-ling was known as Madame Chiang Kai-shek. Chiang's headquarters was in central China, in the city of Chongqing, then romanized as Chungking.

The other was the Communist Party of Mao Zedong, whose links to the Soviets at that time were much debated. Mao's headquarters was in Yan'an, in northeastern China. Both the KMT and the Communists saw each other as a greater threat than the Axis, which they assumed would eventually be defeated by the Allies elsewhere and forced to pull out of China. The analogies to Albania, and Yugoslavia, were clear. As Amery put it to Selborne, he wanted to "apply to the largest country in the world some of the lessons we had learnt in the smallest."

SOE was not yet running operations in China, and so Amery's job would be as a scout: to understand the lay of the land; ascertain the political, bureaucratic, and logistical difficulties; and report back. He was well prepared for such a role, but he needed a good cover.

He found one at dinner when he was still in London. His father had invited Adrian Carton de Wiart to join them at their house in Eaton Square. Carton, Churchill's personal representative to Chiang Kai-shek, was in London to brief the prime minister but soon found himself heading back to Chungking in his own military transport plane.

It was a very diplomatic mission for someone who had not had a very diplomatic career. There were few soldiers who embodied the profession like Carton, who combined the combat bravery of a David Smiley with many more years of practice and a not-quite-healthy dose of disdain for personal safety.

Born in 1880, Carton was the child of an aristocratic Belgian lawyer but was sent to school in England. He decamped from Oxford to enlist, as a private, in the British Army so that he could fight in the Second Boer War. There he was severely wounded in the stomach and groin, invalided home, and given a commission. He refused to complete his studies at Oxford and stayed in the army, taking part in combat with the Somaliland Camel Corps in the First World War, which saw him shot in the face, an experience that lost him his left eye and part of an ear. He transferred to the Western Front, and by the end of the war, he had become a brigadier. On the way, he was shot in the skull and shelled in the ankle, the hip, and the ear (he never mentioned if it was the same one through which he'd already been shot). He was strangely consistent, with six of his woundings occurring on Sundays, a day on which he ever after avoided beginning new undertakings. He also lost an arm, nearly lost a leg, and won a Victoria Cross, the highest honor for bravery in the British military.

Carton bore seventeen different wound scars, as Amery had the opportunity to see when they shared a tent together in Assam. As Amery put it, "He must have been the most mutilated soldier on active service in any army." Yet he also admitted that Carton was far quicker than he at handling luggage and opening doors, despite having one less arm and many more years than Amery. His wounds caused him pain and shortened the fuse on his temper, which had naturally never been long. He was reserved at first, but once you had gained his confidence, "he spoke his mind and without fear of God or devil." His tongue was legendary, and when he lost his temper, his language, according to Amery, "was the most violent and varied I have ever heard. Fortunately, he never lost his temper with me."

Carton was irresistible to his hosts in China. Many men liked to prove their own mettle by simply touching him. As the story went, when one Chinese general asked a colleague what Carton was like, the general was met with this response: "He's very fierce and over a hundred and fifty years old."

Carton agreed to give Amery cover. They flew together to India, staging their journey from Calcutta. Amery stayed with one of his father's friends, who happened to be the Governor of Bengal. Government House, the official residence, was modeled on a grand English home but, for purposes of camouflage from Japanese bombers, had been painted purple, giving it what Amery thought was a "rather surrealist quality."

Amery was told at the time that there were only two ways to get to China: flying over what the pilots called "the Hump," known to the rest of the world as the eastern Himalayas, or traveling through Tibet on yaks. By yak, it would have taken approximately three months to cross all the way to Chungking. Carton and Amery took the risk of flying, which was not insubstantial. The Hump caused dangerous flying weather. The path also overflew Japanese-occupied territory, and the planes at the time, if fully loaded, could barely reach the altitude required to pass over the highest mountains on Earth. Carton once flew over the Hump at twenty-five thousand feet against a one-hundred-mile-per-hour gale; the flight that had been meant to take three hours took five and a half, and one of his staff officers ended up with frostbitten toes, as the plane had been unheated. On their flight, Amery was forced to suck oxygen to keep his stomach in some semblance of order. Hours later, he was rewarded with the sight of red-and-purple mountains emerging from the clouds. "As we came down towards the great lake of Kunming," said Amery, "I fully expected to see dragons playing on the hillsides."

Amery's job was to understand the lay of the land not only with respect to the war in China but also with respect to the work of the Allies there. To that end, his job was to observe, and to listen. He met with the British, with envoys from other Allied countries, and with many Chinese politicians and generals. He also met with Madame Sun Yat-sen, the widow of the great leader.

Carton was generous with his time and introduced Amery to his friends and contacts. Among them were other Allied representatives, including the Russian-born French General Zinovi Pechkoff, a de Gaulle appointee and a close friend of Carton's. Not only had both men lost arms in service to their adopted countries—Carton his left and Pechkoff his right—but they had done so on the same day: May 9, 1915. One day at lunch, Pechkoff asked Carton what Amery's job was. Carton tapped his black patch and said, "He's my missing eye."

Amery's mission, however, was coming to a close. His attempts to visit the Communists in Yan'an had been denied, much to Chiang's embarrassment: the Americans had their fingers in that pie and did not want the British near it. The Allies were soon to split up their spheres of operation in Asia, and SOE was not to operate in China. There was little for Amery to do. Meanwhile, he had received a telegram from his father, urging him to hurry home.

There was a general election on. While he had been in London in 1940, briefing the government as a representative of his boss in Section D, Amery had put his name down on a list of interested candidates for the Conservative Party. As the process went then, he had been interviewed by several selection committees. (British rules did not require candidates to be resident in the district beforehand.) He had not been selected, but his name was on the list, and in 1943, his good friend Randolph Churchill, Winston's son, had asked him to run for the vacant seat (one of two) in his own district of Preston, a constituency on the Scottish border. Amery had agreed, but an election had seemed a long way off then. Now it was here, and he was pledged to stand. Churchill père was rightly anxious about his party's chances in the coming election, and he did not want Amery to be an absentee.

With Amery's mission in China wrapping up, the decision to return to England would have seemed an easy one to make. But just before his father's demand had arrived, Amery had been given a tempting offer by a man named Gordon Etherington-Smith, who was then serving as third secretary to the Embassy. Etherington-Smith (for obvious reasons, even some Foreign Office correspondence abbreviated his name to E-Smith) had been offered the post of British Consul in Kashgar, a city sitting in the northwest of the legendary Chinese Turkestan. He had an allowance for a military attaché; would Amery like the job?

He would, but the impending election, as well as a personal family crisis, forced him to decline. It was a necessary thing, but as Amery wrote decades later, "To have said 'no' to the chance of a year in Sinkiang remains a lasting regret."

Having turned Etherington-Smith down, Amery reconnected with Smiley. They had several meals together, including at Government House and at small Chinese restaurants in town. (Amery had become a fan of the cuisine: "Chinese cooking in its range and delicacy has no superior anywhere and no rival outside France.") What Smiley remembered were the local drinks, possibly because one of his involved a liqueur "reputed to be over a hundred years old, and alleged to be the more delicious because there was a pickled lizard in the bottle."

It was probably from Smiley that Amery learned that Billy McLean had taken himself off, first to SOE headquarters in Kandy and then to Delhi, in order to try to find a suitable mission in China. Amery had one to hand him: the military attaché appointment in Kashgar. The job was McLean's for the taking. He took it.

THE ANCIENT AND MUCH-CONTESTED CITY OF KASHGAR (TO ADD TO the complexity, there was both Old and New Kashgar, then still several miles apart) sat in the northwestern corner of the Chinese province then called Sinkiang, now better known as Xinjiang. The area had been claimed by China for nearly two thousand years, but there was good reason why the name translated to "New Province": various Chinese dynasties had struggled to control it. Since the revolution of 1911, the central Chinese government had held little sway in Sinkiang.

Kashgar was closer to Baghdad than to Beijing. Between it and the central government lay thousands of miles of desert and mountains. Sinkiang itself was both surrounded and bisected by mountain ranges: to the west were the Pamirs, the Hindu Kush, the Indus, the Karakoram, and the Himalayas; the Tien Shan bisected the middle, and the Altai range barred the far north; to the south stood the Kunlun Shan. In the middle was desert. The natural trade routes, despite some of the most formidable mountain ranges on earth, were with the rest of Central Asia, to the west, or with Mongolia to the northeast. Most of the population represented a mix of various Central Asian ethnicities, cultures, and loyalties. They were the people now known as Uyghurs, Kyrgyz, Mongols, Tajiks, and Kazakhs; the term "Turki" was in general use.

There were ethnic Chinese Muslims known as Tungans, whose shared religion with their neighbors did not serve as the basis for good relationships. There were also non-Muslim Chinese settled by the central government. The local warlord was a Manchurian named Sheng Shih-ts'ai. He nominally worked for the central Chinese government, but his closest ties were with the USSR, which he had allowed to invade in the 1930s in order to put down a challenge to his personal rule. The province had been wracked by rebellions and power struggles throughout most of its relationship with China, the most significant being a conquest led by Yakub Beg, who invaded from what is now Kyrgyzstan in the late nineteenth century. Both tsarist and Soviet Russia had held designs on the area. During the Second World War, the Soviets claimed that the province was their prerogative because the Japanese might show up at their back door by crossing eastward from Manchuria through Mongolia and Sinkiang. This was not completely fantasy; the two rivals had fought a battle at Khalkhin Gol on the Manchuria-Mongolia border in 1939. Everyone mistrusted everyone else. Sinkiang was ruled by rumors, like the one circulating in the 1930s that claimed Lawrence of Arabia was working for the Tungans to seize control of the province.

After meeting his Central Asian deserters in Albania (from the

Soviet part of the same region, albeit to the west of the Pamirs), the invitation was irresistible to McLean. He would accompany Etherington-Smith on the journey from Delhi. They would go over land, though despite what Amery had been told, their procession would not involve yaks. It would, however, involve no fewer than eighty-two ponies. Etherington-Smith was tasked with bringing a set of supplies for the consulate, for which there was neither an airport nor a railroad terminus within hundreds of miles. Part of his baggage included 550 gallons of gasoline, presumably for the consulate's electric generators, the ones that went out in high winds.

In 1945, a traveler moving from Delhi to Kashgar could expect to take more than a month to make the trip in good weather. Peter Fleming had made the journey, albeit in the opposite direction, in the mid-1930s. Despite the passage of a decade, his quip that what was then called "the Gilgit road" was a "courtesy title" nevertheless remained true. Ahead of them lay some of the tallest and most precipitous mountain passes in the world.

The journey from Delhi took the men north, through what is now part of eastern Pakistan. The first major pass was the Burzil. At more than thirteen thousand feet above sea level, it was still covered in snow, even on the late June days when McLean and Etherington-Smith traversed it. Most of their going involved only three feet of snow, but in some places, twelve-foot drifts survived in the summer sunshine. Beyond the Burzil Pass lay a journey through Hunza, a land of scree-covered mountains prone to landslides. One British traveler, who had departed the previous fall, thought that "their terror is enhanced by the fact that the Karakoram Hills seem to be crumbling to pieces, causing stone shoots and littering the parris [narrow ledge paths] with slippery stone and rock."

Etherington-Smith, with classic British understatement, called this section the "two rather anxious days when our ponies developed a tendency to fall off the road into the Hunza river." Travelers along the route were treated to the whitened bones of the pack animals whose journeys had ended prematurely. There being no regular postal service, the British Consulate in Kashgar employed men to take the mail in relays over the mountains to India. Several were killed doing so, mostly by avalanches. Ice was as treacherous as snow. McLean and Etherington-Smith crossed two glaciers. This involved four nail-biting hours of guiding the poor beasts of burden along the ice, which Etherington-Smith described as "among my most vivid memories of the journey."

The classic final resting stop on the road from British India was at the foot of the Gul Khwaja Uween Glacier, 14,000 feet above sea level. The next day's passage, across the Mintaka Pass, reached 15,430 feet. Travelers in those days brought no oxygen, and if the day was clear, they could be forgiven for thinking that the view before them was the result of delirium. Stretched out were the Hindu Kush, the Pamirs, the Himalayas, and the Karakoram: hundreds of miles of the tallest land on Earth, running out beneath one's feet. This was the Roof of the World, a sight that, even in today's era of jet planes and spaceships, few have ever seen—and one that still must be earned on foot.

Several days later, the men found themselves descending into the valley that hosted the oasis cities of Sinkiang. Waiting for them were their Chinese hosts: four Chinese soldiers and three Turki police officials, the latter of whom sat proudly astride the very sort of yaks that Julian Amery had been warned about. Etherington-Smith thought them "a remarkable sight, especially when cantering!" After several more days, and with much generous local hospitality, they saw their first motorized transport since India: M. C. Gillett, the British Consul General for whom Etherington-Smith would be taking over, had sent his lorry to pick them up. McLean and Etherington-Smith arrived in Kashgar on August 15. There they were greeted by Gillett himself. He had good news: the Japanese had surrendered. The war was over.

This was not what McLean had been expecting. Despite all the jokes about his languid appearance and his perpetually late arrival to almost all appointments, he was not the sort of man to sit idle. The war with Japan might have been over, but Sinkiang was, if anything, on more of a war footing than ever. Because of the possible Soviet menace to Sinkiang, the Chinese Nationalist central government had been one ally that had not celebrated the end of the war in Europe that May. Would this mean that the Russians would turn their attentions to Central Asia? Since 1944, there had been constant rumors, all duly recorded by Gillett's consulate, about a coming war. There were (frequently true) stories about various raids from the west by Russian-backed Kazakhs. Chinese troops were moved to the area, warnings about aerial bombardment were given to the population, and slit trenches were dug. The economic situation was nearly in crisis, and inflation was rampant. Taxation was through the roof, and conscription was a menace. The excuse for the militarization of the province was nominally the threat from Japan, but all the locals assumed that the real enemy was Russia.

Finally, the Chinese Nationalist central government rid itself of the Soviet-backed local dictator. This did not solve its problems, however, and a new revolt broke out in the fall. Watching from his perch in the consulate, known as the Chini Bagh, or the Chinese Garden, McLean had a front-row seat to it all. Five columns of Soviet-backed Kazakhs invaded across the mountains from the south and, massacring a Chinese garrison along the way, nearly made it to Kashgar. In the north, another thrust approached the regional capital, then romanized as Urumchi. Rebels flanked the city and cut the road from Urumchi to central China.

McLean's brief was not to get involved in this civil war. Kashgar was effectively cut off, so there was nowhere for him to go. In the meantime, he worked on improving his Turkic and introduced himself to the local population. As it often did, McLean's interest in the local culture managed to break through the locals' natural reticence to engage with a foreigner. (In a place like Kashgar, where you never knew who the next ruler would be, caution was warranted.)

He learned falconry from the locals, drank their red pepper tea while sitting on the mud floors of their huts, smoked their homegrown hashish, and even listened to their grievances against their government. With the various mountain passes blocked by the progress of the Kazakh rebels, McLean settled in for what was an unseasonably warm winter for Kashgar but a chilly one for him—the temperature, though reputedly the mildest in fifty years, was still far below zero degrees Fahrenheit.

JULIAN AMERY HAD NOT JUST GIVEN UP THE KASHGAR JOB TO MCLEAN because of the election. His older brother, named John but always known to the family as Jack, had been charged with treason. It was a crime for which there was only one penalty: death.

Jack, who had been living in France, had offered his services to the Germans in 1942. He aided the Nazi war effort in three different ways. One, and probably the most legally damning, was his attempt to recruit British prisoners of war for a special Wehrmacht unit that he meant to call the Legion of St. George. Jack also undertook something of a tour of Nazi-occupied Europe, giving speeches across the continent, including one in Belgrade when Julian was fighting in Albania, not so very far away. But what he was best known for were his speeches on the radio, which were broadcast to Britain. Jack was one of a handful of British traitors who spewed propaganda on the airwaves; the other was William Joyce, known as "Lord Haw-Haw." Both of their shows started with the repeated formula "Germany calling, Germany calling, Germany calling." Jack's had a tripartite setup. First came a baleful antisemitic screed, despite the fact that Jack's own father was of partially Jewish descent. Though Jack himself was raised as a Christian, it is unlikely that he knew nothing of his ancestry. Then came an insistence that Britain could not win against Germany, followed by an argument that the Soviet menace was of far more danger to Britain than the Nazi one.

Upon hearing of Jack's treason, Julian and his father, Leo Amery, had the same first instinct: to submit their resignations. Both were re-jected. When Julian learned that his brother was swanning about Bel-grade as he fought in the mountains of Albania, his position was clear: "Had it lain within my power to ambush his car, I would have done so without compunction."

Why had Jack done it? He would claim, as his mystified and grief-stricken parents would later, that he was a committed anti-Communist who saw the Soviets as the greatest threat. But there was much more to Jack. He had been a source of much woe for his parents for most of his life. His adult behavior, even before committing treason, was egregious.

He had contracted syphilis by the age of seventeen, a feat he topped by marrying a prostitute. He was underage at the time; he and his lover eloped to Athens, where they were legally married. He proceeded to abandon her and, eschewing the formality of divorce, bigamously mar-ried a second member of the same profession who was a French Fascist. In 1943, after a boozy night out in Berlin, she asphyxiated on her own vomit while sleeping next to an equally inebriated Jack. He proceeded then to "marry" a third woman, Michelle Thomas.

Though Jack professed to be part of the film industry, his activities were both more creative and dramatic than even Hollywood fiction. Not a day went by in which he was not hatching some "business" idea or an-other, though what Jack considered to be business, most others would have called either a generic con or some sort of half-baked Ponzi scheme. He purported to own film companies, distribution companies, and even an airport. One noblewoman came begging to Jack's father when she found out that her own son had lost his life savings investing in what Jack had pitched as a business that imported silk stockings to England by air.

He was charged with fraud for passing a bad check in Greece, cost-ing his father thousands of pounds in legal fees. He amassed somewhere in the neighborhood of eighty traffic violations, for infractions ranging from leaving his car in the middle of the road while he drank for three hours at a pub to attempting to mow down a police officer motioning him to stop. In subsequent years, he richly embroidered the space between fraud and treason with a florid variety of other wrongdoings; by 1936, at the age of only twenty-four, he had been declared bankrupt.

But treason was another thing entirely. Jack's actions gutted his family. Successful and well connected, his father hired the best lawyers. Julian quashed his previous feelings and chose to help defend Jack: "There was no room for anger now or even resentment. He was my brother."

Because Jack's actions were so public, and because he refused to deny them (he insisted upon traveling for much of the way back to London in Fascist Blackshirt attire and jackboots), his family and his lawyers had only two avenues of defense: that Jack could not be held accountable for treason because he was not a British subject, or because he was insane.

The first option looked surprisingly promising, as Jack claimed to have been granted Spanish citizenship for helping the Nationalists during the civil war. Julian was duly dispatched to Spain. He came back with some sort of paperwork, but as the fall of 1945 progressed, the possibility surfaced that his brother may have sent him on a wild goose chase. The avenues of law were narrowing.

Julian and Jack had never been close. The younger Amery was not even into his teens when Jack's elopement and Greek arrest made his brother's character clear. They had not had much opportunity to bond earlier. Jack was seven years older, and the boys attended different boarding schools. For his part, Jack, upon meeting his younger brother, had declared that he "would rather have had a kitten."

Julian visited Jack in prison every day and felt that "I got to know him better than in all those years that had gone before." But the legal defenses crumbled. And then Jack refused to plead not guilty.

The scene in the courtroom was dramatic. The trial was meant to begin at half past ten in the morning, but Julian, watching from a corner seat in the back of the small room at the Old Bailey, saw the clock reach a quarter past eleven, and still, nothing had happened. It turned out that the lawyers, the judge, and the Attorney General had been arguing. Both the judge and the Attorney General were opposed to Jack's plan of an unqualified guilty plea. The judge insisted that Gerald Slade, Jack's attorney, make clear to him once more the consequences of such a move.

In the cells for the accused, Slade approached Jack once more. Jack thought that it might be a good idea to declare his guilty plea along with a bitter speech about victors' justice; Slade counseled him against it. "I am caught in a vicious circle here," protested Jack. "Anything I may say in support of my political ideas can only harm my personal prospects and those of my family, while anything I say to help my personal prospects can only be a betrayal of my political ideas."

Guilty pleas without some sort of deal from the prosecution are incredibly rare. Murderers caught in the act plead not guilty. But not Jack. Slade, resigned, turned to go back up the long staircase that led into the small courtroom, where he would stand opposite the dais with leather-upholstered chairs that served as the bench for the judge, magistrates, and chaplain. Then he heard Jack's voice calling him back. Hoping that his client had changed his mind, Slade turned around. Jack said, "I just wanted to tell you how sorry I am that I shall never hear your speech in my defence." The trial lasted all of eight minutes.

Why Jack did what he did—both committing treason and utterly refusing to try to save his own skin—has puzzled most onlookers ever since. His father insisted until his own death that while his older son may have been misguided, deluded, and possibly mentally unstable, his anti-Communist ideals were real, and that his guilty plea was designed to prevent further pain and embarrassment to his family.

Perhaps Jack's refusal to conform to social norms, and to refrain from hurting those around him, was a pathology; perhaps he was fully insane or perhaps merely a psychopath. His family, desperate to save him from the noose, appealed to the Crown, which Jack's father had served so loyally and so long, for mercy.

Revealed were horrifying stories from Jack's youth: that he had been a "hard child," according to his long-experienced nanny; that his kindergarten teacher had thought him an "extremely abnormal boy"; that he had tried to poison his younger brother as a baby by putting his milk bottles in a solution of silver polish; that the headmaster of his boarding school feared he had "a complete indifference to the morals of others." He was frequently paranoid, and he had carried a revolver from a young age. This was aside from the salacious details of his sexuality that had shaken even the experienced prostitute who was his first wife. The psychiatrist who prepared the insanity defense declared that Jack suffered from "moral imbecility." Yet all of these statements were compiled after Jack's guilty plea in an effort by his family to submit an insanity defense. Jack was clearly a man who stuck in the memory. How much his spectacularly public downfall had influenced the recall of those memories is unknowable.

Jack had been effectively expelled from Harrow for bad behavior and had exhausted multiple private tutors. But Jack also showed sharp analytical capacity, self-awareness, and an ability for self-control when he wished to deploy it. He loved, above all, to shock, and he could calculate his behavior to produce the desired response. When Julian first heard that his brother was stuck in German-occupied France, he had said to his friend and colleague Sandy Glen, "There's going to be a disaster. I know exactly what will happen; Jack will go over to the other side."

In his late teens, Jack had confessed to one of his tutors that he held his father in contempt for not taking advantage of his political connections in order to make more money. He was a noted physical coward and an incredibly lazy child, refusing to participate in school sports. Yet he excelled in situations that he enjoyed, such as rock climbing and mountaineering. He was undeniably intelligent and able to apply himself selectively. Despite his checkered educational career, he passed the exams to earn a place at Oxford. He then promptly informed his father that he would not be attending.

For all his stubbornness and bad behavior, Jack was undeniably charismatic. He had been given every advantage in life: the French nanny (like his brother, he was bilingual), the best schools, the private tutors, his father's connections. He could be clever, charming, and utterly convincing. Julian found that "I would go to the prison hoping to cheer him up, and always came away cheered by him." Jack could read people better than they knew.

Julian was amazed at how Jack had converted the prison guards to his side. The chief executioner, a man named Albert Pierrepoint, declared that Jack was the bravest man he'd ever met. For his part, Jack greeted Pierrepoint with the same cavalierness that he had shown his lead lawyer, Slade: "I've always wanted to meet you, although not, of course, under these circumstances."

The insanity defense failed. By pleading guilty, Jack had placed the burden of his salvation on the government. But had the government granted mercy without incontrovertible evidence of a level of insanity that precluded culpability, it would have looked like rank favoritism, given the official position of Jack's father. Jack would be hung on the morning of December 19, 1945. His last words to his father were: "I am your son."

Jack had made a request to be hung in Blackshirt garb and jackboots. The governor of the prison, apparently unfamiliar with Fascist dress codes, initially gave the approval. When the implications were brought to his attention, permission was withdrawn.

Julian Amery sat vigil outside the prison overnight with Michelle, the Frenchwoman whom Jack considered to be his wife. At ten past nine the next morning, the wardens posted the official notice of execution on the prison door, and Amery knew that Jack was dead. To his diary,

Julian committed this memory: "We got home somehow, and I hardly remember how I passed the day. It must be many years since I last cried."

Jack had finally achieved in death what he had so frequently sought in life: to be the explosive, shocking center of attention, the man obsessively followed on the front page, the man no one could figure out and no one could stop talking about. His actions can be read in any variety of ways: as those of a malignant malcontent or a disturbing psychopath or a pitiably insane man. Any true answers died with Jack.

What remained were his actions, and those of his family. For all his atrocious behavior—the lies, the fraud, the bigamy, the careless usage of everyone around him, the vicious antisemitism, the Nazi collaboration—in the end, Jack's decision to die was an undeniably brave choice. Even after his appeals were exhausted, appeals pursued more by his family than by him, Jack refused any attempt to escape.

His family members never wavered in their loyalty to one of their own, and never failed to argue that Jack had been a disturbed man who was nevertheless a committed anti-Communist. Theirs was a remarkable display of forgiveness, of loyalty, of commitment, and of love. Asked at the end of his own life whether the executioner Pierrepoint's characterization of Jack as the bravest man he had ever hung made the pain worse, Julian responded, "No, it was appropriate. He was an Amery."

Jack had chosen a different side. In this, the Amery family's experience was one unusual in Britain but all too common elsewhere. The war against the Nazis eventually turned, as Amery, McLean, Smiley, and Kemp had so clearly found in Albania, into a series of localized civil wars. Julian himself expressed it this way: "Such searing experiences were suffered by many on all sides of the Continent. In Britain, they were mercifully rare." The distinction in Europe was that families caught on different sides could usually identify the motivations that had driven their opposites to such painful choices. With Jack, as ever, even those remained a mystery.

CHAPTER 10

GETTING TO KNOW YOU

In early April 1945, months before the Japanese surrender and Billy McLean's journey across the Himalayas, David Smiley arrived at SOE's special training school for jungle warfare at Colombo, in what was then Ceylon, now Sri Lanka. He was finally preparing for Thailand.

Thailand is a varied territory; much of the north is jungle, but the south has plains. All of it, however, is hot, and it contained wildlife that was unfamiliar to Smiley. Southeast Asia looked different, smelled different, and sounded different than what he was used to. Another officer was leading a column in the region when he felt rather than heard a strange sound in his head. It rose in pitch, with the percussive pressure akin to that of a modern jet plane. It was a shrill throb. As the volume increased, the officer looked and realized that the man beside him heard it too. Soon every man in the column had his hand on his weapon, looking for the enemy, whatever it was. Then, suddenly, the tension was broken by an old Burma hand. "Cicadas!" he declared, laughing. Thailand also had talking lizards (the favorite of all Allied troops who served in the region was called by its cri de coeur, which sounded exactly like the English vulgarity that is the equivalent of a raised middle finger) and deer that barked.

Part of the training school was simply adjusting to the heat. The students stayed in local-style barracks with hard planks as beds. It was just as well, as to Smiley's recollection, they spent most of their time on them just sweating, stripped nearly naked. The camp was so humid that mold grew on every uncovered surface each night. Cobras and pythons lived in the space beneath the floor. Even the unheated showers were quite warm. The sun heated the pipes and water tanks on its own. This was despite the fact that the monsoon season had started and the rains drenched everything in sight on the rubber and coconut plantation that had been co-opted for the camp.

The school was rich in organization and talent. There were reputedly twenty-nine nationalities represented, though as for Europe, only the French, British, and Dutch overlapped with Smiley. He met people from everywhere: Malaya, China, and even Japan. He also, to his approval, finally got to meet some Gurkhas. A warrior people whose diminutive size and genuinely cheerful nature never put even the slightest dent in their lethality, they were beloved by those who fought with them and dreaded by those who fought against them. No manufacturer had yet to make a rifle that could outstrip a Gurkha's preference for his kukri, a curved, and much feared, short blade. As Smiley said, "They operated against us as 'enemy' on a number of exercises, and their performance bore out all I had previously heard about them—including that they were the finest fighting troops in the world."

Smiley paid close attention to the courses on first aid: Albania and his posts in the Middle East and Africa may have had malaria, but the jungles of Thailand held more varied pestilences. There were the usual suspects (venereal disease, malaria, cholera, typhus, smallpox) and the less familiar (snakebite). Albania had not harbored many deadly snakes. At the jungle school, one man found a Russell's viper in his shirt. But what most intrigued Smiley was learning to shoot in an entirely new way. He had already adjusted to the new rifle being distributed, the American .30 carbine.

Now he was taught to shoot the rifle instinctively, like a shotgun. A rifle is traditionally aimed carefully, with one eye closed, to take advantage of the weapon's more precise aim, especially over longer distances. A shotgun, on the other hand, is aimed more generally and often used on difficult but closer moving targets, such as birds; to up the ante, the ammunition is designed as a burst rather than as a single bullet. The logic behind shooting the carbine like a shotgun had less to do with moving targets than with close ones. The jungle was so thick that firefights between soldiers tended to happen at very close range, and as Smiley put it, "A person who fired his shot first usually came off best."

He became quite effective. The theory was put into practice on several training missions in which the students were left to procure their own food (having been taught what was edible and what was not); Smiley brought down wild boars, deer, and "jungle fowl," but he "jibbed at eating a monkey that a French officer shot—it looked uncomfortably human."

SMILEY, PROMOTED TO LIEUTENANT COLONEL, WOULD COMMAND A team across a large swath of Thailand. Primary among his tasks was to arm and train the Thai resistance, which already had a significant and well-organized operation in the country. His other major assignment was to search for and aid Allied POWs and civilian internees.

Thailand was a very different operational territory than Albania, and not only because it was occupied by the Japanese and not the Germans. Thailand was a proud, successful historical anomaly: a small Asian country that had not been fully subjected to the whims of European colonialism. Thailand was, and had always been, independent. Despite a recent anti-monarchical revolution, it had good fortune in its kings, who had deftly managed to keep the Europeans, primarily the British, at a sufficiently friendly arm's length. Reforms had begun to modernize the country, and many Thai princes were sent abroad for

education. This included Smiley's friend Chin, the prince who had recruited him to SOE's Siamese Country Section, which still, in a nod to
some of its royalist members, bore Thailand's old name. Several members of the royal family served in the British forces. By the time Smiley
dropped into Thailand, one had already been killed as a pilot in the RAF.

The Thai government had not been able to stave off the Japanese.
They had invaded in 1942, landing on the coast of what is now Vietnam
and moving westward. Their aim was the jewel of the British Empire:
India. En route lay Thailand, Burma, and the great gates of Imphal,
where British forces (including the all-volunteer Indian Army) stopped
them in the spring and summer of 1944.

This westward sweep was a danger to Thai independence. The country could not stand up to the Japanese invasion. They did the only thing
they could do: they collaborated, at least officially. This included declaring war on Britain. The head of the government, a man named Pibul,
sympathized with Fascism and Japan. Most others did not, including
the statesman whom Pibul considered his greatest rival, the liberal
Pridi. Pridi had been kicked upstairs as the regent to the young and
powerless king. To Allied forces in Thailand, however, Pridi was better
known by his code name as the country's resistance leader: Ruth.

Thailand had an underground so large that even the Japanese sometimes openly referred to Ruth's "private army." The Thais double-crossed
their Japanese occupiers with a cheerful ease that bested even Smiley's
experiences with the Albanian Zogists who had smuggled him in German lorries during his scouting missions. Smiley always got warnings
of impending raids. Even in rural parts of the country, where the sight
of a blond, blue-eyed man was still cause for local gossip, he was never
betrayed by a local.

SOE had been working with the local resistance since long before
Smiley arrived. By February 1945, the local resistance leader, a man
code-named Pluto, who also happened to be the local equivalent of an

MP or a congressman, was reporting that he had recruited 150 potential section leaders for their resistance army.

Smiley dropped in on May 30, 1945, with his favorite wireless operator, the artilleryman "Gunner" Collins, and two Thai resistance fighters, nicknamed Chat and Pun. Smiley's descent, from the relatively low level of five hundred feet, was quick and easy but for the splash on landing. Muddy though it was, the rice-paddy landing was gentle enough by that all-important wartime metric: the bottle of whisky that Smiley had tucked into a pocket of the flying suit he wore over his battle dress was intact.

Smiley descended alone. One of the Thai parachutists had gotten cold feet on the way out and looked quite sheepish when he landed, having been given some physical encouragement upon exiting the plane on the pilot's second run. There to meet them were two other Thai resisters, the local leader Pluto and Kong, who had been Ruth's wireless operator in Bangkok before the regent had sent him north for safekeeping from the Japanese.

For the next month, Smiley, Collins, and their local partners would train guerrillas and lie low until given the signal for an organized uprising against the Japanese. They were assigned a significant swath of territory in northeastern Thailand that was named "Candle" back at headquarters. This represented about one-third of the country, running along the Laotian border in the east and heading west to the railway that went from Korat to Ubon.

By early June, Smiley had inspected two thousand trained fighters. Pluto had organized no fewer than ten training camps, capable of training one hundred men a week in rifles, carbines, and grenades.

ELSEWHERE ON THE CONTINENT, PETER KEMP HAD BEEN FURNISHED with what he called "that sacred gift, Priority," on his way to India. It

landed him promptly in a Karachi hospital with an attack of gout. This
was no less painful or embarrassing for the fact that the disease was he-
reditary. (Once, it had even struck when he was anticipating a German
offensive in Berane; as he recuperated, he could only imagine the propaganda broadcast: "Units of the Wehrmacht occupied Berane yesterday and captured a British major in bed with the gout.") Not to be
outdone, he wrote a poem that ended on these lines: "Prince, when you
have erred from discretion / Your father will tell you—you lout! / Get
the Clap to create an impression, / But never go down with the gout!"

One of Kemp's fellow patients had been captured by the Japanese in
Burma. Set for execution, he had been tied to a tree. The young soldier
tasked with killing him had merely shot him in the shoulder and run
off. The man was rescued by his own side a few hours later. But he was
adamant in his advice: *Do not allow yourself to be taken by the Japanese
at this stage of the war.*

Soon after he was discharged from the hospital and from his omi-
nous roommate, Kemp once again found John Hibberdine. They had
not seen each other since they split in Kosovo, when Kemp was ordered
out to Montenegro. Hibberdine's had been an even rougher road. Struck
by paratyphoid, he had been escorted to the coast by friendly Albanians
and other British officers, who managed to get him there just as Amery
and McLean left on their final departure from the country. Now Kemp
shared what he called Hibberdine's "urbanely cynical company" while
the latter awaited his drop to the Kra Isthmus, at the tip of the Burma-
Malaya border.

The war had also troubled Hibberdine's personal life. His impending marriage had been undone by the vagaries of SOE paperwork. Given
that soldiers on special operations could not let anyone know they
worked for SOE, could not let anyone know where they were going, and
could not communicate from the field at all, some wit had set up a system in which the staff office contacted individuals on behalf of their beloved soldier. Unfortunately, the office used a series of generic messages

that were often mistimed. Hibberdine had prepared messages for his fiancée before his drop into Albania. Three or four months later, they
stopped. Frustrated, she progressed from what one observer called "perplexity to annoyance, and from annoyance to anger." She produced an
ultimatum: respond or she would break off the engagement. To this, she
received the response "I am in the pink." She got engaged to someone
else, and on the day of the wedding, an equally mystifying message appeared: "It's a boy."

It was now Kemp's turn to attend jungle warfare school. There he
set about learning snatches of the Thai language and politely declining
offers to go on a training course bearing a fifty-pound pack. Having escaped several German cordons in his time, once with nothing better
than a pistol and a single magazine, Kemp declared that such a weight
"was a white man's burden that I was not prepared to tote." If it did not
fit into his small haversack, it could be carried on a separate conveyance—
or abandoned. "I never had cause to change this view," said Kemp, who
had plenty of chances to put theory into practice.

His next stop was not the Special Duty flight station but Calcutta,
where one evening he was having drinks on the staff's veranda when he
heard a faint plop and saw that an enormous black scorpion had descended onto the head of the pilot sitting next to him. The pilot, evidently accustomed to split-second decisions, snapped his head to the side,
casting the creature onto his shoulder, where he brushed it off. Death
was averted when someone managed to invert a (barely big enough)
half-pint tumbler over the thing as two young dogs rushed toward it.

David Smiley was also back in Calcutta after his sojourn in Thailand. He summoned Kemp to the Viceregal Lodge, where he was a guest
of family friends, the Wavells. When Kemp arrived, the other man was
a haunting reminder of his own past experience with combat medicine.
Smiley's face and hands were covered in burns, which gave him the appearance of the hapless cartoon villain Wile E. Coyote after his attempts
to blow up his archnemesis Road Runner inevitably fail.

SEVERAL WEEKS EARLIER, SMILEY AND HIS TEAM HAD JUST GOTTEN WORD of a major POW camp full of Allied soldiers near the city of Ubon when his Thai allies came rushing in to warn of unexpected Japanese movement in their direction. Smiley, Collins, and the Thais made to move quickly into the jungle. Smiley packed the sensitive codebooks and other secret documents into a special briefcase while Collins loaded the wireless set onto local laborers.

Smiley's briefcase was the latest from SOE's toy factory, known as the Museum. One officer who saw the Museum in its wartime state in 1945 said that it contained "some of the most diabolically clever machines and devices that it has ever been my lot to clap eyes on." The King himself was said to have spent two and a half hours there on what was meant to be a forty-five-minute visit. This was the shop that produced the ingenious gold buttons and pencil clips that faced north and the concealed jackknives and sewn-in silk maps that had been given to SOE agents in Albania and elsewhere.

Smiley's briefcase was on an altogether different order. It included the regular briefcase fittings, but it also contained five pounds of thermite. It was a bomb. It could be set on a timer in order to be used as a literal suitcase explosive, or it could be used as a document-destruction machine: if one simply placed the relevant materials in the briefcase and pressed the right buttons, the papers would be securely burned.

Or so it was hoped. Most likely there was a short circuit somewhere. Parachuting and the jungle climate had probably not been kind to the stability of a machine that was designed with a permanently installed blasting cap. Even today, explosives experts in special operations carry the blasting caps separately from the explosives, and the two are never paired until an explosion is imminently desired.

Smiley, wearing jungle shorts and his sleeves rolled up on account of the heat, packed his documents as quickly as he could. Then the brief-case suddenly exploded.

Five pounds of thermite flew up into his face and rained down onto his bare arms. Thermite is an incendiary explosive. It goes boom, but it is designed primarily to burn. Smiley managed to close his eyes in the nick of time. His skin blackened and burned. Soon it hardened and crusted, and he was unable to open his eyes. His arms and knees took a beating. His fingernails were burned off, and the bones of three of his fingers were visible.

The Japanese were still coming. Collins led the burned and blinded Smiley into the jungle to hide. It was either a false alarm or the Japanese had passed them by. They returned to their camp (named Heston after the British racecourse—Smiley named all of his camps in Thailand af-ter racecourses, including Ascot), where Smiley was dosed with two in-effective morphine tablets. SOE teams brought no specialized medics. Any doctoring was left to their own training and to the wits and capa-bilities of their local allies.

Smiley's staff officers—much to his relief a competent, friendly, and efficient set of men and women (regardless of their actual jobs, the lat-ter were part of the First Aid Nursing Yeomanry, known as the FANYs) working out of a requisitioned private residence in Calcutta—promised to have him picked up by a Dakota on the landing strip that he and his local allies had recently completed. His caretakers soon exhausted their one small tube of aquaflavine, which did not even cover all of his burned skin. Kong, the Thai wireless operator, rubbed Smiley with coconut oil in the local manner. Another Thai resistance member, code-named Cato, suggested another local remedy of applying the juice of squashed prickly pear cactus. The excruciating pain, caused by damage to the nerves, continued.

Smiley was bathed by hand in salt water per instructions from a doctor in the Calcutta office. Then the maggots arrived, prompting him to hire two local boys to pluck them out with tweezers. Admonished by the radio doctor to let the maggots do their work (they would prevent gangrene from setting in), he had to tolerate their habit of eating into live tissue after they had consumed the dead.

The plane was delayed. After three days, Smiley's burns turned into blisters ranging in size from golf to tennis balls. They burst, leaving raw and uncomfortable skin. At least now he could pry his eyes open just a little. With no pain medication forthcoming, Cato brought him an opium pipe. He smoked it profusely. It relieved some of the pain but produced none of the reputed hallucinogenic dreams. He could eat only through a straw and had next to no use of his hands.

Smiley could barely function. He dictated his misery to his diary through Gunner Collins. He had not slept for three days in a row when Collins came into the room and found him scrabbling to get ahold of his automatic pistol with his weak, lacerated fingers. Smiley had decided to spare his men the burden and "blow my brains out."

Collins took the weapon. Kong and Cato broke security protocol and sent a message to Ruth, the "collaborating" regent. Smiley's team looked up one day to see a Japanese fighter plane descending onto their landing strip. It was a trainer plane, piloted by two members of the Thai resistance, sent by Ruth. It sat only two, but Smiley was tucked into the front with the second officer. The first aircraft to take off from Smiley's clandestine strip bore the roundels of the Rising Sun and contained two members of the Thai resistance, as well as the local SOE commander. They flew about two hundred miles west, where Smiley was treated by a Thai doctor before being sent on (this time by British transport) to Calcutta, nearly three weeks after he had first been burned.

KEMP FOUND SMILEY'S WOUNDS STILL "TERRIBLY EVIDENT," BUT HE HAD made a remarkable recovery. He was mobile, functional, and ready to get

on with planning. The doctors who had received Smiley upon his be-
lated delivery into their care had expected his recovery to span a month
in the hospital, but as he put it, "Luckily, they were wrong."

There was still the challenge of the medical board. Whatever Smiley's preparations were, he failed the physical. To his frustration, he
found that the reason was not physiological. His mother, the formidable Lady Smiley, had intervened by way of Lady Wavell, the Vicereine,
to ensure that her son did not pass his examination.

Lady Smiley had three sons. David was her youngest and by far the
most militant. She may have found him insufficiently safety conscious.
Certainly, a letter he sent to her from Calcutta ("I fully intended to let
you know what had happened when I was better, but I see no point in
telling you when I am half-dead!") indicated that she was less than
pleased at having received the standard War Office telegram but no subsequent news from Smiley himself. Overcome with maternal concern,
Lady Smiley may have temporarily forgotten her son's other character
traits. David had not survived pain that would drive a man like him to
consider suicide only to be thwarted in his ambitions by his own mother.

This was not Smiley's first wartime experience with burns. Several
years before, when serving outside Palmyra with the Household Cavalry, Smiley had watched as a Vichy French bomber was shot out of the
sky by RAF fighters. The pilot's parachute was on fire. He landed badly
burned and moaning in pain. Smiley, stricken by malignant malaria,
looked on as the medic tended to the enemy pilot and cut the burnt skin
all around his wrists, which then came off "just like a glove." Though
Smiley had pronounced himself "so glad" to see the plane shot down,
he "really felt sorry for him then." By morning, the Vichy pilot was dead.

Just before Smiley's evaluation by the medical board, it had been his
turn to submit to the same form of exfoliation. He had gotten to keep
both "gloves" of dead skin as grisly souvenirs. He was now in bureaucratic limbo. He applied for a medical reassessment of his fitness. Kemp,

whose jaw and hand wounds from that mortar bomb in Spain had once relegated him to a role in the Postal Censorship, may have given some advice.

Smiley passed. He shipped the dead-skin gloves that the doctors had cut from his hands to his mother in England. They were a reminder of his determination.

SMILEY FLEW BACK INTO THAILAND WITH THE COMMANDER OF FORCE 136, SOE's designation in the Far Eastern theater. He had a plane that would land them in Bangkok. Kemp was set to drop in by parachute a few days later.

Standing on the tarmac, Kemp was liberally dosed by an RAF doctor. He was suffering from bacillary dysentery and a recurrence of malaria acquired in Albania, but that wasn't going to stop him from reentering the fray. Dropping in with him was a wireless operator named "Spider" Lawson, a Thai resister nicknamed Toy, and Major the Honourable Rowland Winn. Winn was an old friend and a unique character. The heir of Lord St. Oswald, Winn, too, had dropped into Albania. Like Kemp, he had a habit of bad landings. Not long before his mission, in September of 1944, he had jumped off a table in a turn of exuberance at that Cairo party palace Tara and had broken his leg. He narrowly avoided being court-martialed for such risky behavior on the eve of a mission. When he landed in Albania, he broke the leg again. (As he put it, "The tibia went squish and scraped its way along the fibia [sic].") He was treated by a horse doctor, who could easily tell that one leg was shorter than the other, and spent nearly a month recuperating in a shepherd's hut. The veterinarian reset the bone, but Winn retained a lifelong limp.

He was an irascible character whom Kemp had first met in Spain. Winn had so enraged the Republican authorities with his journalistic reporting that he had found it safer to decamp to the Nationalist territories. He had, as Kemp said, "the strongest convictions on most matters of importance, especially on the subject of bullfighting, and would defend his ideas with a pugnacity in argument that was only matched by his courage in the field." Perhaps it was this that led the staff office to misspell the future Lord St. Oswald's name as "Sinn" in the signal summaries for a week. Effortlessly stylish, he also had a habit of "omitting," as Kemp couched it, to brush his hair, but he smelled perpetually of Trumper's aftershave lotion, which he was never without in any theater of war. He would, in the later war in Korea, win a Military Cross for bravery at the Battle of Imjin River.

Winn did the RAF doctor one better on the long, cold flight to their dropping zone in Thailand. He poured the entire contents of a flask of Courvoisier into the miserable Kemp. This distracted Kemp from what he called the "squalor and discomfort of dysentery in an aircraft that had no lavatory." It was also a distraction from the atmospheric acrobatics that often accompanied such flights. The men on the ground got much of the attention, but the pilots who dropped them faced a far higher death rate, mostly from the cumulonimbus clouds that could tear an aircraft to pieces. One Liberator pilot flew into a cloud over Burma, heard a crash, and after a brief blackout found himself flying two thousand feet higher and upside down.

This time they dropped in "chutes." The parachutist got into a slide affixed to the belly of the plane, held himself by the sides, and exited by crossing his arms and proceeding down the incline. Winn could be heard mumbling the verses to Noël Coward's "Mad Dogs and Englishmen" as he went. Kemp nearly hit a wooden hut but ended with a mere splash in a paddy field. He looked up to see Winn finger-combing his unbrushed hair and pulling the jaunty green-and-gold forest cap of the 8th Hussars out of his bush shirt.

Kong arrived and offered the men pony stallions. (It was, according to local custom, bad form to ride the mares.) Kemp was appreciative of their unique combined gait, but at six feet tall, he found his long, dangling legs frequently kicked by his pony's sharp hooves. Still ill, Kemp was cared for over the next several days by Winn and Lawson until they met up with Smiley and Collins in the village of Phannikom. There they were introduced to Pluto, now head of the resistance in their area.

Kemp had forgotten, but Smiley had not. It was August 19, 1945, and it was Kemp's thirtieth birthday. Pluto threw a party at the local schoolhouse, complete with beautiful local dances, beautiful local women, and a rice beer that came in earthenware jars and was sipped through bamboo straws known as *changs*, or elephants. Kemp, charmed by what he called the magnificent hospitality of his hosts, consumed more alcohol than was advisable. He suffered no more than a hangover in the end and was rewarded with Smiley's crisp reassurance: "Don't worry. You're pretty well expected to get plastered on these occasions. Even I have been carried home to bed."

THE ATOMIC BOMBS HAD BEEN DROPPED ON JAPAN EARLIER THAT month, but the country had not yet formally surrendered. In Thailand, no one quite knew what would happen if the underground resistance came out into the open too soon. They needed to avoid an uprising that would both prolong the war and cause unnecessary casualties. The Japanese were thought to be close to surrender, but there were ugly rumors that their impending defeat had not lessened their ferocity in the field toward those who fell prisoner to them. The orders on this account were strict: until the code word *Goldfish* was given, Smiley's teams were to stay underground, working clandestinely.

Winn was sent to the far northwest of the country. Kemp was posted just a bit south, to a town called Nakorn Panom. It sat on the Mekong River, which formed the country's border with French Indochina.

Their instructions were vague: find out as much as possible about what was happening in their areas and across the river from them. "We can keep in touch through the Siamese, who can be trusted not to open our letters," Smiley said, "unlike the Albanian Partisans!"

Smiley stayed farther south, near the town of Ubon. It was here that he received news of the formal Japanese surrender. If Japan had been cowed into submission on the mainland, its armies across Southeast Asia did not feel defeated. In Burma, the Fourteenth Army had pushed the Japanese down to Rangoon; the city had been taken by the Allies in May, not long before Smiley's first drop into Thailand. Yet there were still tens of thousands of armed Japanese soldiers in the field. This was a military culture that did not accept surrender. One British commander in Burma noted that by 1944, thousands of Allied soldiers had been taken prisoner by the Japanese. He estimated that by this same time, the number of Japanese prisoners who had been captured unwounded by the Allies was probably less than one hundred. On that officer's own front in Burma, the number was six.

If the Japanese forces in the area decided to disobey orders, or assumed that the surrender order was a ruse, there would be precious little ability to protect, or extract, SOE agents on the ground. The Japanese already held thousands of Allied prisoners. There was no need to foment a potential bloodbath. After the emperor declared his capitulation, army officers in Osaka took out five downed airmen, brought them to a military cemetery, then shot three and beheaded the others. That same day, on the island of Kyushu, officers used their samurai swords to chop sixteen airmen to death; twelve days later, in Borneo, the Japanese killed the last thirty of the surviving prisoners there.

The prisoners in the POW camp at Ubon weighed on Smiley's mind as he waited. He had a letter smuggled in. It went via the local Thai garrison commander and the very clever resistance courier, a young Chinese woman named Jin, who had a contract to supply the camp with ice and other necessities. In the missive, Smiley outlined the details that he would need in order to organize aid for the POWs. The reply came back on a small scrap of paper, since the Japanese had forbidden all writing materials. There were about three thousand men in the camp, mostly Brits and Dutchmen but a few Australians and Americans as well.

Despite the British understatement of the letter ("we are not in <u>very</u> <u>urgent</u> need of anything"), they nevertheless politely requested, "when convenient," just about all of the essentials they had been denied: clothes, blankets, boots, razor blades, medical supplies, and food.

Smiley wanted to meet some POW representatives. The Thai colonel invited three British POWs to his office. They came under Japanese guard. The colonel kept the lower ranks waiting in the hallway. The Thais, well known for their hospitality, firmly escorted each man to the restroom while the Japanese guard waited in the hall. The "restroom" was upstairs, where Smiley and his staff had been installed in a separate room of their own. The three men were brought up in turn, and Smiley became the first non-POW officer whom they had seen in three and a half years. As Smiley noted in his diary, the POWs were "pathetically glad to see us, and we were so moved with emotion we could barely speak."

With increasing frustration, as well as ill humor due to a canceled supply drop, Smiley waited for two more days to hear "Goldfish." Finally, the order came. Smiley, along with an American OSS officer and another SOE officer commanding the area to Smiley's west, drove down to the POW camp.

In contravention of the Geneva Conventions, the men there had been illegally put to work building an aerodrome for the Japanese. They had already survived constructing their share of the Thai–Burma Railway, more accurately known as the Railway of Death. Through 250 miles of jungle so dense and viscous that it was said an entire elephant corpse would decompose there in just fourteen days, these men had cleared vegetation, graded land, and laid tracks for a railroad with little more than their hands, the crude tools they could cobble together themselves, and the *chunkal*, or local hoe. There was no heavy machinery. There were no bulldozers, Bobcats, or cranes. There weren't even wheelbarrows. There was only human slave labor and suffering. More than sixty thousand Allied POWs worked on the railroad, or 45 percent of the POWs taken by the Japanese in this theater. Fifteen thousand of them died.

David Smiley during parachute training in Egypt. David Smiley in Albania, with his preferred fez.

vid Smiley and Billy McLean in their "individualistic" attire on their first mission to Albania.

Peter Kemp in Albania, third from left.

A too-tall Peter Kemp on an Albanian pony at far right.

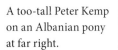

Billy McLean (left) and Peter Kemp (right) with an Albanian guerrilla leader.

David Smiley says goodbye to his mule, Fanny, at the end of his first mission to Albania.

Julian Amery (left) and Billy McLean on the second mission to Albania. Amery's Colt .45 with the etched bone grips from the Bektashis is visible at his waist.

From left: David Smiley, Julian Amery, and Billy McLean during the second mission to Albania.

Abas Kupi (left) sits with Billy McLean.

David Smiley and Julian Amery with some of their Central Asian troops in Albania.

Billy McLean in his "individualistic" attire, holding a captured German MP40 over his shoulder.

Billy McLean with a few Central Asian troops; the beautiful Achmet sits to McLean's left.

Abas Kupi sits with several of his men on Mount Vela before the final evacuation attempts in 1944.

Smiley's crew in Thailand. Top: Gunner Collins, Kong, Peter Kemp, Spider Lawson. Bottom: David Smiley, Pluto.

Rowland Winn
stands next to a
Chinese colonel,
along with David
Smiley and Peter
Kemp, in Thailand.

David Smiley
marries Moyra
Tweedie in
London.

David Smiley greets
Princess Elizabeth
on Malta.

David Smiley as
commander of
the Sultan's forces
in Muscat, Oman.

David Smiley
in Yemen with
a British two-
pounder gun.

David Smiley kitted
out in Yemen.

David Smiley with the Imam (center) in Yemen.

David Smiley's self-portrait on his fiftieth birthday in Yemen.

Billy McLean (right) in Yemen.

It was a substantial part of the reason why Allied prisoners in Japanese captivity had a 27 percent mortality rate; the number under the Nazis was just 4 percent. Prisoners were given little food and no medical care. One set of Americans scrounged up two gold watches and traded them to an interpreter in order to get a Dutch doctor transferred from a camp that already had several medics. The men working on the railway starved, some of them weighing only eighty-five pounds. They had dysentery, malaria, beriberi, and tropical ulcers so bad and infected that many had to have their legs amputated to save their lives, an operation that was itself all too often fatal in such conditions. But their labor was not enough. The Japanese impressed the local population, called the *rōmusha*, whom they treated even worse and who died in droves, with the toll estimated to be three hundred thousand. Given that the Japanese also indulged in public beheadings of civilians, even children, for merely just speaking to Allied soldiers who accidentally walked into their village, this was not surprising.

The treatment was brutal and cruel. Sick men were dragged out and evaluated every day, with more and more being forced to labor as the Japanese, under pressure on the seas from the Royal Navy, pushed to complete the railway that they hoped would save their supply lines in Burma. One Dutch doctor asked a Japanese guard whom he was treating for syphilis if he could keep any extra medication, since the doctor could use the surplus to treat malaria as well. The guard let the doctor finish, then grabbed the vial, threw it on the floor, and smashed it with his boot. A prisoner who shouted "Snake!" in the night upon finding a python in his bed was rousing his fellows not out of fright but because he knew the whole barracks would come down on the creature in order to kill it for food. Their clothes were long gone. Most wore only G-strings and "ball bags." It was a horror story that far surpassed the details in the movie that made it famous: *The Bridge on the River Kwai*.

The day before Smiley arrived, the POWs had stood silent, stock-still, and defiantly unresponsive as the Japanese commandant informed them that the war was over. The men were soon rejoined by their officers, including their colonel, Philip Toosey, whose leadership and management of the Japanese many people credited with the prisoners' survival (after, of course, their own sheer determination and strength).

Toosey lined his men up on parade. They had the sunken chests and the distended bellies of the starving. Many were barefoot or shod in homemade clogs. As Toosey called them to attention and the Japanese flag was hauled down, the men produced a Union Jack, hidden throughout the war. They hoisted the flag and sang "God Save the King." Smiley struggled to hold back the only tears of emotion that ever threatened his composure throughout the entire war.

THE POWS, DESPITE THEIR TREATMENT AT THE HANDS OF THE JAPANESE, were surprisingly lenient toward their former captors. Several Australians took the ultimate revenge on two of them, but that was the extent of it. Aside from the physical abuses suffered by the prisoners, Smiley was appalled to find that none of the Red Cross mail, welfare correspondence, or medical packets had been delivered. "A despicable performance," he declared. The former camp commandant made the mistake of offering Smiley a Red Cross cigarette, which he refused.

Smiley recruited several POWs to help him identify war criminals. The Japanese, and the Korean guards whom they had employed, were lined up and carefully identified by the men whom they had mistreated. After using Dutch soldiers to determine which men had beaten the POWs building the airstrip near Ubon, Smiley turned to their commanding officer. "Major Sensui, you are the last. Hand over your sword." He had been the worst offender of them all. The Dutch were delighted with Smiley's performance.

The POWs were sent home in groups, as it was difficult to find enough transportation to move them all at once. Many were stuck waiting in Ubon. Being men of a certain age, they were very anxious to confirm that their constituent parts were still in working order. David Smiley, lieutenant colonel, ordered up several brothels. There were a handful for the troops and one for officers, christened "the Chinese Hotel." Ten thousand packets of condoms, referred to then in common slang as "French letters," were delivered to minimize damage.

The Dutch then invented one of the best uses of military red tape in history. They borrowed official requisition forms, requisitioned a girl in the brothel, and paid her with the forms as a sort of IOU. The girl delivered the documents to Smiley.

Not to be outdone by the Dutch, Smiley called a meeting with the woman nominated to represent her peers and the chief of police, who had overseen the opening of Ubon's newest entertainment establishments. Smiley had a neat solution to the problem. One of his administrative chores had been shipping home used parachute panels. These were the sort made of real silk, a valuable commodity. Bandits had robbed the latest train on which the parachutes had been packed, providing themselves with thousands of pounds in profit. Smiley made an offer: he would pay three parachute panels per performance. This was a generous price. The panels were worth about a pound each, making the equivalent in inflation-adjusted dollars about $180 per session. The professionals were well paid, the Allied governments did not need to produce cash, and no more bandits stole parachutes off trains.

One day, fifteen young Korean women arrived at Smiley's house in Ubon. They were the so-called comfort women, Koreans who had been stolen from their country and trafficked as sex slaves for the Japanese forces throughout the Pacific theater. They had nothing to do with Smiley's brothel system, which employed willing local participants. They wanted to be liberated from their captors, the Japanese, who claimed to have paid them for services that had not been rendered and were still owed. Smiley wrote out his own version of bureaucratic paperwork, declared the debt null and void, and housed them in town with a Thai police guard. They would come to his house to sing in the evenings when he entertained the POW officers from the camp.

The last of the POWs left at the end of September. Smiley's focus shifted to managing and disarming the Japanese. The army sent one of its most resourceful and unusual officers to help. His name was John Hedley, though he was known to Smiley's staff as "the Mad Major."

Hedley was an Old Etonian and an old Burma hand. No one who crossed his path ever seemed to forget him. Older than most of his fellow soldiers, he was in his late thirties. He had the kind of physical stamina and energy that defied description. He used a double-time marching pace and regularly refused rides in lorries. He had lungs of iron and often dropped and wore out men half his age. He could always be found with his jungle uniform (shapeless hat, bush shirt and slacks, jungle boots), a full kit that likely weighed in at seventy pounds, and his rifle, an old .303 Lee–Enfield, even when invited to dinner by the local dignitaries.

He was fluent in several of the local languages, including Burmese and Thai. There was vanishingly little that escaped his notice. One of Hedley's former commanding officers realized that he had been reassigned to a new area because the intelligence briefings coming up the line were so detailed that no one else could have produced them. Nothing was ever good enough for John Hedley. When sent to do overnight road reconnaissance, he took advantage of finding a Japanese driver sleeping in a lorry, shot him in the head, and then carefully cataloged the contents of his truck in order to include the details in his intelligence report.

He was adamant in his opposition to the Japanese. If he was not graceful under pressure, he was undeniably effective. During the retreat from Burma in 1941, one officer noticed him lying flat on his belly, facing away from everyone else and in the direction of the Japanese. Asked what he was doing, he replied, "Captain Hedley, sir, Burma Rifles, attached to the [he named a notorious Indian regiment]. We were ordered to hold this line. Someone fired a shot in the jungle and the whole Blank Battalion of the Royal and Bright Yellow Blanks—buggered off." Ordered to abandon his post, he refused until the officer in question proved himself to be the colonel in command of the rear guard.

His manners were unusual. He walked into one staff office on a new assignment, seeking his brigadier, and asked for "the manager. The Bara Sahib. The Big Cheese. The Boss." He introduced himself to another brigadier by demandingly asking, "Have you brought my mail?" Answered in the negative by the flustered general, Hedley replied, "Humph! Somebody in Bangkok ought to pull their fingers out." He regularly offended the local Thai officers, which tended to leave Smiley, not naturally inclined to diplomacy, profusely apologizing in his wake.

He came to Smiley after fighting with the Chindits in Burma. Smiley could have had none better. Disarming the Japanese was, on the one hand, straightforward: their reputation for discipline was well earned, and when given orders, they followed them. But Thailand also suffered from a long-standing bandit problem. Thefts were increasing at a rate that seemed to require a dramatic response, especially as the robbers were well armed.

On a visit north to check on Rowland Winn, Smiley gifted a Japanese sword to Winn's invaluable local boatman. Sitting with brandies after dinner, Smiley and Winn were interrupted by the boatman, who had been guarding Winn's supplies. "He appeared late at night with the sword dripping in blood, stating that he had found a robber in our store and had cut his head off," Smiley said. "He had."

The banditry got so bad that the British rearmed some Japanese soldiers in order to use them as guards. But the Japanese were afraid that they would not be supported (or would be hanged as murderers) if they used lethal force, and the lawlessness continued. Finally convinced of

British support, they came to Hedley and Smiley one morning announcing that they had "bagged a stiff!" Smiley, Hedley, and the Thai police and army representatives all went out to look.

To Hedley, the scene was obvious: Robbers had approached the supply store. They were warned off. The language got heated. (Or, in Hedley's phrasing, "It soon became clear there was an imperfect communion of spirit between the two bodies of men.") A Japanese sentry fired a shot, hitting one bandit in the liver; he managed to get about sixty yards down the road. The Japanese sentries had clearly marked the blood trail by ringing each drop with leaves. "But the most irrefutable evidence of all came at the sixtieth yard," Hedley noted. There they found "the stiff in situ." The Japanese were complimented for their work. Smiley was amazed to find that the local governor was "delighted," as he professed to have been "longing for someone to be shot *pour encourager les autres.*"

CHAPTER 11

CRY HAVOC

In Nakorn Panom, in the south of Thailand, Peter Kemp was faced with a different sort of prisoner, and a different side of postwar Japanese cooperation. When Imperial Japan began its invasion of much of Asia in the late 1930s, the country proposed a "Co-Prosperity Sphere" of Asian solidarity. This campaign cloaked itself in a half-Wilsonian language of nationalism and self-determination. It brought prosperity to the Japanese alone and replaced Western colonialism with a Japanese model. It nevertheless helped to either create or encourage revolutionary and independence movements in Southeast Asia, movements that some disgruntled Japanese officers continued to support even after their country had surrendered.

This became a problem for Kemp and Smiley because the nature of their work meant that they were involved in the region's political stability, or lack thereof, a problem familiar to them from the Albania missions. Thailand was not so much of a problem, but its neighbor was, and crossing the border was as easy as rowing a boat across the river; customs and border checks did not exist in their areas. They were about to be ensnared in the earliest days of a conflict that bogged down first the French and then the Americans for decades: the Vietnam War.

Right next door to Thailand—unfortunately for Kemp, right across the Mekong River—was French Indochina. That colony included the lands that today make up Vietnam, Cambodia, and Laos, and there the French methods of colonialism made Japanese arguments all too palatable. Lawrence of Arabia, himself no fan of colonialism, noticed that the British at least appreciated cultural variation, while their Continental cousins saw "the Frenchman as the perfection of mankind" and demanded slavish imitation but would never admit mastery. France's "civilizing mission" assumed a French superiority that refused to admit many locals into administration.

The French connection with Indochina began in the sixteenth century, but it remained a trading and missionary relationship until the late eighteenth century. In 1787, Louis XVI formally involved the French state in a colonial role. Two years later, a revolution came for King Louis, and his head. Nearly two hundred years later, another was about to come for the French Empire.

When the Japanese invaded French Indochina, the Vichy government ruled the colony. On paper, the Japanese were allies of Axis-oriented Vichy. The Japanese took functional control and mostly left their outnumbered allies alone. A small and brave resistance formed, including part of the army, but the majority of the French armed forces followed orders to cooperate. They did not fear the Japanese so much as a local revolution backed by a rising tide of anti-French sentiment.

That sentiment was led by a group then called the ethnic Vietnamese. In Vietnam, they were a majority, but their position was complicated. Today's Vietnam retains over fifty different minority groups, despite allegations, after the end of the Vietnam War in 1975, of ethnic cleansing against those the ethnic Vietnamese called *moi*, meaning "savages," including the Montagnard hill tribes who fought with first the French, and then the American Special Forces, against their oppressors. French Indochina included the complexity of not only Vietnam but also Cambodia and Laos, right on the Thai border. There were small minorities of ethnic Vietnamese living on the French side of that border as well, right across from Kemp's and Winn's areas.

The Vietnamese who organized and fought were known as the Viet Minh, the Communist revolutionaries led by Ho Chi Minh. The Viet Minh were also partners of the Japanese, especially since the Japanese had decided, by March 1945, that the French forces in Indochina posed a threat. On March 9, they gathered the French together, executed almost all the men whose technical expertise they did not need to keep the country running, and interned the women and children.

Smiley had repatriated the POWs on his side of the river, but nearby French civilian internees were another matter entirely. The civilian internees were not of much interest to the Japanese, but they were to the Viet Minh.

If the Japanese mostly followed orders and played by the book with Smiley at Ubon, the same was not true farther north, on the border. There the anti-Western revolution that had begun with the Co-Prosperity Sphere still burned in the minds of Japanese who did not feel themselves defeated in the field. The Viet Minh's revolution gave them a way to avoid total defeat. French civilians became easy starter targets. The British officers were tasked with helping the French.

ONE DAY, KEMP SAW A DAKOTA FLY BY. HE LATER LEARNED THAT IT HAD dropped a French officer, entrusted with a mission similar to his own, and the officer's wireless operator. A few weeks later, they made contact. The Frenchman's name was François Klotz. He had been stuck in a cave with the wireless operator—"who is a she," he carefully explained— attempting to touch base with their local mission. But the batteries needed to be charged, and the conditions were miserable, so Kemp invited the pair to move into his house in Nakorn Panom, across the river from the Laotian town of Thakhek, in what was then French Indochina. Delighted, Klotz accepted.

He was young, only twenty-five, but a careful and practiced officer. Calm, somber, and possessed of a stocky build and a dark, sturdy face, Klotz spoke slow but nearly perfect English. He was kind and charming, and as an Alsatian, he was familiar with border wars and complex territories.

With Klotz was a young woman named Edith Fournier. Kemp noted that she was lovely and feminine in appearance, with an abundance of chestnut hair but a scarcity of English. He also recognized that she was a tough second lieutenant in the French army and wore the badged battle dress to prove it. Fournier was an excellent wireless operator and code worker. They labored together seamlessly, handling the heavy traffic of the combined missions.

Jock Rork, Kemp's wireless operator, lived with them as well. He was a twenty-year veteran of the Royal Corps of Signals. His red hair matched his independent and sometimes stubborn streak, but he was warm-hearted and absolutely fearless. They were first joined in the house by a savage monkey, a live gift from a local contact and an animal whom Kemp succeeded in taming. Later, they added two male gibbons. Enchanting, soft, and sweet, the gibbons loved to ride around the house with their arms wrapped around the necks of whichever secret warriors they so chose, cuddling up against their keepers and picking imaginary parasites from the humans' hair.

Soon came news of French internees in distress on the other side of the river, in French Thakhek. Kemp had been struggling to help the French civilians from his side of the river. David Smiley arrived from Ubon, driving one of the giant American cars that he had requisitioned from the Japanese. Together, the British and the French crossed the Mekong in one of the small boats that served as a ferry.

In the whitewashed houses of Thakhek, they found the imprisoned families of the overthrown French forces in what had once been a typical convent. Housed on the refectory floor were a host of miserable people. Eighteen women, fourteen children, five nuns, three men, and one priest, all French, were massed together with around forty mixed-race orphans of both French and local descent, all under the care of the nuns.

The women and children surrounded Smiley, Kemp, and Klotz. Exhausted, underfed, and fearing for their lives, they wore clothes that were little better than rags. They begged for news of their husbands and their fathers, whom they had not heard from in many months.

Their appearance gnawed at Kemp. These women could not actually be as old as they looked. The daily fear and anxiety had worn them down. "We had to say we knew nothing," he recorded, "for we could not tell them that we believed all their men to be dead." They had likely been victims of the March 9 coup. These women and children were civilians, but they were in French Indochina as the dependents of either French officers or local French colonial administrators. Their roots in the country were not deep, and they were now caught in the crossfire of a civil and anti-colonial war.

The Viet Minh could not decide if they wanted to hold the French civilians hostage for a potential negotiation with the French government or execute them in a war of ethnic cleansing. The country was a mess after the Japanese had executed their coup but then lost the war. Ho Chi Minh would reputedly later say that the Viet Minh had never seized power, because there was no power left to seize.

"I THINK, GENTLEMEN, YOU HAVE ONLY JUST ARRIVED IN TIME," SAID Madame Collin, the unofficial leader of the prisoners. "The [Viet Minh] guards who have replaced the Japanese have become extremely menacing. They show us their knives and make gestures of cutting our throats." Thin, fair, and of quiet disposition and gentle voice, she knew the cruelty of her tormentors. Unlike the others, she was aware that the Japanese had beheaded her husband six months before.

Smiley went outside with Klotz to negotiate with the Viet Minh's self-titled "delegates" for the release of the civilians. One of the requirements of the recently signed armistice was that the Japanese remain legally responsible for the protection of civilians under their control until those civilians could be handed over to the Allies. The Viet Minh were not interested in technical treaty rules. Complicating the situation was their own position in Thakhek. The Viet Minh controlled the city, but they did not control much more. An ethnic minority within the borders of the Laotian section of French Indochina, the Vietnamese who made up the Viet Minh tended to be grouped around different urban centers. They were not well liked by the majority Lao population.

The Japanese, now outnumbered and outgunned by their former local allies, had little control of the situation. The only hope for the civilians was evacuation across the Mekong to British-controlled Thailand. In order to accomplish this, Smiley would have to convince the Viet Minh that they had no other choice.

Smiley's argument was simple: *The civilians are legally under my control, and I must take them away.* It was, as the French would say, a fait accompli. The Viet Minh insisted that this was not so. They even tried to claim that the French were not party to the armistice. For two hours, the two sides shouted at and cajoled one another. Finally, Smiley had a breakthrough. He could take the civilians.

Out of nowhere appeared a group of armed Japanese soldiers. They were loud, rude, uncouth, and visibly drunk. They rounded up the European officers, including Kemp, who was still inside trying to calm the women and children, and marched them roughly down the street. Japanese bayonets in the Allied officers' backs prodded compliance.

Taken inside a house a few blocks away, they were introduced to a young Japanese officer named Captain Nakajima. Sitting in a room furnished only with a spare desk, he bowed. He was handsome and followed formal procedure flawlessly. In halting English, with an enviable poker face, he apologized for being unable to allow them to remove the French civilians. He did not yet have orders to this effect, and without superior orders, he was afraid that his hands were tied.

Kemp and the other officers protested. This was madness, as was their treatment only moments before. Nakajima smiled thinly; his soldiers would be punished. But the French civilians could not leave. Smiley, exasperated, offered to solve Nakajima's problem for him. Smiley would undertake the long drive back to Ubon and return with orders from Nakajima's superior in the morning. He insisted that Nakajima replace the Viet Minh guards with his own men in the meantime. The captain agreed.

Back outside, Smiley was irate. Growling to Kemp and Klotz, he said, "Obviously, he's been tipped off by the [Viet Minh] and is scared of them because they outnumber his men."

Walking back to the convent to oversee the mounting of the Japanese replacement guard, they caught a Japanese soldier trying to snatch a watch off a young French nun. Smiley grabbed him. The soldier, drunk, swung around at Smiley and tried to stab him with a bayonet. Smiley held the soldier back and shouted for a Japanese officer. A corporal appeared, and Smiley watched him perform an "interesting piece of Japanese discipline": he slapped the soldier's face silly. An officer repeated the process. The nun retained her timepiece.

Satisfied that the traditional brutality of Japanese military discipline would be carried out on the guards in question and not on the civilians, Smiley and Klotz set off on the 170-mile journey to Ubon. Kemp was left as an additional, overnight guard. His job, as Rowland Winn later put it in a dispatch to headquarters, was "to protect the women from a fate worse than Kemp."

After explaining the plan and offering what reassurance he could, Kemp stayed the night with the men of the group, including the priest. One of them was the French electrician who had been in charge of the local power station. Just before the armistice, he made the mistake of not only picking up a leaflet that Klotz had dropped by plane a few weeks beforehand but also waving to the pilot. A local Viet Minh member saw this and reported him to the Japanese. He, his wife, and their young child were arrested and bundled into a car. He told his family to run for the tree line as soon as the car stopped. But the child was too little to run fast. The electrician's wife and child were caught and executed on the spot. Their bodies were buried next to a highway marker. Distraught, the electrician plowed into the jungle. He stopped at a local villager's hut. The Viet Minh man who lived there hacked at him with a machete for good measure before turning him over to the Japanese. They were planning to shoot him until a stern letter from Kemp arrived. That was two weeks earlier. The electrician had instead been sent to the convent with the other civilians. This evening marked the second time that Kemp had saved his life, assuming they all survived the night.

The priest opened two bottles of Communion wine in Kemp's honor. They drank them both and went to sleep.

THE NEXT MORNING, SMILEY RETURNED FROM HIS MISSION AND WAS relieved to find everyone still safe. His approach to the convent had been lined by scowling, sullen Viet Minh. Despite the Japanese guard, they still lurked all around the building, intimidating with both their numbers and their obvious malcontent. The presence of a Japanese lieutenant next to Smiley smoothed the way, but only barely.

The superior orders were clear. Captain Nakajima was to release the civilians; furthermore, he was to clear the Viet Minh out of town so that the next day the civilians could be evacuated in peace. He did so. The following morning, Smiley arrived in a boat belonging to the governor of Nakorn Panom. The French civilians embarked, and the Thais took them to the local hospital to await evacuation to Europe. They were, Smiley said, "pathetically grateful." Freed, the civilians blossomed. Even Kemp noted how, with just a bit of makeup and some ingenuity, they looked quite lovely. "I began to regret that present circumstances did not allow me to cash in on my position as their liberator and protector," he said wistfully.

Kemp soon received word of seven more French civilians being held hostage by the Viet Minh near a set of local tin mines. He, Klotz, and Smiley requisitioned a Japanese officer and escort, complete with a light machine gun, and set off to release them. Entering the village, they saw a Viet Minh platoon pouring fire into what appeared to be the local schoolhouse. The Viet Minh declared that the town had been attacked by bandits.

Smiley convinced the Viet Minh to cease their fire. As Kemp's heart pounded in his throat (and by Smiley's own confession his did as well), Smiley walked forward slowly, shouting in French, "Don't shoot! I'm an English officer!"

Smiley passed the bodies of four Viet Minh, dead on the ground, and slowly climbed the steps to the schoolhouse. He was covered by the rifles of ten fierce Lao soldiers inside. With them was a mixed-race sergeant and one young French officer in jungle battle dress.

They were remnants of the French resistance in Indochina, during which French officers of the colonial army had led local troops against the Japanese and their Vietnamese allies. The Viet Minh who had served in the colonial army had abandoned it, but many of the Lao, who had no love for their Vietnamese neighbors, had stayed to fight it out. When the Japanese had turned on the French in March, attempting to intern the civilians and slaughtering the officers, some had escaped. They had been fighting a rearguard action ever since. Most, especially in Tonkin, in the north of what is now Vietnam, had tried to make it to the Chinese border. Refused aid by the Americans who controlled the skies in that region, they had been decimated by combat casualties and disease. These men had been living in the jungle and were now fighting to take back Indochina.

Smiley was impressed with their professional performance. Despite being badly outnumbered, they had managed to kill four Viet Minh and suffered only two wounded of their own. The Viet Minh were furious that Smiley had uncovered their attempt to pass off their attack on the

French unit as policing banditry. They offered their dead for close inspection. Smiley noted that "they must have been unattractive enough when alive." The civilians and the Lao wounded were evacuated with the Allied officers. The French forces melted back into the jungle.

This was not the first instance of Viet Minh attacking French interests. Days before, Kemp and Klotz had rescued a teenage girl and an older man who had each been cruelly shot and left to slowly die by the Viet Minh. The officers packed the wounded into a tiny Citroën car, found a doctor, and eventually had them evacuated to Bangkok. Soon Kemp would hear from a colleague of the schoolhouse's French resistance officer. His name was Tavernier, and he led a similar group of Lao resistance guerrillas in the jungle. They operated across the Mekong from Kemp's headquarters. Tavernier was in desperate need of money, arms, and medical supplies for malaria and dysentery. A new war was brewing as the insurgents jostled for control of France's dying empire, and it looked like the civil war might spill across the borders into Thailand. The British government, which always feared the disorder of a power vacuum, was adamant about supporting French rule. Orders from SOE headquarters were clear: "You will give French all possible assistance short of becoming involved yourselves."

TO COMPLICATE MATTERS, AMERICAN SPECIAL FORCES HAD A STRONG presence in Southeast Asia as well. Kemp and Smiley had an excellent working relationship with one local OSS man, an older former missionary named Halliday, and Smiley had also worked easily with other American officers to evacuate the Ubon POW camp. But then a new American OSS officer arrived, landing near Rowland Winn, just north of Kemp. Winn found this new officer frustrating to deal with. He had a habit of receiving drops in Winn's drop zone without informing him first, which did not help. Nor did his habit of encouraging the Viet Minh against the French, who he insisted must "cease their aggression." Winn encouraged the new OSS party to move southward, hoping the Americans would find a space of their own. But southward was also toward Kemp's area. "He would never have done it if he could have foreseen the consequences," Kemp said later.

Kemp, Smiley, and the documents of the British staff office knew him as "Aaron Banks," but showing a linguistic preference that may have matched his blooming sense of self-regard, he styled his surname in the singular: "Bank." He held the rank of major in the OSS, the same as Kemp and Winn in SOE, though he had far less to show for it. An unusual soldier, he was in his early forties. In his memoir, he omitted to mention what he did in the years between lifeguarding at Biarritz as a young man and joining the army in 1942, but he did speak fluent French. He was hard-charging, determined, effective, and highly organized as a planner, qualities that would serve him well in a later career as a staff officer.

He had made it into the OSS on account of his strong European language skills but had not arrived in Europe until 1944, when he was dropped into southern France as part of a Jedburgh team, tasked with preparing the way for the seaborne invasion that became known as Operation Dragoon. With that completed, Bank, by his own description, spun his wheels in London until an assignment came through in Southeast Asia. Frustrated by proposed but repeatedly canceled operations, he was practically crawling out of his skin to get into some action.

In France, he had worked with the Communist maquis that formed the French resistance in his area, operating on the ground for three months before his role was complete. Like many OSS officers, he was energetic, idealistic, and convinced of the righteousness of his own convictions. These very same qualities were shared by the French in their colonial adventures, and they had not ceased causing friction between the two competing beacons of revolutionary republicanism since the Marquis de Lafayette arrived to aid George Washington.

The tension with the Americans stretched far beyond that of Bank and his strong dislike of the French. For reasons that have never been made clear, the American president Franklin D. Roosevelt was adamantly opposed to the Free French leader, General Charles de Gaulle. It wasn't until 1943 that the United States stopped recognizing the government of Vichy France, which was collaborating with the Nazis. Possible explanations have run the gamut. Perhaps it was personality conflicts (de Gaulle did not charm everyone in his path, and neither did Roosevelt). Perhaps it was personal resentment (of the increasingly ill Roosevelt, often wheelchair-bound when the cameras were put away, toward the towering soldier de Gaulle). Or perhaps it was America's hypocritical ambitions to replace the old empires with its own (opening up China and Southeast Asia to American commercial dominance).

Whatever the reason, Roosevelt's White House (and often Roosevelt's State Department) was decidedly anti-French. The American general posted to Chiang Kai-shek's headquarters in China was told to give the French no help at all. The position of China complicated matters as well, as did the inherent nature of any joint operation. There was conflict between the American generals in China and the elegant and competent royal relation Lord Louis Mountbatten, head of the South East Asia Command (SEAC, which the Americans uncharitably said stood for "Save England's Asiatic Colonies"). During the Second World War, Chiang was fighting both the Japanese and a civil war, which he would lose to the Communist Mao Zedong. His eyes were far larger than his stomach, but he nevertheless had his own designs on Southeast Asia. He complicated matters by telling different stories to both the Americans and the British. This was not unique to Chiang. As one historian put it, "The Chinese are noted for historically playing one set of barbarians off against another."

In practice, this meant that SOE officers on the ground in Thailand thought it was their exclusive operational area. The OSS thought it had free rein as well. The OSS was an organization, much like SOE, that was designed for sabotage and resistance work. Since it was American, as ever a country rightly proud of its own revolution, it had a tendency to support revolutionary and anti-imperialist parties. The Americans thought nothing of this, but they also frequently forgot that their revolution was unique in that it did not destroy the underlying social structures that had birthed it and made it so successful. Most revolutions end by eating their own children, as the French had good reason to know.

Tavernier had already complained to Kemp about Bank, who had been holding conferences with the Viet Minh delegates. Bank had promised that the Americans would use their Chinese allies to disarm the French and, as Kemp put it, force them to cease "what he called French aggression." Bank had crossed the Mekong, confronted Tavernier at a roadblock, and insisted that he withdraw.

"He spoke to me as I would not dream of speaking to a servant—in front of my own soldiers and the [Viet Minh], all of whom understand French. He called me a pirate, and threatened that if I did not withdraw my men, he would send Chinese troops to disarm us," protested Tavernier.

Kemp signaled to headquarters in Calcutta, requesting advice. He was informed that Bank should not be operating in his area and that he should tactfully request Bank's removal. Meanwhile, SOE's headquarters would refer the issue to Mountbatten's staff at SEAC, running the issue up the chain of command.

To Kemp fell the task of informing Bank. In his most polite English bearing, he begged Bank to desist and reminded him that the French were their shared allies. "Tavernier and his men have held out with great endurance against the Japanese, to whom the [Viet Minh] gave their wholehearted collaboration," said Kemp.

"So did the French collaborate," Bank snapped back. "Why, I was betrayed myself by a traitor in France! It damn nearly cost me my life," huffed the man with three months of operational experience to the man who had nearly ten years of it.

Kemp was relieved when Bank crossed the Mekong and set up shop in Thakhek. But Bank was not yet done stirring up trouble, and Kemp had issues corralling Klotz as well. Bank insisted that Klotz stay away from the eastern shores of the Mekong. Klotz was apoplectic: "I can certainly go to Thakhek if I wish! I am a French officer and Thakhek belongs to France."

Tavernier could wait no longer. Kemp and Klotz set off together one morning for a meeting on the Thakhek side of the river. In a recent airdrop, Kemp had received medical supplies that Tavernier needed. With them came one of Bank's men, Lieutenant Reese, a young American officer who had come over to their side of the river that same morning.

They floated across the monsoon-swollen Mekong in the governor's boat. The white houses of Thakhek stood in sharp contrast to the vivid green jungle. In the distance, mountains formed the backdrop. It was warm and cloudless, a good afternoon, given the state of the local roads, to meet Tavernier.

As they stepped from the docking ramp onto the road, the sleepiness of the town was broken with a sharply barked "Halt!" Pouring out of the front door of one of the houses to their left was an entire platoon of Viet Minh. The delegate, whom Kemp recognized as a former employee of the electricity plant, stalked up to them with a pistol in his hand. Dressed in khaki shorts with a questionable gray hat, he would have cut a ludicrous figure in any other circumstance, Kemp thought. But here he was, full of self-importance and armed to the teeth.

"Bien!" spat the delegate as Kemp noticed the rotting, blackened teeth against his gums, stained red from betel leaves used to wrap tobacco. "Who are you?"

"I am a British officer, as you know," Kemp replied evenly.

"And you?" he asked Reese.

"American."

"You," said the delegate in a leading question to Klotz, "are French?"

Klotz nodded. The delegate then declared that Klotz, as a Frenchman, was under arrest but that Kemp and Reese could go. Kemp was aghast. If Klotz was given over to the Viet Minh, he would almost certainly be killed. Reese, meanwhile, sauntered through the platoon and took a position propping up the wall of a house on the other side of the street.

"Don't be ridiculous," said Kemp, trying to sound both calm and confident. "The British, Americans, and French are all allies, and we are certainly not going to let you arrest our friend. Isn't that so, lieutenant?"

Reese couldn't meet his eye. Kemp was convinced that he was acting under orders but still found his response unbelievable. "I don't know," he muttered. "I guess we're neutral." He looked miserable.

Kemp realized that he had been sold out. Every man in this Viet Minh platoon had a rifle, and they all had the jump on both Kemp and Klotz, who carried only pistols and would still need to unholster them. What he would have given for just a few British or Indian troops in that moment, thought Kemp.

"François," he said, "you and I are going back to the boat. There doesn't seem any future in staying here."

Klotz's hand rested on his pistol holster. They had little chance of successfully shooting it out. But it takes quite a bit of courage to relinquish the illusion of control that shooting back, no matter what the odds, can give. Would it not be better to take their chances? What if the Viet Minh were bluffing . . . or what if they were cowards? One well-placed shot could drop one of these trumped-up riflemen. They all wanted to kill a Frenchman, onto whose person they had lumped all of their grievances—some real, most imagined. The French had not invented the minority position of the Viet Minh in Laos, though like all rulers they took advantage of local infighting. For these men, Klotz, who had been in the country for mere months, represented all the ills of colonialism. But just how many of them were willing to die for the privilege of killing this one Frenchman?

Klotz, smiling tightly, removed his hand from his pistol holster.

Kemp, putting on his best senior British officer show, turned to the delegate and said, "Monsieur Tu, since our presence here is unwelcome to you, my friend and I are returning to Siam. Au revoir." Kemp bowed, put his arm firmly around Klotz, and wheeled him toward the ramp.

"No!" screamed the delegate. "You may go, but he stays here."

Kemp decided to ignore him. "Keep moving," he muttered firmly to Klotz, who kept his calm expression, though it masked a roiling interior. It was a game of nerves. They were practically standing on the international border between French and British territory. The Viet Minh would be delighted to kill every Frenchman they could find, but they could not risk antagonizing the British, who controlled the territory next door.

The loading of a rifle makes a recognizable sound as the bolt slides back, catches the round, and slides forward again, chambering the bullet. It is a metallic sound, somewhere between a click and a thud. A thumb-guided movement to the side locks the bolt in. That sound again. That was the sound—multiplied by the strength of the platoon—that Kemp heard as they kept on walking.

Please, dear God, Kemp thought, *look after us now.*

The fusillade went over their heads. *For show, thank heavens,* Kemp said to himself. *We'll make it. Hurry.* The little boat was just a few yards away, tucked under its dirty canvas awning. Kemp began to time the launch. They needed just a small shove to make it to the current that would carry them to the Thai side. They could shelter in the boat, behind her flanking sides. He pressed Klotz on, walking nearly behind him. The Viet Minh would not dare to shoot a British officer. He was a human shield.

He had not counted on the fury, or the foolishness, of the Viet Minh. One soldier slowly crept up behind them. The soldier shoved his rifle under Kemp's arm, against Klotz's back, and fired, point-blank. Klotz stumbled. Gasped.

"Oh, Peter!" he whispered. "Oh, Peter!"

Blood bubbled from the corners of his mouth. It stained the front of his shirt. It spread all over Kemp, desperately trying to keep Klotz level in his arms. Wrenching himself away, Klotz lurched toward the boat. He fell to his hands and knees and began to drag himself. Kemp picked him up again, dragging him onto the dock. He lay there, face down. Half a minute later, he was dead.

KEMP SPUN AROUND AND CHARGED UP THE RAMP. THERE HE FOUND only Reese, joined by a major, acting as Bank's second-in-command. Voice shaking, he spat, "I hope you're proud of your [Viet Minh] friends." Pointing at the corpse, he cried, "*That* is the direct result of your work!"

The major slowly said, "I guess we better have a company of Chinese paratroopers down here right away. I'll go call Hanoi."

There was nothing left for Kemp. The mission to Tavernier was impossible. The Americans remained obdurate; no help would come from that quarter. The major uttered no hint of an apology. Kemp ignored him, along with the terrified little American NCO who clearly wanted nothing more than to get out of there as quickly as possible.

He now had a new mission. He must escape with Klotz's body before the Viet Minh could fashion it into a macabre trophy.

The two Thai boatmen who had helped them cross the river reappeared. They had hidden when the shooting started. They helped Kemp load Klotz's body into the little launch. Kemp sat next to him, resentfully swatting away the flies that were already buzzing over the bloodied corners of Klotz's mouth. As he sat there, fighting a losing battle with the pesky scavengers, he could not help but second-guess himself. He was alone in his own mind. Already, he replayed his decisions. Maybe they should have tried to shoot it out; maybe the odds had not been as bad as they looked. He had misread the Viet Minh. The confident air of British authority that he had depended on to save them had not quailed the bloodlust. Yet Klotz had chosen to trust him. In his rational heart,

Kemp knew his choice to be the only one he could have made. A shoot-out would have left both of them dead for sure. But to Kemp, sitting in the boat, memorizing the lines of his dead friend's face as he waved his shaking hand to deter the flies as they drifted over the Mekong, the thought held no consolation.

WHEN THE LITTLE BOAT LANDED, HE DISPATCHED THE BOATMEN WITH a note to the governor. The body should be taken to the local nuns, who could lay Klotz out properly and prepare a funeral. Kemp walked slowly back to the house. On the veranda were the two wireless operators, Fournier and Rork. Kemp approached the porch. Klotz's blood stained his shirt all the way down his chest and arms. Fournier stood. She looked at him. Quietly, voice low, she asked the question to which she must have already sensed the answer. "Where is François?"

"François is dead." He could barely meet her eye.

Fournier stood still and quiet. The pain seemed to absorb into her body. As she held herself erect, the tears slowly welled into her eyes. In French, barely audible, she cried, "This is the second time, monsieur! The second time!" Her previous partner had been taken by the Gestapo.

Leaving the crying Fournier in the hands of the gruff, kind, older Rork, Kemp retreated to his room. Collapsing on his own bed, he allowed himself just a few minutes for his own despair.

Then he rose and went back to work.

THE NUNS WASHED AND LAID OUT KLOTZ'S BODY WHILE KEMP DRAFTED signals to Calcutta, reporting the incident. One was in the clear so that the Americans could not help but hear the British reporting. The other, in code, was a more detailed and private report. Kemp included his suggestions for setting the matter right.

There was a Catholic cemetery to the north of town where Klotz's funeral would take place and where he would be buried. The next day, as he was about to leave for the funeral, Kemp found the neutral Lieutenant Reese on his doorstep. The American saluted, then said gravely and determinedly, "I've come, major, to attend Lieutenant Klotz's funeral."

"That's very good of you, lieutenant, I'm sure. But—but—do you know what you may be letting yourself in for? The French here are pretty indignant and—"

"I know. But I'd like to be there."

After the tricolor-draped coffin was lowered into the ground, after the volley was fired and the dirt shoveled in, the young American turned, saluted the grave, and walked away. As Kemp put it, "Whatever may be said about him, he showed that day no lack of dignity or courage."

Smiley confronted Bank personally.

"Apart from everything else, he can't tell the truth," Smiley complained. "He swore to me that he had never called the French officers bandits or ordered them to give themselves up to the [Viet Minh], but he didn't know that I had in my pocket a letter written by him to the French at Savannakhet in those very words."

Smiley sent an urgent signal to his staff office, requesting Bank's removal. What Smiley, Kemp, and Winn did not know, though the local Viet Minh may have, was that there was another coup going on in Saigon at the same time. The British had sent several Gurkha rifle regiments of the Indian Army, under the command of General Douglas Gracey, to ensure calm in the city. But Gracey rapidly found that it was impossible to keep the calm without taking sides. The Americans did not want to see the French regain their empire. The French and the British did not want to see a power vacuum that ended in the rise of a radical Communist government under the Viet Minh.

Aware that doing nothing was as much of a choice as doing something, Gracey sanctioned a French coup against the Viet Minh. Armed

French officers took back control of the city. They were not gentle about it, keeping even women and children detained with their hands above their heads for hours after the shooting stopped. Fighting was sporadic. The Viet Minh struck back in the Cité Héraud district. There, Vietnamese whom the Communists insisted were "bandits" entered the local houses and pulled out and murdered about 150 French civilians, many of them women and children. All of this happened two days before Klotz was killed. It could not have failed to add to the frustrations of the local Viet Minh.

The French also registered their outrage over Klotz's murder. Theirs even appeared in *The New York Times*, where the Gray Lady reported that the French had tartly requested that "instructions be sent to these officers, who are presumably cut off from their bases and acting on their own authority." The final blow had already come from the White House. The ill and overtaxed Roosevelt had died in April. He had been succeeded as president by Harry Truman, who was no fan of the OSS, which he called a "Gestapo" organization. He had issued an order on September 20, a week before Klotz's death, disbanding the OSS. Bank—who in his own memoir couldn't seem to tell the difference between Winn, Kemp, and Tavernier; who never bothered to learn Klotz's name; and who declared that "the Frenchman was asking for it"—was back in Calcutta by early October.

"The Frenchman" was not the Viet Minh's only casualty, despite the OSS's cozy relationship with Ho Chi Minh himself. The day before Klotz was killed, an American OSS officer, Colonel Peter Dewey (a relation of the presidential candidate behind the famous "Dewey Defeats Truman" headline gaffe), was driving in his jeep to the OSS villa outside Saigon. Gracey had warned him many times about the danger of the location, but he failed to heed those warnings. Approaching a Viet Minh roadblock around lunchtime, he and another OSS officer were shot at point-blank range by a light machine gun. As a warning, Dewey had reportedly shouted in French, "I'm American!" But the damage was done. Dewey lay dead; the other officer managed to crawl away to safety. In hindsight, Dewey was labeled the first American casualty of the Vietnam War. Bank's thoughts on whether he deserved it went unrecorded.

SMILEY CHANGED KEMP'S ORDERS. SOE'S STAFF OFFICE WAS WILLING TO take up one of the suggestions that Kemp had made on the evening of Klotz's death. The British would supply the French and Lao resistance fighters with arms, as well as medicines and other nonmilitary supplies. After Klotz's funeral, Smiley sat down to inform Kemp. "By the way, Peter, you're not to go to Thakhek again," Smiley said as they finished. "The Viet Minh are after your blood, and they've put a price on your head."

"How much?"

"I can't quite make out. It's either five hundred pounds or half a crown, depending on the rate of exchange."

Kemp might have been offended by the lower end of the estimate. When the staff reported his response in their weekly situation reports, they declared that as Kemp did not think his enemies' courage to be "equal to their cupidity, he is not in the least perturbed."

The Viet Minh tried to assassinate Kemp four times. As Kemp's new orders required him to undertake, as he called them, "the perils of a gunrunner," they had good opportunities. Their best one came when Kemp, under the cover of darkness, was smuggling arms across the Mekong in a small convoy with the help of several local boatmen and some of Tavernier's Lao soldiers. They were installed in a pirogue, a long, low, elegant Thai vessel with a shape similar to that of a Viking longboat.

As they floated upstream, Kemp noticed an island in the river. Suddenly, machine-gun fire pierced the night, striking the paddler of the leading pirogue and sending him overboard as the man steering slumped over, fell, and capsized the whole boat, drowning a third man aboard. The subsequent bursts were high—a regular habit of untrained troops with machine guns, as Kemp had reason to know. Kemp, who at that surreal moment wondered whether there were crocodiles in the Mekong, later reflected, "I imagine that a smuggler can have few more disagreeable experiences than that of coming under heavy fire at close range in a flimsy canoe on a fast and turbulent river." He rolled to his stomach and began shooting back.

By subterfuge, Kemp avoided a second ambush on his return. The grateful but worried Tavernier, disturbed to realize that they had obviously been compromised by some of Kemp's agents (all too often double agents, to his chagrin), suggested that they use only his men as couriers. The neighborhood was becoming dangerous. Tavernier's Franco-Lao soldiers who were caught by the Viet Minh as they traveled on leave to visit their families either disappeared completely or were found beheaded. In a scene eerily similar to that of the American colonel Dewey, Rowland Winn survived his own ambush (his fourth one) when he was attacked while driving in a jeep with a French officer and his Lao soldiers. Winn broke his wrist, the officer his shoulder, and one of the Lao a leg. The jeep had overturned, which provided Winn and the other wounded with cover while the uninjured soldiers ran for help. They were pinned down for two hours by Viet Minh, who failed to press the attack home and melted away at the sight of the Lao soldiers coming to Winn's rescue.

One evening, Kemp was sitting on his veranda in a pair of newly washed khaki drill slacks when sniper fire tore across the darkness. He indignantly spilled a glass of good local rum on his fresh pants. But the assassins missed.

Kemp's gunrunning could not take his mind off revenge. He had been plotting to capture the two men he felt most responsible for the death of François Klotz: the Viet Minh's local chief delegate, a man named Long who went by the alias Le Hoq Minh, and Delegate Tu, whose screeching voice had accosted them at the landing platform and who had given the deadly command to fire on the fleeing pair.

Kemp tracked both in their crossings of the Mekong. He knew that if he had good enough intelligence, he and his small command could catch one or both. They would either deliver them to Tavernier or dispose of them on their own. "I suppose I must seem no better myself than the men I was pursuing, but so bitter was my hatred for those two that I could not feel I was contravening the teachings of my education and religion," he later wrote in his memoir.

In that memoir, Kemp confessed that he had received unofficial and cautious approval of his plans, but when he finally had good enough intelligence to capture Le Hoq Minh and requested formal approval (what the office euphemistically called an "arrest"), he received what he described as a disappointing denial "in one word of cabalese: 'Unoff-bump.'"

What Kemp did not record in his memoir was another story, one that he had reported in the Top Secret files collected by the staff office. On October 30, Viet Minh attacked Tavernier's group but were fought off. Then, the report said, the Viet Minh attacked Tavernier again two days later.

With the guns that Kemp had provided, the French overpowered their assailants. They killed what was initially reported as twenty Viet Minh and later as thirty. This was the better part of a platoon, the same size of the unit that had killed Klotz. The Viet Minh had either begun with a unit far larger than a platoon or pressed home an attack with high-casualty tactics that were uncharacteristic of the guerrillas' operations. Perhaps it had been merely a Vietnamese platoon, but in their excitement over their success, the French had mixed up who was ambushing whom when they relayed the story.

In the battle, the French took one prisoner. He confessed that the Viet Minh were aiding an underground movement by the Japanese to destabilize the area and had been using Chinese vehicles and flags to conceal their movements.

In his memoir, Kemp also left unrecorded something that turned out to be very convenient for the French: the single prisoner, left unnamed in the signals, also happened to be the leader of the party that had killed Klotz. The staff office summary left no ambiguity as to the outcome: "The French killed the prisoner."

CHAPTER 12

THE MOST MARVELOUS JOB THE ARMY HAS EVER GIVEN ANYONE

B ritain was shortly to conclude its peace treaty with Thailand, leaving no role for SOE officers on the ground. Slowly, they prepared to hand over their operations to the regular Allied occupation forces. In November 1945, Smiley and Kemp took a flying visit to Bangkok, the country's capital, to see some of the more senior officers stationed there.

If Kemp had known anything about Smiley's track record with planes, he probably would have offered to walk. It wasn't as if Smiley were a neophyte. He had his own private pilot's license and, before the war, had owned a Miles Whitney Straight. But trouble seemed to follow him once the wheels were up, as it had on his way out to Asia.

There was the time in 1941 when, on his way to rejoin his cavalry unit in Habbaniya, he hitched a ride on an RAF Vickers Valentia that he thought looked "almost too old to fly." The intercom didn't work, and the batteries went dead, then the radio. There were about a dozen things wrong with the engine, and the plane was flying low to avoid patrols of German and Italian fighter planes. Then, "to cheer us up," Smiley recalled dryly, the pilot announced that they were lost. The passengers were asked, as darkness fell, to look for the lake that would indicate their landing zone. "All I could see," Smiley later wrote, "were the flames from the engines which looked exactly as if they were on fire."

Then there was the time when Smiley got a seat on a Dakota back to Cairo after visiting his older brother in Eritrea. The pilot abandoned his takeoff preparations and rolled back down the runway. Smiley, as the most junior officer aboard, was booted off by an impatient brigadier who took his seat. As he flew on the next plane to leave over the desert, the pilot came on the speaker to ask the passengers to keep an eye out for the plane that had left ahead of them. It had not checked in. It was found the next day, crashed, with no survivors.

Asked in India to join an RAF flight over Thailand as an observer, Smiley had once found himself putting out flames alongside the dispatcher and the rear gunner when a fire broke out in the Liberator's fuselage. They were not able to save the parachutes, so there would be no bailing out if they failed. They were forced back to base after shutting off one of the engines, which had a bad fuel leak. In Thailand, he'd had two other accidents, including one in a Japanese bomber that overturned on landing. Later, while serving in Oman, he would nearly crash in a sandstorm that enveloped his plane at five thousand feet. The pilot would land with ten minutes of fuel to spare.

Now heading to Bangkok after the end of the Second World War, what Kemp saw before him was the small Mitsubishi plane that had been allocated to Smiley's use in Thailand and that Smiley had already deemed "temperamental." It was piloted by a young Thai officer called Prang, whose name happened to match the British slang for "crash." On the leg from Ubon to Bangkok, the plane's engine cut out at five thousand feet above dense jungle. As the plane sank, the pilot engaged in some "feverish pumping" and managed to restart it, only to have to repeat the process five more times. By the end, they were flying at no more than two hundred feet. Kemp and Smiley were looking at each other, in Smiley's estimation, "resignedly."

Kemp, as a matter of fact, was running over the only useful RAF advice he could think of, which was to attempt to land in bamboo if there was no paddy available when crash-landing in the jungle. "Do you see any bamboo down there?" Kemp demanded, much to Smiley's amusement.

They landed at Korat, about halfway to their destination. The tail-wind pushed them forward. The plane bounced, a wheel came off, and a wreck ensued. They were on the ground and, aside from the aircraft, in one piece. Prang climbed out of the pilot's seat with what Kemp described as a "bashful, apologetic, and wholly disarming smile."

Fortified by very stiff drinks and a different plane, they flew on to Bangkok. On the way back, they were lent another Mitsubishi, which Smiley piloted himself. In midflight, they hit a very large bird and nearly lost control, forcing another near-emergency landing in Korat, where they found a gash three feet long and nine inches deep in the metal of one wing. Smiley finally got them back to Nakorn Panom. As they were about to land, the engine once again cut out.

"What was the cause of that?" Kemp asked some time later.

"Oh, it seems they forgot to fill her up at Korat. She was clean out of gas when the engine cut," Smiley said. "Aren't we the lucky ones?"

KEMP RETURNED TO UBON TO WRAP UP HIS MISSION. ALONG WITH THE Mad Major John Hedley, a captain from the War Graves Commission, and several sappers, he spent a night playing poker and drinking local whiskey and rum. Before heading to bed, Kemp stepped out onto the veranda for some fresh air.

The next thing he knew, he was waking up in a dark and highly questionable smoke-filled local hut. He had no idea where he was. He was not tied up but detained in a different way: his trousers were missing. Slowly, he sensed movement. Across from him was an old man. They looked at each other, and then the man disappeared, slipping out the hut's door.

Kemp had no idea how he had arrived at his present location, but he was certain that, no matter how much he may have imbibed before stepping onto that veranda, it had not been voluntary.

The pain and fuzziness in his head reminded him of his concussion upon landing in Albania. He had no idea if he was one mile from his own bedroom or one hundred miles, but he had to move. He grabbed a burlap-style bag, attempted to cover himself, and crept out the entrance.

He was relieved to find a road. Then he heard noise. It was a party of police or soldiers. They could only be heading back to the exact same part of Ubon where he intended to go. But Kemp, despite Smiley's jokes about the irregular nature of his commission, was a British officer to the core. It never occurred to him to run out and ask for help. "Of course it would never do for them to find a British officer of field rank wandering about the countryside at half past one in the morning without his trousers," he later declared. He let the group pass and then slunk along behind them.

After ten minutes that felt like an hour, he made a final mad dash into the barracks and his room. Collapsing onto the bed, he found himself overcome with hysterical laughter of relief and amusement. Creeping home half-covered in a burlap bag had reminded him of the code name of his Mission: Sackcloth.

Kemp came in for quite a bit of ribbing over this incident, which included all sorts of jokes about local women taking advantage of a British officer for his public drunkenness. ("They produced several theories to account for it, the simplest and by far the most popular being that I had left my trousers in a brothel.")

"We'd better find that hut," said Hedley, the only one who was not laughing.

Little escaped Hedley's attention, though the hut itself was never found. He soon pieced together the likely details: Somebody, or probably two somebodies, had recognized Kemp standing on the veranda and had decided to collect the sizable Viet Minh reward for his delivery.

They likely thumped him on the back of the neck, dragged him away, and deposited him in the local hut. Unprepared, they stole his trousers, hoping that British pride and modesty would keep him caged when more formal restraints could not. But his captors either panicked or were unable to bring a Viet Minh guard in time. "Whatever the reason," Kemp wrote, "I am heartily thankful for it; I have heard too many stories of Viet Minh irregulars disemboweling their prisoners." Hedley packed him into the next available transport to Bangkok: a railcar in a goods train, which Hedley had outfitted with some wicker chairs.

Smiley had already gone through Bangkok on his own way home to attend the Staff College back in England. In Bangkok, the SOE and Tara crowds were reassembling once more, along with the Thai allies Pluto and Cato. Alan Hare was there, as were Billy Moss and John Hibberdine, who had served on the Kra Isthmus, the peninsula that joins Thailand to what was then Malaya.

It was 1946, and everyone else was going home. Kemp was offered another job. He would later say it was "the most marvelous job I think the Army has ever given anyone." Promoted to lieutenant colonel, he was finally granted a non-SOE role: to accept the Japanese surrender and act as interim governor of the island of Bali.

KEMP HAD HEARD BALI CALLED "THE LAST PARADISE." DESPITE KEMP'S habit of using that line about the "marvelous job" whenever he wanted to distract questioners from other aspects of his service, the island at the time was anything but serene. Bali was part of the Dutch East Indies, now Indonesia. The Dutch had been as unprepared for the Japanese invasion of their Pacific colonies as they had been for the German one of their homeland, and the colony was quickly overrun by Axis forces in 1942.

As in French Indochina, the Japanese had taken control and found local allies in violent, nationalist anti-colonial movements. Also as in

French Indochina, this was complicated by the residencies of multiple ethnic groups within a small space. The Javans who inhabited the main island were not the same as the Balinese. There were also plenty of Chinese residents and other ethnicities as well. The habits of the European colonizers made the argument of the revolutionaries only too easy. If the French were much worse colonizers than the British, so, too, were the Dutch less loved than the French.

The Japanese surrender kicked off what became known as the Indonesian War of Independence, or the Indonesian National Revolution. There were Communist and non-Communist elements. There was also plenty of ethnic hatred against Europeans, Eurasians, and other disliked ethnic groups, such as the Chinese. For nearly a year, ethnic-based bloodletting would rend Indonesian society in what came to be called the Bersiap.

This made life more complicated for the Allied forces that landed to take control from the Japanese. In order to increase military efficiency and plan for peace in the postwar period, Indonesia had been placed into SEAC, under Lord Mountbatten's responsibility, at the Potsdam Conference in July of 1945. It thus became a British problem. One brigadier was murdered by local revolutionaries who staged an uprising. A battalion of his men were overrun and killed. Women and children were chased into the officers' club and murdered in the bathrooms. Further bloodshed was only prevented by the arrival of General Robert Mansergh of the 5th Indian Division and a large body of troops, who prevented the massacre of more than a thousand civilians, mostly women and children, who had been herded into a local jail that the revolutionaries were in the process of setting on fire. Mansergh's Indian troops blasted a hole in the wall and hauled them out.

Bali was spared much of the carnage, which was concentrated on the main island of Java. But it could not escape the tensions that underlay the violence.

KEMP'S BRIEF HAD TWO MAIN TASKS. THE FIRST WAS TO ACCEPT THE formal (though not, in the language of the time, official) surrender of the Japanese. Then he would oversee the signing of the instruments of surrender. The official version, with a review of the troops, a ceremonial handover of swords, and so on, would be accepted by General Mansergh after the Dutch landing in a week's time.

On no account was Kemp to let the locals know that the Allied landing force would be Dutch. It might start a revolt. He was to produce intelligence for Mansergh's staff office. Kemp would have a handful of his own staff officers and British soldiers, but he would mostly need to use the Japanese to rule. It was a delicate task. As one of the officers briefing Kemp cheerfully put it: "If they chop you up, we'll know we'll have to be more careful with the next lot."

The surrender over which Kemp would preside was not the fancy ceremony that would be videotaped and preserved for history. It was the formal surrender nonetheless, and with the relevant signatures, Kemp would become, in Western eyes, at least, the temporary ruler of a Pacific island. He, his staff, and his small contingent of British troops approached Bali via the frigate *Loch Eck* one bright February morning. In a scene that could not have been encouraging to Kemp, left to worry if "we were right in our easy assumption that they would obey me, or if our reception was going to be warm rather than friendly," a frustrated Japanese officer pulled up alongside them. He informed the Royal Navy captain and his crew that sufficient information had not been passed to the Japanese garrison. Would they kindly wait a moment? The British landed in the afternoon, with the surrender set for the following morning. Kemp was both relieved and disturbed to see how pleased the Japanese officers were to hand over responsibility.

Aboard the ship the next day, Kemp and his fellow officers stayed seated during the well-staged surrender. The flags were lowered and raised, the ship gleamed, and the table and rows of chairs were set out precisely. The five-page-long "Formal Instrument of Surrender" lay on the table, which the Japanese officers, after a short conference, approached and signed in their turn. Kemp, who had fought hard to join the British Army after his adventure in Spain, had been ridiculed by friends before the Second World War for his choice to fight for the Nationalists' cause, and who had spent so much time since proving his loyal British bona fides, now gratefully thought that "I could not suppress a surge of pride at the thought of the small but historic role I was allowed to resume."

Kemp's eyes drifted to the Japanese Admiral Shizuo Okuyama, the senior officer signing the surrender. His signature complete, the elderly Okuyama sat still, hands on knees, head bowed, tears streaming down cheeks that bore the signs of his old age. Kemp, who had spoken with the POWs at Ubon, knew of the cruelty of the Japanese war effort, albeit only secondhand. He had been well warned about not allowing himself to be taken alive by the Japanese. Yet he had never fought them himself. Still, watching Okuyama, he could not help but feel overwhelming pity: "Now, in my unearned hour of triumph, I felt ashamed to watch this veteran sailor, who had spent his life in a service with a great fighting tradition, weeping openly over his humiliation at the hands of a jumped-up young lieutenant colonel who had never even fought against him."

Okuyama proved to be an officer and a gentleman. His help was valuable to Kemp, who still needed to prepare for the Dutch landing. Civil administration had broken down. The beaches the Dutch meant to land on were insufficiently prepared. Defenses (manned by the still-armed Japanese) would have to be organized. An airstrip sufficient for landing Dakotas needed to be upgraded. And a lid had to be kept on the simmering volcano that was the civil war, even if it so far appeared to be mostly instigated by outsiders from Java and not the local ethnic Balinese. Kemp, sitting down to review his tasks, was still at his desk when the next dawn broke.

The Dutch were convinced that they would be opposed on landing, but one week later, Kemp was delighted to see that his preparations had worked. The land approaches to the beach had been carefully guarded by Japanese troops since the previous evening. Kemp had warned the Dutch not to let any stray shots from enterprising young radicals turn a symbolic resistance into a bloodbath, but there were no shots to be heard. Tall, blond Dutchmen strode off the landing craft alongside their determined Dutch-Indonesian soldiers.

They had brought a British videographer to capture the scene, Bali beautiful even in silent black and white. A welcome party of Japanese officers waited for the Dutch. Kemp and his crew, along with a Swiss painter and his Balinese wife, stood separately. The videographer captured the Dutch peacefully unloading ships and moving into town unopposed. He let his camera linger on the painter's wife, the only woman on the beach. Peter Kemp stood just off camera. As he shook the hand of the Dutch Colonel Fritz ter Meulen, he later said, "I could almost feel the weight of responsibility roll from my shoulders."

In the span of barely a week, Kemp had struggled to maintain control of a situation that he admitted he did not understand. Bali seemed peaceful, but there were signs of violence under the surface. Before Kemp's arrival, the Japanese had been attacked by groups seeking their arms; the perpetrators were thrown in jail. Language of freedom and liberation merged with threats of ethnic violence. Kemp was warned to use as little force as possible. The British did not want to oppress the locals for the Dutch. Local dignitaries, threatened with execution, feared helping him. One raja summoned Kemp in a panic, afraid that his town would be overrun by men bearing both guns and spears. Kemp managed to diffuse the situation, but only barely. Everywhere he went in Bali, he was warned to be forceful so that he wouldn't appear weak. Caught between the rock and the hard place of Western liberalism and local expectations, he walked a tightrope that he was only too happy to relinquish to the Dutch commander.

Kemp was soon packed off to the nearby island of Lombok, even smaller than Bali at just thirty miles by forty-five. There the natives of Lombok feared rule by the Balinese, who on their own island feared rule by the Javans. No one trusted the Dutch, though men with property and trading interests appreciated the prosperity of peace under Dutch rule.

As Kemp prepared to hand over his staff operations, terrorist-style violence spiked. It was not safe to be out at night. Men were robbed and murdered for things as trifling as cameras or wristwatches. One European, a longtime resident who had good relationships with his local neighbors, went out looking for a missing man. He was found later in a rice paddy, a rope around his neck and more than thirty sword slashes across his body. It would turn into a civil war that would continue until the Dutch relinquished control in 1949.

KEMP RECEIVED A LETTER FROM THE WOMAN WHO WAS NOW BARELY his ex-wife, Lizzie Phillips. She was getting remarried. Kemp, who had just completed his official responsibilities for SOE, finally felt the full force of the emotional blow that he had held off for so long. "Now I felt the full pain and desolation—mixed, let me be honest, with a large dose of hurt pride—of this news which I ought to have expected but had somehow never foreseen," he said.

He did not elaborate, but he left clues about the details. Kemp and Lizzie had not been married long. They could not have known each other for long before they were wed. Kemp arrived back from Spain in 1938, then still badly wounded. Their wedding was in the fall of 1941.

Kemp had arrived in London from Albania in the late spring or early summer of 1944 and was presumably reunited with his wife. They were together that June, when Kemp had been sent to visit King Zog. The dethroned monarch was living the suburban life in Marlow, to the west of London. This was where Kemp's wife had left her wedding rings in the hotel bathroom, by intention or omen, never a good sign. Curiously, it was Kemp, not Lizzie, who made the call to the hotel to rectify the error; he was "most apologetic."

Perhaps it was the Polish mission that finally did them in; perhaps this is what Kemp had meant when he said, "Bitterly I cursed the selfishness and obstinate determination to go my own way that had wrecked my marriage and destroyed our love." He had spent so much of the war on operations. He could have had a staff job if he had wanted to stay home. That was what some other officers who had served in Albania chose to do. Perhaps she had pressed him to take that route as well. If so, he must have refused. By October 1944, he had left for Bari and was waiting to drop into Poland.

A few months earlier, in May, Lizzie had applied to SOE herself. Her paperwork indicated an application for a FANY role in motor transport. The security clearance would have taken time to work out. There were apparently extra checks and processes when employing two married individuals in the same secret unit.

The record does not indicate whether she was eventually employed by SOE or not. But her contacts there had expanded. Peter Kemp had reasons beyond the usual to be hurt, and embarrassed, by his ex-wife's remarriage. Her new husband was none other than George Seymour, whom Kemp had called in his Albanian report the possessor of "one of the finest pairs of moustaches in the British Army," behind whom Kemp had jumped into Albania, and with whom Kemp for weeks had shared a tent.

This time, the announcement was more subdued than the status flag waving notice of Lizzie and Kemp's elaborate nuptials. It simply proclaimed the engagement of "Major G. V. Seymour and Mrs. H. E. Kemp" and did not share the ceremony date.

Had Kemp introduced them? It is possible. It seems that, at one point, Kemp and Seymour had been slated to go to Slovakia and Hungary on another Eastern European mission, which was canceled before Kemp was reassigned to the Poland mission. Seymour may have arrived in London before Kemp. Perhaps Seymour met Lizzie then. Perhaps she met him when she was applying for the FANY job at SOE. Or perhaps he was the reason she applied for the FANY job at SOE. Glamorous Seymour, a regular cavalry officer, a member of a noted noble family, far richer than Kemp, and the possessor of those mustaches, stayed on in London as a staff officer when Kemp went to Poland.

Kemp never mentioned exactly when his wife requested a divorce. In his memoir of his time in Albania and Poland, there are no indications that something was amiss. Maybe during those periods he didn't know. They were still married, and apparently still together, when he left for Poland that October. But by the time Kemp made it out of Poland and NKVD jail and met David Smiley in the Arab restaurant in Cairo where he was recruited to the Thailand mission less than six months later, he knew that his marriage was over. Until he received her letter in Lombok, however, he had seemingly not guessed why. Ever the gentleman, he was too polite to mention it. In none of his papers, private or public, would he ever say that she had left him to marry a man whom he had considered a friend and comrade, a man whom he had apparently asked to look in on his wife. In Bali, Kemp "took no pleasure in this paradise, but brooded in a deep pit of loneliness and despair, and abused my fate, and hated myself, and wept a little, and drank too much, and wept some more."

His duties complete, Kemp returned to Batavia, where General Mansergh granted his overdue orders for demobilization. "You've earned an air passage," the general said. "I'll sign an order now to give you priority." He was two months shy of his thirty-first birthday and had been at war for nearly ten years.

David Smiley noted, when the two parted in Thailand, that Kemp was "in a very bad way. I have never seen him so neurotic and drinking so much." His personal troubles aside, the death of François Klotz had left a permanent mark. Kemp was also suffering, though he did not know it yet, from the early stages of tuberculosis.

CHAPTER 13

OLD FRIENDS AND NEW BEGINNINGS

The summer of 1945 brought "victory days" in Europe and the Pacific, but conflict did not end that year. There were already early rumblings of the wars of decolonization to come. The Cold War, too, began its birthing pangs.

To Western intelligence establishments, Albania once again looked like a potentially valuable strategic piece on the chessboard of Europe, just as it had been before, when David Smiley and Billy McLean were deployed there in 1943. By 1949, Enver Hoxha and the Albanian Communist Party held complete control of the country.

But Josip "Tito" Broz, the Communist dictator of Yugoslavia who had exerted such outsize influence over Hoxha, had split with Stalin. This was a rupture in the Soviet world, the first inkling the West had that Stalin might not wield the kind of control to which he aspired. For Hoxha's Albania, it meant that the geopolitical map had become far more complicated. Stalin, like Tito, had always treated Albania like a Yugoslav satellite, a lesser moon of Balkan Communism.

Hoxha promptly renounced his former protector, allying himself with Stalin. But while the USSR was a large and powerful ally, it was very far away. It was also literally on the other side of Yugoslavia. Albania was surrounded by Tito to the north and east. To the south was Greece, a state that claimed part of southern Albania and was itself in the middle of a civil war between Communist and non-Communist factions. To the west was the Adriatic Sea, and Italy.

Hoxha's sinking of two British warships in 1946 (they hit illegal mines in the international waters of the Strait of Otranto, the narrow strip of water between the eastern edge of the Italian boot and the Albanian coast) did not endear him to the Western powers. This, combined with the fact that Albania was small, isolated, and not a crucial USSR-bordering state like Poland, meant that Albania suddenly looked far more attractive to members of the Western intelligence establishments interested in active resistance to the Soviet threat. Hoxha was also sheltering Communist rebels who were raiding across the border into Greece, then functionally a British protectorate, and prolonging the civil war in the cradle of Western democracy. What were the chances that Hoxha, who made the lives of his people so miserable, could be overthrown?

It was this project in which Billy McLean and Julian Amery soon found themselves engaged. Amery had lost his parliamentary election in 1945; McLean had resigned his commission after the war in order to pursue politics but had not yet found a seat either. In the meantime, Amery had written a book called *Sons of the Eagle*, a cri de coeur on the team's experience in Albania. Its publication in 1948 arrived just in time to give an extra push to those interested in removing from power the man who had become such a false partner.

McLean and Amery had time on their hands, as well as valuable experience in the region and with Hoxha himself. They also had extensive, and sympathetic, contacts within both the British government and British intelligence. The latter had a habit of using people who operated unofficially, and off its traditional payroll, to get work done. Amery and McLean took the lead and did the initial legwork on their own, although MI6 paid their bills. Once official, the project would be called, on the

British side, Operation Valuable. The basic idea was simple: find and train groups of patriotic Albanian exiles willing to be delivered back to their homeland, collect intelligence about the likely success of an insurrection, foment dissent, and then slip across the Greek border for extraction.

The plan would eventually involve partnering with American "cousins" at the CIA, who would carry on a version of the operation long after the British ceded the field. (The CIA also helped with financing. As McLean was told by one British official, "Church mice do not make wars.") But the initial challenges to the plan involved far more local allies. The first was the Greek government, fighting for its survival against Communist guerrillas, many of whom were being sheltered by Hoxha's men across the border in southern Albania. This was the same border that Smiley and McLean had traversed in 1943, when Smiley was briefly detained on suspicion of being a Greek spy.

The next challenge involved both the Albanian talent and the Italian government. Italy was still full of internment camps holding displaced refugees, and some of the camps outside Bari held Albanians. This was the only available population from which the operation could recruit: they would need to find men with sufficient strength, interest, and reliability. The Italian government, which hosted the refugees, would have to either agree or be convinced to look the other way.

And then there was the issue of Albanian leadership. It would help no one to organize an operation that appeared to be merely a Western incursion running on the backs of brave Albanian patriots. Both Amery and McLean were well aware that there were a host of exiled Albanian leaders who wished for Hoxha's downfall. They would need to support the creation of an Albanian National Committee to which credit could be given.

McLean and Amery began with the Greeks, for without their support, there could be no operation. In the spring of 1949, the two flew to Greece to gain permission, and backing, for an underground war. Such a thing is not exactly the sort of meeting that goes on official paperwork in fancy offices and published minute books. Amery, with much experience in that part of the world, realized that they would be better off seeing a power behind the throne. He arranged for a rendezvous with a well-known arms dealer, a man named Bodosakis, who was known to have extensive influence among top Greek military brass.

There were no meetings in stuffy conference rooms. McLean and Amery met the arms dealer for lunch at a taverna twenty miles outside Athens, near the sea. They pitched their plan to the gunrunner, who, convinced after three hours, promised to bring their proposal to the field marshal. It was Bodosakis who proposed the system by which he would signal to the British men the fate of their plans. Bodosakis said, "If it's no, I'll leave one bottle of brandy in your room at the hotel. If it's yes, I'll leave six." Within a few days, Amery entered his room and found six bottles.

The British government would deal with its Italian counterparts, but it was left to McLean and Amery—alongside fellow SOE veterans and then MI6 agents Alan Hare and Harold "Perks" Perkins—to organize matters with the Albanian exiles. This was, by nature, a complex and challenging task; for all that could be said against the Communists, they had been united and organized where the non-Communist forces often had not. The Ballists of the republican Balli Kombëtar were still in competition with Abas Kupi's Zogists. Moreover, the Americans wanted to support certain pro-Italian factions that had collaborated with the Italian occupation, which had chased out King Zog.

The idea of missions that were primarily of the reconnaissance and intelligence-gathering sort was not to the initial taste of Abas Kupi, who argued for a flat-out strike force. He pledged his own money, men, and organization, but it was when the warlord asked for tanks that Amery noticed even the gung-ho Perks's face contort into "a picture." Yet the real challenge was not Kupi's desire for open warfare but King Zog's desire for both control and prestige.

As McLean explained it, the decision had been made to go to the rest of the exiled Albanian leaders first in order to form an organization, gain their blessing for the operation, and obtain their help in getting it off the ground (such as by recruiting the appropriate men). McLean's opinion was that, in the grand tradition of begging for forgiveness rather than asking for permission, Zog's acquiescence would have to be secured last. Otherwise, the man who still called himself king would naturally insist upon being in charge, which would destroy the ability of the other exiled leaders, especially the republicans, to work in concert.

One day that spring, Amery, McLean, and an American CIA operative named Robert Low decamped to Cairo to visit the exiled monarch. Dethroned though he was, Zog was no shrinking violet. He had become king on the strength of his own personality and ambition. The son of a local notable who had revolted against the then Ottoman rulers of Albania, Zog had been taken hostage and raised in the Ottoman court, where he learned intrigue from the masters themselves. Sent back to Albania, he participated in a declaration of independence, fought for the Austrians against the Ottomans, and ascended to the presidency of Albania in 1925. He declared himself monarch three years later. At the time, a story circulated that Zog had been attacked by an assassin on the steps of an opera house in Vienna. As Amery commented, "Some kings have walked calmly on when shot at. Others have taken evasive action." But not Zog. As the story goes, he pulled out his own pistol and shot the man dead. "Such a man, I thought, deserved to be king," Amery later said.

Apocryphal though it likely was, the story (and its afterlife) said something about the way Zog perceived himself and how he expected to be treated. When Low, McLean, and Amery arrived with news of Operation Valuable, Zog's reaction was not one of welcome. He rose, angrily declared that he had made Albania and not some self-declared government-in-exile in Rome, and demanded that his guests leave his lavish villa immediately. The American Low moved to depart. Amery, who, as his biographer put it, "could always be relied upon to keep his nerve on these occasions," stayed put. Zog had been schooled in the greatest court of intrigue the modern world has seen: the dying days of the Ottoman Empire. Amery recognized an opening gambit classic to Eastern methodology.

Lawrence of Arabia had once claimed that Englishmen abroad tend to fall into two categories: the John Bull types, who become more English the farther they get from home and end up as caricatures of themselves, and the kind who "go completely native." The brilliant Lawrence, who spoke fluent Arabic, chose Bedouin robes over his British uniform, and once embarrassed King George V by declining a knighthood in person, fell into the latter category. Amery was the rare bird who could float above the fray: always impeccably English, he was nevertheless well versed in the manners of the relevant local diplomacy— and able to wield them.

Before he joined Smiley and McLean in Albania in 1944, Amery had undertaken an extensive tour of intelligence, intrigue, and deception operations throughout the Mediterranean. Posted to Belgrade, he had formed relationships with not only the ruling party but also the competing agrarian parties. He once spent Christmas Day watching a peasant party politician give a speech; curious about the Brit, the politician had taken Amery trudging through the snow to meet the regular rural people of Serbia. He had a warm relationship with the man who was then the Serbian Agrarian Party's leader, Milan Gavrilović, to whose family Amery had once brought a pair of Dalmatian puppies. ("Nothing I have ever done before or since has met with such enthusiasm," he later said of the gift.) In fact, he was technically a member of Gavrilović's party—a fact that allowed him to elicit shock and discomfort from colleagues who liked to lazily dismiss him as an arch-reactionary. Speaking at Parliament in 1992, Amery enjoyed the astounded looks on the Labour front bench as he declared his membership, dating back to 1940, in the Peasant International. "Honourable members may not have always seen me as a peasant," he remarked.

He knew something, too, of politicians in exile. Organizing relationships and operations with the exiled Yugoslav government from Jerusalem in 1941, he opened the door to a man named Kosta Todorov, who declared, "You look very young. But never mind, at your age I had been condemned to death twice," and then organized diabolically clever ways to get his political opponents to recognize him. (One tactic involved convincing a Greek leader that as their mothers were both from Crete, the men must be cousins.)

Amery was accustomed to thinking on his feet. When a Serbian politician slated for Operation Bullseye in 1941 bailed at the last minute, Amery decided to solve the problem by going straight to the Yugoslav Director of Intelligence, but he was again nearly thwarted, this time by a malfunctioning elevator that held him and a colleague hostage for twenty minutes. The Yugoslav intelligence officer in question was in bed, not alone, and indisposed, but Amery talked him into providing the tough men who ultimately landed on the Montenegrin coast with Bill Hudson.

Amery had helped smuggle a Bulgarian politician from his native country to Istanbul by "diplomatic bag" (in this case, a large trunk that was purported to contain the British Embassy's archives). He learned how to patiently listen to older men, long out of politics, who retained their connections and, out of power, were willing to speak their minds. He preferred Balkan-flavored Belgrade to Austrian-inspired Zagreb, and realized, as Metternich had put it, that "east of the Lindenstrasse the Orient begins." In his autobiography, he recounted how once, when held up by a customs officer who questioned his profession of "diplomat" on a mission to Romania just before the fall of that country in 1940, he "thought it wiser to avoid answering questions of this kind" and "accordingly took the high line" in his reply: "You are quite right.

Diplomacy is not a profession. It is a career." Julian Amery was not discouraged by King Zog.

Amery soothed the monarch, promised him a referendum after Albania was freed from the Communist noose, and apologized prettily for "usurping the royal prerogative." Zog, mollified, agreed not to interfere with the work of the committee. The CIA officer Low called it "quite the most dazzling display of verbal diplomacy I have ever witnessed."

The Albanians, sans Zog, were brought to London for further discussions while the operational side of the program was planned out. This brought in Peter Kemp. Having contracted tuberculosis toward the end of the war, he had recently spent a miserable several months in a sanatorium in Switzerland. "This sanatorium enjoyed a high reputation," Kemp said, "though I could never understand why." He had been working in Rome for an aircraft manufacturer, but his illness put a stop to that. Coming out of the sanatorium, he reconnected with a friend who asked him to join a life-insurance company, for which Kemp ostensibly worked for the rest of his career.

Kemp had also reconnected with another old friend: Harold "Perks" Perkins, the MI6 officer who had been working with McLean and Amery and for whom Kemp had worked in Poland. Kemp, like seemingly everyone else who worked with the man, adored and respected Perks. The men were close personal friends. Kemp was roped into the new Albania mission.

His first job was to receive the members of the nascent Albanian National Committee in England. This caused almost immediate problems. Abas Kupi, as per usual, was carrying the pistol that was perpetually concealed in his pocket, a habit that David Smiley had noticed back in 1944. It fell to Kemp to explain to the customs officers at RAF Northolt, an airport just west of London, that this illiterate, non-English-speaking Albanian warlord posed no threat to the British populace. (Kupi's weapon was temporarily confiscated.)

The second problem concerned an essential that came second, after weapons, in all wars: food. Kemp ushered the group back to his flat in London, around the corner from the BBC's offices. Despite the end of the war, strict rationing was still in place, and drumming up enough food to feed an impromptu crowd took some doing.

This became the temporarily triumphant labor of Kemp's new wife, Cynthia. Despite his previous misadventures in matrimony, Kemp met Cynthia on his return from Bali, and the two were soon in love. They married at the end of November in 1946. It was a quiet wedding, quite different from Kemp's first. Cynthia, a year younger than Peter, was by all accounts a kind and generous woman.

She was also resourceful and creative, having managed to wrangle through her ration cards a sufficient quantity of ham mousse from Harrods for the party—only to be told that many of the guests were Muslims and therefore could not partake of the pork. "However," as Kemp dryly noted later, "Muslim or non-Muslim, they drank plenty of our alcohol."

While the details were being ironed out, it fell to Kemp to play host; he showed the group around the famous tourist traps that beckoned even in bombed-out postwar London (the Tower being a noted attraction). While official receptions were off the table, the Albanians were visited by various members of the intelligence establishment. Julian Amery hosted a garden party at his aunt's home in Kent, where Kupi had not one but two guns on him at the table. The Albanian warlord noticed a snake and, with what Amery called "great peasant skill," picked it up and terrified the intellectual townsman and committee leader Mid'hat Frashëri. As Amery later recounted, this became known as "the lunch where they chased each other round the garden with a snake."

Perks flew to the British-occupied zone of Germany and consulted another MI6 officer: Xan Fielding, one of the former residents of Tara, who had once playfully competed with David Smiley for the hand of the beguiling Polish countess Sophie Tarnowska. Fielding and Smiley had been, and remained, great friends. Perks wanted Fielding to help recruit Smiley.

Smiley was the only member of the crew who had stayed in the army after the close of hostilities. He had been to the Staff College at Camberley, having been recommended by his friend Lord Wavell. Self-deprecatingly, Smiley declared that he had been "lucky to pass out," as his crammed six-month college course had coincided with a happy introduction to a woman named Moyra Tweedie. They had met at a dinner hosted by her cousin Gavin Astor. Always known as Moy, she was the granddaughter of a duke on one side of her family and the granddaughter of a former Viceroy of India on the other. Independent and formidable, she had been raised in Kenya, where her father was the elected leader of the white settlers before the war. She had served as a cipher clerk in East Africa and was mentioned in dispatches in the same list as Smiley, then fighting in the Middle East. By this time, she was working at Bush House for the BBC's East European section.

She was also a widow and the mother of two young children, Gavin and Anna. Her late husband, whom she had met and married in Africa during the war, had been killed in Germany during the last weeks of the conflict. A major in the Scots Guards, he had been out with another officer, looking for somewhere the company could stop for the night, when he was ambushed. Three years younger than Smiley, Moy was whip-smart, unflappable, ambitious in the best way, and as well connected as Smiley himself. She was also, as one of his junior officers couldn't help but note even years later, tall and beautiful. Married in 1947—it was a ceremony attended by the Duke and Duchess of Gloucester, uncle and aunt to Princess (soon-to-be Queen) Elizabeth and related to both bride and groom as well—Moy and Smiley were a brilliant match.

Personal happiness aside, though, Smiley was beginning to get frustrated with his posting. His colonel had retired. Though he was next in line, Smiley was deemed too young to take command of the regiment.

He had done intelligence work in the past. Just before his marriage to Moy, he had been sent as an intelligence attaché to Warsaw, a stint that ended badly when he proved to be too good at his job. He was illegally arrested and roughed up, then declared persona non grata and expelled. In an extra bit of cruelty, Smiley's secretary, an older Polish woman, was sentenced to fourteen years of hard labor. At her age, this was tantamount to a death sentence. Perks, who had probably gotten Smiley's name from Kemp, had played a role in this posting, as well as in another year that Smiley had already spent on secondment to MI6. When Perks and Fielding came knocking and Perks laid out his proposal over a glass of brandy, Smiley took no time in saying yes. "I admit, I rather jumped at it," he recalled.

To Smiley fell the task of training the Albanians, who were codenamed "the Pixies" on account of their size (their naturally small stature having been exacerbated by the poor conditions of displaced-persons camps). Smiley, with his guerrilla experience in the war and recent MI6 experience, was well qualified for the task.

Where to put them was another question. All would have to take place with absolute secrecy. This was to be a deniable operation, one that needed to be effective without kicking off World War III. They were already recruiting Albanians from the refugee camps in Italy, and Italy was, from a geographic perspective, most convenient. But placing the trainees there, which would not only risk security but also rightly unsettle an irritable Italian government, was quite out of the question. The British settled on a convenient Mediterranean island: Malta, then still part of the British Empire.

Malta sits in the central Mediterranean, on an imaginary line between Tripoli and the southeastern coast of Sardinia. Home to human civilizations of antiquity greater even than Egypt's, Malta has seen Phoenicians, Romans, Carthaginians, crusaders, Arab traders, and probably a host of pirates, privateers, and smugglers as well. Like the (also then British) island of Cyprus, it was a crucial point of naval control during the Second World War. As the Cold War dawned, it held a strategic location whose value seemed unlikely to wane.

With the exception of Operation Valuable, Malta in 1949 was a fairly standard (if gloriously well-situated) peacetime outpost. But it also boasted some illustrious residents. Admiral Lord Mountbatten, an uncle of Prince Philip's, was then posted to Malta. So, too, was the prince, along with his wife, then still Princess Elizabeth. She had given birth to her first child, Prince Charles, less than a year prior. Given the climate, work started and ended early. There was polo, which Smiley made sure to partake in each afternoon. Amid this shimmering and very British outpost, how were nearly fifty non-English-speaking Albanians going to train covertly?

Anywhere near garrison headquarters in Valletta was out of the question. But Malta, despite its small size, had a surprising variety of territory. At one point during the nineteenth century, a line of fortifications had been built across the island, a veritable wall with linked strongholds. They never ended up being used, but despite being de facto abandoned, they still held their line. One of them, Fort Benjimma, was borrowed to serve Smiley's purpose.

The fort came complete with its own moat. While Smiley oversaw the training operation, he was not doing all the work himself. The MI6 apparatus kicked in to find staff for running the operation. Two of the men in charge of firearms training discovered that the moat was the perfect range: not only the proper size but also a natural silencer capable of muffling sounds from live-fire practice with submachine guns. Smiley, for his part, was not yet willing to give up direct action entirely. He provided the training in explosives.

Cover remained a problem. There was no reason for an officer of Smiley's rank to be wandering off to a disused fort. Why, in fact, was a cavalry officer on the island of Malta at all? He was given cover as a deputy chief of staff at the garrison headquarters in Valletta. This came with an office in what Smiley called "a lovely old building formerly belonging to the Knights of St. John [otherwise known as the Hospitallers]." The modern crusader had to put in an appearance at his "office" each morning, making himself visible by pointedly saying hello to everyone he saw before slipping out to his duties at the fort. Mostly, his cover was that of a not-very-hardworking cavalry officer, an image Smiley was only too happy to burnish through afternoon polo matches with royalty. Both he and Moy participated in the extensive social life expected of a field-grade officer and his wife.

Moy was in on the scheme far beyond attendance at dinner parties. The operation needed secure signals, and those required a cipher clerk with a security clearance. Moy already fit the bill, so she was given a refresher course and set up with her own equipment. The fact that she had just given birth in May to her third child, and David's first son (named Xan, after Fielding), was no hindrance. She declared, "We had a girl to help with the children, so there was no problem over that"—an appropriate acknowledgment but a nevertheless breezy take on the mental and physical acrobatics of running the ciphers for several hours before dawn, then maintaining the cover of an "ordinary officer's wife" in public, despite the odd sleeping hours.

The Pixies would need to be landed in Albania by ship. The Royal Navy was enlisted in the cause but only temporarily. Its job was to take groups of Albanians from Malta and transfer them at sea to a less conspicuous delivery vehicle, a sailing ship outfitted with an almost obscenely large engine and christened *Stormie Seas*.

Two Brits, Sam Barclay and John Leatham, served as the delivery pilots. Both were former naval officers who had done some unofficial gunrunning in their time. Wanting a lifestyle that afforded them independence, the pair had begun building a boat for charters. Approached by MI6, who paid for the engine, they were hired to deliver the Albanian scouting groups to the coast.

It helped that both men had previous experience doing clandestine landings. It also helped that Barclay's wife, Eileen, was available (along with their dog, Lean-To) to make the operation look slightly less suspicious. As Barclay put it, "If you find a yacht anywhere with just half a dozen men on board, it's a bit funny, a bit suspicious." It was also Eileen who distracted an irritated duo of Greek customs guards. Offering them cigarettes but realizing that she didn't have any, Eileen found herself in what might have been a stage comedy as a hand—fully belonging to a man who wasn't supposed to exist—extended out of the engine room, holding the promised gift.

The Italians, who had seen the transfer from the Royal Navy ship to the yacht, were angry. The ordinary Greek customs and naval officers knew nothing of Amery's agreement with the brandy-bearing arms dealer and his military contacts. In any situation, the Greeks and Albanians did not get along, with each frequently having designs on the other's territory. The Albanian men may have been going home, but they were well aware that they were going into hostile territory. Enver Hoxha's secret police, the Sigurimi, operated a reign of terror. The Pixies had been given new watches, which not only told time but also provided a convenient compartment, fastened to the inside of the wristband, for a cyanide pill.

It was imperative that the landings be made as quietly as possible, a difficult task, considering that one of the British trainers was almost certain that none of the Pixies had ever seen a boat before. The Albanians, despite their possession of a beautiful coast, were not a seafaring people. It was not for nothing that when he made his escape in 1944, Abas Kupi had to hire a Montenegrin captain. The Albanians had been trained, and would be landed, by two former Royal Marines. One of them, a man named Terence Cooling, always known as "Lofty," had delivered his fair share of raiding parties as a member of the Special Boat Section during the war. Along with a partner named Darby Allen, he would deliver the scouting teams to shore at the same point where Smiley and McLean had been evacuated after their first mission, the cove nicknamed Seaview.

The initial British operations took place in late September. Silence was of the essence. Even small transfer dinghies don't exactly roll all the way up onto a beach; one must still jump out into the water and walk ashore. But it would make no sense for men pretending to be shepherds to be caught with literal wet feet. As Cooling put it, "My job was going to be to piggyback them ashore, to make sure they didn't start on their first night's march going squelch, squelch."

The landing itself was successful, though some of the men suspected they'd seen a light that quickly shut back off. In all, the British landed six teams by the end of October. Smiley, his initial training job done, moved to another cover on the Greek island of Corfu to await the scouting parties as they came across the Greek border to report.

Of the six different teams that Smiley had trained, none came out intact. Of the first set to be landed, one group was ambushed near the village of Dukati, and all were killed; another group suffered significant losses and split up. Those who survived straggled across the Greek border. Meanwhile, at least one of the groups had managed to get a brief message off to Smiley via the wireless: they had been "expected."

For five months in 1949, after the Pixies started deploying to Albania, Smiley ran his safe house in Corfu. Much like the seaborne Greek customs officers to whom the mysterious hand had offered cigarettes, the Greek border guards had not been briefed about the sub-rosa Albanian deal. When several survivors came straggling across from Albania, it was Smiley's job to bail them out of Greek prison and make the necessary excuses. Meanwhile, he, Moy, and the children kept up their double lives, with Smiley appointed a new cover role at the local British Military Mission, which was liaising with the Greek forces battling Communist guerrillas.

The British Foreign Office claimed satisfaction with the operation, producing optimistic paperwork. Smiley and Alan Hare were beginning to get nervous. Hare, who ran the radio on Corfu, was concerned about the lack of contact. With the surviving Pixies now scrambling out of Albania, it was clear that there was a problem.

The Americans plowed ahead with their side of the plan. In Washington, it was called Operation Fiend, or Valuable Fiend. It would continue into the early 1950s, with Albanian teams being trained in Germany and parachuted into the north of the country. Smiley returned to his regiment in Germany.

Julian Amery, running for Parliament again and finished with his initial responsibilities in Operation Valuable, had returned to England. Peter Kemp had come out to Rome in the fall, continuing his liaison job with the Albanian leaders. But, as Smiley had noted years earlier, trouble tended to follow Kemp. His tuberculosis recurred. It may have been the result of an operation he underwent in Italy in which the doctors gave him too much ether that subsequently settled into his lungs. Or it might have been the reason for the surgery, though this was unlikely. Kemp was several years into his new marriage, so the procedure might have been done to treat infertility caused by a case of mumps in Kemp's youth. Either way, the tuberculosis sidelined him. He was pulled off the case, replaced by the man he had been sent out to relieve: John Hibberdine, his old companion from Kosovo.

Billy McLean had also wrapped up his work on Operation Valuable but was in Rome for other reasons. Declaring that Roman Catholicism was the only truly "grown-up" religion, he was waiting to be married off by a monsignor who had formerly served as a secretary to the pope. McLean's bride had once been declared "the Pearl of Dubrovnik," a moniker that ever after followed her in the British press. Her real name was Daška Kennedy. Born in Dalmatia to a family called Ivanović, she identified as Yugoslav, child of one fortune and stepchild of another. She had been raised partly in London and partly in Dubrovnik. Bilingual, beautiful, and immensely rich, she had ended up as Billy's seatmate at a dinner party in London. Enchanted, he asked to see her again. As she dropped him off on her way home from dinner one night, she found herself falling in love with him and he with her.

Her abrupt question—"How old are you?"—took McLean by surprise. He quickly answered, "Twenty-eight," only to realize the implications behind the query. He rapidly amended his response with, "And three quarters!"

He was probably not expecting hers: "Well, I'm thirty-two, and I'm married and have four children."

Neither was able to stay away from the other, though both were reluctant to break up a marriage. But the situation soon became untenable, and Daška filed for divorce. Her twin daughters, Marina and Tessa (upon birth, the girls, reflecting their mother's unofficial title, were referred to as "the seed pearls"), first met McLean in the back of a London taxi. Marina remembered nothing of Billy that day, but she did recall saying to her mother, "I've never seen you looking so happy!" Daška's divorce decree was officially issued that July 4, which she declared, in a telegram to McLean, as "Independence Day!" They were legally married at Caxton Hall and then, in November, wed at the Church of Saints Luca and Martina, just across from the ancient Roman Forum, by Daška's cousin, the monsignor. Two days later, they returned to London so that McLean could stand for his election campaign with Julian Amery.

In Germany, the failure of the Albanian mission gnawed at Smiley, who felt responsible for the men involved. There was a leak somewhere. But Smiley could not figure out where.

He would have no closure until 1963. That was the year in which a very senior former MI6 officer called Kim Philby defected to Moscow from his flat in Beirut. He betrayed both an astonished country and his own best friend, a man named Nicholas Elliott, who had been sent to take Philby in.

Philby was the most famous of the spies who became known as the Cambridge Five, friends who had been recruited at the eponymous university in the 1930s. Along with Philby, they included Donald Maclean,

Guy Burgess, Anthony Blunt, and John Cairncross. Nicknamed in his boyhood after a Rudyard Kipling character who is likewise a natural-born deceiver, Philby was the son of a prominent Arabist. Tall, intelligent, and successful, he played up a stammer, drank hard, and fooled everyone. He went through women like he did his liquor. Other spies have done it for money, for glory, for ideology, for protection. What Kim Philby got off on was deception itself.

In his self-aggrandizing memoir, *My Silent War*, he crowed about how he nearly got to the top of MI6. He ran counter-Soviet espionage operations while working for the Soviets. He had (proverbially) stabbed one of his own colleagues in the back to get the job that involved Albania: liaison between MI6 and the CIA. In his book, he implies that he had had a strong hand in the mission's failure. Friends with James Jesus Angleton, the CIA officer who would become the most famous mole hunter besides Senator Joseph McCarthy, Philby glided smoothly down the corridors of espionage and power. He and Angleton lunched each week at Harvey's, in Washington, DC. Years later, those involved came to the conclusion that Angleton accidentally "gave Philby over drinks the precise coordinates for every drop zone of the CIA in Albania."

This was an exaggeration: there was no reason why someone like Angleton would have had such technical operational details. For Smiley, it was very much enough. Thereafter, he blamed the failure of the operation on "that bloody man Philby."

There were certainly other reasons why the operation might have failed. It was not the best idea to use the same landing zone that SOE had used during the war. The Sigurimi, the Albanian secret police, had the country locked down tight. The locals may have been so afraid that they turned state's evidence the moment they realized something was happening. There were other security issues as well. While the Pixies had every reason to be as careful as possible—they were, after all, going into the lion's den themselves—recruiting from émigré communities is always challenging. As one intelligence officer put it, "Émigrés have few people to talk to, and you cannot trust them not to gossip." Someone else in Malta could have noticed it odd that a whole group of non-English-speaking men were lurking about an abandoned fort in Royal Pioneer Corps dress and gym shoes. There were also other governments involved. The more people there are with some sort of access to information, the greater the potential for a leak, or several leaks.

FOR SMILEY, THE EXPLANATION HINGING AROUND KIM PHILBY'S BE-trayal was so convincing because it felt so familiar. He had seen it before with James Klugmann, the NKVD agent stationed in the SOE staff offices of Cairo and Bari.

Klugmann, with his organized (if sometimes unwitting) fellow travelers in the office, had seen his desires realized: British policy shifted from supporting the royalist Mihailović in Yugoslavia to the Communist Tito, and from backing various groups in Albania to exclusively supporting Enver Hoxha's Communist Partisans. There were other factors that goaded Churchill into changing his mind about Yugoslavia, not the least of them being the Top Secret ULTRA decrypts. Like Philby with Operation Valuable, Klugmann could not claim complete credit for the coup. But neither man could be accused of not trying his utmost.

Klugmann was not satisfied by Tito's victory. In addition to his manipulation of the staff office, he himself had passed information to Tito's headquarters. He provided both specific military intelligence and broader advice. He told Tito and his men how to "adapt their tactics"— not against their enemies but with British officers in the field, like Churchill appointee Fitzroy Maclean. Klugmann told the Communists how to present the most attractive face to his own superiors, however false that image might be. He knew what the senior British officers were looking for, and by revealing what that was to Tito's men, he was setting the other British officers up to hear only what they wanted to hear.

Klugmann had been delighted on the "great day" in the spring of 1944 when SOE's headquarters had recalled all British missions to the Chetnik (nationalist, royalist, and conservative) resistance in Yugoslavia. Tito had already defeated the royalist leader Mihailović. Now he had captured him and was putting the royalist on trial for his life. A guilty verdict was guaranteed. No one doubted that the sentence would be execution.

Klugmann was incensed to learn that a few British officers who had served with the royalists were being allowed to send factual evidence in support of Mihailović. Those officers believed that he had been framed as a collaborator. Many downed American pilots spearheaded a Western mission to give evidence. Klugmann demanded to be able to send his own evidence, though he had never been in the field.

Why Klugmann felt the need to supply evidence against a man whose trial was fixed was unclear. Klugmann had been so clever, so subtle. Now his hand slipped ever so slightly.

MI5 was onto him again. His moves against Mihailović appeared to be the straw that would break the camel's back. But, again, Klugmann was lucky in his friends. Guy Burgess warned their shared handler that Klugmann had been recorded in damning conversation.

Then, Roger Hollis, head of MI5, received several phone calls from an officer in the upper reaches of MI6. The MI6 officer asked MI5 to wave off. There was really nothing to see here. He reminded Hollis of their conversation in a cover note to the transcripts examining Klugmann's attempts to testify against Mihailović. The MI6 officer signed his cover sheet "H. A. R. Philby." He was better known as Kim.

THE STORY OF THE CAMBRIDGE FIVE GAVE US *TINKER TAILOR SOLDIER SPY*, put on-screen with the brilliant Alec Guinness as John le Carré's master spy, George Smiley. It is a work whose fiction nevertheless very much reflects its own time, no more so than in the escapist fantasy of the mole's violent end. The Cambridge Five and Klugmann, by contrast, all got away with it.

In Britain, it was difficult to get a conviction without either having a confession or catching the perpetrator red-handed. This was the secret to the escape of the Cambridge Five spies, as opposed to the spy and later defector George Blake, who was convicted and incarcerated after his full confession. Blake somehow managed to break out of Wormwood Scrubs and make his way to Moscow. As the onetime Soviet handler of several of the Cambridge Five said of John Cairncross, the "atomic spy" whom Klugmann had recruited: "If [he] was never brought to trial, the reason must be that there was insufficient evidence to convict him. In other words, our side had done a first-rate job from beginning to end."

McLean, Smiley, Kemp, and Amery were certain of Klugmann's treason. They alluded to it in their memoirs and in interviews given years after. In 1975, Amery received a letter from a friend named Hugh Clifford, who had been a POW in Libya and Italy. He had escaped and ended up in some of the nasty fighting alongside Italian (Communist) Partisans in northern Italy near the end of the war. Clifford had noticed in Amery's 1973 autobiography the story of a Communist mole who'd had a Yugoslav agent killed. Clifford had also deduced that this was a reference to James Klugmann. He passed Amery a letter from their mutual friend Archie Jack, who had served with the Chetniks and had firsthand experience of Klugmann's machinations. Jack was, on this subject, utterly consistent: he told the same story when he was interviewed by the Imperial War Museums more than a decade later.

In addition to being a former officer and a combat veteran, Hugh Clifford also happened to be the thirteenth Lord Clifford of Chudleigh, member of an ancient family that had invaded England with William the Conqueror and, as dedicated Roman Catholics under a monarchy that turned to Protestantism, had suffered much for their beliefs. This furnished him with a seat in the House of Lords, a family history of principled stands, and a certain amount of protection from any blow-back over what he wanted to say. On February 26, 1975, in the Lords, Clifford told to Parliament the story of James Klugmann's treason and his role in the murder of the Yugoslav agent.

The story would surface again in 1996, when David Smiley and Basil Davidson, one of Klugmann's sympathizers in the Bari office, sparred publicly in the letters section of the *London Review of Books*. Those not in the Lords were never able to be very specific, or very aggressive. The public battles had an oddly restrained feeling to them, perhaps because the editor of the magazine had asked Smiley about "potential legal consequences" before publishing his correspondence. It was only in private, such as in Archie Jack's letter to Hugh Clifford, that the gut punches came out—as when Jack opened a newspaper in the mid-1950s to see a photo of Klugmann, boldly featured as a leader of the Communist Party of Great Britain. This decorum was due not to a lack of anger or conviction but to the British libel laws at which the editor had hinted. Safe from these, Clifford would be the only man ever able to call Klugmann a murderer—or a spy—in public while he still lived.

Though he did not feel the need to defect until 1963, Kim Philby was publicly accused as the "Third Man" of the Cambridge Five in 1955. MI5 had finally forced MI6 to dismiss him several years earlier, but Philby had stayed under the radar and was never charged with a crime. Infuriated by Philby's lack of punishment (the Americans executed moles like the Rosenbergs for far less), the FBI's J. Edgar Hoover slipped his name to a tame American journalist, who printed it. Soon after, Philby was named by a cantankerous Labour MP, Marcus Lipton, in Parliament. Philby's supporters insisted that Lipton repeat his charges "outside," by which they meant outside Parliament, where there was no immunity from lawsuit for either libel or slander. The whole affair generated a firestorm and required a response from the government in the House of Commons. But there was no "smoking gun" on Philby, as there almost never is in cases of espionage. Without a smoking gun, the

Secretary of State for Foreign Affairs was cornered into giving a speech exonerating Philby.

Upon his public "clearance," Philby gave a masterful press conference that, as the story goes, is still used for training by MI6. Philby invited reporters to his mother's house. Opening the door to an absolute throng at the appointed time, the master of deception exclaimed, "Jesus Christ! Do come in." Dashing and neat in a perfectly tailored suit, he grandly asked a male reporter seated near him if the newsman would give up his seat for a female reporter standing in the doorway. The man leaped up. Philby began talking. As the writer Ben Macintyre put it, "There was no trace of a stammer, no hint of nerves or embarrassment. Philby looked the world in the eye with a steady gaze and lied his head off." It was a brilliant performance.

Philby, threatening to sue Lipton, forced the MP to retract his earlier statements. But Lipton had been right, and the government had been wrong. Philby's elusive smoking gun finally showed up almost a decade later, and he defected in 1963 as one of the most successful and productive agents in the history of the USSR.

The Secretary of State for Foreign Affairs who had made the speech exonerating Philby was a man named Harold Macmillan. He was well known to McLean, Smiley, Kemp, and Amery. In January 1950, Amery had married his daughter.

One day in the spring of 1949, Amery had rung up the Macmillan household looking for his old friend Maurice, with whom he had attended Oxford. Maurice was out, but his sister Catherine answered the phone. Amery promptly asked her to lunch instead.

Catherine, seven years younger than Julian, was smart, charming, and pretty. Within two months, they were engaged, Amery having received a "clear and favourable" indication from the oracle at Delphi during his Greek mission to set up Operation Valuable. Billy McLean stood as best man.

Her father, Harold, would have to live out his life as the man who had declared that one of Britain's most notorious traitors, who later wrote a book crowing about his "achievements," was innocent. Amery, McLean, Kemp, and Smiley were intensely aware of pushing their arguments too far. Even after Klugmann's death, he had living associates like Davidson who could still sue them. As frustrating as the lack of prosecution against Klugmann might have been, bungling it in the manner of Philby would have been worse.

Klugmann spent many years after the war under surveillance by MI5, which at one point even tried to use John Cairncross to draw him into a confession. Yet in the bruising and demoralizing aftermath of not only the revelations surrounding the Cambridge Five but also the general decline of British power after the Suez Crisis, even MI5 was unwilling to name Klugmann as the "Sixth Man," though by either a literal or figurative accounting, he most certainly was. Clever as always, Klugmann held out: he would not sit for an interview with MI5, and he evaded Cairncross's attempts to snare him. But he ended up a sad and bitter man. Alienated from many of his fellows by his support of Stalin in the Stalin-Tito split, he became a more and more doctrinaire supporter of the Soviet Union. A gay but likely celibate man, "even his sexuality seems to have been repressed from an early age because of damage he perceived it would cause the Party." He died in 1977, alone and unrepentant, still carrying water for a system that killed millions in pursuit of what had always been both an impossible dream and an authoritarian nightmare—and failed.

CHAPTER 14

A SEAT OF MARS

Peter Kemp was woken from nightmares and fitful sleep by a sound that had haunted his dreams for twenty years: the slow, dull, inescapable rumble of approaching tanks. It was late October 1956, and he was in Hungary.

Both Kemp and the tanks—it was unclear if his dreams discerned make and model, but these were the ubiquitous Russian T-34s and T-54s—had arrived for what became known as the Hungarian Revolution. Unplanned, unorganized, and very nearly leaderless, it was a spontaneous eruption against not just Communism but the foreign domination of Hungarian Magyars by Russians. It had been triggered accidentally by the Russians themselves.

The death of Stalin three years earlier had caused a reckoning in the Soviet Union and its satellites in Eastern Europe. The ensuing power struggle in Moscow led first to the rise of the serial rapist and murderer Lavrentiy Beria and then to his much longer-lived successor, Nikita Khrushchev. It was Khrushchev who gave the "Secret Speech" to a closed session of the Communist Party Congress that denounced the excesses and, in Communist-speak, "errors" of Stalin's regime and prompted the movement known as de-Stalinization.

Like so many things intended to be secret, the contents of the speech spread like wildfire. The real-world implications arrived soon enough: not in Hungary but in Poland. There, a clever political operator named Wladyslaw Gomulka seized power. Gomulka was interested in reforms, but he was no democrat. When Khrushchev, panicked over a potential loss of control, threatened to send in the troops and flew to Warsaw, the Poles called the Russians' bluff. Gomulka went toe to toe with Khrushchev on the airport tarmac and informed the Soviet leader that he had no intention of renouncing either Communism or the Warsaw Pact, the USSR's false equivalent to NATO that helped control the countries shrouded by the Iron Curtain. Gomulka also informed Khrushchev that he had no intention of relinquishing power. Khrushchev let Gomulka be. A strong leader who could keep Poland under firm Communist control worked for Moscow.

The same was not to be in Hungary, which had labored under the dictatorship of Mátyás Rákosi for years. Rákosi's violence and repression have not earned the fame of his mentor Stalin's, but they should have: on a per capita basis, Hungary suffered under a comparatively vicious and dangerous cult of personality. One of Rákosi's habits was the encouragement of a secret police unit known as the AVO, which would play a large role in the revolution, and its repression.

De-Stalinization had set off a power struggle in Moscow that reverberated in Hungary. The Stalinist Rákosi was replaced with the Stalinist Ernö Gerö (the saying in Budapest was that "they have replaced a bald Rákosi with a thin one"). Gerö and Kemp had one thing in common: they had both fought in Spain and, strangely enough, against the same enemy. Gerö had been sent by Stalin to purge "Trotskyites" and in so doing became known as "the Butcher of Barcelona."

Gerö was in power on October 23 when Budapest broke into revolt. Spontaneous and leaderless, it was sourced from among the two groups most prized by the Soviets yet who, in Hungary, were nevertheless miserable: students and factory workers. It began at the radio station, where students demanded to have their Sixteen Points read on air. The AVO turned the protest into a bloodbath, and the revolution was on. Street fighting exploded across the city. The Hungarian military was called out. Tanks rolled through the ancient streets. Some of the military, including the most charismatic figure of the revolution, the Colonel (soon-to-be General) Pál Maléter, went over to the protesters.

The Russians had never left the satellites to defend themselves on their own. Tens of thousands of Soviet troops were already stationed in Hungary. They were Soviet tanks that fired on the civilians, and they were Soviet tanks that the civilians began to target. A tank is a formidable weapon, but a tank is most effective when it moves with infantry. A tank stuck in a narrow city street, with restricted movement and visibility, is a sitting duck. This the brave Hungarians rapidly discovered. They burned out tanks with Molotov cocktails, grabbed weapons from their own conscripted soldiers, and went to war. They began to call themselves "freedom fighters," a label casual and common now but new then. "That phrase originated in Hungary," Kemp wrote in 1976 in a barbed reference to several decolonization movements that had been hijacked by oppressive, and frequently Soviet-backed, regimes, "where it truly meant fighters for freedom, not, as it does today, any group of thugs with Kalashnikovs and a sense of grievance."

The streets were filled with young people hurling makeshift weapons at the tanks. Using underground passages and the buildings themselves to their advantage, the quick-moving revolutionaries rained fire down on their enemy. The "flower of youth" is an overused phrase, but on the streets of Budapest, it was true and in stark evidence. Children as young as twelve fought in the city's Corvin Passage. One fighter there, old among his peers at twenty-four, admitted that there were many times when he wanted to slip away and go home. "And I did start to go. But when I saw children, dead, I couldn't. I was in the services for two years. I know how to handle a gun. Am I going to leave these kids to die? The shame kept me there."

By the end of the month, thousands were dead in the streets. Atrocities raged: the civilians, venting a decade's worth of fury over repression by the secret police, killed AVO members who had been taken prisoner. They hung one man from his heels and set his body on fire. For their part, the AVO fired elsewhere on unarmed, peaceful protesters. They began to hunt the freedom fighters. By late October, the facades of the beautiful old buildings of Budapest already bore the bulk of the scars that many of them retain to this day. An enormous statue of Stalin was torn down, leaving only his bronze boots still standing. The revolution spread. Soon the revolutionaries held most of the country west of the capital, the territory known as Transdanubia.

The Russians were regrouping in more ways than one. The Russian tanks pulled out of the capital, and the Soviets appointed Imre Nagy—a committed Communist who had spent many years exiled in Moscow but was nevertheless a reformer popular among protesters—to lead the government.

Peter Kemp, meanwhile, was rushing to get to Budapest, hoping to make himself useful to a cause that he believed in, a habit he had established during his early days in Spain. By 1956, he officially worked for a life-insurance company, a position that both he and most observers found quite amusing, given how uninsurable his life always seemed. Yet the company turned a remarkably blind eye to Kemp's habit of traveling for reasons other than insurance sales, a tradition long appreciated and cultivated by British intelligence, with whom Kemp had many contacts. He soon got himself press credentials from a small Catholic weekly, *The Tablet*, and flew to Vienna. As he prepared to leave, he received a postcard with an excerpt from Ezra Pound's poem "An Immortality": "For I would rather have my sweet, / Though roses die of grieving, / Than do high deeds in Hungary / To pass all men's believing." He neglected to mention which friend sent it, but the lines provided no deterrence. Kemp was determined to go.

This was how he had found himself waking in Győr to the rumble of Soviet tanks heading west in order to seal off the border. He had been deposited in Győr, a city fairly close to the Austrian frontier, by a fellow British journalist whom he had come across in Vienna. Now he found himself another ride, with another Brit. This one was an opera singer named Nigel, optimistically en route to give a concert in Budapest.

"It'll be a hell of a squash," Nigel warned. He was also bringing along another British journalist (a young man who, as Kemp put it, produced such a look that "I forbore to ask the name of his paper"). Nigel was transporting, too, a young Hungarian couple, who were desperately trying to get to Budapest so that they could tend to the girl's dying brother, who had been fighting with the revolutionaries.

Shoved into the back of Nigel's Morris Minor, a very small economy car typical of 1950s British production, they made it to the capital after a harrowing experience with a drunk Russian soldier who nearly shot the two Hungarians at a checkpoint for reasons that never became known. Kemp had watched as the soldier unsteadily held his pistol, hammer cocked, just inches from his own face.

They were relieved by the arrival of a calm young Russian officer, who let them pass. Kemp arrived in Budapest in time to find one of his former SOE colleagues, Basil Davidson, in the capital. Davidson had reverted to his prewar career as a journalist. He was as declarative, as confident, and as wrong as ever.

"Everything's settled," said a very satisfied Davidson. "The Russian troops are pulling out. There's to be another conference tonight to discuss the logistics of withdrawal."

THE RUSSIANS BENEFITED NOT JUST FROM THEIR OWN RUTHLESSNESS but from another, unexpected source: a war in the Middle East. In late October, not long after the Hungarian Revolution had started, Israel attacked Egypt and occupied the Sinai in what initially looked like an extension of the skirmishes that the two countries had been engaged in for months. In fact, it was a concerted effort with both Britain and France to set the preconditions for a European invasion of the Suez Canal Zone. Gamal Abdel Nasser, then the leader of Egypt but in truth a trumped-up colonel who had participated in the coup that overthrew the hapless King Farouk only four years earlier, had nationalized the canal that July.

That day in London, Julian Amery, who'd been busy serving as a Conservative MP since his election in 1950 after the Operation Valuable debacle, had a full schedule. At his home in Eaton Square, he hosted a lunch that was attended by other Conservatives; the prime minister of Iraq, Nuri al-Said; and Billy McLean, who had also been keeping busy as a Conservative MP, having won a seat in 1954 for Inverness, Scotland. After lunch, Amery was walking to Parliament with a colleague when they ran into a group of people on the street who asked, "Have you seen the tape?" Rushing to the House of Commons, they learned the news off the wire: Nasser had nationalized the Suez Canal.

It was a possibility that both Amery and McLean had been fighting against for years. The Suez Canal, built by a Frenchman named Ferdinand de Lesseps in the late nineteenth century, snaked 101 miles through the shoulder that connects Africa to Arabia. It reduced the journey from England to India by a third; through it flowed much of Europe's Middle Eastern oil supply. Caught up in the pressures of decolonization and Nasser's coup, the British government had worked out a deal just two years earlier that produced a timetable for withdrawing British forces, who had been stationed in Egypt since Admiral Lord Nelson's time, from the Canal Zone. The nationalist forces in Egypt whom Nasser claimed to represent saw any British presence as imperialism. Men like Amery and McLean saw the lurking hand of Soviet influence (Nasser would soon accept Soviet-made weapons from Czechoslovakia) and an attempt to create a dangerous power vacuum that would harm British interests.

Amery had opposed the measure that agreed to withdraw British troops from the Canal Zone by June 1956. The agreement indicated that

Britain would be allowed to return troops in the event of an emergency, but Amery presciently noted that "it can be quite difficult to stay put in a place, but it will be a damned sight more difficult to get it back." He was correct: Nasser nationalized the canal a month later.

Amery's objection was joined by McLean's. Making his own maiden speech (Amery thought it "much the best speech of the debate") in the House of Commons that spring, McLean had told the legend of the last Nasrid sultan of Granada. Having lost the city to the Spanish Catholic Reconquista, he wept over his loss on a hill outside the city, his eyes lingering on the prize that he had lost. Beside him, his mother admonished, "Well may you weep like a woman for what you could not defend like a man." McLean ended the speech pointedly: "Let that never be said of us in this country."

It was this conclusion that ruined his friendship with Anthony Eden, then the prime minister. Eden had presided over the Suez negotiations and evacuation. Eden had also been in the Foreign Office when Amery, McLean, and Smiley were in Albania; it was he to whom they had attempted to appeal to save Abas Kupi (and who characteristically declined to take a decision after they had landed back in Italy, sending them to the military authorities instead). Eden was a Conservative highflier with a reputation that often outmatched his skill. Handsome, highly intelligent, and extremely well educated, Eden was overshadowed by the domineering figure of Winston Churchill, his own indecisiveness and effeminacy, and a serious addiction to methamphetamines. He also had a thin skin. Eden congratulated McLean on his speech (in public he could do no other); in private he never spoke to him again.

When both McLean and Amery heard of the joint invasion of Suez, they were encouraged. Perhaps now the earlier mistake would be rectified. In government but not in the Cabinet, they weren't privy to secret negotiations. The Israelis, the French, and the British had made a deal. The Israelis would attack the Sinai and trigger the clause that allowed the British to reoccupy the Canal Zone. But a day later, the operation was over. The French, who loathed Nasser's encouragement of the rebels fighting for independence from France in Algeria, wanted to continue the assault. But the British government had backed down, forcing the French to do so as well. It was a humiliation of the highest order, one brought about at the hands of the Americans, who had demanded a halt. As Winston Churchill later put it, "I don't know whether I should have dared to start. I would never have dared to stop."

Amery was mortified. Running into a Cabinet member named Selwyn Lloyd in the halls of Parliament, he snapped, "How's the second Bordeaux Government feeling?" Lloyd turned back and said, "We reckoned with Soviet hostility. We never thought the Americans would be with us but I had not reckoned on their open hostility."

The Eisenhower administration, which was happy to work with Britain in Europe but hostile to Britain's interests elsewhere, had thrown down its cards. The Americans threatened a run on sterling. Eden caved. As one British diplomat later put it to Kemp in a comment by no means limited to Hungary, by the end of that fateful autumn week it became clear that "the last great revolt of the satellites is over."

THE REST OF THE JOURNALISTS STARTED LEAVING HUNGARY IN DROVES. Suez was now the big story; Budapest seemed to be, as Basil Davidson had so smugly declared, all settled. While the United States had always insisted that British imperial adventure in Suez had prevented it from being able to support the Hungarians properly (how could it complain about one colonialist adventure while its allies indulged in another?), Kemp had always denied that Suez was the distraction that prevented the West from helping in Hungary. The real issue seemed to be the short attention span, and queasy stomach, of the West. Despite the aggressive pronouncements of Radio Free Europe, the Eisenhower administration, up for reelection in a matter of days, had no intention of starting an entanglement, or engaging in something that could start World War III, in either Europe or the Middle East. It was unfair, as one saying went at the time, to say that "the Americans were willing to fight communism to the very last Hungarian," though one could see how the freedom fighters felt betrayed.

Kemp realized, bitterly, that although the freedom fighters' war against what he saw as some of the worst and longest-lasting oppression since the Mongols had earned the admiration of the world, their support would stop at admiration only. There would be no troops, no supply drops, no help. The Hungarians fought alone, in Milton's phrase, "preferring hard liberty before the easy yoke." They died for it. They had no weapons and little training but a host of courage. In the industrial suburb of Csepel, they fought to the last bullet, and the workers organized strikes for weeks and weeks thereafter. But it was not enough.

In the early morning of November 4, the Soviets rolled back into Budapest. This time, they came with the tanks, the infantry, the artillery, and even the planes. Russian MiGs swooped over the city, adding a new terror from above. Though no one knew it yet, the leaders of the Hungarian government, including the heroic General Maléter, had been detained. Along with Nagy, who had sought refuge in the Yugoslav Embassy, they would later be executed. So would almost anyone who had dared fight against the regime.

Stirred this time by machine-gun fire and shell explosions, Kemp was still in Budapest. As the Russians crushed the revolution, the remaining journalists, Kemp officially among them, were ordered to stay in the British Embassy, for fears that the Russians would target them in reprisal. They did not. But after a week, the fighting was over. The slaughter, however, went on.

Most of the remaining journalists now left. Kemp stayed, ostensibly to report on the blooming repressions. The relieved ambassador said, "As long as a few of you chaps can hang on here, the Hungarians won't feel themselves completely abandoned."

The repressions were brutal. It was said that in the aftermath perhaps fifty thousand Hungarians had been killed, both in the fighting and also in the repressions that followed. The AVO ruthlessly hunted all who had questioned their power.

Their victims were either executed or shipped off to hard labor camps. Age lent no mitigation: some children would be held until their eighteenth birthdays, only to be executed, like pigs slowly fattened before the slaughter. For some of them, the wait was years on a teenage death row, absent either appeal or hope. On the radio, Kemp heard of the hanging of one seventeen-year-old girl, condemned for killing the Soviet soldiers who had invaded her city. Her name was Erzsébet Mengyi. He could still recall it decades later.

A few weeks later, Kemp received a phone call from a contact whose name he never put into writing. Kemp was nominally still in Budapest under a reporter's cover, but he had yet to file any stories. He blamed this on telegraph lines no longer working, which made cost-prohibitive long-distance phone lines the only way to get stories out. Yet someone was still paying for Kemp's keep and, crucially, for his very difficult-to-get rental car, as well as the equally elusive fuel to fill it. Like his insurance firm, the newspaper providing his credentials was also willing to look the other way, another tradition long appreciated by British intelligence.

"I have something to show you, if you are interested in the Russian repressions," said the unnamed contact to this very unusual journalist, who was collecting information in a war zone but not producing anything for publication.

Kemp followed the instructions of the contact and found himself in a tiny one-room apartment facing three young people whose soft faces were prematurely aged by the experiences of the last few weeks. Two boys and one girl, they looked haunted, horrified, scared: once predators, they were now prey. If he never again saw children as terrified as these three, Kemp thought, he could be satisfied with the work he had done in the world.

They had been sentenced to hard labor, his contact explained. Hungarian partisans had derailed their deportation train, and in the ensuing confusion, they had managed to escape. But now they were being carefully stalked by the AVO, and even their own families would not take them in. An earlier escapee from the train had been beaten to death in front of them. Now here they were, back in the heart of Budapest, but they could not hide in plain sight for long. The city was patrolled by Soviet troops, Hungarian troops acting under Soviet orders, and by the AVO themselves. They were marked men. Streets, and especially the crucial bridges over the wide, blue Danube that splits the city in two (a divide from which it receives its name—Buda and Pest are on either side of the river), were policed by checkpoints. There was no free movement. Papers were required everywhere. The only hope was to flee: first to Győr, close to the Austrian border, and then to the West.

Kemp's contact introduced the oldest boy as Balázas, their leader. A medical student, he was nineteen years old. The other boy, Dénés, was a mechanic's apprentice. Magdi, the contact explained, was Dénés's fiancée.

"Good God!" Kemp exclaimed, eyeing the small, plump girl, still pretty despite the evident strain on her face. "How old are they?"

"Seventeen and sixteen. Our people marry very young these days, you know."

Yet they seemed like such children. In an alternate life, perhaps a gentler one not mired by war, they could have been *his* children. He had turned forty-one that August. Married twice, he was unable to have children of his own. He knew what was coming next.

"Time is running out for them," his contact said. "Is there *anything* you can do to help get them out?"

WHEN HE HAD TOLD THE BRITISH AMBASSADOR THAT HE WAS GOING to stay, the diplomat had reminded Kemp of one very important thing:

the NKVD, the Soviet secret police, had a file on him from his time in that Polish prison. Then, the Soviets had merely been trying to keep the SOE team from reporting inconvenient information during the Yalta Conference. Kemp's questionable presence in Budapest as a journalist would not likely end with a similarly benign release. Last time, he had been treated to a drive-by of the infamous, looming Lubyanka, the NKVD's central secret prison in Moscow. This time, if caught, he might well become a resident there.

The ambassador's warning about the NKVD's file rang in his head. Any presumed spy caught in the country at this moment would be shot. Any attempt to evacuate the trio would require proceeding through dozens and dozens of checkpoints. The border might be closed. Getting involved would be an extreme risk.

The haunted faces of the three children stared back at him. He had seen those eyes before. He had been a soldier for many years. He had followed orders that he found odious to further the good of the mission. Those were the eyes of the Northern Irish deserter from the Republican ranks that his Spanish Foreign Legion detachment had captured during the Spanish Civil War. Unfortunately for the deserter, the Nationalists had just recently decided to apply the same rules as the Republicans: they were going to shoot all non-Spaniards who had come into the country to fight for their enemies.

Kemp was given the job of overseeing the execution precisely because he had argued against it. His colonel had sent two legionnaires behind him to make sure that he ordered his own men to finish the job. Walking beside the man from Belfast, Kemp explained, miserably, that he had failed to win his reprieve. He would have to have him shot.

"Oh my God," whispered the man, barely audible. It was the voice of simultaneous shock and recognition, the voice that Kemp would hear not ten years later on the lips of Edith Fournier as he told her of the death of her partner, François Klotz.

Those were the closed yet defiant eyes of the young Polish machine gunner who had saved Kemp from the Nazis, and from a fate even worse than that of the NKVD prison, on another morning when Kemp woke to the muted siren of lumbering tank treads. Not far down the road were four German tanks—and one hundred German soldiers, an entire company.

Ordered to retreat so that they might salvage the intelligence apparatus of the mission, Kemp and his team ran for the tree line. "If there is any more disagreeable experience in warfare than that of running away under fire, I hope I never meet it," Kemp later remarked. They would have been wiped out by a single well-aimed burst from one of the tank's machine guns, but those guns had been occupied. An intrepid, and very young, Polish soldier had taken up a strategic point with his Bren, a British-made light machine gun. Along with a few other Polish riflemen, who numbered not more than twenty-five in total, he attacked. Kemp could hear the characteristic sound of the Bren. And then he could hear it no more.

Kemp and the team escaped. The Germans, stunned by the level of resistance, slowed their approach. The Poles got away with a single casualty: the young Bren gunner. He had been killed instantly by a burst from one of the tank guns.

They buried him at first light the next morning. As his body, wrapped in the Polish flag, was lowered and the dirt slowly shoveled in snug around his cold, lifeless form, Kemp wondered how they "could hope to justify this man's sacrifice for our safety." The grave began to fill as the chill Polish sunlight made the red rims of their eyes that much more glaring. And then, remembered Kemp, "we felt the full shame and bitterness of our flight." They could not even notify the young man's family, who lived too far east, past the line that demarcated Soviet control. As Kemp knew bitterly, that fateful line was named not for a Pole or even a Russian but for a British diplomat, George Curzon. The son's grave was marked with only a little wooden cross. Poland was not Sparta. Still, Kemp thought that he deserved the epitaph for the three hundred at Thermopylae, who had fought bravely against equally hopeless odds.

A little wooden cross, too, had been the final marker for the barely twenty-five-year-old François Klotz. The Viet Minh, not satisfied to see Klotz dead, face down on that little river ramp into the Mekong, continued to cross the river to steal his cross time and time again. Klotz, who had died in Kemp's arms, whom Kemp, despite his best attempts, had failed to save. There were the members of his first Commando team, wiped out on a raid along the French coast that he should have been on but that a combat injury had prevented him from joining. There were his Albanian interpreters, sacrificed by his command to the demands of their "ally" Enver Hoxha, who only grew into a more and more brutal Communist dictator. There was the Spanish Civil War soldier who had given up his spot in the hospital in deference to the Englishman who had come so far to help, only to die in the ambulance that evacuated him. And there was his own brother, lost when German Stukas bombed HMS *Illustrious* in the Sicilian Channel. So many of them were young, some many years younger than he. Kemp was weary of surviving better men.

HE LOOKED AT THE THREE FREEDOM FIGHTERS HUDDLED ON THE BED. He had been forced to abandon allies before. He had failed to save his friends. The whole world had deserted the Hungarian rebels. There was no cavalry coming, no fifth column to save them. But whatever mysterious source was behind Kemp's expense account, there were no official superior orders here. He had what many sensitive special operators are designed to have: deniability. There was no one's neck on the line but his own.

"Now, I have a suggestion for you: I am willing to drive you in my car to Győr," Kemp said. "There is a possibility that when they see my

British flag the guards at the checkpoints will let us through; there is the further chance that if they do stop us they will be satisfied with my British passport and press card, and won't bother about anyone else in the car. I have seen that happen before. I admit it's a pretty desperate gamble and you may very well be caught. So if you have any other plan of escape I strongly advise you to stick to that. Otherwise, if you'd like to try your luck with me, you're welcome."

It was a Hail Mary of the highest order, but it was the only chance they had. They leapt up to shake his hand. He told them to be ready in an hour.

What followed was a journey of modest distance but epic terror. Kemp, at the wheel, first could not find the students at the rendezvous point. They claimed he was late (Kemp was not naturally the most punctual of men), but they had also been scared off by the presence of a Russian patrol. They had good reason to be nervous; they had seen an escapee beaten to death by the AVO. Finally collecting them, Kemp began the drive out of Budapest.

It was at a checkpoint on the Kossuth Bridge, crossing the wide Danube, where they first ran into trouble. There was Kemp, once again trying to cross a river with young allies. Once again, he had no choice but to bluff his way through. His only hope could be that this time would be more successful than the last, when François Klotz had died in his arms on the banks of the Mekong.

The checkpoint was manned by the Russians, who had an AVO official alongside them. Kemp's blood pressure could not have been improved by the visible concern of his passengers, whom he barely knew and whose ability to keep their cool he'd had little opportunity to assess. "Angliski journalist," he called out, handing his passport to the Russian soldier and cavalierly removing his hat to assist in identification. When questioned as to his destination, he glibly answered, "The Ministry for Foreign Affairs," where he did at least often have occasion to call in.

Sweating as his papers were looked over by the AVO officer, Kemp lit a pipe to add to the air of nonchalance, though "my mouth was so parched that smoking it was out of the question." As the Russian soldier handed back his passport, Kemp spied the AVO man looking more closely at the car. From a distance, the policeman would not have noticed the passengers, but if he approached, he would soon realize that they were not all English. Betting it all, Kemp took the initiative. "Thank you very much!" he called in his posh English accent as he let out the clutch. They rolled through the checkpoint unmolested.

There were more to come but none as terrifying as this. In what seemed a comedy of errors, the car's axle broke while crossing railroad ties west of the city. They were quickly rescued, first by a group of workers who towed the car and then by a pair of Red Cross men who escorted them to the town of Szony and made arrangements for the students to get to a lightly inspected railway station, where the train would take them to Vienna. After another hair-raising incident in which the students nearly missed the train when they panicked at the sight of a Russian tank near the platform, they were safely swept out of the country. Kemp gave them the address of a friend in Vienna, who called two days later. "Your pals have arrived. They're staying with us here for the moment. They're a grand bunch and the little girl's a smasher—you dirty old man!"

SOMEONE, SOMEWHERE, HAD DECIDED THAT KEMP WAS NOT THE SORT of journalist they wanted in Hungary. The next time he called at the Ministry for Foreign Affairs to renew his visa, his application was denied. It was mid-December, and a blizzard was howling. It was noon as he approached the desk for what he thought had become routine paperwork.

"Permission to renew it has been refused. You must leave today," Kemp was told. The blizzard would earn him no respite. He would have to move himself across the 130 miles to the frontier, but his little rental car had not yet been repaired. Protesting got him nowhere.

"That's your problem. But heaven help you, Mr. Kemp, if you are still in this country after midnight."

The British Embassy came to his rescue. Not wanting either the bad press or the headache of having to bail him out of the Hungarian version of the Lubyanka, the British Embassy provided both car and driver. In the midst of the blizzard, they barreled across the roads toward the Austrian border. They made it with fifteen minutes to spare.

CHAPTER 15

LORD OF THE
GREEN MOUNTAIN

Uniform soaked straight through with sweat and dark glasses fogged, David Smiley thought ruefully about how he had been towing his children on skis over twelve feet of frozen Baltic—with his car—a mere weeks beforehand. The country he now found himself in contained an area rumored to be the hottest place in the world. Called the Elphinstone Inlet, its heat could kill a man, drive him mad, or both. This was Oman, 1958. It was one of the princely kingdoms on the shores of the eastern corner of Arabia once known as the Pirate Coast, and Smiley was the new commander of the armed forces of the Sultan himself.

It was a job far more challenging, and significantly less grand, than it looked on paper. The challenge involved a guerrilla war in a desert dotted with nearly insurmountable mountains and roads littered with the insurgents' mines. As for the grandeur, when the Sultan promoted Smiley from Chief of Staff to Commander, or Caid, he did so on the basis of putting Smiley in charge of not just his army but his air force and navy as well. This expanded Smiley's arsenal by the grand array of two Pioneer airplanes and what Smiley called "the single motor launch that comprised his navy."

Smiley was in Oman courtesy of the new Undersecretary of State for War, Julian Amery. Both Amery and Billy McLean were still serving in Parliament, having been elected in 1950 and 1954, respectively. Peter Kemp was still officially employed in the insurance industry, where his firm still turned a blind eye to his continued unofficial intelligence roles. Smiley, meanwhile, continued his rise in the British Army.

Amery had been faced with a dilemma. Oman was one of the poorest countries in the world. The Sultan, Said bin Taimur, did not even allow hospitals in his domain on the grounds that both he and his country were too poor, and that saving lives to grow the population would only lead to starvation (though he did permit the establishment of a small clinic run by a few missionaries, which he did not have to pay for). But Oman had been, and still was, strategically crucial to Britain for two reasons, one old and one new. First, its coasts guarded the route to India. This was the reason behind the long-running British association with Oman's sultan, a relationship that went back more than a century. Oman's neighbors to the north were then called the Trucial States, after the agreement that stopped their depredations on British shipping by offering sufficient incentives, both carrot and stick. The piracy eventually waned. (The Trucial States later became the United Arab Emirates.) With India now independent from Britain, the significance of Oman in the 1950s had a new and far richer basis: oil.

As Amery put it when opponents of British involvement in Oman complained: "No oil, no welfare state. No oil, no pensions." Oil, or at least the Buraimi Oasis, a section of land attractive to prospecting, was the source of Amery's dilemma. The Saudi government had staged a small invasion of the oasis several years before. They were backed by the Americans, who were betting on a Saudi victory, and thus access to the oil for themselves. Negotiations in Geneva fell through when, as one of Smiley's junior officers put it, the Saudis attempted to make up for "their lack of cogent legal argument by a liberal distribution of cash," a perfectly acceptable tradition at home that was unsuitable on the international stage. The small conflict in the Buraimi Oasis continued. It intersected with another, longer-standing tension in Oman: that of the competition between the Sultan (whose control was primarily along the coasts) and the Imam (whose mountain tribes occupied the interior). The new Imam, a man known as Ghalib bin Ali, had a brother, Talib, who happened to be a gifted insurgent commander. Together, backed by Saudi money and American equipment, they were challenging the government of the Sultan, Britain's ally.

Amery had already visited the Sultan and had been involved with the Oman problem for some time. He had been unimpressed by the Sultan's former commander. For many years, the Sultan had employed British officers seconded from Her Majesty's armed forces to command his troops, some of whom were locals (mistrusted by the Sultan) and most of whom were men recruited from Baluchistan, part of modern-day Pakistan. The erstwhile British commander had not only failed to conquer the rebels but had also gotten his forces chewed up in the process. Amery, in a scathing nod to his own World War II experience, had considered that former commander not just unfit for the job but "essentially a staff officer." He had a better man in mind.

That was how Smiley, on leave from his job as military attaché in Sweden (as an intelligence officer, he had posed his beautiful wife, Moy, on bridges across the country in order to photograph and document them for potential demolition purposes in the event of a Soviet invasion), found himself recruited by Amery for a job half a world away.

To give Smiley's predecessor credit, Oman was a difficult operational environment, starting at the top. The Sultan was a complex and sometimes contradictory figure. On the one hand, he was a charming and exceedingly well-educated man. (Smiley himself said that the ruler "spoke an English so faultless that it could never have come from an Englishman"; he had learned that spotless English at a boys-only boarding school often dubbed "the Eton of India.") On the other hand, he was neither decisive nor charismatic, both distinct challenges for a leader, especially one under pressure. His typical canned response to Smiley's suggestions for improvement, innovation, or both consisted of two paired phrases that Smiley ever after associated with him: "I see, Colonel Smiley, I see. I will think about it." When Smiley requested permission to train some of the Sultan's own men for higher ranks so that he would not have to rely on British officers, the Sultan firmly refused. "You must know, Colonel Smiley," he said, "that all revolutions in the Arab world are led by colonels. That is why I employ you. I am having no Arab colonels in my army."

The Sultan presided over abysmal conditions. He eschewed almost all modernization but had an extensive prison, known as Jalali, where he kept both criminals and political prisoners. Smiley was so appalled by the state of the prison that he issued extra water rations to his own men, who guarded the exterior, so that they could slip hydration to the desperate prisoners inside. But despite directing such cruelty, the Sultan was also curiously gentle-mannered and easily embarrassed. He refused to spend much time in front of his subjects because his budget did not allow for the largesse of giving the sorts of gifts expected on state occasions. He was a proper man who liked to thank Smiley with presents, such as silver coffeepots and an incense burner, all manufactured in London by Mappin & Webb.

The Sultan was correct in his suspicions that men drawn from the local population did not make the most effective fighters. The soldiers from Baluchistan were better, but the British officers commanding them often encountered language barriers. Many of the officers working in Oman spoke some Arabic, but the days when many British officers boasted fluency in the various tongues of the empire were long gone. One junior officer who had been assigned Baluchi troops rummaged through the bookshops in Bloomsbury when home on leave. Near the British Museum, he found, to his delight, a dusty old hole-in-the-wall whose proprietor had a box of mint-condition books titled *A Grammar of the Baloochee Language*, printed in the 1880s. He bought half a dozen and took them back to Muscat, where "at last we could communicate with our soldiers."

As Smiley pointed out, the Baluchi troops were brave and excellent defenders, though they needed to be well led in attacks. But misunderstandings inevitably occurred. The one instance of what technically may have been desertion in the face of the enemy was better labeled, Smiley thought, "a misunderstanding." Faced with the offender after the fact, Smiley was treated to the following angry defense: "When I joined this army, Sahib, it was not explained to me that I should have to fight!"

The heart of Smiley's military challenge was the Jebel Akhdar, or the Green Mountain. The Jebel Akhdar lay in the north-central sector of Oman, part of the ridge of mountains running up and down the coast that forms the softly sloping half U just south of the Strait of Hormuz, across the Gulf of Oman from Iran, where Smiley had briefly served during the Second World War, when that country was still commonly called Persia. The Jebel was called "green," though it was anything but. One of Smiley's young Arabic-speaking officers thought the color designation of the local mountains (there were red and black jebels too) had to do with the way that colors were described in the language itself. The Jebel was not green: it was yellow, and orange, and light brown, and beige, and all the other colors that made up the sharp rocks that could cut even good boots to shreds in days. But it was, apparently, more green than much else around, and so the "green mountain" it was.

The Jebel rose out of a formidable plain flanked with wadis and small valleys and difficult approaches. The villages surrounding it were hostile. The roads and passages were literally explosive, courtesy of mines. The reason for the military focus on the Jebel rested at the very top. There the three leading rebels—Ghalib, the Imam; his brother, the insurgent commander Talib; and their local ally Suleiman—were comfortably ensconced in their headquarters, having fled to the peak after Smiley's predecessor had failed to defeat or capture them. The Jebel was larger in area than Cyprus. Its cliffs were made of sheer rock face. The only paths up were suitable for very nimble goats and little else; they were so narrow and so littered with rocks that to hold the pass against even a massive army would not have required the legendary three hundred Spartans who had held the pass at Thermopylae. These passes could be held, as one of Smiley's officers said, by "two men and a boy."

The Jebel was widely considered to be impregnable. The last time that it had been successfully assaulted was under the Persian Empire, nearly a thousand years before. It took an entire army to mount an assault that conquered the defenders at the top only by taking a level of casualties acceptable to despots and slave-drivers, which many of their enemies had accused the Persians of being. But Smiley had no such man-wasting inclinations, and no such resources. He also had to contend with something the ancient Persians had found more manageable: the climate.

To say that Oman was hot was an understatement. Temperatures regularly reached 100 degrees Fahrenheit in the shade and 125 in the sun. British troops stationed in Oman and in the surrounding Gulf areas were forbidden from serving for more than two months straight. This system, much to Smiley's chagrin, did not apply to officers. Forty-five of the fifty British troops on loan to Smiley for an operation had to be evacuated over time for heat exhaustion; two others died. Shorts were forbidden in public in deference to local custom. Air-conditioning was rare; most troops lived in tents. There they contended with spiders eight inches long that came equipped with two waving arms to catch prey in addition to the traditional six appendages of the arachnid family, with a beak like an octopus with which to consume their meals. One officer said, upon seeing his first emerge from a crack in a wall, that "if I had been alone I would have forsworn alcohol from that day on." There were also the scorpions. Smiley found a colony living in his lavatory, which at the time was an unplumbed palm hut. While he waited for a regular toilet to be installed (the first of its kind in the area), he "had to share this lavatory—and on several occasions nearly the seat" with the scorpions.

In a frustrating turn of karma for Smiley, his army was attacked by the mines on the roads. Given that one of the tasks of the Sultan's armed forces was to provide safe roads for the oil company's trucks, this was a problem. At first, the issue was expensive and frustrating but not lethal. Only 158 were detonated during the Jebel operations, and they killed more camels and donkeys (five) than humans (three). One was even set off by a thrown stone.

Still, they damaged vehicles and stuck a thorn in the side of military and oil operations. The small mines that the Saudis were supplying to the rebels would blow the wheels off Smiley's vehicles, but the harm tended to be isolated to the vehicles alone. When the mines began to get larger—these were well-made American mines—the destruction was more serious. Smiley had several close calls in convoys. In a letter to Amery, still Undersecretary of State for War, he requested "more mine detectors," as he was in "an excellent place for live trials."

For his part, Julian Amery had been spending a frustrating amount of time fending off hand-wringing from the Foreign Office, which was concerned that British involvement in Oman would lead to charges of imperialism in the United Nations. The late 1950s were still a moment when even many conservative diplomats of the Western powers believed the United Nations to be more substantial than the talking shop and anti-Western echo chamber that it would ungracefully age into as the Cold War dragged on. In response to a friend and colleague warning of UN opprobrium, Amery replied, "Don't mind much."

Working on a plan to eliminate the rebels, their mines, and their commanders atop the Jebel, Smiley regularly kept Amery apprised of both progress and challenges. He sent an ambitious shopping list. He wanted armored-car units (like the ones he had briefly served with in another desert during the Second World War). Possibly thinking of the soldier who had seemed confused about the relationship between armies and fighting, Smiley also asked for more regular British troops to add to the few already on loan. Told that regulars were hard to come by, Smiley simply upped his offer: Could he please have a single squadron of the SAS?

The SAS was the Special Air Service. It was founded during the Second World War by an extremely intrepid young officer named David Stirling. Early in the war, his older brother had been one of Peter Kemp's colleagues in the Commandos, and Stirling himself had once been one of Kemp's students at a special-operations training school in Scotland. Stirling had designed the SAS as an airborne hit squad to target German and Italian forces behind the lines in the Western Desert. He and his men destroyed so many enemy planes during night raids that one wit suggested Stirling be awarded the Distinguished Flying Cross. Though Stirling had insisted that his men have airborne training, the SAS stopped doing combat jumps after a disastrous initial one during the war. But it had retained the name and ever since proved the mettle of its members in intense combat all over the world.

Amery sent two SAS squadrons. En route home from the insurgency in Malaya, they were well trained, combat-rich, and heat-acclimated. One officer who worked with them said, "They were the coolest and most frightening body of professional killers I have ever seen—the ordinary Commandos were perfect gentlemen in comparison. A company of these battle-hardened toughs was worth a regiment of infantry and probably a division of our staunch but stolid and unintelligible Baluchis." For Smiley, they were soon to once again make good their motto: "Who Dares, Wins."

Despite the increasing involvement of the RAF (the value of the planes blasting propaganda became questionable when the rebels sent down a message saying that the speakers were faulty, and bombing was no more a panacea then than it is now), it became clear that the only way to get the insurgents off the mountain would be to walk right up there and take it from them. Smiley began to assemble everything his growing assortment of troops might possibly need. There were the Baluchis and the locals of the Sultan's Armed Forces, the Trucial Oman Scouts, a set of Life Guards with their Ferret scout cars, some Royal Marines, and the SAS. There was also a drove of little Somali donkeys. (They were purchased as pack animals but, despite Smiley's best intentions, would turn out to be useful in only one very surprising way.) The operations against the rebels increased. The flights continued. The rebels began to get nervous.

Someone had found a way up the mountain. It was a very small track, but the SAS operators were willing to climb it. The donkeys were assembled, ready to resupply the men making the assault. They carried both loads of ammunition and, ever crucially, water, of which there was none on the ascent. By then, Smiley had had to recruit stronger Omani mountain donkeys, as the Somali ones were too small and weak.

It would be a combined land and air assault, with planes strafing any visible pockets of resistance and two medical evacuation helicopters on standby. But most of the work would be, as Smiley put it, "a straight slog up the mountain face." They would begin at 8:30 p.m. Then, just days before the assault, one of Smiley's intelligence officers came up with a brilliant plan to deceive the enemy.

"I'm prepared to bet," said the officer, "that if we call leaders of the donkey men together on the night before the assault and tell them in strictest confidence and under the most ferocious penalties that the following night they'll be leading their donkeys up the Tanuf track, Talib will have the news within twenty-four hours." The moles did the intelligence officer one better. Talib had the erroneous news in twelve hours.

Slog up the mountain they did. It was a journey that took nearly twelve hours of hard climbing. Faced with a cliff that previous scout units had found impassable, the SAS operators rigged rappelling ropes and slipped right on down. Enemy resistance collapsed completely in the face of the brilliant deception plan, the unstoppable SAS, and the sight of parachuted supplies, which the rebels mistook for paratroopers. Ironically, the supplies were only dropped because of the uselessness of the little Somali donkeys, who proved to be accidentally worthy in the end.

Smiley evacuated two SAS casualties by helicopter, which landed under mortar fire. Smiley's forces suffered few casualties, though both of these SAS men later died. His troops overran the mountain and its hinterland. Though the three rebel leaders escaped, control was safely back in the hands of the Sultan and his British supporters. The local leader, Suleiman, was so "criminally careless," as Smiley put it, that he had even abandoned an entire cave full of crucial operational documents. This was an operational coup for Smiley. Before leaving the cave, each man took a souvenir. Smiley's was a round brass coffee tray. Years later, in retirement, he was still using it to serve coffee to guests at his home in Spain.

Though the assault on the Jebel ended the major conflict in Oman, Smiley's job was not done. He served a three-year tour for the Sultan, the latter part of which involved dealing with more insurgent mines. They were American ones, far bigger and more dangerous. The mine layers' tactics were clever, and Smiley was chagrined to find himself the mined rather than the miner. At one point, a set of smugglers brought a whole lorry load of material into Oman, sailing easily past the checkpoints. Smiley confronted his men, only to be informed that the drivers were dressed "as soldiers—as *your* soldiers!" Even in his frustration, Smiley had to admit that it was an impressive piece of work. The rebels had stuffed, as he put it, "four Browning .50 antiaircraft guns, nine heavy mortars, thirteen Bren guns and their ammunition, three wireless sets, and not less than forty men" into an old British three-ton truck, making them the world's most creative packers, brilliant used-car mechanics, or both.

The mines brought back memories of Albania in more ways than one. Insurgents would plant mines (as the Albanian Communist Partisans had staged raids) near the villages of their enemies, hoping to elicit reprisals. Tracking guerrillas remained as difficult as ever. Smiley's most effective tactic was simply paying for any mine that was turned in, up to the sum of £200, depending on the type. This yielded a new black-market trade in infiltrating mines purely for the purpose of collecting the reward, but it worked.

In another happy accident involving working animals gone wrong, Smiley had imported from Cyprus what he thought were trained bomb dogs to help track mines, but the Alsatians that had been delivered to him were actually guard dogs and very intolerant of the heat. By the time they were retrained, it was far too hot to put creatures with such heavy coats to work in Oman, so back they went. In their wake rode a rumor that Smiley had been importing lions from Kenya in order to eat the mine layers, a morsel of misinformation he had little incentive to correct.

At the end of his tour, Smiley took leave of the Sultan, parting with him amicably and never expecting to return to Arabia. He was offered command of the SAS, but in a move that he would later admit was born of a chip on his shoulder, he turned it down, as the War Office refused to give him the promotion to brigadier that should have accompanied the role. The budget, he was told, simply would not pay for a brigadier. And so Smiley retired. For a time, he found himself living in Scotland with his wife and children and reviewing restaurants for *The Good Food Guide*. He was just getting restless again when, in May of 1963, he received a call from his old friend Billy McLean.

"David? How would you like to come with me to the Yemen?"

THE YEMEN—THE DEFINITE ARTICLE WAS THEN STILL PART OF ITS OF-ficial name—lay on the opposite, southwestern corner of Arabia from Oman. Known in ancient times as Arabia Felix, or "Happy Arabia," it was home to the biblical Queen of Sheba and the trade in luxuries such

as frankincense, balsam, and myrrh. No western expedition had ex-
plored the hinterland during the time between the destruction of a Roman legion in the first century BC and an almost equally doomed
Danish one in the mid-eighteenth century. It was ancient even in Alexander's time, but its fortunes had been on the wane since 700 BC, when
the Egyptians introduced trade across the Red Sea, eliminating the need
for the caravans that had made the Yemen rich and laying the vulnera-
ble land open to successive invasions by various neighbors. Yet the Yemen, with its combination of desert plains, craggy jebels (much like
Oman's), and fiercely independent tribes, was difficult to control, even
for the locals who tried to unite and rule it for themselves.

McLean had already made one tour of the Yemen. His journey was
thanks to yet another set of political upheavals, this time also related to
the neighbors. The Yemen had been ruled for many years by a heredi-
tary imamate. The old Imam, much to the surprise of almost everyone
around him, had managed to die peacefully in his bed, an unfitting end
for a violent old man. His son, Muhammad al-Badr, had previously engaged in a bit of political flirtation with Nasser in Egypt. Nasser spoke
of a unifying Arab nationalism that was more accurately a cover for his
own megalomaniacal desire for empire. It rankled him that other more
powerful Arab kingdoms, such as Saudi Arabia and Hashemite Jordan,
stood in his way. Taking over the Yemen would be an excellent way to
challenge his neighbors. It would also challenge the British, who still
held a protectorate over the crucial port of Aden, to the south.

When al-Badr decided that murdering and overthrowing his father
was not a step he wanted to take, Nasser was forced to find an alternate
route. The old man died anyway, but al-Badr was not the puppet that
Nasser wanted. In the autumn of 1962, Nasser found his solution in one
of the new Imam's palace intriguers, who organized a coup that nearly
succeeded. The Imam, however, heard the telltale click of a gun's safety
being switched off behind him. Dashing into his room, he foiled the

most important part of the plotters' plan. He not only lived but also escaped to the mountains to rally his loyal tribes.

The rebels backed by Nasser called themselves Republicans and claimed to represent a new, democratic government in the Yemen. With Nasser's colonizing ambitions and Soviet backing, this was not true, but the terminology was attractive. The US government, which had always struggled to tell the difference between democratic nationalism and international Communism, formally recognized the new government in the Yemen and pressed Britain to do the same.

McLean and Julian Amery decided to do a bit of homework. McLean was already in the Middle East. Both were still members of Parliament, though Amery had shifted into a role as the Secretary of State for Air, which gave him oversight of the RAF and kept him usefully involved in all things related to armed conflict. Radio Cairo and the propagandists of the rebel Republicans were insisting that they held a majority in the country and should be formally recognized. McLean went to see for himself.

McLean visited Jordan and Saudi Arabia in addition to the Yemen. If McLean did not quite have the gift of gab that had allowed Amery to settle King Zog in the lead-up to Operation Valuable, he had something just as desirable: real connections in the Middle East. McLean truly enjoyed, and perhaps preferred, the company of his foreign friends, an affinity that had begun when he started learning Amharic in Ethiopia during the Second World War. McLean had connections in Kurdistan, Iraq, Iran, Turkey, Syria, Jordan, and Saudi Arabia, to name just a few. His ability to operate, and the extensiveness of his Rolodex, would have put the foreign offices of most Western nations to shame.

On this trip, he was twice the guest of King Saud, who had McLean brought to one meeting in a car that drove him through the marble-pathed royal gardens, over what McLean noted as "an enormous Persian carpet," and right up to the audience chamber. When McLean cabled his observations home, the messages had to be translated, then locally encrypted and passed through the Saudis and Jordanians before being retranslated and delivered to the British ambassador in Amman. The King of Jordan proudly told McLean that he himself had done the final translation. McLean was beloved by far more than royalty. During McLean's many trips to the Yemen over the succeeding years, delighted cries of "Colonel Billy!" frequently went up from the tribal fighters who recognized him, probably not least because he had a jocular way of lifting spirits. Once, when a shell fragment had (not dangerously) nicked a friend next to him, he'd reacted by waving his precious box of now bloodstained cigars and saying, "Dammit, Wilfred, look what you've done now!"

What McLean found bore no resemblance to the Nasser-backed propaganda. The Imam's Royalists commanded the loyalty of the tribes. Outside the towns, the Republicans had little support. As the tribes represented the majority of the population, not to mention the vast majority of Yemeni history and culture and an even larger majority of the armed men, the Republicans had little claim to either democratic government or the state's prerogative of a monopoly on violence. "In the Yemen, power does not lie in the towns," McLean said in a debate in Parliament. "Damascus may be the key to Syria, as Cairo is the key to Egypt, but Sanaa is not the key to the Yemen."

McLean was convinced that with a little British and Saudi support, the rebels could easily be eliminated. They claimed to control the military, but the tribes had the rifles and the better shots. The Republicans did hold the country's air force, but this consisted of thirty old planes so mothballed that McLean was told "mouses jumped out" when their covers were taken off. Flying them was also moot, as the one pilot trained to do so had been banned from takeoff for apparently having "fallen down three times."

The Egyptians already had a few thousand men in the country, with modern, Soviet equipment. These soldiers had been told that "they were being sent to the Yemen to fight the British." In McLean's judgment, the rebels, led by the palace intriguer, could "only survive with Egyptian help," and even then they would not be "able to subdue the greater part of the country or gain the support of the majority of the population."

His warning arrived in time to prevent British recognition of the rebels. But there was still much fighting to come in the Yemen; by the time the war was over, Nasser was fielding over fifty thousand men per year there. By the following May, McLean, with Amery in the background, had recruited Smiley to the Yemen as well.

Smiley's visits started as observational. By this point, the Saudis and the Jordanians, who had no desire to see a Nasserite foothold in Arabia, were backing the Royalists. They financed the journeys of Smiley and McLean. Smiley's role was to travel the country, figure out what was going on in the war, and give his hosts a frank assessment of how they could improve their military operations.

There was no easy way to get from London to the Yemen in 1963, so McLean and Smiley flew first to Beirut. Almost exactly twenty years after they had boarded another plane in the dark of night to drop into Albania, they were, as Smiley reflected, "about to launch ourselves into a guerrilla war in another unknown country." From Beirut, they flew to Jeddah in Saudi Arabia, where they were whisked from the plane and never once dealt with customs. The first person Smiley saw in the hotel lobby the next morning bore a face that was familiar to him from only images—the face of Talib bin Ali, rebel commander of the Jebel Akhdar in Oman. He was sitting down to read the newspaper.

Commanders in war spend their time trying to get into the other side's head, trying to figure out what their adversaries will do, and when, and why. Their actions can be mysterious even in hindsight. And there he was: the respected opponent, ripe for the asking.

"Billy," Smiley whispered, "there is my old enemy Talib bin Ali! You remember—the brother of Ghalib, the Imam of Muscat. I fought against him for three years. I must go over and talk to him."

"You'll do nothing of the kind," McLean insisted. "That would be very bad security and could lead to all sorts of complications." The opportunity did not repeat itself.

In Oman, Smiley had fought for the Sultan against Saudi-backed rebels. Now he would help the Saudis support Yemeni Royalists fighting against Egyptian- and Soviet-backed rebels. Nevertheless, he was surprised when McLean introduced him to Amir Faisal, soon to succeed Saud, by saying, "You know, Sir, Colonel Smiley commanded the Sultan of Muscat's army, and was fighting against your people?"

A bemused Faisal replied in the affirmative. "Colonel Smiley was only doing his duty. And he did it very well." Faisal was wise enough to realize that the best man to employ was the one who had defeated him the last time.

McLean was needed in Parliament for a vote, but on his first tour of the Yemen, Smiley saw quite enough to produce cogent advice. He toured the country in the company of the Royalists. They were spartan journeys, often at night, by truck, donkey, and foot. Over several weeks, Smiley trekked to meet with the Imam and the various emirs who commanded the Royalist forces from their redoubts in the desert mountains. It was difficult going, though Smiley was at least pleased to find that the sandstone mountains of the Yemen were kinder on his feet than the hard rocks of Oman.

At one point, he and his small group were surrounded by men who claimed to serve the Imam but in reality were merely brigands. The brigands rummaged through their gear, stole Smiley's binoculars, and insisted that the travelers drop their weapons. Outnumbered nearly three to one, Smiley held his semiautomatic rifle carefully and faced the prospect that this could finally be the end of the line. He determined that, "if I had to be killed, I would first shoot a great big black-bearded villain who kept shouting insults at me and, moreover, now had my binoculars." They were saved by the arrival of two hundred of the Imam's actual troops, who appeared at the top of a nearby hill.

Reconnecting with McLean at the end of his tour, Smiley found that they had come to the same conclusions. The Imam's forces were hampered by three things: tactics that focused on taking towns for prestige instead of effective guerrilla attacks on supply routes and the limited roadways; a lack of coordination due to sparse communications (much like the Omani rebels had, the Yemeni Royalists took up perches in mountain caves); and a poor supply system for ammunition and small arms in particular.

What followed in the Yemen was a hiccupping war, scarred by failed truces, by what Smiley and McLean suspected was Egyptian use of aerial bombing with chemical weapons, and by UN denunciations of perceived British imperial designs in the face of actual Egyptian ones. The Republicans proved no less repressive than the despotic old Imam, father of the current one. A Swedish general who had been sent over as the head of a UN observer mission judged the stability of the Republican regime by the number of heads (their orifices stuffed with cigarette butts by the local children) posted on the main city gate in the capital each day. The same number of heads indicated continuity, but more heads—"a fresh batch," minus those offed for petty criminality, as the Swede put it—meant that "a number of backsliding Republicans or unfortunate Royalist supporters had been taken to task."

It was a war with very strange bedfellows, and one that lasted into the late 1960s. The Americans, bogged down in Vietnam and fighting Communism there, initially backed the Egyptians—who were also, in turn, backed by the Soviets. The Saudis supported the Royalists. The Israelis did too, but so professionally and quietly that it was imperceptible. The Jordanians provided support as well, including for an endeavor that involved Smiley, Amery, and McLean: the recruitment of European special-operations mercenaries to train the Imam's forces.

This project never involved the British government proper. While McLean had managed to convince the government to withhold from the rebels official recognition, there was still a contingent in the Foreign

Office that was susceptible to public foreign criticism, especially from the US and the United Nations, of actions that served its own country's interests. (As the aforementioned Swedish general also noted, the new states born of decolonization and recently admitted to the UN "were reveling in the politically inspired largesse of the great powers, and had discovered how well it paid to shout and snarl and be abusive.") Faced with inaction, McLean, Amery, and several of their colleagues did something that, in this day and age, seems both scandalous and illegal but was, at the time, nothing of the sort: they organized a solution on their own.

With the unofficial acquiescence of the prime minister, Amery and McLean, joined by David Stirling (the SAS's founder) and several others, met at White's in London. The club, as described by Amery's biographer, was "then well known for operating along the intersection between the intelligence services, the Conservative Party, and the aristocracy." The Yemenis needed expertise. It was to be "a *war* that never was." One of the men tasked with recruiting the purely private unit quietly cashed a check from the Yemeni Foreign Minister via the manager of the Hyde Park Hotel. The check was for £5,000, the equivalent of more than £150,000 today.

"Why do you need so much money?" the manager demanded.

"I know it's a lot," came the bland response, "but my daughter's getting married." The bride in question was then eight years old.

Though it took some time, David Smiley was the eventual commander of the mercenaries in the Yemen. While much has been made of the role of former or "on leave" SAS men fighting in the Yemen (there was even a movie made, an espionage thriller starring Robert De Niro and Jason Statham, that conflated this conflict with a later one in Oman), most of the mercenaries were actually French or Belgian. There were never more than fifty of them, and their main role was to train the local troops.

Smiley thought the French offered the best value: former men of the

French Foreign Legion who had fought at Dien Bien Phu and in Algeria, they were quiet professionals who had no problem with the "mercenary" label. The story at the time was that they split their year between Yemen (where they were well paid but where both women and alcohol were forbidden by local custom) and the war in Congo, where the women and booze were plentiful but the payment less than regular.

The risk-averse segments of the Foreign Office, subject to American criticism even while the war in Vietnam raged, were not pleased with Amery's "uncanny ability to cut across their conventional lines of communication." One official sent an underling to Amery's office to demand that he "immediately desist" from his "activities" in the Yemen. Amery made the appropriate "soothing noises" and did nothing of the sort; much to the chagrin of the junior messenger, the senior official "did not seem to notice or mind!" In the meantime, Smiley commanded the mercenaries while McLean, by the end, spent more time in the Yemen than in England trying to keep the complex, unofficial diplomacy operational.

What Amery, McLean, Smiley, and the whole assortment were doing in the Yemen was the last gasp of the tradition that had built the British Empire in the first place. Lord Salisbury, the former prime minister and Conservative giant of the late nineteenth century, had defended the Englishman's right to "get his throat cut where and when he likes." It was that notion, more so than "the fit of absentmindedness," that had built an empire. From Robert Clive to the East India Company to Cecil Rhodes, Canadian fur trappers, and even those fiercely independent British American colonists, Brits willing to exchange personal risk for fame, fortune, adventure, religious freedom, or their own liberty more generally had planted seeds across the world. The successful ones were eventually backed by the full force of the government, but British imperialism had never been organized along the fiercely centralized, "civilizing mission" lines of, say, Britain's closest neighbor.

The war in the Yemen was technically never won, though it was not for lack of trying. Certainly, the Egyptians, for whom the Yemen became a sort of Vietnam, did not win it, their great Soviet-sponsored military might bogged down by tribesmen armed mostly with rifles. As McLean once put it, "President Nasser's idea of expanding Arab socialism, or Egyptian imperialism, or whatever you want to call it, has foundered on the rocks of traditionalist Islam in the Yemen."

Still, the Royalists saw no triumph either. By 1968, they were losing the war, and the tribes were fracturing. The Saudis, tired of the expense of supplying the Royalists (and buying off their tribesmen), organized a coalition government. While the British, in the meantime, had given up the crucial port of Aden, the Saudis had at least managed—then—to create a government that was willing to work with the West and also quite suspicious of the Soviets, who had backed the Egyptians even though they'd been so violently disposed toward the USSR. The Imam retired to Britain. Smiley, Amery, and McLean signed his application for citizenship.

CHAPTER 16

HEIRS THROUGH HOPE

H er name was *Startide*, and she was not Billy McLean's first choice of boat. She did not even have her captain present. But since his last charter—on a boat owned by his mother-in-law and named for his wife, no less—had fallen through, she would have to do. There was nothing wrong with the previous vessel. But her captain had hemmed. Her captain had hawed. He had argued that an American ship was blocking the harbor, that there was a leak, engine trouble, probably that Mercury was in retrograde. The real issue was that the captain had gotten wind of what McLean was up to, and he wanted no part in it.

It was January 1965, and McLean intended to sail from Spain across the Mediterranean, all the way to North Africa. His goal on arrival was to spring a rebel dissident from jail in Algiers and smuggle him out of the country.

It was a project of sufficient import to pull McLean away from his activities in the Yemen, which were also occupying him at the same time. The incarcerated rebel in question was named Hocine Aït Ahmed; he had been part of the National Liberation Front (FLN) leadership that had recently wrested Algerian independence from the former French colonial overlords. But like all revolutions, this one, too, had devoured its children, and Ahmed was imprisoned not by the French but by his own side. No one ever figured out exactly who roped McLean in, or precisely why, but the money materialized from somewhere, and he was off on another assignment.

The original crew, aside from the reluctant captain, included McLean's wife, Daška; Peter Kemp; and a young barrister named Simon Courtauld, a friend of Daška's nephew whom McLean had met when both happened to be in Tehran. After the failure of his first attempt to charter a boat, McLean had called another friend who was then living in exile in Spain: King Leka of the Albanians.

Leka was the only son of King Zog. Leka, uncrowned but by no means diminished (he was, it was said, nearly seven feet tall), was an enterprising sort of gentleman. He produced the boat, a new captain, and a young woman who served as cook and was thus known as Cookie.

Springing a man from jail in a country that has no diplomatic relations with one's own, and where one does not speak the language, is a bold endeavor. Daška was sent home for safety's sake. Kemp was qualified, but McLean soon sent him back to Spain to monitor operations from dry land. This was a demotion of his own doing: Kemp had been drinking far too much.

Prophetic words that had been imparted by one of the surgeons who had operated on Kemp in Spain nearly three decades before, after his gruesome mortar wound in the Spanish Civil War, were now coming true. Pain that could only then be quelled by alcohol had fueled a habit that had given way to addiction. By Kemp's own admission, this was what had ended his second marriage to the kind and supportive Cynthia. "If remarriage is, as they say, the triumph of hope over experience, my hope, at least, was fully justified," Kemp wrote, "though I'm afraid few could say the same for her. Cynthia was a wonderful wife and put up with me for twelve years. She should have had a medal."

The barrister Courtauld was dispatched by plane to Algiers, and outdated sea charts notwithstanding, the remaining party arrived in port just in time to raise all the suspicions of the local gendarmerie. Despite advance planning that involved the aid of a local redheaded Scottish schoolteacher who was meant to smuggle messages into the jail wearing a burka, someone was clearly onto them. The mission was waved off. McLean attempted to bundle the young Courtauld into the boat for the return journey, but the thought of an unsettled hotel bill (and the dinner jacket he'd left behind in his room) gave Courtauld the courage to pay the tab, fetch his luggage, and brazen it out by flying home.

McLean, Leka, and the now-horrified second captain were treated to a helicopter buzzing overhead, an escort by a local police boat, and observation from several Soviet gunboats as they pulled out of the harbor. A gray sludge began to emerge from *Startide*'s refuse pipe. McLean had burned his papers in a bucket and was now flushing them down the toilet. Leka opened his golf bag to reveal not clubs but a set of submachine guns. (The "food" tins that he'd brought were instead full of hand grenades.) The captain briefly considered throwing the royal giant overboard as they escaped.

It was not for nothing. Their bungled mission had been the result of a somewhat friendly rivalry. The boyfriend of the red-haired Scottish schoolteacher turned out to be a CIA man, and Hocine Aït Ahmed was sprung from prison (in much the same fashion) by the Americans, who wished to take credit, four months later.

IT WAS NOT THE FIRST TIME THAT KEMP AND MCLEAN HAD OVERLAPPED on interests in Africa. A few years before, each had been in what was then known as the Belgian Congo (later Zaire and today the Democratic Republic of Congo). After the Belgians handed over independence with what Kemp called "precipitate and undignified haste" in the summer of 1960, the country fell apart. Factions developed in different regions of that vast country. Congo seemed as if it would split into pieces. One backed continued connections with Europe for the purposes of profitable mining and stability. Another flirted with the Soviets. All were led by Congolese. Leaders were murdered, the army rioted, and the remaining Europeans were terrorized on the street. The UN, still attempting to work out what "peacekeeping" would mean in practice, sent in troops—not to quell the violence but to forcibly preserve the same borders that had been imposed upon the country by Western imperialism. European mercenaries arrived to back the pro-stability secessionists. In the midst of all this, the UN's first Secretary-General, Dag Hammarskjöld, was killed in a plane crash whose cause is debated to this day.

As an MP, McLean visited the pro-stability (and pro-European) state led by the Congolese politician Moïse Tshombe, who called it Katanga. McLean arrived in the late fall, just a few months after independence was granted and everything began to collapse.

Kemp arrived a few months later, staying for "six very disagreeable weeks" in 1961 for what he claimed was "an English Sunday paper now long since defunct," continuing his tradition of serving as an insurance salesman who managed to linger in more global Cold War hot spots than most actual journalists ever did (or would ever want to). In Congo, Kemp and McLean would have crossed paths with the same French mercenaries whom David Smiley would command in the Yemen just a few years later. There they also would have seen the UN's inability to hold itself above the Cold War fray, absorbing a lesson that McLean soon put to very practical use a continent away.

The two men had likewise overlapped in Southeast Asia on other missions. McLean visited Indonesia, Cambodia, and Vietnam, arriving in the later days of the French war with the Viet Minh in the early 1950s. Watching French troops, especially the crack Foreign Legion, fight in the guerrilla conflict, he was reminded of fighting with his Abyssinian patriots in the Second World War. Sometimes he forgot that others' sense of an appropriate level of danger was not the same as his own. Promising his wife, Daška, who had flown out to meet him in Saigon, that the town was "safe as houses," he had barely finished speaking before an explosion shattered the glass and brought down the ceiling plaster.

Kemp, who would make several trips, first arrived in the 1960s. Again he traveled ostensibly as a journalist seeking to observe some of the hottest parts of the Cold War. He purported to have been given a £1,000 advance for a subject ("Piracy and Rebellion in South East Asia") that his own agent had thought better for an article than for a book. Somehow a paperback firm produced the advance, which works out to more than $20,000 in today's currency—even more mysteriously, for a book that Kemp never wrote. Someone, somewhere, thought it well worth it to send a man of Kemp's experience to Southeast Asia in the 1960s.

Kemp visited Chiang Kai-shek's Taiwan, then called Formosa. After learning about slavery and piracy in Indonesia, he made a daring journey in an open boat called a *kumpit* to North Borneo, took another boat to Singapore, and then infiltrated himself into Laos. He finally crossed from Thailand to Laos in a pirogue, much like he had done in 1945. But now there was an outboard motor. Years before, in the dead of night, rowing hard against the current, the journey had taken forty-five minutes. This time it took seven, no rowing required.

He reconnected with a Lao prince he had known during the war, then smuggled himself into the city of Vientiane, slipping past control posts and getting to the city center under what Kemp, who well knew, called "ferocious artillery and mortar bombardment." Laos was, at the time, in the midst of another civil war that was also part of the Cold War. Much as in Vietnam, a Communist insurgency threatened the government. That was but a small part of a longer story in the region, wherein the Lao were frequently impinged upon by their larger neighbors, especially the Vietnamese. This time was no different, and the North Vietnamese showed few qualms about expanding their war against their non-Communist southern neighbor into bordering Laos.

Did this unwritten book warrant an illegal border crossing (Kemp had omitted to obtain a visa) and a risky dash under fierce fire to get to the city center? While he mentioned his dismay at the loss of civilian life in Vientiane, Kemp never explained what story was so pressing as to propel him into the middle of such a large firefight. Perhaps it was an operation similar to the one that he had begun to help McLean with in Algeria, and to the one that he had successfully carried out for those three frightened teenagers in Budapest. Whatever it was, Kemp was too professional to say.

By 1965, he was back, this time to visit the Americans in their war in Vietnam. He boarded a helicopter to be flown into a remote Special Forces camp ("I've ordered the pilots to get us in there at all costs," the colonel escorting him said cheerfully) and on landing was warned to get off the LZ because three men had recently been shot there by the resident enemy sniper. One young pilot who took Kemp on a mission in a Forward Air Control (FAC) aircraft was delighted by Kemp's composure in the midst of heavy ground fire.

"But that wasn't a dangerous flight, surely?" Kemp sputtered upon receiving hearty congratulations.

"But you're an *old man*, Mr. Kemp," the pilot explained. Peter Kemp, veteran of two hot wars and one cold one, was then nearly fifty.

BILLY MCLEAN MANAGED TO COMBINE HIS DUTIES AS AN MP BETWEEN 1954 and 1964 with involvement in not just Algeria, Congo, Vietnam, Cambodia, and Indonesia but also Ethiopia, Iran, Iraq, Kurdistan, Turkey, Jordan, Cyprus, Libya, Pakistan, and Afghanistan. Some of his connections, such as with Ethiopia, reached back to World War II. He had long had ties to unrecognized Kurdistan, where he had met rebels on his journey home from Kashgar, and where he returned in 1965. It was in Iran that he bumped into Simon Courtauld, whom he had roped into his Algeria mission. And that ill-fated attempt at a jailbreak had not been McLean's first time in the country; a photograph from 1962 shows him and a few journalists taking cover in a ditch during an ambush by the nationalist forces. The journalists, with worried expressions, duck behind a concrete wall. McLean sits on his heels, peeking over the top of a more forward position and looking bored. His left hand rests, relaxed, across his knee. His right hand, outstretched, holds a newspaper that he looks about to crack back open to read.

His travels, for what one parliamentary colleague called his role as an "unpaid undersecretary for the Foreign Office," meant that he was often gone for long periods of time. This was regularly a trial for his wife, Daška, less so because of his absence itself than because of his reluctance to commit pen to paper (long-distance calling then being both expensive and, in many of McLean's posts, unavailable). McLean was not a habitual writer. While Smiley, Kemp, and Amery all kept detailed diaries, McLean kept scraps of papers, remainders of calendars and appointment books, and snatches of observations. He wrote reports when required, especially on his trips to the Yemen, but he did not enjoy writing. Simon Courtauld later became a writer at *The Spectator*. He recalled once inviting McLean to lunch, where the latter was to hand over an article on one of his latest missions. McLean arrived for lunch—but sans article, which never materialized.

Likewise, he had difficulty in writing to his wife, who complained that David Smiley, another man of action, always managed to write to his. It was not that McLean did not remember; at the end of one long report on the Yemen, he wrote to his contact, "Please could you send a telegram to my wife at 17 Eaton Square saying I am well but will not be back for Christmas." It was then already mid-December.

Daška's younger brother tried to help McLean rectify this situation. He drafted postcard-style letters on McLean's behalf. "Dear . . . Dearest . . . Darling . . . Daška," they began (McLean was instructed to circle one), "I am staying . . . at the British Embassy . . . in a hotel . . . in a cave. I shall return . . . next week . . . in six months . . . next year."

If it was not a traditional way of handling things, it was one that nevertheless worked well for the McLeans. And McLean was not always away. He was recruited by no less than Julian Amery to host, in one of his final acts as an MP, an unusual set of guests at his large house in Inverness, Scotland. In his role as Minister for Air, Amery had been given a gracious reception in Moscow and wanted to return the favor. McLean found himself hosting a Communist delegation in Scotland, complete with Nikita Khrushchev's son Sergei.

McLean put on a full Highlands party, keeping some of the delegates to himself and billeting the others (knowing, as his biographer put it, "the secret weakness of communists for the aristocracy") on noble friends with grand country houses nearby. One of those was an old colleague of Peter Kemp's from the Commandos: Lord Lovat, who had landed on the beach on D-Day with his bagpiper going full bore. McLean was delighted to learn through Daška that the young Khrushchev spoke perfectly decent English—but only in front of her and never in the company of the other Russians, to whom he feigned ignorance, insisting upon a translator. "Splendid!" said McLean on hearing the story, bemused as always by the Soviet obsession with secrecy and the resulting hypocrisy.

JULIAN AMERY CONTRIBUTED FAR MORE TO HIS POST AS MINISTER FOR Air than a British-Soviet travel exchange. It was Amery who was crucial in getting one of the twentieth century's most famous aircraft designs contracted, funded, and flying: the supersonic Concorde, which cut the time for flights between Europe and North America in half. An integrated Anglo-French project, it was a fitting assignment for a man who had grown up bilingual and was as comfortable in France as he was in England.

Amery's talent for negotiations and cooperation went well beyond his relationships with the French. It was also Amery who, in the midst of a messy civil war in Cyprus, settled a crucial security issue for Great

Britain. In Cyprus, nationalist Greeks warred against British control and insisted upon *enosis*, or union, with Greece, something that was anathema to the other faction on the island, which preferred Turkey. Amery secured agreement for continuing British bases on that strategic Mediterranean island in what turned out to be one of his proudest and most lasting geopolitical accomplishments. Other men had been exhausted by negotiations with the country's wily president, Archbishop Makarios III. Through a series of forty meetings that saw him living in Cyprus for nearly four months, Amery convinced the nationalist leader to accept independence rather than *enosis*. His father-in-law, the Prime Minister Harold Macmillan, declared it "a superb job."

In the late 1960s, Amery hosted a series of clandestine meetings. Israel and Jordan were at loggerheads. Both knew that they needed to make peace with each other, but neither knew how to make the approach. In the end, it was Amery who served as middleman for delicate, high-level negotiations that took place during a series of meetings in his first-floor parlors at 112 Eaton Square.

By then, both Amery and McLean were officially out of office, McLean having lost his seat in 1964. Peter Kemp had attempted to join them in the early 1950s, but as he put it, his interview with the local Conservative committee was "foiled by the erratic behaviour of my false teeth," a legacy of his terrible wound from the Spanish Civil War. Amery served from 1950 to 1966 and again from 1969 until 1992, when he retired and accepted a seat in the House of Lords.

All four men had always thrived upon the unofficial. While Amery never achieved either Cabinet rank or the post of Foreign Secretary to which he seemed all too well suited, his father-in-law had a more sanguine approach to Amery's career: "I wouldn't worry about Julian," Macmillan said. "Julian has his own Foreign Office." When once asked if he felt that his career had fallen short of what it should have been, Amery replied, "In life one learns that the prizes don't always go to the ablest or to the ones who were right; they go to people who are better connected, or have the ear of the powers that be. It's stupid to be disappointed." Amery was subtle and sophisticated enough to realize that, for both himself and postwar Britain, influence was always preferable to power.

DAVID SMILEY RETIRED FOR GOOD AFTER HIS ADVENTURES WITH BOTH Billy McLean and Julian Amery in the Yemen. He and his wife, Moy, had initially planned to settle on a farm in Kenya, but given the geopolitical situation there and airfares that, as Smiley put it, "would have ruined us" if they had chosen to send their children to school in England, they decided on something closer to home. Picking the Spanish coastal countryside, they initially built a house that Smiley christened Tara in homage to the original. The second Tara was later sold, and the pair bought a larger homestead close by, where Smiley became a gentleman farmer, growing olives and almonds with Moy's aid.

Smiley was not the only one drawn to Spain. During one of McLean's various missions abroad, his wife, Daška, had decided to build a house on Majorca, across a gorgeous bay from her brother Vane. It was here where friends and family would gather. McLean himself became an expert spear fisherman, his favorite quarry being moray eels. The family tried eating them once, his stepdaughter Marina recalled, but they were "not very nice." Spearfishing was a pastime that Smiley had indulged in as his "favorite relaxation" activity during his service in Oman. And it was an obsession, too, for Daška's brother Vane. Amery's son, Leo, recalled that a tongue-in-cheek rumor went round that Vane would take his scuba gear, encase the newspaper in plastic, and then sit on the seafloor reading in peace. Exaggeration though that may have been, Vane's skills and developments in the world of underwater exploration were real. When he was finally introduced to the famous undersea filmmaker Jacques Cousteau by the Prince of Monaco, the Frenchman rushed up to Vane and exclaimed, "At last!"

For his part, Peter Kemp preferred to keep his maritime accomplishments topside. If he did not indulge in Vane's spearfishing habit, he did enjoy sailing, where he may have felt closer to his deceased brother, Neil, a Fleet Air Arm pilot killed by German bombers in 1941. Vane and Kemp had just missed overlapping at Cambridge in the 1930s, but they met in Italy during the war, when Vane was serving with British military intelligence. Despite Kemp's laconic response to Vane's question about what he thought of Albania ("What can one think of a nation whose emblem is a two-faced buzzard?" Kemp had said, misidentifying Albania's double-headed eagle), the men became close friends. Kemp subsequently wrote his first two books aboard one of Vane's cargo ships, Vane having inherited his stepfather's massive shipping firm. On that journey, he had traveled from Europe to the West Coast of the United States and back, and he was still thanking Vane and Daška for help with his final book, published just before his death.

Billy McLean never had children of his own, but he served as godfather to Julian's son, Leo, and earned the adoration of the children in his own adopted and extended families. Everyone recalled that McLean enjoyed children; he was willing to both play with them on their own terms (he would hide behind doors and pretend to ambush little passersby, one of his stepdaughters recalled) and treat them very much like adults. Amery once sent an apprehensive Leo to the McLeans' place for dinner when the then teenager wanted to leave Eton early. McLean entertained Leo in standard adult style, with the result being that as Leo walked home, filled with more brandy and cigar smoke than he was accustomed to, he saw the clock tick two in the morning. (He also stayed at Eton.) The Amerys and McLeans lived directly across from one another on Eaton Square, a walk of merely one hundred yards between them. When McLean's stepdaughter Tessa came of age and began her successful career as an interior designer, it was she whom Amery invited to redecorate the family home. McLean was a constant presence at the Amery residence, reading the paper in an armchair and participating in the official and unofficial political life that formed the heart of the house.

ARABIA DID NOT MARK THE END OF AMERY AND MCLEAN'S FOREIGN partnerships. In the late 1970s, they traveled to China together, and 1984 saw them land in Pakistan for a visit with several high-ranking generals and government officials there. They took Leo with them. By then a grown man with his own career, he sometimes served as a discreet notetaker for his father. The occasion was the Soviet invasion of neighboring Afghanistan. In the twilight of their lives, McLean and Amery were still on the front lines of the Cold War, putting heads together with allies to figure out how best to give the Russians hell. They meant to return to the region, but by the time the trip was arranged, Billy was too unwell to travel.

His heart had plagued him for years; his indulgence in sweet liqueurs and some of the tastier delights of the various countries that made up his collection of foreign interests had caught up with him. He died on November 17, 1986, the only member of the group not to see the fall of the Berlin Wall and the collapse of the Iron Curtain across Europe.

His funeral, at St. Margaret's in Westminster, was attended by an abundance of friends, among them some glitterati: the Crown Prince and Princess of Yugoslavia, the Imam of the Yemen, representatives of the King of Jordan, the Crown Prince of Ethiopia, the Speaker of the House of Commons, and King Leka of the Albanians. But in the end, the close circle remained. David Smiley gave a reading, and Julian Amery gave the eulogy. He remembered Billy as a modern-day beau sabreur, a dashing swashbuckler, man of wit, and man of action in the tradition of Lawrence of Arabia. The future, Amery warned, would need many more like McLean.

One soon appeared on the big screen in the form of the character Westley, incognito as the Dread Pirate Roberts, in the cult favorite *The*

Princess Bride. Ridiculously handsome, utterly charming, unfailingly loyal, impossibly courageous, and unflappably calm, he was the fiction where McLean was the fact. Yet there was something quite real to Westley. The actor was Cary Elwes, Billy McLean's stepgrandson.

IN NOVEMBER 1989, THE BERLIN WALL FELL. WITH A RAPIDITY THAT shocked nearly everyone, the Soviet hold on Eastern Europe collapsed, and soon, too, did the USSR itself. The following year, Julian Amery received an invitation from the new leadership of a country he had not seen in a long, long time: Albania. Would he, the new government inquired, be interested in visiting again?

Amery quickly convened a lunch at home with Peter Kemp, David Smiley, and Alan Hare. Kemp must have declined the invitation. It was not for a lack of interest in travel. After one last mission to Southeast Asia, in the so-called Golden Triangle at the intersection of Laos, Burma, and Thailand, where an opium gang mistook him for a narcotics bureau agent and tried to assassinate him, he had focused his missions on Africa and Central and South America. In 1979, he visited what was then still Rhodesia (now Zimbabwe) and was dismayed to find that the rugged, elite, racially integrated, and controversial Selous Scouts considered him too old (he was then in his sixties) to accompany them on a combat parachute drop. Kemp, whose previous drops had involved getting dragged on landing (training in England), a concussion (Albania), a wrenched knee (Poland), and accompaniment by dysentery and malaria (Thailand), had only been concerned about the weather. Should he, Kemp inquired of friends before leaving, bring one pullover or two? And while he was there, would a suit be necessary, or would it be acceptable to wear casual tennis gear to the local Umtali Club?

He had spent time with the Tupamaros, a group of urban guerrillas in Uruguay, interviewing dissident leftist leaders who were being pursued by Soviet-backed enforcers. (The Soviets, as he pointed out, had little love for leftist groups that were not their own, as none other than Che Guevara discovered.) He also traveled to Nicaragua, where he learned, to his delight ("Stoke well . . . the furnaces of Hell!"), that the Albanian dictator Enver Hoxha had met his demise in 1985. And he had traveled, in 1990, to Kosovo, which was then part of soon-to-disintegrate Yugoslavia and today insists upon a highly contested independence from its Serbian neighbor. As Kemp put it at the time, "Unfortunately, Serbs seem to enjoy—and *enjoy* is the word—bad relations with their neighbours." Standing on the street with a group of student protesters in the capital of Pristina, he was bemused when the young people urged him back inside.

"It is dangerous for you here in the street," they said.

"But you're here in the street," Kemp replied.

"Yes, but we are young. We can run," they said, laughing.

Youthful though his spirit might have been, Peter Kemp's health was failing. He still looked marvelous; a photograph from the wedding of the young journalist who accompanied him to Kosovo shows him slim, elegant, and charming in morning dress, characteristically standing next to a beautiful Montenegrin woman. But another trip was not to be.

DAVID SMILEY EAGERLY TOOK JULIAN AMERY UP ON THE INVITATION TO return to Albania. Using a botanical expedition as cover, he had previously attempted to get himself back there while Hoxha's Communists still ruled. Ever straight and honest, he was confronted by a questionnaire. Have you ever visited Albania before, it asked, and where did you stay? "Yes," responded Smiley. "In a cave." His application was denied.

Smiley, Amery, and Hare returned to Albania in 1991. They were warmly greeted by the government, which put on a generous picnic at one of SOE's former dropping grounds in Bixha. Smiley surveyed the tree against which he had cracked his back as they had landed—McLean and Amery with the cotton parachutes—almost forty-five years before.

Then, emerging slowly, the visit's biggest surprise appeared. Walking with a cane, still bearing the plummy accent imparted by so many conversations with Alan Hare, was Shaqir—one of the interpreters whom they had been forced to leave on the beach. Smiley had searched for him in the decades since, only to grow convinced that the man had been executed. Shaqir had spent twenty years in prison.

"Half a century, my dears," Shaqir said in greeting.

Smiley was overcome. "This is one of the happiest days of my life," he said, "to find you when I thought you were murdered." The shame that had haunted him for decades was now, at least partially, resolved.

IN PRESS CUTTINGS ABOUT HIS BOOKS—WHICH KEMP SAVED AND donated, along with his other personal papers, to the Imperial War Museums—there is a telling story in a review by the author Gavin Maxwell:

My earliest impression of Mr. Peter Kemp was as a small boy at preparatory school; he was pink-and-white and cherubic and he was using a pen nib to tattoo his forearm with the words *pro patria mori*. The ink, doubtless, wore off in time, but the idea remained, for from the days of his late adolescence, when he fought in Spain for the Nationalists and somehow survived terrible wounds, he has devoted himself with extraordinary single-mindedness to being killed as violently as possible.

Maxwell exaggerated; Kemp was a romantic, not a daredevil, though the life-insurance job did always seem incongruous.

He did not, in the end, meet a violent death. Peter Kemp died at a hospital in Chelsea, London, on October 30, 1993. The cause was officially listed as septicemia, but Kemp had cancer as well. His death certificate was signed by Elizabeth Moore, the woman to whom he credited his recovery from alcoholism in the 1960s, but of whom he characteristically said little else. He had his body cremated: a fitting mirror to the final resting place of his beloved brother, Neil, who was buried at sea in the Mediterranean.

A child sent from India to England by his parents at the age of four, Kemp did not meet his father again until he was fifteen. His father died while he fought in Spain. His brother, Neil, was killed in the Second World War. His mother died in 1946. Two marriages ended in divorce. There were no children, his infertility the result of a childhood case of mumps. Yet Kemp had, undeniably, one of the richest of lives. And while he left very little behind, he was not alone.

Liz Moore, the mysterious woman who signed his death certificate, was beautiful, effortlessly organized, and assertive in the most attractive of ways. Divorced herself, she had two grown children. Her relationship with Kemp was long and rich but officially unofficial. Kemp credited her with saving both his sanity and his life. He rented the flat that she kept at the top of her house in Chelsea; he once nearly burned the place down when he put his pipe out in a wastepaper basket. (He also once absentmindedly knocked it out in another man's pint glass.)

Liz was only four years younger than Peter but so charming—and so disarming—that Kemp's nephew, Ian, assumed the age difference was far greater. He also had no idea that Liz worked, officially, for the Ministry of Defence. She was, in her own way, quite traditional. One night, over several whiskies, Ian became privy to what was clearly not the first iteration of this conversation: "Liz," Peter said, "let's get married." "No, Peter," Liz replied. "You've had too many wives already."

If Liz was irresistible, so, too, was Peter. Years later, Peter told Ian in passing that a new tenant had taken up residence in the flat at the top of Liz's house. Ian, with characteristic Kemp family reserve, omitted to ask about Peter's new address. When he became very ill and was admitted to the hospital in the last months of his life, it was Liz who went every day to feed him his meals. The death certificate that Liz signed asked for Kemp's address, and hers. They were the same. Kemp called her "my closest friend and my most candid critic," the person to whom "I owe a debt I can never hope to repay." Their relationship, however defined, had spanned the better part of thirty years.

IT FELL AGAIN TO JULIAN AMERY TO GIVE THE EULOGY. THIS TIME, HE told a fuller version of the story about his first impromptu meeting with Kemp in that ditch, under shellfire, during the Spanish Civil War. "Amery, Eton and Oxford," the younger man had said upon shaking hands. "Kemp, Wellington and Cambridge," replied the English *alférez*.

Time was closing in on Amery as well. His had been a long, full, rich life in terms of both family and politics: a long and happy marriage, four wonderful children, the career of a true statesman. Toward the end of his life, an interviewer asked him if the signing of the Concorde deal had been his proudest moment. "No," responded Amery. "My proudest moment was when Nasser proved me right about the Suez Canal, and I was able to say in the House of Commons, much more politely than I'm saying it now, 'I told you so.'" But he had one final task, one final thing left undone.

Not long before he died in 1996, Amery invited the Home Secretary to lunch at his storied house on Eaton Square. He had an unusual request. Would it be possible, Amery asked, to disinter and cremate his older brother, Jack, so that his ashes might be scattered in France, as Jack had wished?

It had been half a century. Amery had dealt with Jack's treason, and demise, in a characteristically calm and measured way. His son, Leo, recalled that no one mentioned Jack's existence until he and his three sisters were old enough to have a proper conversation about it. Then they did so at length and in depth. He also recalled that there was only one photograph of Jack in the house: as a child, before the Fall.

If Amery's request was unusual, it was also entirely legal. A bit of paperwork had to be completed first, but in the end, the wishes of both Amerys were satisfied. Julian Amery died in his sleep later that year, not long after he had woken from a vivid dream in which he felt a tremendous sense of calm.

IT WAS FITTING THAT DAVID SMILEY, THE SOLDIER'S SOLDIER, REMAINED the last. He lived another decade, watching the euphoria of the post–Cold War world settle into a new age of unsettled global politics. As that new world struggled to turn into an order, tragedy came for the Smileys, for whom service was such a family tradition.

Hugo Tweedie, the first husband of Smiley's wife, Moy, had been a major in the Scots Guards. In the final months of the Second World War, he was killed in Germany while seeking out a harbor site for his troops. With Tweedie, Moy had had two children, Anna and Gavin, whom Smiley had raised as his own alongside his two sons with Moy. Gavin's son, Alex, had joined Smiley's old regiment, the Household Cavalry. The unit, while still the senior regiment in the British Army, had evolved since Smiley had last served in it. Smiley was there for the evolution from horsed cavalry to armored-car units (with which he had broken through the German lines in the Western Desert). Alex would be there for the fully armored version.

Alex was a tank lieutenant, and he was heading right back to where Smiley had started: Iraq. There he joined the initial pushes of the invasion in the spring of 2003. On April 1, he was leading his troops over a difficult stretch of terrain when the ground beneath his tank crumbled, collapsed, and pitched the tank, upside down, into the bordering ditch, where they were trapped under five feet of water. His lance corporal, a man named Shearer, was killed. The medics got Alex breathing again and evacuated him to Scotland. But he never woke up. He died three weeks later at a hospital in Edinburgh.

By this time, Smiley was quite old and struggled with mobility. He and Moy had since moved back to England and were living in a flat in the leafy London suburb of Earl's Court. But Smiley was never one to be deterred from life, and so in 2003, he also found himself back in the desert, invited to Yemen to share his story of the civil war with researchers there.

An uncomplicated patriot, as one of his sons put it, David Smiley retained his classic, unrelenting spirit to the end. He died in 2009, three months shy of his ninety-third birthday. At his funeral, his son Xan said, "I'm proud that some of my father's exploits may go down in the annals of military history; and of course I'm proud of his bravery. But I think I'm proudest of all of the simpler virtues of his life: his disarming modesty, his uncomplicated patriotism, his down-to-earthness, his instinctive decency, above all his absolute straight-as-a-die honesty."

THIS PENDANT WORLD

When Peter Kemp was first picked up by the Soviets in Poland in 1945, his captors were driving a Dodge truck granted to them by the American Lend-Lease program. It was emblematic of the experience that Kemp and his fellow teammates had during the Second World War. It was also emblematic of the forces against which they would fight in the decades to come.

Hitler and his shiny boot-wearing, goose-stepping Fascists were an easy enemy for the West to understand. Their evil was raw, their oppression wicked, their totalitarianism obvious. It was worth partnering with the Soviets to defeat them. They constituted a threat to the world order and a danger to basic human decency, actively pursuing what Churchill called "the abyss of a new Dark Age."

The SOE quartet fought against that Dark Age, and then kept on fighting. Together, they ambushed the Germans in Albania, took the local surrender of the Italians, and tried their best to harry the German retreat from the Balkans. Even before that, they had fought Rommel in the desert, conducted Commando raids on the Channel Islands, and clashed with the Italians in Abyssinia. In the Far East, Kemp and Smiley

saw firsthand the horrors of Japanese crimes against Allied POWs when
they rescued some of the men who had built the railway bridge over the
River Kwai. In different parts of China, Amery and McLean saw a different side of Allied complexity.

In Southeast Asia, and in Albania, all four men saw the thing that
their superiors had hoped to ignore, at least for a little while longer: the
beginning of a new war. Whereas the Germans were an obvious enemy,
what the warrior Gurkhas of Nepal called *dushman*, the Communists
and their whispering manipulations were not. Stalin was a monster, to
be sure. No one could help but notice the more than three million
Ukrainians he had slowly murdered through starvation imposed by col-
lectivization. Others were killed more quickly, charged with being "ku-
laks," a term that was reinvented, like so many others, to serve a new
purpose. The show trials of the 1930s sent chills up the spine. So did
sometimes sending only half of your men into battle with rifles and
shooting anyone who tried to run for his life.

But the Soviet Union also spoke for progress, for modernity, for
equality. To the liberal West, inherently self-reflective and self-critical,
this was a far more difficult enemy to face for the fact that it was so hard
to face it at all—especially in 1945, when all anyone wanted to think
about was ending the war and going home. The USSR said all the right
things. It spoke of good values that good men wished to reflect. And the
West was not perfect, was it? These empires—heavens, look at the French
in Indochina! And did the British need to rule everything?—were simply unfair. The Americans, raised on a proud revolutionary tradition,
were especially susceptible. That the West's real flaws were honestly
exposed while the Soviets and their Communist allies around the world,
from Hoxha to Tito to Ho Chi Minh, lied through their teeth about everything from the economic figures to the gulags to the liquidation of
millions mattered little.

THE SOE QUARTET'S WAR BROUGHT THE FOURSOME INTO CONFRONTA-
tion with one of human psychology's most dangerous habits: wishful
thinking. This bogeyman chased them through Albania and into
Southeast Asia. It only got worse as formal hostilities came closer and
closer to ending.

Take, for example, the Albania story. It was presented in the staff
office, and has been presented by many since, as binary: nationalists versus Communists, progress versus empire, good versus evil, black versus
white. But dreams of progress had never held a candle to the antedilu-
vian attractions of power.

For all their protestations about pinning down German divisions
and fighting the Hun, the Communists collaborated and shared information with the Germans when it suited them. So, too, did various nationalist groups. In a small space, each saw outsiders, on both sides of
the "main" conflict of the Second World War, as potential arms dealers
in a local power struggle.

The ambitious young men in the staff office, like Eliot Watrous, did
not wish to admit that their fashionable progressive politics (which, in
a tribal way, led them to despise and abuse men from conservative and
traditional backgrounds, such as McLean, Smiley, Amery, and Kemp)
were being manipulated by a force at least as totalitarian as the one they
thought they were fighting against. As one SOE officer in London put
it, the operations of SOE's staff offices—first in Cairo, then in Bari—
sometimes "did not seem to be quite what Mr. Churchill meant by setting Europe ablaze."

Keble and his obsession with rank, Klugmann and his slavish
service to raw totalitarian might, Watrous and his chairborne paper-
pushing, Kupi and his warlordism, Hoxha and his megalomania—what
they all sought was not progress but personal power. Even how the story

was told and who got to tell it—in competing memoirs and in those letters to the editor—was an expression of power, one in which no one was
whiter than white. In all of the Balkans, it was perhaps only David Smiley who desired to do nothing other than kill Germans. In Albania and
Yugoslavia, pro-Communist British policy began to indulge in the same
wishful thinking as its junior American cousins—assuming that ideas
could stand in for politics and that ambitions of sheer power were a
thing of the past.

Wishful thinking followed Amery to China, where the Americans
deftly kept him out of Mao Zedong's territory. It haunted Kemp and
Smiley in Thailand. There, American—or, at the very least, OSS—
support for the Viet Minh led directly to the death of the French officer
François Klotz, who died in Kemp's arms. Indirectly, that support, which
allowed Ho Chi Minh to consolidate power, would lead to the deaths of
nearly sixty thousand Americans in Vietnam two decades later. They
watched from perches throughout the developing world as the UN was
reduced to a talking shop, mostly for criticism of the West—and frequently with the West's encouragement, like the new men of the Foreign Office who wrung their hands over Amery's work in the Yemen.
Meanwhile, ordinary people were persecuted at the behest of ruthless
leaders backed with guns and tanks sold to them by the Soviets. There
are a surprising number of places in the world today where you can buy
an AK-47 for the price of a chicken.

THEY LEARNED THE HARD WAY THAT WISHFUL THINKING COULD LEAD
to duplicity, and that the consequences of duplicity were very, very real.
Sometimes the people you hoped to trust the most—your staff office,
your head of counterintelligence, your own family—were the ones you
could trust the least. Smiley may have laid too much credit at the feet of
Kim Philby. Yet it would have been hard to give too much credit to the

role that traitors played in their own lives, a fact that never diminished their determination to serve.

They were quiet professionals. Xan Smiley, the extremely sharp tack who is David's oldest son, knew Kemp well throughout his life. Despite a journalism career that saw him serving in senior positions for *The Economist*, *The Telegraph*, and *The Times* in Washington, Africa, the Middle East, and Moscow, the postwar Kemp, in Xan's impression, was "a busted flush," a reformed alcoholic who became fussy about teapots in his old age. Kemp worked hard to maintain that illusion, often distracting anyone who had questions about his service with a regaling turn of topic: "Did I ever tell you about the time I became military governor of Bali?" Kemp's own nephew, his only surviving family member, had no idea of his extensive activities for British intelligence. Just years before he died, Kemp was sitting at a café in Kosovo with his experienced journalist escort. When a full-blown riot not twenty-five meters away was attacked by police, the escort firmly told him that it was time to go. "Can't I finish my beer first?" asked Kemp, who was expected to write a full report upon his return.

Kemp was only the most extreme example. The work of Smiley, McLean, and Amery in Arabia was effective but often unofficial. In the Yemen, they helped prosecute a "war that never was." They engaged in some of the first clandestine activities of the Cold War in Albania, on the mission betrayed, at least in part, by Philby. They worked, together and separately, in Africa, the Middle East, Southeast Asia, and South America. Near the end of his life, Amery was asked by an interviewer if he had ever been a spy. "The word is derogatory," the statesman sniffed.

They were quiet men in other ways as well. Kemp never mentioned that his first wife ran off with George Seymour, and nor did anyone else. Julian Amery wrote a chapter about his treasonous brother, Jack, for his autobiography, then cut it from the final manuscript. He also never mentioned how he felt about the fact that his brother—undeniably a traitor—paid the ultimate price, while James Klugmann, who put far more of his own countrymen in harm's way than did the miserable Jack, never paid any. Only to his diary did Smiley commit his nightmares, including the one about his older brother being dead. Smiley was lucky: of the group, his were the only brothers to survive the war.

When, in his grief, Peter Kemp mixed up the date of his nephew's birth, he never mentioned that he had missed his own brother's wedding because he had been at a hospital in Spain, nor that his brother's death had involved decapitation from a bomb fragment. Julian Amery brilliantly recounted his assault with the Turkestan Legion soldiers on a German machine-gun nest, but even as he described watching the beautiful Achmet gleefully cut down a young German soldier, he never mentioned that he, unlike the rest of the team, had never killed a man in combat. Billy McLean did not mention the sad details of his younger brother's death, just two hours after arriving at a British hospital following the evacuation from Dunkirk. His own godson did not even know that he had a younger brother. No one mentioned that Peter Kemp did all of his parachute drops with a set of false teeth, or the scars all over the left side of his face. It is nearly impossible to find a photograph, or even a drawing, of his left profile.

DID THEY WIN? THE COLD WAR IS OVER, THE SECOND WORLD WAR WON. Their most specific enemies have been vanquished: Hoxha and his regime in Albania, the Soviets in Russia and Eastern Europe. Thailand is thriving and Vietnam possibly on the road to success. Yet there is a reason why so many of the places in which they operated remain conflict zones to this day. Abyssinia, now Ethiopia, is in the middle of another civil war, hopefully about to draw to a close. So is Yemen, now without the article in its name. Albania is free and Kosovo nominally independent, though Kemp's line about the country's Serb neighbors "enjoying" bad relations remains true. Sinkiang is now Xinjiang, still suffering for the central government's anxieties over its loyalty. The successors to SOE's Polish allies watch the latest iteration of Russian imperialism in Ukraine, wondering if they are next. All these places sit on political fault lines, their borders having been contested for generations. In many cases, the Cold War froze a process of frontier reckoning that began with the First World War but was never completed.

Their ultimate lesson lies not in their victory but in their longevity and determination. Today we like to speak of the Greatest Generation, and these men were excellent exemplars of it. But we think of that generation as a snapshot: men in a youthful version of their prime, with the clock stopping in the summer of 1945. The proper metaphor is not a snapshot but a film strip. They kept going. The SOE four were among some of the first to realize, often in frightening and trying circumstances, that a victory for freedom and peace and security could not be gained by defeating the Nazis alone. The Soviets started the Cold War before their eyes, if not under their noses. They spent the rest of their lives fighting it, in and out of uniform.

Much of our world would look unrecognizable to them. One thing would look very familiar: a resurgent Russian imperialism, the Great Game resurrected and rearing yet again its ugly, callous head. To the surprise of almost everyone, including itself, the West has stood its ground, backing Ukraine with everything other than fighting troops. Nearly seventy years before, Peter Kemp wrote that the freedom fighters of Hungary had won the admiration of the world, but "alas, only the admiration." The West feared escalation then; the Russians try to use it now. So many of the tactics are the same. The whisper campaigns designed to get the West to do Russian bidding bear an eerie similarity to their Soviet antecedents. *Isn't it unreasonable that the Ukrainians won't negotiate?* one line goes. *Isn't hunting collaborators bad? Are the Ukrainians really being nice enough to journalists? Won't Western support just*

lead to nuclear catastrophe? go some others. The ears seem less recep-
tive this time.

When they came limping out of Albania, Julian Amery reflected
on how they had managed, despite the dominance of the brutal Hoxha,
to sow a seed. "And one day," he promised, "there will be a harvest."
Perhaps, just perhaps, it is here.

ACKNOWLEDGMENTS

"I am at your disposal," said Xan Smiley when we first spoke, and he meant it. Xan generously shared his connections, his advice, his memories, his stories, and his family; without his aid, this book would be a shadow of its current self. I cannot possibly hope to repay the debt I owe to both Xan and his very lovely wife, Jane, for their hospitality, their knowledge, their trust, and their kindness in welcoming me into their home and letting me range through David Smiley's incredible personal collection of papers and photographs. In their home, I held in my hands the tiny letter smuggled to David by the POWs in the camp at Ubon, and read his diaries while listening to his great-grandchildren tell very English jokes in the next room.

Leo Amery provided insights and delightful stories that I never would have otherwise come across; his family's commitment to, and candor in, preserving their history for others is exceptional. To Annie Walsh, I owe another debt of hospitality. To Ian Kemp, I am grateful not only for his memories and otherwise undiscoverable clues about the clandestine life of his uncle Peter, but also for the delightful and serendipitous blooming of friendship. My country owes him a debt as well. He came to fight for us in Vietnam, serving two tours when men including future presidents were doing their best to stay away. He won a Silver Star for bravery, a decoration that probably would have been higher had he not been a foreigner.

For telling stories, passing along priceless documents and photos, and in general sharing their remarkable families and friends with remarkable generosity, I am grateful to Tessa Boteler, Caroline Cobbold, Marina Cobbold, Pat and Carol Coulcher, Simon Courtauld, Tessa Kennedy, Lizzie and Murky Hare, Charles Moore, and Lucy Moore.

Artemis Cooper kindly pointed me in the right direction in the early days. Richard Bassett shared not only his extensive knowledge about what seemed an impenetrable subject to an American interloper but also his quiet and careful wisdom. Stacy Schiff's thoughtfulness and willingness to share her advice lit a far brighter beacon than she knows. Tom Jehn and Karen Heath gave me that most impossible of all gifts: time.

Clive Jones, Mark Seaman, and Roderick Bailey lent their knowledge about SOE, its sources, and other historical arcana. This book would not have been possible without the work of Raluca Oprean. As always, I am indebted to the National Archives, the British Library, and the Imperial War Museums. The oral history interviews conducted by the inimitable Conrad Wood are gems. I am also grateful to the staff of the Churchill Archives Centre: Katharine Thomson, Sophie Bridges, Jessica Collins, and Nicole Allen, who helped me with Julian Amery's voluminous and wonderfully cataloged papers. Libraries are the lifeblood of writers, so I thank the Boston Public Library, the Minuteman Library Network, the Harvard University Library, and especially the London Library, whose collections and memberships are a brilliant boon to the independent writer.

I will always owe a great debt to Candida Moss, whose friendship has been invaluable for nearly twenty years. Elise Franklin, miraculously wise and good-humored, edited the whole thing at the drop of a hat. Through his reading, Ying Xiao lent his ever-insightful eye as well. And, of course, I must thank my daughter, who has gracefully accepted my seemingly endless associations with people from the past. At the very least, I have incorporated her previous criticisms: this book has pictures in it.

I would have gotten nowhere without Roger Freet, agent extraordinaire. Rick Kot and Terezia Cicel have been the most generous of editors. And I am grateful to the entire team at Viking and Penguin Random House, including Camille Leblanc, Maya Petrillo, and copy editor Lauren Morgan Whitticom. I am grateful as well to Jeff Ward for his beautiful maps. Permission for use of the papers of Billy McLean has been granted by Marina Cobbold; permission for the papers of David Smiley, by Xan Smiley; permission for the papers of Peter Kemp, by Ian Kemp; permission for the papers of Julian Amery, by Leo Amery; and permission for the papers of Alan Hare, by Murky Hare. Photographs have been reproduced with the permission of Leo Amery, the Churchill Archives Centre, and Xan Smiley.

Nearly thirty years after the publication of *The Spy Who Came in from the Cold*, John le Carré finally admitted, most of all to himself, that "by telling an ingenious tale, I was making some kind of bitter order out of my own chaos." One of the truths I have learned from the men of this book is that so often the deepest and most personal parts of life are the ones left off the printed page; these are honored by their own absence. I owe similar debts, bear similar allegiances, and, strangely enough for a writer, maintain a similar preference for the untold. But as that talented talespinner Tim O'Brien once wrote: "It *wasn't* a war story. It was a *love* story."

A NOTE ON SOURCES

How do we know what we know about the past? Historians are notorious for their love of documents. It is not for nothing that schoolchildren
are taught that "prehistory" is the time before the written record. Yet no
one is fool enough to think that there is neat and written evidence for
everything. The fashion for the written record and "the archive," especially official government ones (raised to the venerable level of the pseu-
doscientific, like most things in the academy, by a nineteenth-century
German man), will always clash with other ways of knowing about the
past: memory, personal experience, memoir, oral tradition, oral history,
personal photographs, family lore, diaries, newspapers, eulogies, epi-
taphs, stories that still may not be printed, basic human compassion.
We deceive ourselves if we think that an official archive is preferential
to the unofficial, or that there is a bulletproof answer to anything. History, too, requires an act of faith.

Take, for example, the records of the Special Operations Executive.
Under lock and key for decades, they tantalized historians seeking to
understand what happened during the war of dirty tricks. They are a
red herring. Many early SOE Cairo records were burned during the
war, when Erwin Rommel advanced on Cairo during the "Great Flap."

(Many officers attempted to burn papers, only to have them float, half-incinerated, over the city, proclaiming their classified status as they fluttered and flew.)

The surviving documents of the official SOE archive have never presented the neutral, explanatory filter of the chaos on the ground that historians so desire. Staff documents reflect what the staff office understands (or wants to understand), and no more. That is one reason why many papers seem to have never made it into the official archive—including Smiley and McLean's report on Albania, which was not to the taste of those supporting the Partisans. McLean's own personal archive preserved it; so, too, did the Foreign Office and the War Office, though the SOE archive somehow failed to capture it.

Staff paperwork tells its own narrative. The competent Siam Country Section's sanitized version of the story of Tavernier's clash with the Viet Minh who killed François Klotz is but one example. Or take a story told by Terence "Pat" O'Brien, the Special Duty Squadron pilot who dropped men and supplies (including Smiley and Kemp) into Southeast Asia. O'Brien was called to a staff meeting with an American pilot. Both men agreed on the operational plan of the mission. Yet the staff insisted that the pilots were in disagreement. Various acrobatics were required to satisfy this narrative, which the staff committed to the official record. As O'Brien put it, "Politicians and staff officers produce the documents that military historians rely upon for their studies of old campaigns, and participants in such events can often be mystified by the picture those authentic documents present."

Staff office documents represent a tension present since Agamemnon and Achilles clashed: the split between staff officers and field operators. In their deepest, darkest hearts, the staff officers accuse the field operators of being stupid, and the field operators accuse the staff officers of being cowards. Only the staff officers create the official record. Academics, especially the younger generation, who rejected the early work of veterans like M. R. D. Foot, have found a natural attraction to the cerebral staff officers.

SOE's Cairo and Bari staff offices posed an additional problem. Even the Second World War was not intense enough to quash the nemesis of bureaucratic infighting. To this was added at least one mole (who had his own NKVD code name before the war even began) and those staff officers whom he manipulated to his own ends. When we throw in the basic fact that any official archive necessarily prizes certain voices above others—staff officers who produced rivers of paper over field officers who did the grunt work, male officers in general over the women FANYs who did the decryption but whose thoughts rarely made it into the official files—we have a valuable but dangerously incomplete record. Relying on this official archive to judge the experience of the men on the ground is about as wise as a medical student studying female anatomy by way of Picasso. Both are representative, but both are distortions.

The value of diaries and memoirs and the like is suspect, but the value of any source is suspect. The value of the troves of alternative archives that the true grunts of SOE generated lies in their volume, their corroboration, their misfit nature. Like the Dead Sea Scrolls, they unsettle by their very existence. They force us to think differently about the canon. They force us to make our own decisions, the uncomfortable ambiguity of reality laid cold and bare.

NOTES

INTRODUCTION

xxvii **At a private dinner:** Julian Amery, *Approach March: A Venture in Autobiography* (London: Hutchinson, 1973), 224.

CHAPTER 1: A RUGGED NURSE OF SAVAGE MEN

1 **A Rugged Nurse:** This title is an allusion to a line about Albania from Lord Byron's *Childe Harold's Pilgrimage.*

1 **His feet dangling:** David Smiley, 1943 diary, 1, Private Papers of David Smiley (hereafter cited as PPDS).

2 **the No. 52 Middle East:** David Smiley, *Irregular Regular* (London: Michael Russell Publishing, 1994; Leeds, UK: Sapere Books, 2020), 41. Citations refer to the Sapere edition.

2 **Smiley and the company:** Smiley, *Irregular Regular*, 41.

2 **That strange noise:** Smiley, 42.

2 **The Italian force had fled:** Smiley, 43.

3 **He was making terrible:** David Smiley, 1941 diary, 31, PPDS.

3 **Smiley gave permission:** Smiley, 1941 diary, 31, PPDS.

3 **"A shot through the head":** Smiley, *Irregular Regular*, 43–44.

4 **"unintelligible in fourteen languages":** Xan Fielding, *One Man in His Time: The Life of Lieutenant-Colonel NLD ('Billy') McLean, DSO* (London: Macmillan, 1990), 13.

4 **Not only did this allow:** Fielding, *One Man in His Time*, 20–21.

5 **They called the unit:** Fielding, 21–22.

5 **On November 27:** Fielding, 23–24.

5 "Italian relics in the form": Associated Press, "Gondar Captured," British Movietone, archival footage from January 1, 1942, streamed on July 21, 2015, YouTube video, 0:57–1:00, https://youtu.be/uQbhsY5T7iQ?si=0mDVZtZ TIpNuvbsn.

5 "He now looked twice": W. E. D. Allen, *Guerrilla War in Abyssinia* (New York: Penguin Books, 1943), 124.

5 "This officer is a born": Fielding, *One Man in His Time*, 25.

6 "one felt as if one": M. R. D. Foot, *SOE: The Special Operations Executive, 1940–1946* (London: British Broadcasting Corporation, 1984; London: Mandarin, 1990), 4. Citations refer to the Mandarin edition.

7 SOE employed thirteen: J. G. Beevor, *SOE: Recollections and Reflections, 1940–1945* (London: Bodley Head, 1981), 29.

7 If those failed: David Smiley, *Albanian Assignment* (London: Chatto & Windus, 1984; Leeds, UK: Sapere Books, 2020), 23. Citations refer to the Sapere edition.

7 They had files: Smiley, *Albanian Assignment*, 23.

9 The Albanians lay ancestral: Julian Amery, *Sons of the Eagle: A Study in Guerrilla War* (London: Macmillan, 1948), 12.

9 "no place amongst decent people": Tajar Zavalani, *History of Albania*, ed. Robert Elsie and Bejtullah Destani (London: Centre for Albanian Studies, 2015), 130.

9 As a British observer: Amery, *Sons of the Eagle*, 11.

10 "with reluctance rather than regret": Amery, 12.

11 had an excess of flesh: Smiley, *Albanian Assignment*, 74.

11 eyes to be "savage": Enver Hoxha, *The Anglo-American Threat to Albania: Memoirs of the National Liberation War* (Tirana, Albania: 8 Nëntori Publishing House, 1982), 39.

11 he shared Hoxha's ferocity: Smiley, *Albanian Assignment*, 73–74.

12 The Germans were on: Smiley, 16.

12 The Germans and Italians were: Smiley, 16.

12 "old-fashioned English": Smiley, 18.

13 The result was a broken: Smiley, 26.

13 The pilot had lived up: This was Jimmy Blackburn, the squadron leader. In the small-world department, he was one of Peter Kemp's friends from school.

13 "indeed Greek to me": Smiley, *Albanian Assignment*, 27.

14 It was all he could: Smiley, 35.

14 the industrious teenage daughter: Smiley, 35.

15 His arm obligingly gave: Smiley, 50.

15 Colt .45 in the holster: While Smiley called it a Colt, it may not have been. There have long been rumors about the pistols carried by the men of SOE. Made after the Colt design, they were, as the story goes, actually formed of scrap metal from the German "pocket battleship" *Graf Spee*, scuttled in December 1939, just outside the harbor at Montevideo, Uruguay, where it had been trapped by a group of British and New Zealand cruisers. British intelli-

gence had managed to quietly contract an Argentinian firm to create a set of pistols made out of metal salvaged from the Nazi vessel. (See Michael J. Parker, "Investigation of a Legend: The *Graf Spee* and the Ballester-Molina," *American Rifleman*, January 30, 2014, https://www.americanrifleman.org/content /investigation-of-a-legend-the-graf-spee-and-the-ballester-molina/.) Of unexpected design, they were the perfect weapons for covert operations.

15 **more impressive than he:** Smiley, *Albanian Assignment*, 51; and Smiley, 1943 diary, May 18 and 19 entries, PPDS.

16 **an Italian bomber spotted:** Smiley, *Albanian Assignment*, 72.

16 **Those Italians crashed:** Smiley, 73.

16 **Smiley called them:** Smiley, 148.

17 **he had learned how:** Fielding, *One Man in His Time*, 16.

17 **His younger and only:** Fielding, 9.

17 **Gillian made it:** "The Fallen Old Bryanstonians: Patrick Barnard Gillian McLean," Bryanston, accessed June 22, 2022, https://www.bryanston.co.uk /page/?title=Patrick+McLean&pid=861.

17 **All that would await:** "Second Lieutenant Patrick Bernard Gillean McLean," Commonwealth War Graves Commission, accessed June 22, 2022, https:// www.cwgc.org/find-records/find-war-dead/casualty-details/2450546/patrick -bernard-gillean-mclean/.

CHAPTER 2: AN OFFICER AND A GENTLEMAN

19 **To gather more intelligence:** Amery, *Approach March*, 311.

19 **"I replied gravely":** Amery, 29.

20 **"the work that I had":** Amery, *Sons of the Eagle*, 23.

20 **He offered to collect:** Amery, *Approach March*, 158–59.

20 **"Our staff in Belgrade":** Amery, *Sons of the Eagle*, 25.

21 **he had been involved:** Amery, *Approach March*, 241.

21 **While in Palestine:** Amery, 280.

21 **He personally accompanied:** This was called Operation Bullseye. See Amery, *Approach March*, 242–56.

22 **Permission was denied:** Amery, 265.

22 **He then began making inquiries:** For more details, see David Faber, *Speaking for England: Leo, Julian and John Amery—The Tragedy of a Political Family* (New York: Pocket Books, 2007), 397–446; and Amery, *Approach March*.

22 **as one biographer put it:** Richard Bassett, *The Last Imperialist: A Portrait of Julian Amery* (York, UK: Stone Trough Books, 2015), 81.

23 **As one staff officer:** Bickham Sweet-Escott, *Baker Street Irregular* (London: Methuen, 1965), 73–74.

23 **Anyone who was allowed:** On Keble's physical description and nickname, see Basil Davidson, *Special Operations Europe: Scenes from the Anti-Nazi War* (London: Grafton Books, 1987), 147–48.

24 **"a globe-shaped little"**: Xan Fielding, *Hide and Seek: The Story of a Wartime Agent* (London: Secker & Warburg, 1954; Philadelphia: Paul Dry Books, 2013), 69. Citations refer to the Paul Dry Books edition.

24 **Keble had access to:** There may not be much that is very glamorous about spying on a road, but the LRDG's twenty-four-seven monitoring of all traffic passing along the coastal roads was arguably the most effective special-operations mission of the entire war. The LRDG's members were unrivaled desert operators, and it was among the famous "private armies" of the war that gave rise to the special-operations community as it exists today. Equipped with radios, specially modified Chevrolet trucks, and a large amount of specialized desert knowledge bolstered by sheer determination, the men of the LRDG went quite a long way toward making the defeat of Rommel possible.

24 **This information was backed:** Artemis Cooper, *Cairo in the War, 1939–1945* (London: John Murray, 2013), 150–51.

24 **She was built:** Cooper, *Cairo in the War*, 150–51.

24 **Unable to axe:** "Parker, Joseph Donald (Oral History)," interview by Conrad Wood, May 20, 1988, Imperial War Museums (hereafter cited as IWM), catalog no. 10183, audio reel 4/6, https://www.iwm.org.uk/collections/item/object /80009963. See also Peter Wilkinson, *Foreign Fields: The Story of an SOE Operative* (1997; repr., London: I. B. Tauris, 2002), 132–33. Citations refer to the reprint edition.

25 **Keble had retained:** Foot, *SOE*, 332–34. See also "Parker, Joseph Donald (Oral History)," audio reel 4/6.

25 **Deutsch seemed to specialize:** On Klugmann and the Cambridge Five, see Christopher Andrew and Vasili Mitrokhin, *The Mitrokhin Archive: The KGB in Europe and the West* (London: Allen Lane, 1999; New York: Penguin, 2000). Citations refer to the Penguin edition.

26 **surprised to see a talented:** Foot, *SOE*, 64–65.

26 **Even Smiley later had:** See "Smiley, David de Crespigny (Oral History)," interview by Conrad Wood, 1988, IWM, catalog no. 10340, audio reel, https://www.iwm.org.uk/collections/item/object/80010120; and "Glen, Alexander Richard (Oral History)," interview by Conrad Wood, March 21, 1991, IWM, catalog no. 11915, audio reel, https://www.iwm.org.uk/collections/item/object /80011656.

26 **His big goal:** While voluminous research by respected and senior scholars, such as M. R. D. Foot and David Martin, has pointed to Klugmann's influence on changing policy in Yugoslavia, there have been a few dissenters, from mainly three angles. One is an overreaction to the overreaction that was McCarthyism; in this, Klugmann—who was an admitted NKVD agent as early as the 1930s, and whose work (both recruiting other spies and, perhaps even more controversially, creating "legends" for Soviet illegal immigrants) was

considered so sensitive by the KGB that it was not admitted until 1998, years after the fall of the USSR itself (see Andrew and Mitrokhin, *Mitrokhin Archive*, 83)—is excused on his own grounds. The other angle is rooted in the classic academic anxiety that constantly produces new "angles" of argument where none are needed, but alas, no one has ever been granted tenure for agreeing with one's forefathers. In this version, Klugmann is excused using language terribly similar to his own lies to the security officers who examined him, as well as the hairsplitting argument that senior British policymakers had sources other than Klugmann's intelligence that influenced their thinking on Tito. The final protest is that there was no direct evidence that Klugmann was working for the Soviets while in SOE, though the evidence provided via Mitrokhin's defection seems a serious counter to such a claim. Regardless, there is almost never direct evidence in espionage cases—that is the name of the game. This should not disturb professional historians; after all, researchers have never found the sought-after "Führer's order," but no one doubts that Hitler ordered the Holocaust. None of the apologist arguments in Klugmann's favor deal with the obvious point, which is that Klugmann's loyalties were to his Soviet handlers and that his efforts and intentions were to serve not British policies but Soviet ones. Field officers like those on the McLean Mission suffered as a result.

26 **Klugmann meant to keep:** Transcript of taped conversation between James Klugmann and Bob Stewart, 8 August 1945, Norman John Klugmann Security Service file for 1945-08-25 to 1947-03-13 (hereafter cited as KV 2/791), Records of the Security Service (hereafter cited as KV followed by the relevant file number), National Archives, Kew, UK (hereafter cited as TNA).

27 **Explaining it later:** See Davidson, *Special Operations Europe*, 162; on Klugmann and Yugoslavia more broadly, see 103–80.

27 **"a group of about ten":** Klugmann and Stewart conversation, 8 August 1945, KV 2/791.

27 **"as a result of mass recruiting":** Klugmann and Stewart conversation, 8 August 1945.

27 **"betrayal of information":** Sir David Petrie to Stewart Menzies, 29 August 1945, KV 2/791, TNA.

27 **With the characteristic flexibility:** See Yuri Modin, *My Five Cambridge Friends: Burgess, Maclean, Philby, Blunt, and Cairncross by Their KGB Controller* (New York: Farrar, Straus and Giroux, 1994), 106. Klugmann was both clever and coward enough to always insist that he worked for the Communist Party—a decent enough cover in the West, where the idea of freedom of political conscience was taken seriously. Even his Soviet handlers found this occasionally exasperating, but they were happy to "trot out" (their words) the leader of the British Communist Party when Klugmann, probably with an eye toward the security of his own skin, insisted that he needed official orders.

The fiction of the distinction between the party and the totalitarian regime thus worked for everyone.

27 **He lived in a large:** Davidson, *Special Operations Europe*, 110.

28 **They had lost:** See, for example, the various attempts of security to prevent his work in intelligence, which are documented in the Norman John Klugmann Security Service file for 1934-10-12 to 1947-02-17 (hereafter cited as KV 2/788), TNA. The traditional entry paperwork caused no problems. As Kemp noted, just like all SOE recruits, Klugmann would have been asked to sign a statement swearing that he was neither a Fascist nor a Communist. Of course, as the historian who also happened to be an SAS veteran, former POW, and Croix de Guerre recipient put it, "As a good communist he knew his duty to tell a lie." See Foot, *SOE*, 65.

28 **Klugmann was "thoroughly reliable":** Letter from Brigadier Keble to Colonel Maunsell, 12 January 1943, KV 2/788, TNA.

28 **"I should be very sorry":** On bundling Klugmann into the toilet stall, see Davidson, *Special Operations Europe*, 50–51. On Keble defending Klugmann, see Keble to Maunsell, 12 January 1943, KV 2/788.

29 **"Following a natural":** Amery, *Approach March*, 261.

29 **Then he wound up:** Amery, 261. Amery refused to name names in his autobiography but made it quite clear that the evidence pointed to Klugmann's involvement.

CHAPTER 3: THE ALFÉREZ

31 **He was accompanied:** Smiley, *Albanian Assignment*, 84–85.

31 **Kemp was thus:** Smiley, 85.

31 **"in spite of this":** Smiley, 85.

32 **"I hate being shot at":** Peter Kemp, *The Thorns of Memory: Memoirs* (London: Sinclair-Stevenson, 1990), 3.

32 **"This is really very amusing":** Letter to Lt. Col. G. M. Ormoerod, 23 January 1932, Peter Mant MacIntyre Kemp Security Service file (hereafter cited as KV 2/4418), TNA.

32 **Leaving his pistol's safety:** Peter Kemp, *Mine Were of Trouble* (London: Cassell, 1957; Albuquerque: Mystery Grove Publishing Co., 2020), 130. Citations refer to the Mystery Grove edition.

32 **Their men had been known:** Kemp, *Mine Were of Trouble*, 92.

33 **"I had not the face":** Kemp, 140.

33 **He was speaking to his:** Kemp, 149.

33 **His mind nearly separated:** Kemp, 150.

33 **They smiled and put him:** Kemp, 151.

33 **"When I sent you off":** Kemp, *Thorns of Memory*, 137.

33 **One Spanish surgeon:** Kemp, *Mine Were of Trouble*, 152.

33 **Kemp brought a bottle:** Kemp, 154–55.

34 **"I knew enough of war"**: Peter Kemp, *No Colours or Crest* (London: Cassell, 1958; Albuquerque: Mystery Grove Publishing Co., 2020), 2. Citations refer to the Mystery Grove edition.

35 **said the satyr**: Kemp, *No Colours or Crest*, 78. Characteristically, Kemp both recorded and published the ensuing conversation as it happened in French, *sans* translation.

35 **an open-necked shirt**: Kemp, *No Colours or Crest*, 78.

35 **"Few were the messages"**: Kemp, 80.

36 **"A good deal"**: Kemp, 81–82.

36 **"There's one little"**: Kemp, 82.

36 **"What are you going"**: Kemp, 83.

37 **When he arrived at**: Kemp, 65. The declaration-wielding staff officer was Basil Davidson, the one and future journalist.

37 **"be very careful"**: Kemp, *No Colours or Crest*, 85.

37 **"Of course they must"**: Kemp, 1.

38 **"and a serious attitude"**: Kemp, *Thorns of Memory*, 4.

38 **"Sometimes I think that God"**: Kemp, *Mine Were of Trouble*, 6.

38 **"I couldn't believe"**: Kemp, *Thorns of Memory*, 146.

38 **Neil was decapitated**: Charles Lamb, *To War in a Stringbag*, rev. ed. (1977; repr., London: Bantam Books, 1980), 145. Citations refer to the reprint edition.

38 **As a fellow pilot**: Lamb, *To War in a Stringbag*, 145.

38 **The pilots dodged**: Lamb, 121–22.

39 **When she had married**: "A Stalbridge Bride," *Western Gazette*, August 19, 1938.

39 **Neil had never met**: The loss of Neil was a crushing blow to his family, who had also lost Neil and Peter's father while Peter was fighting in Spain. Neil's death in action dealt a crushing blow to the service as well. One fellow pilot remembered him as "a fine chap who would have made a wonderful admiral had he lived." (See Lamb, *To War in a Stringbag*, 145.) Other fellow officers wrote more than a column and a half's worth of tributes, which appeared in the prestigious *Times* newspaper in the weeks after his death. They extolled his professionalism, his flying skills, his technical mastery, his character. Neil had the sort of sense of humor that made everyone love him; he was "always ready for a skylark, ashore or in the mess." (See W. S. D., "Personal Tributes: Lieutenant N. McI. Kemp, R.N.," *Times [UK]*, January 29, 1941.) He was a natural mentor, a man destined for the highest ranks of the Royal Navy. Perpetually cheerful, he was also a savagely hard worker for whom, in wartime, there was no "off duty." When his previous ship, the HMS *Courageous*, was torpedoed and sunk in the Atlantic, Neil could be seen passing a nearby cork life vest to a weaker swimmer, even though he was nearing exhaustion himself. "His cheering words heartened and revived all those men in the water who were within hail of his voice." He was a ballsy pilot, the kind of man whom

his compatriots compared to the Elizabethan pirate Sir Francis Drake in terms of both his adventurism and his loyalty to the crown. Neil's preference was for the "singeing of beards" type of raid, and thus the sinking of the Italian fleet at Taranto, during which he flew in the first wave, was the perfect sort of mission. As a friend wrote, "He had a fine brain and a stout heart which would admit no difficulties too great to be overcome." While his eulogist did not know it at the time, Neil Kemp had indeed scored his hit on the fleet at Taranto. Yet no confirmation was needed: "I know how the stout heart of Lieutenant Neil Kemp sang as he 'put her nose down' to the waters of Taranto Harbour. I know that he thrilled as he levelled out and steered an unerring, unwavering course for his chosen target. I know how he would shout, as was his way, when he released his torpedo. For that moment had he devoted hours, days, weeks of training. Of this I am convinced—that the torpedo sent on its way by him scored a hit. The Neil Kemps of this world—and there are few—do not miss their targets." (For all heretofore unattributed quotes and details in this note, see "Lieutenant N. McI. Kemp, R.N.: A Friend's Tribute," *Times [UK]*, February 5, 1941.)

39 "Reserved in manner": Kemp, *No Colours or Crest*, 85.
39 "in the most dangerous": Kemp, 85.
39 "It was quite successful": Kemp, 86.
40 "Of course this was just": Kemp, 86.
40 "If you do an ambush": Smiley, *Albanian Assignment*, 81.
40 "My men have not": Smiley, 82.
40 Smiley was pleased: Smiley, 82.
40 "was delighted to": Smiley, 83.
40 The Albanians finished off: Smiley, 82–83; and Kemp, *No Colours or Crest*, 86.
40 "too close to be healthy": Kemp, 86.
41 recovering the next day: Kemp, 87.
41 "the longest and most boring": Smiley, *Albanian Assignment*, 87.
41 "but no such luck": Smiley, 87.
42 "You do that": Kemp, *No Colours or Crest*, 91–92; and Smiley, *Irregular Regular*, 10–12.
42 Kemp "admired their detachment": Kemp, *No Colours or Crest*, 92.
42 "disagreeably startled by": Kemp, 92.
42 "We must withdraw": Kemp, 92.
42 "my first action": Smiley, *Albanian Assignment*, 89.
42 "Do you mean": Smiley, 89.
42 "some plainly audible": Kemp, *No Colours or Crest*, 93.
42 only eighteen Germans: Smiley, *Albanian Assignment*, 89–90.
43 "I'm damned if": Kemp, *No Colours or Crest*, 93.
43 was "sheer exasperation": Major P. M. M. Kemp, BLO report, 1944, 2, Records of Special Operations Executive (hereafter cited as HS) 5/144, TNA.
43 One of the mulemen: Kemp, *No Colours or Crest*, 93.

43 "let 'em have it": Kemp, 94.
43 "Give me covering fire": Kemp, 94.
43 "Don't be so damned windy": Kemp, 95.
43 McLean's smile froze: Kemp, 95.
43 "On our way": Kemp, 95.
43 confessed himself "very jealous": Smiley, 1943 diary, August 25 entry, PPDS.
43 Toward the end of August: Smiley, *Albanian Assignment*, 90.
44 "We're being attacked": Kemp, *No Colours or Crest*, 97.
44 not exactly a: Kemp, 37, 97.
44 Smiley took a few: Kemp, 97.
44 "Pack it in": Kemp, 97–98.
44 "If I had been entranced": Kemp, 98.
44 A teenage boy had: Kemp, 98.
44 "He seemed greatly": Smiley, *Albanian Assignment*, 92; and Smiley, 1943 diary, August 27 entry, PPDS.
44 whom Kemp tried to: Kemp, *No Colours or Crest*, 98.
45 Those troops were some: Kemp, *Mine Were of Trouble*, 104–5, 107–9.
45 "began to run wildly": Kemp, 108.
45 "kept throwing himself": Smiley, 1943 diary, August 28 entry, PPDS.
45 Smiley decided this: Smiley, August 28 entry. The word *windy* is slang for "cowardly," or "chicken."

CHAPTER 4: WITH FRIENDS LIKE THESE

47 One thing that everyone: Kemp, *No Colours or Crest*, 112.
47 "having smartened myself": Smiley, *Albanian Assignment*, 95–97.
47 The Italian commander had: Smiley, 97–99.
48 The Germans appeared: Peter Kemp, "Set Europe Ablaze," interview by Henrietta Sophia March-Phillips for the BBC, September 30, 1983, IWM, catalog no. 12299, audio reel 1/2, 05:09–05:19, https://www.iwm.org.uk/collections/item/object/80012034.
48 He blew up: Smiley, *Irregular Regular*, 125.
48 Beating a rapid: Smiley, *Albanian Assignment*, 104.
48 He hauled himself: Smiley, 104.
49 Smiley took no orders: Smiley, 106.
49 "A pity there is": Smiley, 1943 diary, October 7 entry, PPDS.
49 Told to remove: Smiley, *Albanian Assignment*, 99.
49 "The smell was awful": Smiley, 100.
49 "I suppose the Partisan": Kemp, *No Colours or Crest*, 89.
49 He patched them up: Smiley, *Albanian Assignment*, 102.
50 The priest took his Sten: Smiley, 102; and Smiley, 1943 diary, October 3 entry, PPDS.
50 "He is such good": Smiley, 1943 diary, August 16 entry, PPDS.

51 "These were divided": Kemp, *No Colours or Crest*, 88.

51 He found that he was: Kemp, 121.

51 Davies himself chose: Smiley, *Albanian Assignment*, 110–11; and Kemp, *No Colours or Crest*, 132.

51 Some of the Communist: This detail about the nickname's perceived sinisterity derives from an interview with Alan Victor Hare by John Halliday. The interview is preserved in the Hare family's private papers, which were shared with the author.

52 "on the receiving end": Kemp, *No Colours or Crest*, 132.

52 What Smiley proclaimed himself: Smiley, *Albanian Assignment*, 110.

52 By their own admission: Smiley, 113.

52 "You're getting as untidy": Smiley, 113.

53 "expressed his pleasure": Smiley, 113–14.

53 Nicholls thought he: Smiley, 114.

53 Despite Davies's insistence: Edmund Davies, *Illyrian Venture: The Story of the British Military Mission to Enemy-Occupied Albania, 1943–44* (London: Bodley Head, 1952), 47.

53 "In Cairo I had been": Davies, *Illyrian Venture*, 62.

53 "Our Albanian bodyguards": Smiley, *Albanian Assignment*, 115.

53 Kemp noticed how devoted: Kemp, *No Colours or Crest*, 87.

54 Taken from a ways: Davies, *Illyrian Venture*, 68.

54 Smiley whipped his feet: Smiley, *Albanian Assignment*, 120.

54 He vowed never: Smiley, 120.

54 Politicking was never: Smiley, 115.

54 The Partisans would insist: Kemp, *No Colours or Crest*, 82.

54 Unable to resist: Smiley, *Albanian Assignment*, 75.

55 It was a captured: Smiley, 1943 diary, October 28 entry, PPDS. Interestingly, the self-censored and redacted copy of the diary in the National Archives omits that the document was copied and passed on. See Major Smiley's diary, October 28 entry, HS 5/143, TNA.

55 This meant evading conflict: Smiley, *Albanian Assignment*, 117–18.

55 Hoxha was not above: Blendi Fevziu, *Enver Hoxha: The Iron Fist of Albania*, ed. Robert Elsie and trans. Majlinda Nishku (London: I. B. Tauris, 2017), 52.

55 Smiley and McLean soon passed: Smiley, 1943 diary, October 29 entry, PPDS.

55 "It is just like": Smiley, October 29 entry.

56 Smiley was reduced: Smiley, November 13 entry.

56 "By my reckoning": Smiley, *Albanian Assignment*, 124–25.

56 "It was soon": Amery, *Approach March*, 158.

57 As the two strandees: Alexander Glen, *Footholds against a Whirlwind* (London: Hutchinson, 1975), 151.

57 "Oh yes we can": Glen, *Footholds against a Whirlwind*, 151.

57 Smiley rowed as hard: Smiley, *Albanian Assignment*, 126.

57 Just as it sank: Smiley, *Irregular Regular*, 133.
57 watching the scene from shore: Glen, *Footholds against a Whirlwind*, 151.
57 "George!" Kemp called: Kemp, *No Colours or Crest*, 130.
57 When he arrived back: Kemp, 133.
58 When Davies moved: Kemp, BLO report, 1944, 22, HS 5/144.
58 He had no intention: Kemp, *No Colours or Crest*, 134–35.
58 "The whole affair": Davies, *Illyrian Venture*, 91.
58 "The only result would be": Davies, 91.
58 Kupi and his Zogists: Kemp, *No Colours or Crest*, 135.

CHAPTER 5: A STATELY PLEASURE-DOME

59 A Stately Pleasure-Dome: This title is an allusion to the second line of Samuel Taylor Coleridge's poem "Kubla Khan."
59 There they had been "deloused": Smiley, *Albanian Assignment*, 127–28.
59 As the Blitz raged: Cooper, *Cairo in the War*, 5.
59 When one officer: Cooper, 5.
60 "did not have to be": Cooper, 9.
60 Since the nineteenth century: On the background of Egypt, see Cooper, 9–20.
60 ruling at the turn of: On the linguistic abilities of Fuad, see Cooper, 21.
60 Also as in Paris: Cooper, 10, 27.
60 Not a weekend went: Cooper, 62.
60 grand villa's garden: Cooper, 231.
61 The diplomat said it was: Cooper, 231.
61 After listing his titled: Cooper, 231.
62 She agreed to come: Cooper, 294.
62 They carried with them: Andrew Tarnowski, *The Last Mazurka: A Family's Tale of War, Passion, and Loss* (New York: St. Martin's Press, 2007), 103.
63 who had been close friends: Smiley, *Albanian Assignment*, 128. On Sophie's background, see "Lives Remembered: Sophie Moss," *Independent*, February 22, 2010, https://www.independent.co.uk/news/obituaries/lives-remembered-sophie-moss-1906518.html; and "Obituary of Sophie Moss," *Telegraph*, December 3, 2009, https://www.telegraph.co.uk/news/obituaries/military-obituaries/6716412/Sophie-Moss.html. On the whole family story, see Tarnowski, *Last Mazurka*.
63 While he was working on: Amery, *Approach March*, 319.
63 "Life at Tara was luxurious": Amery, 319.
63 Whether the fault rested: "Obituary of Sophie Moss."
64 Egypt's King Farouk: Cooper, *Cairo in the War*, 295–96.
64 "the conversation became tedious": Wilkinson, *Foreign Fields*, 138.
64 There was also a story: Wilkinson, 138.
64 the mongoose got loose: Cooper, *Cairo in the War*, 295.
64 who happened to possess: Tarnowski, *Last Mazurka*, 222.

64 **McLean did not make:** Cooper, *Cairo in the War*, 295.
64 **Not long thereafter:** W. Stanley Moss, *A War of Shadows* (London: T. V. Boardman, 1952; Philadelphia: Paul Dry Books, 2014), 136–37. Citations refer to the Paul Dry Books edition.
65 **General Friedrich-Wilhelm Müller:** Roderick Bailey, "Introduction," in Patrick Leigh Fermor, *Abducting a General: The Kreipe Operation in Crete* (New York: NYRB, 2014), xxii.
65 **Moss and Leigh Fermor:** Cooper, *Cairo in the War*, 311.
65 **Their current task:** Clive Jones, *The Clandestine Lives of Colonel David Smiley: Code Name 'Grin'* (Edinburgh: Edinburgh University Press, 2020), 113.
65 **In the fall of 1943:** Amery, *Approach March*, 272.
66 **"All organisations tend to":** Amery, 265.
66 **This was one of Brigadier:** "Parker, Joseph Donald (Oral History)," audio reel 4/6.
66 **Amery maintained that:** Amery, *Approach March*, 265.
66 **referred to as simply Fitzroy:** On Fitzroy's impressive antics, see his memoir: Fitzroy Maclean, *Eastern Approaches* (London: Jonathan Cape, 1949; Chicago: Time-Life Books, 1980). Citations refer to the Time-Life Books edition.
67 **Keble had now graduated:** On the miscalculation regarding the tanks in the desert, see Wilkinson, *Foreign Fields*, 132.
67 **He faked a signal:** David Martin, ed., *Patriot or Traitor: The Case of General Mihailovich: Proceedings and Report of the Commission of Inquiry of the Committee for a Fair Trial for Draja Mihailovich* (Stanford, CA: Hoover Institution Press, 1978), 125.
67 **He admitted to his:** Klugmann and Stewart conversation, 8 August 1945, KV 2/791.
67 **"I'd do what I was":** Klugmann and Stewart conversation, 8 August 1945.
67 **This was a curious:** Klugmann first passed information to Tito's headquarters through a man known as Ivo Lola Ribar, whom Klugmann had met at an international Communist conference years earlier. After Ribar was killed, Klugmann passed his information through a man named Vladimir Velebit. (Klugmann and Stewart conversation, 8 August 1945, KV 2/791.) It was an effective gambit. Those watching from the other side realized that "much influenced by Velebit's advice, Tito showed great skill in adjusting his attitude to [Fitzroy] Maclean's." (Fitzroy was Churchill's personal representative.) See Vane Ivanovic, *LX: Memoirs of a Jugoslav* (New York: Harcourt Brace Jovanovich, 1977), 261.
68 **When reminded that Amery's heart:** Letter from Julian Amery to Leo Amery, 14 November 1943, file 3/1/8 (Letters from JA to Leo Amery from 1942-01 to 1948-12), Papers of Julian Amery (hereafter cited as AMEJ followed by the relevant reference code), Churchill Archives Centre, Cambridge, UK (hereafter cited as CAC).

68 **Amery helped McLean and Smiley:** Julian Amery to Leo Amery, 22 December 1943, AMEJ 3/1/8.

68 **McLean and Smiley were off:** Julian Amery to Leo Amery, 22 December 1943.

68 **Following Julian Amery's introduction:** On lunch, see Smiley, *Albanian Assignment*, 133.

69 **This was to become:** Jones, *Clandestine Lives*, 116.

69 **Smiley stressed a more:** Jones, 115.

69 **Hare's succinct response:** Smiley, *Albanian Assignment*, 57.

CHAPTER 6: THE BATTLE FOR KOSOVO

71 **Peter Kemp was dreaming:** Kemp, *No Colours or Crest*, 152.

71 **moments before had come:** Kemp, 143.

71 **All Kemp had left:** Kemp, 151.

71 **"There are some men coming":** Kemp, 152.

71 **Kemp leaped up:** Kemp, 152.

72 **Somehow they made it:** Kemp, 152–54.

72 **allowing harm to come:** Zavalani, *History of Albania*, 132.

72 **But Kemp's Italian interpreter:** Kemp, *No Colours or Crest*, 154.

72 **In the nearest village:** Kemp, 154; and Kemp, BLO report, 1944, 39, HS 5/144.

72 **Looking down on:** Kemp, *No Colours or Crest*, 154.

73 **of rightfully Serbian land:** Peter Kemp, "Waiting for a Bloodbath," *Spectator*, May 5, 1990, 14.

74 **"In their turn they":** Kemp, *No Colours or Crest*, 184.

74 **With help from the regional:** Kemp, 154. The root of Bajraktari's surname traces back to a medieval title of Ottoman provenance. It is better known today under a different spelling, Bayraktar, which is the name of the Turkish-made TB2 drones used by Ukraine in its defense against the Russian invasion. Their inventor shares the same name.

74 **Hasan warned Kemp:** Kemp, *No Colours or Crest*, 164.

74 **Associated with the Yugoslav:** Kemp, 165.

74 **Albanians like the Gheg chieftain:** Kemp, 158.

75 **One of them was a:** Kemp, 123.

75 **When the British NCOs:** Kemp, 124.

75 **Hoxha never would have:** Fevziu, *Enver Hoxha*, 42.

75 **Even in 1945:** Fevziu, 128, 134.

76 **The signal had come:** Kemp, *No Colours or Crest*, 167.

76 **Kemp rapidly signaled:** Kemp, 167.

76 **"The others were suitably":** Kemp, 167.

76 **They later showed one:** Davies, *Illyrian Venture*, 171. The others were purported to be Richard Riddell and Tony Simcox.

77 **In what Kemp described:** Kemp, BLO report, 1944, 45, HS 5/144.

77 In what was probably: Kemp, BLO report, 45.

77 As he was soon to: Kemp, *No Colours or Crest*, 171.

77 a "musical comedy routine": Kemp, BLO report, 1944, 45, HS 5/144; and Kemp, *No Colours or Crest*, 172.

78 When they arrived at Hasan: Kemp, *No Colours or Crest*, 172.

78 Kemp was mortified: Kemp, 172–73.

78 "If you want to play": Kemp, 173.

78 The language was sometimes: Eliot Watrous to Alan Palmer, 8 June 1944, HS 5/39, TNA.

80 The Germans would be onto: Kemp, *No Colours or Crest*, 173–74.

80 "That such stimulus": Kemp, 176.

80 The irredentists insisted: Kemp, 181.

81 Trying to keep up: For more, see Amery, *Sons of the Eagle*, 68–70.

81 "Enver was full of charm": Davies, *Illyrian Venture*, 146.

82 "It is impossible": Davies, 148.

82 By the dint of: On Davies's war, see *Illyrian Venture*, especially 196–99.

82 The officer denied it: Davies, 147.

82 told both men to contact: Smiley, *Albanian Assignment*, 134.

83 "I have grown inured": Letter from Julian Amery to Leo Amery, 6 December 1943, AMEJ 3/1/8, CAC.

83 "Please call at my office": Amery, *Approach March*, 327.

83 "it seemed fitting": Amery, 328.

83 He was once saved: Kemp, *No Colours or Crest*, 183–84.

83 They suggested that their mission: Diary of John Hibberdine, 19 January 1944 entry, IWM.

84 The Kosmet Partisans executed: Kemp, *No Colours or Crest*, 185–86.

84 Kemp and Hibberdine doubted: Kemp, 188–89.

84 "Gani convinced me": Kemp, 189.

84 The British officer was saved: Kemp, BLO report, 1944, 53–54, HS 5/144; and Kemp, *No Colours or Crest*, 189–90.

85 been acting with "defiance": Kemp, BLO report, 1944, 53, HS 5/144; and Kemp, *No Colours or Crest*, 189.

85 Gani Kryeziu attempted to: Kemp, 190.

85 "shattered all my hopes": Kemp, 190.

85 The reason aligned: Kemp, 190.

85 Only just that morning: Diary of John Hibberdine, 24 January 1944 entry, IWM.

85 "I thought 'tactfully' was good": Kemp, BLO report, 1944, 54, HS 5/144.

85 "Only staff officers": Kemp, *No Colours or Crest*, 190–91.

86 The passage was dangerous: Kemp, 192.

86 "I tried to explain": Kemp, 193.

86 "I looked back": Kemp, 195.

87 "Have some raki": Kemp, 201.

87 "The next thing they'll do": Kemp, 209.
87 "In view of misunderstanding": Kemp, 210.
87 "We could not feel": Kemp, 211.
88 Kemp admitted that: Kemp, 211.
88 "the most abject": Kemp, 211.
88 "We said goodbye": Kemp, 211.

CHAPTER 7: THE SUBURBS OF ARMAGEDDON

89 The Suburbs of Armageddon: See John Masters, *The Road Past Mandalay* (London: Michael Joseph, 1961; London: Cassell, 2002), 165. Citations refer to the Cassell edition. This chapter's title is an allusion to a line from Masters's memoir of fighting with the Chindits in Burma. Masters went to Sandhurst with Smiley and to Wellington with Kemp, and he fought in Iraq at the same time as Smiley during the beginning of the war. They were men cut from the same cloth.
89 "he damned well": Kemp, *No Colours or Crest*, 215.
89 "was inclined to be vague": Smiley, *Albanian Assignment*, 138.
89 For eight runs: David Smiley, 1944 diary, April 16 entry, PPDS.
89 "Are you quite all right": Smiley, 1944 diary, April 16 entry, PPDS.
90 "made us all feel": Smiley, April 16 entry.
90 All four men were: Smiley, April 18 entry.
90 The count had invited: Amery, *Sons of the Eagle*, 78.
90 Amery noted that: Amery, 78. On the names, see Smiley, *Albanian Assignment*, 139–40.
90 "We were very relieved": Smiley, 139.
90 covered in black ash: Smiley, 140; and Smiley, 1944 diary, April 19 entry, PPDS.
90 parachutes were supposed to be: Smiley, *Albanian Assignment*, 140–41.
90 "felt one-up because": Smiley, 141.
91 It was a "small comfort": Smiley, 141.
91 "For the ways are many": Amery, *Sons of the Eagle*, 76. A photograph of the pistol was privately shared with the author by Leo Amery.
91 The son of a Cabinet: See Kemp, *No Colours or Crest*, 212. As Kemp had put it after hearing that the gifted political animal Amery would be joining the mission, "I was delighted at the news, for I reasoned that the British Government would not send so powerful a mission to Kupi unless it was intended to give them full support." Nosi, with anger rather than delight, may well have reasoned the same.
91 "We were not unkind": Smiley, *Albanian Assignment*, 141.
91 "They looked and acted": Smiley, 145–46.
92 "poacher might turn gamekeeper": Amery, *Sons of the Eagle*, 32–33.
92 He carried no outward weapon: Smiley, *Albanian Assignment*, 144.

92 "Each time I met him": Smiley, 144.

92 The feeling appeared to be: Smiley, 144.

93 "We Albanians are few": Amery, *Sons of the Eagle*, 88.

94 Power was not absent: Amery, 11.

94 "Let the King send": Amery, 124.

94 "typical F.O. message": Smiley, 1944 diary, June 4 entry, PPDS.

94 "an operation which": Amery, *Sons of the Eagle*, 174.

94 a previous suggestion: Amery, 174.

94 "He wants us to fight": Smiley, *Albanian Assignment*, 163.

95 "I wish he'd bite": Smiley, 163.

95 "David seems to be": Smiley, 157.

95 "you shall have action": Amery, *Sons of the Eagle*, 177.

95 After treating Amery: Signal no. 53, 12 July 1944, AMEJ 1/1/37 (SOE: Albanian Telegrams In, Bari to Field, 1944-05–1944-10), CAC; and Amery, *Sons of the Eagle*, 179.

95 Moving down to the piers: Smiley, *Albanian Assignment*, 158–59; and Amery, *Sons of the Eagle*, 180.

95 waited for the mule party: Smiley, *Albanian Assignment*, 159.

95 He sent the man: Amery, *Sons of the Eagle*, 181.

96 Germans firing off: Smiley, *Albanian Assignment*, 159.

96 were getting nervous: Smiley, 159.

96 "was tiresome enough": Smiley, 160.

96 "One German reminded us": Smiley, 160.

96 By three o'clock: Amery, *Sons of the Eagle*, 181.

96 They hoped to trap: Smiley, *Albanian Assignment*, 161.

96 from the grinning Jenkins: Smiley, 160.

96 The explosion was so large: Smiley, 1944 diary, June 22 entry, PPDS.

96 all of the traffic: Amery, *Sons of the Eagle*, 182.

97 "I am bitched": Smiley, *Albanian Assignment*, 167; and Smiley, 1944 diary, July 15 entry, PPDS.

97 "Tell me what": Amery, *Sons of the Eagle*, 238.

97 A literal militant priest: Smiley, *Albanian Assignment*, 156; and Amery, *Sons of the Eagle*, 178–79.

97 "there is no way out": Julian Amery, 1944 Albanian diary (top-copy typescript), August 8 entry, AMEJ 1/1/32, CAC.

98 It was "essential": Signal no. 60, 14 July 1944, AMEJ 1/1/37, CAC.

98 "I knew my house": Julian Amery, 1944 Albanian diary (top-copy typescript), July 15 entry, AMEJ 1/1/32, CAC.

98 "I feel very sorry": Smiley, 1944 diary, August 13 entry, PPDS.

98 Eyewitness testimony from: Kemp, *No Colours or Crest*, 124–25.

99 "Why do you have to": Kemp, 214.

99 Soon after he returned: Davies, *Illyrian Venture*, 98.

99 "a most fortunate accident": Kemp, *No Colours or Crest*, 221.

99 "obtain authority to hold": Watrous to Palmer, 8 June 1944, HS 5/39.

99 "informed of developments": Watrous to Palmer, 8 June 1944.

99 Hoxha declared that: Signal no. 164, 27 August 1944, AMEJ 1/1/37, CAC.

100 Smiley recorded the only: Smiley, 1944 diary, August 27 entry, PPDS.

100 Had McLean done anything: Signal no. 164, 27 August 1944, AMEJ 1/1/37.

100 To the Central Asians: Kharkov is now Kharkiv, Ukraine. It has become, alas, the renewed site of an assaulting Russian army.

100 The number would eventually: Smiley, *Irregular Regular*, 148.

100 bizarre dream come true: Amery, *Sons of the Eagle*, 276.

100 Now they had murdered: Amery, 274.

100 "Disregarding the fate": Smiley, *Albanian Assignment*, 180.

101 "interesting insight into": Smiley, 181.

101 The Central Asians appealed: Smiley, 181.

101 The quiet was suddenly: Amery, *Sons of the Eagle*, 275.

101 The Mareschal was dead: Amery, 275.

101 Amery saw the Liverpudlian: Amery, 275.

101 with Kupi's son Petrit: Smiley, *Albanian Assignment*, 182.

101 "What matters is what": Amery, *Sons of the Eagle*, 281.

102 His troops followed: Amery, 282.

102 One of his countrymen: Amery, 283.

102 "A Zogist officer with": Amery, 284.

102 They burned the German camp: Smiley, *Albanian Assignment*, 183.

102 a "lunatic message": Smiley, 1944 diary, September 9 entry, PPDS.

102 Amery was to remain: Signal no. 200, 9 September 1944, AMEJ 1/1/37, CAC.

103 They had harangued him: Eliot Watrous, the young and green staff officer (who'd been promoted to major after he took over from the dead Philip Leake), had heard a rumor that Julian Amery, technically a captain, was also wearing a major's crowns in the field. Watrous could have only gotten this information from someone communicating through the Partisan camp, likely via the spy Frederick Nosi. Perhaps it was inexperience or insecurity that pushed Watrous to such a source. Certainly, it revealed frustration from the staff office in Bari. As the issue clogged traffic on precious signal lines in the midst of a much-needed evacuation discussion, it also exposed a disagreeable inclination to punish for punishment's sake. McLean patiently explained the obvious: that as Amery's last name was so famous in Albania, he had merely meant to head issues off at the pass. Having already run one mission there, he knew that the rank of captain meant little in the mountains. Before they dropped in, McLean had asked Leake to promote Amery. Leake told McLean that it could be done in the field. Perhaps McLean had interpreted this as an unofficial advance promotion. Perhaps he had simply taken a good look around the rank-obsessed tribal society in which he operated and chosen a when-in-Rome approach. Or perhaps he had thought that Leake was about to put the paperwork in anyway. But then Leake was dead. Perhaps the issue was

not really Amery's embellished crowns. There were still elements in Bari and
Cairo who had never wanted Amery to get into the field at all. There was also
the issue of preference for the Communists. As the staff office signaled to
McLean, "This action on your part made work of A.L.O.s with Partisans extremely difficult." (See Signal no. 230, 2 October 1944, AMEJ 1/1/37, CAC.)

103 **"papers could be mine"**: Signal no. 74, 2 September 1944, AMEJ 1/1/36, CAC.
103 **He also probably could**: Eliot Watrous to Alan Palmer, 11 September 1944,
HS 5/39, TNA. Watrous also left McLean in the dark on a crucial local development. The officer with Hoxha, Alan Palmer, was receiving information
about what was known as Operation Ratweek, a major Allied air offensive
against German lines of retreat in Yugoslavia. Nowhere in the signals was
McLean given even a hint of such information. Operation Ratweek was run
by Fitzroy Maclean, the officer that the choleric Brigadier Keble had tried, and
failed, to keep away from Tito. The connections between the Yugoslavs and
Hoxha's Partisans were as tight as ever, both in the Balkans and in Bari.
104 **"We knew that this meant"**: Smiley, *Albanian Assignment*, 164.
104 **Another British officer with**: Amery, *Sons of the Eagle*, 314–15.
104 **Smiley feared it would**: Smiley, *Albanian Assignment*, 176–77.
104 **There had already been**: These men were not the only ones who mistrusted
the staff office in Bari. Fitzroy Maclean, the brigadier sent to Tito in Yugoslavia, said quite explicitly after the war, "I can assure you that I did not take the
first parachute that was offered me." See Martin, *Patriot or Traitor*, 125.

There were other stories as well. In a dramatic accusation, Rowland Winn
(later Lord St. Oswald), a British officer who was friends with the group, reported that Reginald Hibbert, a British officer serving with the Partisans and
a man whom Winn believed to be a Communist sympathizer, had told him
during a discussion that life was going to get unpleasant for him. "He said that
he had arranged with James Klugman [*sic*], who was with SOE in Bari, for
Smiley, Amery and McLean to leave the nationalists and move into partisan
territory," Winn wrote. "Then, he said, there would be a 'mistake' and all
three would be shot." See Nicholas Bethell, *The Albanian Operation of the CIA
and MI6, 1949–1953: Conversations with Participants in a Venture Betrayed*,
ed. Robert Elsie and Bejtullah Destani (London: McFarland & Company
2016), 140.

Other versions of that story, relayed to the author verbally, indicated that
an "airstrike" would take care of McLean and Smiley. Since the Partisans had
no air force of their own, this could have only meant intentionally calling in
friendly fire from the RAF . . . or giving information to the Germans, which
would have looked much like the Luftwaffe raid that killed Philip Leake.
104 **They had been warned**: Signal no. 34, 25 September 1944, AMEJ 1/1/36, CAC.
104 **Amery bought some**: It was a stratagem that was recognized as such by the
staff officers. They promptly turned around, changed the contents to make it
look like some sort of Amery family cabal, and delivered the doctored version

to the BLOs serving with Enver Hoxha: "At last the Zogists are moving. They have launched an attack on a bridge. They have blown up the bridge. Smiley, Amery and I took part in it." It was marked "Please show this personally to the Secretary of State for India." See Bethell, *Albanian Operation*, 98.

104 **"Wound no worse":** Signal no. 8, 10 September 1944, AMEJ 1/1/37, CAC.

105 **They now had seventy:** Smiley, *Albanian Assignment*, 184.

105 **They destroyed fifteen:** Smiley, 185.

105 **Set up along an S-bend:** Amery, *Sons of the Eagle*, 290.

105 **Even the hard-bitten Jenkins:** Amery, 291–92.

106 **The people shooting at him:** Smiley, *Albanian Assignment*, 186.

106 **The only local who would:** Smiley, 186.

106 **"most inveterate enemies":** Amery, *Sons of the Eagle*, 292.

106 **Then he was shot:** This was Llazar Fundo, who was captured alongside Said Beg Kryeziu, both with the British officer Tony Simcox. Fundo was a long-time political player in Albania. He had known Enver Hoxha for years and in fact had been one of the earliest members of the Communist Party in the country. But Fundo saw the flaws in Communism and left the party in the late 1930s—or so he thought. The Partisans had recognized Fundo when they forcibly detained Simcox and the rest of his mission and marched them to the Partisan headquarters at Berat. Fundo never even made it that far. Hoxha put the order to kill him in writing. Given to histrionics, like so many vicious petty dictators, Hoxha was specific: "Torture Zai Fundo to the brink of death and then execute him." The rest of the order betrayed Hoxha's anxieties. "Ask him questions about the following: Why did he go to Kosovo? Who sent him there and what instructions had he received? What are Gani [Kryeziu] and the English aiming to do? He must be held to account for his former activities and his treason. Send us his deposition with a trusted person. Then have Zai killed on the spot. Enver." All dictators order murder. Few sign their names. See Fevziu, *Enver Hoxha*, 52.

106 **Not long beforehand:** Fifty-three were evacuated in August (Signal no. 144, 17 August 1944, AMEJ 1/1/37, CAC) and 150 in June (Eliot Watrous to Alan Palmer, 17 June 1944, HS 5/39, TNA).

107 **The office was set up:** Letter from David Smiley to Roderick Bailey, 21 August 1999, PPDS.

107 **He'd had a friend:** Smiley, 1943 diary, February 26–April 9 entries, 124, PPDS.

107 **She later paid a price:** Smiley, 1944 diary, June 7 entry, PPDS. Her name was Linda Morse.

107 **"in order to test":** Smiley, October 26 entry.

107 **he was ambitious:** Even the British officer Reginald Hibbert, who was himself very supportive of the Communists to whom he was then assigned, found Watrous to be appallingly ambitious. See Reginald Hibbert, *Somewhere Near to History: The Wartime Diaries of Reginald Hibbert, SOE Officer in Albania, 1943-1944*, ed. Jane Nicolov (Oxford: Signal Books, 2020), 216.

108 **"keep you informed"**: Watrous to Palmer, 8 June 1944, HS 5/39, TNA.

108 **"Once the Partisans knew"**: Smiley, *Albanian Assignment*, 195–96.

109 **"Inshallah! We shall play"**: Amery, *Sons of the Eagle*, 327. *Inshallah* is a transliteration of an Arabic expression that means "God willing."

109 **Amery recorded his last**: Amery, 1944 Albanian diary, October 26 entry, AMEJ 1/1/3.

109 **"Their chief motive"**: Smiley, *Albanian Assignment*, 150.

109 **It went not to Eden**: Smiley, 197. Others, perhaps embarrassed by their own manipulation by Klugmann or their own sympathies with his politics, have hotly debated this or blamed the story on the conservatism of McLean and Amery, both of whom eventually served as Tory MPs. See, for example, Basil Davidson's *Special Operations Europe*; and Roderick Bailey, *The Wildest Province: SOE in the Land of the Eagle* (London: Jonathan Cape, 2008; London: Vintage, 2009). Citations refer to the Vintage edition.

109 **Her boss had made**: "Smiley, David de Crespigny (Oral History)," audio reel 4/7; and Smiley, 1994 diary, October 30 entry, PPDS.

110 **a "very nice girl"**: Smiley, 1944 diary, October 30 entry, PPDS.

110 **His name was John Eyre**: Smiley, October 30 entry. See also Nicholas Bethell, "Colonel David Smiley," interview in Bethell, *Albanian Operation*, 155. Smiley is quite safe as a source, beyond the contemporaneous nature of his diary entry. He was so politically disinterested that he preferred dangerous reconnaissance missions to conferences, even with Kupi, and was notably unable to keep signs of annoyance and boredom from his face during the endless political discussions with the Communist Partisans, even back when he and McLean were on good terms with them. (See Kemp, "Set Europe Ablaze," audio reel 1/2, 12:23–12:59.) Smiley was constitutionally disinclined to flights of fancy and possessed absolutely no reservoir of neuroticism. It was, after all, his own wife who later said, "David had no imagination, and that's why he was so brave!" (See Jones, *Clandestine Lives*, 333.)

110 **he was later sent home**: Kemp, *No Colours or Crest*, 212.

110 **He stood for the Communist**: Bailey, *Wildest Province*, 284.

110 **Smiley heard one**: Smiley, *Albanian Assignment*, 197.

110 **Even the languid McLean**: Amery, 1944 Albanian diary, October 29 entry, AMEJ 1/1/32.

110 **"I agree with you"**: Amery, *Sons of the Eagle*, 336.

111 **Nor would he ever**: Amery, 336–37.

111 **Hoxha succeeded in eliminating**: Hoxha liquidated everyone from the Communist "deviant" Mustafa Jinishi, felled in the north by an operation meant to look like a German ambush (though there were no Germans in the neighborhood). The Communists sold Gani out to the Germans at Gjakova. Once Gani was in Communist custody, Hoxha used him to capture Hasan. As Kosovars, both were eventually killed on the orders of not Hoxha but Tito: Hasan quickly, Gani more slowly. Said, evacuated by the British officer Tony

Simcox to Italy, was the only Kryeziu brother to survive. See Amery, 1944 Albanian diary, October 9 and 16 entries, AMEJ 1/1/32.

111 **Too much exposure:** Amery, October 28 entry.

111 **"Average? There is no such":** Glen, *Footholds against a Whirlwind*, 172–73. It was not Glen's only exposure to such brutality. In Bari, he found one of Klugmann's fellow travelers trying to repatriate a group of terrified and hysterical Dalmatian women and children to Tito. Glen prevented it, but only by pulling a gun on the other officer and informing him that the women and children would go over his dead body. They stayed. See "Glen, Alexander Richard (Oral History)," audio reel 7/8.

111 **The Soviets were taking:** One notable exception to the ban on foreigners in Central Asia was the indomitable Fitzroy Maclean, whose bold journeys (and fluent Russian) were part of what recommended him to Churchill for the Yugoslavia mission.

111 **Amery took them away:** Bassett, *Last Imperialist*, 112.

111 **And then he turned:** Amery, *Approach March*, 404–5.

CHAPTER 8: GO EAST

114 **They would have improved:** Kemp, *No Colours or Crest*, 219.

114 **The weather going over:** Kemp, 222.

114 **For several days:** Kemp, 223–24.

114 **"It is well known":** Kemp, 226.

114 **"cold but correct":** Kemp, 227.

115 **"have the opportunity of":** Kemp, 224.

115 **Often chased from:** Kemp, 235.

116 **"Sorrowfully we took":** Kemp, 243.

116 **"with all fittings":** Kemp, 251.

116 **"this is it":** Kemp, 250.

116 **Between what Kemp briskly:** Autobiographical notes, n.d., Private Papers of Lieutenant Colonel PMM Kemp, DSO, MC (hereafter cited as PPPK), IWM; and Kemp, *No Colours or Crest*, 251.

116 **"Poker was impossible":** Kemp, *No Colours or Crest*, 251.

116 **It was a game:** Kemp, "Set Europe Ablaze," audio reel 2/2.

116 **Stalin had wanted:** Kemp, *No Colours or Crest*, 253.

117 **That was how Kemp:** Kemp, 256.

117 **The alluring Polish countess:** Smiley, *Irregular Regular*, 158.

117 **Smiley had taken her:** Smiley, 1944 diary, early 1944 section, 3, PPDS.

117 **"various changes of heart":** Smiley, November–December entry.

118 **Her wedding to Billy:** Tarnowski, *Last Mazurka*, 226.

118 **their marriage was over:** Tarnowski, 308.

118 **His name was Prince Subha:** Smiley, *Irregular Regular*, 155.

118 **Smiley brought him to lunch:** Moss, *War of Shadows*, 59.

118 "a delightful person": Moss, 59.
118 "short of extending": Smiley, *Irregular Regular*, 167.
118 But the Thai resistance: Smiley, 167–68.
118 "I could not have wanted": Smiley, 158–59.
119 "Looking back from time's": Kemp, *No Colours or Crest*, 33–34.
119 Her father had died: For details on the Phillips family, see Eva-Marie Kröller, *Writing the Empire: The McIlwraiths, 1853–1948* (Toronto: University of Toronto Press, 2021), 334–46.
119 "I don't mind": Kemp, *No Colours or Crest*, 2.
119 "we were far from": Kemp, *Thorns of Memory*, 3.
119 A Russian headdress: "Captain P. M. MacI. Kemp and Miss Phillips," *Times* (UK), October 6, 1941.
120 She was also either forgetful: "Telephone Check on Marlow 121," 22 June 1944, KV 2/4418, TNA.
120 "There were plenty": Peter Kemp, *Alms for Oblivion* (London: Cassell, 1961), 3.
120 Their first flight: Smiley, *Irregular Regular*, 159.
121 "was a nuisance, but": Smiley, 159.
121 Then an outfit called: Masters, *Road Past Mandalay*, 36–37.
121 "In their most earnest": Masters, 37.
122 cooked on the scalding: Smiley, *Irregular Regular*, 69.
122 This last one was: Smiley, 84.
123 Of those recalled: For these stories and more, see Terence O'Brien, *The Moonlight War: The Story of Clandestine Operations in South-East Asia, 1944–5* (London: William Collins, Sons & Co., 1987; London: Arrow Books, 1989). Citations refer to the Arrow Books edition.
123 "But if any pilot": O'Brien, *Moonlight War*, 320.

CHAPTER 9: THE SILK ROAD

125 Smiley was waiting in Calcutta: Amery, *Approach March*, 429.
126 "apply to the largest country": Amery, 410.
127 Born in 1880: Amery, 417.
127 He was strangely consistent: Adrian Carton de Wiart, *Happy Odyssey: The Memoirs of Lieutenant-General Sir Adrian Carton de Wiart, V.C., K.B.E., C.B., C.M.G., D.S.O.* (London: Jonathan Cape, 1950; Yorkshire, UK: Pen and Sword, 2020), 54. Citations refer to the Pen and Sword edition.
127 Carton bore seventeen: Amery, *Approach March*, 417.
127 "He must have been": Amery, 411, 417.
127 He was reserved at first: Amery, 417–18.
127 His tongue was legendary: Amery, 418.
128 "He's very fierce": Amery, 418.
128 "rather surrealist quality": Amery, 412.
128 Amery was told: Amery, 412.

128 **Carton once flew:** Carton, *Happy Odyssey*, 267.

128 **"As we came down":** Amery, *Approach March*, 413.

129 **Not only had both men:** Carton, *Happy Odyssey*, 265.

129 **One day at lunch:** Amery, *Approach March*, 420.

129 **He had not been selected:** Faber, *Speaking for England*, 482–83.

130 **"remains a lasting regret":** Amery, *Approach March*, 428.

130 **"Chinese cooking in its range":** Amery, 426.

130 **"reputed to be over":** Smiley, *Irregular Regular*, 173.

130 **He took it:** Fielding, *One Man in His Time*, 54.

131 **Sinkiang was ruled:** On that rumor, see Peter Fleming, *News from Tartary: A Journey from Peking to Kashmir* (New York: Charles Scribner's Sons, 1936; Evanston, IL: Marlboro Press, 1999), 171. Citations are to the Marlboro Press edition.

132 **Part of his baggage:** Letter from Gordon Etherington-Smith to First Secretary of the British Embassy in Chungking, 23 August 1945, 12/2407, Political and Secret Department Records, India Office Records (hereafter cited as IOR/L/PS followed by the relevant reference number), British Library, London, UK (hereafter cited as BL).

132 **Despite the passage:** Fleming, *News from Tartary*, 338.

132 **Most of their going:** Etherington-Smith to First Secretary of the British Embassy, 23 August 1945, IOR/L/PS 12/2407.

132 **One British traveler:** Letter from KPS Menon to Olaf Caroe, 25 October 1944, IOR/L/PS 12/2407, BL.

132 **"two rather anxious":** Etherington-Smith to First Secretary of the British Embassy, 23 August 1945, IOR/L/PS 12/2407.

133 **Several were killed doing:** On the dangers of the mail route, see Lady Macartney, *An English Lady in Chinese Turkestan* (London: Ernest Benn, 1931; Oxford: Oxford University Press, 1985), 112–13. Citations are to the Oxford University Press edition.

133 **This involved four nail-biting:** Etherington-Smith to First Secretary of the British Embassy, 23 August 1945, IOR/L/PS 12/2407.

133 **Stretched out were:** On the view, see Menon to Caroe, 25 October 1944, IOR/L/PS 12/2407.

133 **Waiting for them were:** Etherington-Smith to First Secretary of the British Embassy, 23 August 1945, IOR/L/PS 12/2407.

133 **"a remarkable sight":** Etherington-Smith to First Secretary of the British Embassy, 23 August 1945.

133 **The war was over:** Fielding, *One Man in His Time*, 58.

134 **The excuse for the militarization:** For details, see Kashgar Weekly Reports, 1944–1946, IOR/L/PS 12/2384, BL.

134 **Rebels flanked the city:** Fielding, *One Man in His Time*, 59.

134 **he worked on improving:** Fielding, 60.

134 **He learned falconry:** Fielding, 60.

135 With the various mountain: Fielding, 60.
135 Upon hearing of Jack's: "In Which I Remember John Amery," annotated draft chapter of Approach March, 1967–68, AMEJ 8/3/48, CAC.
136 "Had it lain within": "In Which I Remember John Amery," annotated draft chapter of *Approach March*, 1967–68, AMEJ 8/3/48.
136 He purported to own: Faber, *Speaking for England*, 282.
136 One noblewoman came begging: Faber, 292.
136 He amassed somewhere: Faber, 281, 283.
137 In subsequent years: Faber, 282–96.
137 "There was no room": "In Which I Remember John Amery," annotated draft chapter of *Approach March*, 1967–68, AMEJ 8/3/48.
137 "have had a kitten": Amery, *Approach March*, 25.
137 Julian visited Jack: "In Which I Remember John Amery," annotated draft chapter of *Approach March*, 1967–68, AMEJ 8/3/48.
137 But the legal defenses crumbled: See, for example, Julian Amery, typescript diary from October 1945 to December 1946, 20 November 1945 entry, AMEJ 4/1/1, CAC.
137 The trial was meant to: Amery, typescript diary from October 1945 to December 1946, 28 November 1945 entry, AMEJ 4/1/1.
138 "I am caught": Amery, 28 November 1945 entry.
138 "I just wanted to tell": Amery, 28 November 1945 entry.
138 The trial lasted: Rebecca West, "The Crown versus John Amery," Reporter at Large, *New Yorker*, December 15, 1945, 78.
139 Revealed were horrifying: Faber, *Speaking for England*, 126–32.
139 He was frequently paranoid: Faber, 293.
139 This was aside from: Faber, 293–94.
139 The psychiatrist who prepared: Faber, 504.
139 and he could calculate: Faber, 127.
139 "There's going to be": Faber, 440.
139 Jack had confessed to one: Faber, 199.
140 He then promptly: Faber, 200.
140 "I would go to the": "In Which I Remember John Amery," annotated draft chapter of *Approach March*, 1967–68, AMEJ 8/3/48.
140 The chief executioner: "Naim Attallah Talks to Lord Amery," interview, *Oldie Review of Books*, November 27, 1992, 23; and Faber, *Speaking for England*, 512.
140 "I've always wanted to": Faber, 512.
140 His last words: Amery, typescript diary from October 1945 to December 1946, 18 December 1945 entry, AMEJ 4/1/1.
140 When the implications: Faber, *Speaking for England*, 512.
140 At ten past nine: Amery, typescript diary from October 1945 to December 1946, 18 December 1945 entry, AMEJ 4/1/1.

141 **"We got home somehow":** Amery, 18 December 1945 entry.

141 **Asked at the end:** "Naim Attallah Talks to Lord Amery," 23.

141 **"Such searing experiences":** "In Which I Remember John Amery," annotated draft chapter of *Approach March*, 1967–68, AMEJ 8/3/48.

CHAPTER 10: GETTING TO KNOW YOU

143 **Getting to Know You:** This title is an allusion to a tune from Rodgers and Hammerstein's Broadway musical *The King and I*, set in what is now Thailand.

143 **"Cicadas!" he declared:** Masters, *Road Past Mandalay*, 182.

144 **Cobras and pythons:** Fielding, *One Man in His Time*, 53.

144 **The sun heated the pipes:** David Smiley, 1945 diary, April 11 entry, PPDS.

144 **This was despite the fact:** Smiley, *Irregular Regular*, 161.

144 **"They operated against us":** Smiley, 162.

144 **There were the usual:** Kemp, *Alms for Oblivion*, 9.

144 **Albania had not harbored:** Smiley, *Irregular Regular*, 163. Smiley did, however, kill a quite sizable one before his first extraction from that country.

144 **At the jungle school:** Kemp, *Alms for Oblivion*, 9.

145 **The jungle was so thick:** Smiley, *Irregular Regular*, 164.

145 **The theory was put into:** Smiley, 164.

146 **By the time Smiley:** Smiley, 155.

146 **Thailand had an underground:** It was not the first set of strange bedfellows; for a variety of reasons, many of them due to a personal hostility toward Charles de Gaulle, President Roosevelt had recognized the actual collaborators running Vichy France until 1943.

146 **By February 1945:** CANDLE report of 2/17/1945, HS 1/68, TNA.

147 **Muddy though it was:** Smiley, *Irregular Regular*, 178.

147 **This represented about:** Smiley, 169.

147 **Pluto had organized:** CANDLE report of 6/4/1945, HS 1/68, TNA.

147 **Elsewhere on the continent:** Kemp, *Alms for Oblivion*, 7.

148 **it had even struck:** Kemp, *No Colours or Crest*, 210.

148 **Not to be outdone:** "A Ballade against the Gout," July 9, 1945, PPPK, IWM.

148 **But he was adamant:** Kemp, *Alms for Oblivion*, 7.

148 **Now Kemp shared:** Kemp, 10.

149 **"perplexity to annoyance":** Moss, *War of Shadows*, 156.

149 **"I am in the pink":** Moss, 156.

149 **She got engaged:** Moss, 156.

149 **"was a white man's burden":** Kemp, *Alms for Oblivion*, 9.

149 **Death was averted:** Kemp, 9.

150 **One officer who saw:** John Hedley, *Jungle Fighter: Infantry Officer, Chindit & S.O.E. Agent in Burma, 1941–1945* (Brighton, UK: Tom Donovan, 1996), 99.

150 **The King himself:** Hedley, *Jungle Fighter*, 99.

151 **His fingernails were burned:** David Smiley, 1945 Operation Candle diary, June 23 and 24 entries, PPDS.

151 **Smiley's staff officers:** Smiley, *Irregular Regular*, 166–67, 195.

151 **His caretakers soon:** Smiley, 1945 Operation Candle diary, June 24 entry, PPDS.

152 **Admonished by the radio:** Smiley, *Irregular Regular*, 196.

152 **It relieved some of:** Smiley, 196.

152 **"blow my brains out":** Smiley, 1945 Operation Candle diary, June 27 entry, PPDS; and Smiley, *Irregular Regular*, 196.

152 **The first aircraft to take:** Smiley, *Irregular Regular*, 197.

152 **They flew about two hundred:** Smiley, 197.

152 **Kemp found Smiley's wounds:** Kemp, *Alms for Oblivion*, 10.

153 **The doctors who had received:** Smiley, *Irregular Regular*, 198.

153 **"I fully intended":** David Smiley to Lady Smiley, 17 July 1945, PPDS.

153 **He landed badly burned:** Smiley, *Irregular Regular*, 78–79.

153 **stricken by malignant malaria:** Smiley, 1941 diary, June 27 and 28 entries, 68, PPDS.

153 **Though Smiley had pronounced:** Smiley, June 27 and 28 entries, 68.

153 **He had gotten to keep:** Jones, *Clandestine Lives*, 167.

154 **He shipped the dead-skin:** Jones, 167.

154 **Standing on the tarmac:** Kemp, *Alms for Oblivion*, 12.

154 **"The tibia went squish":** Bethell, *Albanian Operation*, 140.

154 **"the strongest convictions":** Kemp, *Alms for Oblivion*, 11.

155 **He poured the entire:** Kemp, 12.

155 **"squalor and discomfort":** Kemp, 12.

155 **One Liberator pilot:** Smiley, *Irregular Regular*, 162.

155 **Winn could be heard:** Kemp, *Alms for Oblivion*, 13.

155 **He looked up to see:** Kemp, 124

155 **Kemp was appreciative:** Kemp, 14.

156 **Pluto threw a party:** Kemp, 18.

156 **He suffered no more:** Kemp, 20.

156 **"We can keep":** Kemp, *Alms for Oblivion*, 18.

157 **He estimated that:** Masters, *Road Past Mandalay*, 163.

157 **On that officer's own:** Masters, 163.

157 **After the emperor declared:** Gavan Daws, *Prisoners of the Japanese: POWs of World War II in the Pacific* (New York: William Morrow, 1994), 336.

157 **That same day:** Daws, *Prisoners of the Japanese*, 336.

157 **It went via the local:** Smiley, *Irregular Regular*, 204–5, 215–16.

157 **The reply came back:** Smiley, 205.

158 **Despite the British understatement:** "To the British Military Mission from the Senior Medical Officer, POW Camp UBON, Thailand," n.d., PPDS.

158 **The three men were brought:** Smiley, *Irregular Regular*, 207.

158 **"pathetically glad to see":** Smiley, 1945 Operation Candle diary, August 24 entry, PPDS.

158 **More than sixty thousand:** Daws, *Prisoners of the Japanese*, 184; and John Dower, *War without Mercy: Race and Power in the Pacific War* (New York: Pantheon Books, 1986), 48.

158 **Fifteen thousand of:** Dower, *War without Mercy*, 48.

159 **One set of Americans:** Daws, *Prisoners of the Japanese*, 186–87.

159 **The Japanese impressed:** Dower, *War without Mercy*, 47.

159 **Given that the Japanese:** See, for example, the story of the Burmese village of Sinthe, recounted in O'Brien, *Moonlight War*, 59. As O'Brien writes in his war memoir, "I had to remind myself of another Japanese army captain. He was the one who one day went into the village of Sinthe, where we had stopped for half an hour; he ordered his men to seize the headman and all his family, together with four other complete families—twenty-one people in all, men and women and children—and he took them back down to Bhamo. And there, in the public square, he cut off their heads."

159 **The guard let the doctor:** Daws, *Prisoners of the Japanese*, 192.

159 **A prisoner who shouted:** Daws, 204.

159 **It was a horror story:** The French novel on which the movie was based was translated by Xan Fielding, Smiley's close friend from Tara and an SOE officer in Crete, France, and later Thailand.

159 **The day before Smiley:** "Doy, Cyril (Oral History)," interview by Peter M. Hart, August 2002, IWM, catalog no. 23812, audio reel 15/17, https://www.iwm.org.uk/collections/item/object/80022020.

160 **Smiley struggled to hold:** Smiley, *Irregular Regular*, 209–10.

160 **Several Australians took:** Jones, *Clandestine Lives*, 176.

160 **Aside from the physical abuses:** Smiley, *Irregular Regular*, 211.

160 **The former camp commandant:** Smiley, 211.

160 **"you are the last":** Smiley, 223.

161 **There were a handful:** Smiley, 214.

161 **Ten thousand packets:** Jones, *Clandestine Lives*, 180.

161 **Bandits had robbed:** Smiley, *Irregular Regular*, 214–15; and Smiley, 1945 Operation Candle diary, September 16 entry, PPDS.

161 **fifteen young Korean:** Smiley, *Irregular Regular*, 223.

161 **Smiley wrote out:** Smiley, 223.

162 **They would come to:** Smiley, 223.

163 **"Captain Hedley, sir":** Masters, *Road Past Mandalay*, 137.

163 **Ordered to abandon:** Masters, 137.

163 **He walked into one:** Masters, 136.

163 **"Have you brought my mail?":** Kemp, *Alms for Oblivion*, 78.

163 **He regularly offended:** Smiley, *Irregular Regular*, 220.

163 **"He appeared late":** Smiley, 1945 Operation Candle diary, November 5 entry, PPDS.

163 **Finally convinced of:** Hedley, *Jungle Fighter*, 120.

164 **"It soon became clear":** Hedley, 121.

164 **"But the most irrefutable":** Hedley, 121.
164 **Smiley was amazed:** Smiley, 1945 Operation Candle diary, October 20 entry, PPDS.

CHAPTER 11: CRY HAVOC

165 **Cry Havoc:** This title is an allusion to a line spoken by Mark Antony in Shakespeare's *Julius Caesar*: "Cry 'Havoc!' and let slip the dogs of war."
166 **himself no fan of:** T. E. Lawrence, *Seven Pillars of Wisdom* (London: Jonathan Cape, 1935; Hertfordshire, UK: Wordsworth Editions, 1997), 337. Citations refer to the Wordsworth Editions edition.
166 **That sentiment was led:** The term at the time, disused today and considered derogatory, was "Annamites," referring to the Vietnamese people from Annam. For simplicity's sake, I have used *Vietnamese* throughout.
167 **The Vietnamese who organized:** Not all Vietnamese people were Communists, though most of the Communists in the region were indeed Vietnamese. The danger posed to the French could be Communist, nationalist, ethnic, or all three combined.
167 **The Viet Minh's revolution:** Peter Dunn, *The First Vietnam War* (New York: St. Martin's Press, 1985), 67–68.
167 **Kemp saw a Dakota:** Kemp, *Alms for Oblivion*, 27.
167 **He had been stuck:** Kemp, 28.
169 **were massed together:** Kemp, 32.
169 **"We had to say":** Kemp, 33.
169 **Ho Chi Minh would reputedly:** Dunn, *First Vietnam War*, 67.
169 **"you have only just":** Kemp, *Alms for Oblivion*, 33.
170 **He could take:** Kemp, 34; and Smiley, *Irregular Regular*, 226–27.
170 **In halting English:** Kemp, *Alms for Oblivion*, 34.
171 **"he's been tipped off":** Kemp, 35. On the outnumbering and menacing Viet Minh, see Smiley, 1945 Operation Candle diary, September 7 entry, PPDS.
171 **A corporal appeared:** Smiley, *Irregular Regular*, 227.
171 **The nun retained:** Kemp, *Alms for Oblivion*, 35.
171 **"to protect the women":** Kemp, 35.
172 **This evening marked:** Kemp, 35.
172 **The presence of a Japanese:** Smiley, *Irregular Regular*, 227–29. His name was Hosada, and he would soon be charged with war crimes in a separate incident.
172 **"pathetically grateful":** Smiley, *Irregular Regular*, 228.
172 **"I began to regret":** Kemp, *Alms for Oblivion*, 42.
173 **requisitioned a Japanese officer:** Kemp, 40.
173 **As Kemp's heart pounded:** Smiley, 1945 Operation Candle diary, September 11 entry, PPDS; and Kemp, *Alms for Oblivion*, 41.
173 **Despite being badly:** Smiley, *Irregular Regular*, 231.

174 "they must have been unattractive": Kemp, *Alms for Oblivion*, 41.

174 Tavernier was in desperate need: Kemp, 31.

174 Orders from SOE headquarters: Kemp, 44.

175 find a space of their own: Kemp, 46.

175 "He would never have done": Kemp, 46.

175 he omitted to mention: Aaron Bank, *From OSS to Green Berets: The Birth of Special Forces* (Novato, CA: Presidio Press, 1986), 2.

175 He was hard-charging: Aaron Bank was a gifted organizer and a master of US Army bureaucracy. It was he who, after serving as a staff officer in the Korean War, founded the legendary special-operations unit best known as the Green Berets.

175 With that completed: Bank, *From OSS to Green Berets*, 63–104.

176 The American general posted: On this saga, see Dunn, *First Vietnam War*, 69–118.

176 "The Chinese are noted": Dunn, *First Vietnam War*, 118.

177 Bank had promised that: Kemp, *Alms for Oblivion*, 48.

177 "He spoke to me": Kemp, 48.

177 "Tavernier and his men": Kemp, 49.

177 "So did the French": Kemp, 49.

178 "I can certainly go": Kemp, 49.

178 As they stepped from: Kemp, 49.

178 "Bien!" spat the delegate: Kemp, 50.

179 "Don't be ridiculous": Kemp, 50.

179 "I don't know": Kemp, 50.

179 "you and I are going": Kemp, 50.

180 putting on his best: Kemp, 50.

180 "No!" screamed the delegate: Kemp, 51.

180 *look after us now*: Kemp, 51.

180 "Peter!" he whispered: Kemp, 51.

181 "I hope you're proud": Kemp, 51–52.

181 The major slowly said: Kemp, 52.

182 But to Kemp: Kemp, 52.

182 "Where is François?": Kemp, 53.

182 Her previous partner: Kemp, 53.

182 Kemp included his suggestions: Kemp, 54.

183 The American saluted: Kemp, 54.

183 "But I'd like to be": Kemp, 54–55.

183 "Whatever may be said": Kemp, 55.

183 "Apart from everything": Kemp, 55–56.

183 Smiley sent an urgent: Smiley, *Irregular Regular*, 234.

183 But Gracey rapidly found: Opinions on Gracey's actions in Saigon differ, but his character is uncontested. By all accounts, he was a fluent Gurkhali speaker

beloved by his troops. He was no reactionary, and eventually the young government of Pakistan personally requested that he be the commander in chief of their army at independence. See Dunn, *First Vietnam War*, 164.

184 **They were not gentle:** Dunn, *First Vietnam War*, 195.

184 **Vietnamese whom the Communists:** Dunn, *First Vietnam War*, 203.

184 **Theirs even appeared:** "French Fleet Aids Indo-China Move," *New York Times*, October 4, 1945.

184 **He had been succeeded:** Truman was encouraged in this view by a jealous J. Edgar Hoover, head of what was then his own empire, the FBI.

184 **He had issued:** Richard Harris Smith, *OSS: The Secret History of America's First Central Intelligence Agency* (New York: Dell Publishing Co., 1973), 364.

184 **who in his own memoir:** Bank, *From OSS to Green Berets*, 123, 127–31.

184 **Approaching a Viet Minh:** Dunn, *First Vietnam War*, 215. The story of the circumstances surrounding the death of Colonel Dewey has been much contested. The Americans have blamed Gracey, claiming that he did not allow Dewey to fly flags. The British have argued that this was standard procedure and that Gracey did take steps to protect Dewey: for one, by suggesting that Dewey append the Stars and Stripes to the front of the jeep, where it would be more visible than a fluttering flag, and for two, by repeatedly trying to move him into the safety of the city.

185 **"I can't quite make out":** Kemp, *Alms for Oblivion*, 56.

185 **When the staff reported:** FIC sitreps for the week ending on 17 October 1945, HS 1/100 (Sitreps: March–November), TNA.

185 **machine-gun fire pierced:** Kemp, *Alms for Oblivion*, 64.

185 **The subsequent bursts:** Kemp, 65.

186 **"I imagine that a smuggler":** Kemp, 64.

186 **The grateful but worried:** Kemp, 65.

186 **were found beheaded:** Kemp, 76.

186 **In a scene eerily similar:** Smiley, 1945 Operation Candle diary, November 4 entry, PPDS.

186 **They were pinned down:** Smiley, November 4 entry.

186 **He indignantly spilled:** Kemp, *Alms for Oblivion*, 76.

187 **"I suppose I must seem":** Kemp, 77.

187 **what the office euphemistically:** FIC sitreps for the week ending on 1 November 1945, HS 1/100, TNA.

187 **"in one word of cabalese":** Kemp, *Alms for Oblivion*, 77.

188 **The staff office summary:** FIC sitreps report for the week ending on 7 November 1945, HS 1/100, TNA. David Smiley's private diary from the same period confirms the real story: "Heard the fighting yesterday consisted of a patrol of Lao from Tavannier's [*sic*] band attacking a houseful of Annamites and killing fifteen without loss and setting the house on fire. It was being used as an Annamite HQ." See Smiley, 1945 Operation Candle diary, November 2 entry, PPDS.

CHAPTER 12: THE MOST MARVELOUS JOB
THE ARMY HAS EVER GIVEN ANYONE

189 "almost too old": Smiley, 1941 diary, 49, PPDS.
189 There were about a dozen: Smiley, 49.
189 "to cheer us up": Smiley, *Irregular Regular*, 62.
190 "All I could see": Smiley, 62.
190 Then there was the time: Smiley, *Albanian Assignment*, 15.
190 It was found the next: Smiley, 15.
190 not able to save: Smiley, *Irregular Regular*, 172.
190 he'd had two other: Smiley, 239.
190 The pilot would land: David Smiley with Peter Kemp, *Arabian Assignment* (London: Leo Cooper, 1975; Leeds, UK: Sapere Books, 2020), 63–64. Citations refer to the Sapere Books edition.
190 Now heading to Bangkok: Smiley, *Irregular Regular*, 238.
190 It was piloted by: Smiley, 238.
190 As the plane sank: Smiley, 238.
190 they were flying at no: Smiley, 238.
190 was running over the only: Kemp, *Alms for Oblivion*, 69.
191 "Do you see any": Kemp, 69.
191 Prang climbed out: Kemp, 70.
191 they hit a very large: Smiley, 1945 Operation Candle diary, November 2 entry, PPDS.
191 "it seems they forgot": Kemp, *Alms for Oblivion*, 71.
191 Along with the Mad: Kemp, 79.
192 The pain and fuzziness: Kemp, 80.
192 "Of course it would never": Kemp, 82.
192 Creeping home half-covered: Kemp, 82.
192 "They produced several theories": Kemp, 82.
193 "I am heartily thankful": Kemp, 83.
193 Hedley packed him: Kemp, 78.
193 "the most marvelous job": Kemp, "Set Europe Ablaze," audio reel 2/2, 24:42–24:46.
194 Indonesia had been placed: Kemp, *Alms for Oblivion*, 85.
194 Mansergh's Indian troops: Kemp, 87–88.
195 "If they chop you up": Kemp, 89.
195 In a scene that could: Kemp, 93.
196 "could not suppress a surge": Kemp, 96.
196 "in my unearned hour": Kemp, 97.
196 sitting down to review: Kemp, 97–98.
197 Peter Kemp stood just off: "Dutch Landings on Bali," directed by Desmond Davis (UK: SEAC Film Unit, 1946), IWM, catalog no. JFU 531, 35-mm film reel, https://www.iwm.org.uk/collections/item/object/1060034738.

197 **"I could almost feel"**: Kemp, *Alms for Oblivion*, 156.

198 **He was found later**: Kemp, 178–79.

198 **"Now I felt the full"**: Kemp, 172.

198 **They were together that June**: Kemp, *No Colours or Crest*, 216–17.

198 **This was where Kemp's wife**: "Telephone Check on Marlow 121," June 22, 1944, KV 2/4418, TNA.

199 **he was "most apologetic"**: "Telephone Check on Marlow 121," KV 2/4418.

199 **"Bitterly I cursed"**: Kemp, *Alms for Oblivion*, 172.

199 **A few months earlier**: "Hilda Elizabeth Kemp," June 3, 1944, KV 2/4418, TNA.

199 **"one of the finest pairs"**: Kemp, BLO report, 1944, 10, HS 5/144.

199 **It simply proclaimed**: "Major G. V. Seymour and Mrs. H. E. Kemp," *Times* (UK), July 1, 1946.

200 **In none of his papers**: Notes from an interview between Roderick Bailey and David Smiley, June 2000.

200 **"took no pleasure"**: Kemp, *Alms for Oblivion*, 172. The story has a sad ending on all sides. Lizzie and Seymour had one child who lived for only a day before perishing. Their second was born posthumously. George Seymour died at his desk from a heart attack while serving on headquarters staff in Singapore in July of 1953.

200 **"You've earned an air passage"**: Kemp, *Alms for Oblivion*, 181–82.

200 **"in a very bad way"**: Smiley, 1945 Operation Candle diary, November 21 entry, PPDS.

CHAPTER 13: OLD FRIENDS AND NEW BEGINNINGS

203 **"Church mice do not"**: Nicholas Bethell, "Billy McLean," interview in Bethell, *Albanian Operation*, 117.

204 **"If it's no"**: Nicholas Bethell, "Julian Amery," interview in Bethell, *Albanian Operation*, 19.

204 **Within a few days**: Bethell, "Julian Amery," 19.

204 **the republican Balli**: On this, see Bethell, "Billy McLean," 118.

204 **He pledged his own**: Julian Amery's notes from 21 May 1949, AMEJ 1/1/65 (SIS Adventures, 1948-03–1950-04), CAC.

205 **the man who still called**: Bethell, "Billy McLean," 118–19.

205 **"Such a man"**: Amery, *Approach March*, 311.

206 **"could always be relied upon"**: Bassett, *Last Imperialist*, 139.

206 **The brilliant Lawrence**: On this, see Scott Anderson, *Lawrence in Arabia: War, Deceit, Imperial Folly and the Making of the Modern Middle East* (New York: Anchor, 2014).

206 **He once spent Christmas**: Amery, *Approach March*, 151–55.

206 **"Nothing I have ever done"**: Amery, 149.

207 **"Honourable members may not"**: Bassett, *Last Imperialist*, 247.

207 "You look very young": Amery, *Approach March*, 239.

207 The Yugoslav intelligence officer: Amery, 247–48.

207 Amery had helped smuggle: Amery, 226.

207 "east of the Lindenstrasse": Amery, 150; and Bethell, "Julian Amery," 18.

207 "thought it wiser": Amery, *Approach March*, 194.

208 Amery soothed the monarch: Bassett, *Last Imperialist*, 139.

208 "quite the most dazzling": Bassett, 139.

208 "This sanatorium enjoyed": Kemp, *Thorns of Memory*, 314.

208 The men were close: Nicholas Bethell, "Peter Kemp," interview in Bethell, *Albanian Operation*, 105.

208 It fell to Kemp: Nicholas Bethell, *The Great Betrayal: The Untold Story of Kim Philby's Biggest Coup* (London: Hodder and Stoughton, 1984), 102. It was not the last time that a Kupi, a handgun, and British-style laws would come into conflict. Years later, it fell to Julian Amery to detangle Abas Kupi's son Petrit from a capital charge in Australia, where the younger Kupi had shot dead a man who had killed his uncle. See Nicholas Shakespeare, "Return to the Land of Zog," *Daily Telegraph*, October 5, 1991.

209 It was a quiet wedding: See "Lieutenant-Colonel P. Kemp and Miss C. Henry," *Times* (UK), November 18, 1946.

209 She was also resourceful: Bethell, "Peter Kemp," 106.

209 as Kemp dryly noted: Bethell, "Peter Kemp," 106.

209 Julian Amery hosted: Bethell, "Julian Amery," 16.

209 "great peasant skill": Bethell, *Great Betrayal*, 102–3; and Bethell, "Julian Amery," 14.

209 "the lunch where they chased": Bethell, "Julian Amery," 16.

210 Smiley declared that: Smiley, *Irregular Regular*, 248.

210 Always known as Moy: Jones, *Clandestine Lives*, 198–99.

210 Independent and formidable: Jones, 198.

210 She had served as: Jones, 199.

210 she was working at Bush: Jones, 199.

210 A major in the Scots: John Retallack, *The Welsh Guards* (London: Frederick Warne, 1981), 141.

210 tall and beautiful: P. S. Allfree, *Warlords of Oman* (London: Robert Hale, 1967), 113.

211 At her age: See Jones, *Clandestine Lives*, 201–4.

211 When Perks and Fielding: Bethell, *Great Betrayal*, 44.

211 "I rather jumped at it": Bethell, 44.

213 "a lovely old building": Smiley, *Irregular Regular*, 250.

213 "We had a girl": Nicholas Bethell, "Moy Smiley," interview in Bethell, *Albanian Operation*, 157.

213 The Pixies would need: This was the way that the British, who took responsibility for the operation in the south, would land them; a larger and longer American operation would involve parachute drops in the north.

213 **Both were former naval:** Ben Macintyre, *A Spy among Friends: Kim Philby and the Great Betrayal* (New York: Broadway Books, 2014), 126–27.

214 **"If you find a yacht":** Nicholas Bethell, "Sam Barclay," interview in Bethell, *Albanian Operation*, 27.

214 **Offering them cigarettes:** Bethell, "Sam Barclay," 28.

214 **It was imperative:** Nicholas Bethell, "Terence Cooling," interview in Bethell, *Albanian Operation*, 52.

215 **"My job was going":** Bethell, "Terence Cooling," 53.

215 **The landing itself was successful:** Bethell, "Terence Cooling," 54.

215 **Those who survived straggled:** See Jones, *Clandestine Lives*, 234.

215 **they had been "expected":** "Smiley, David de Crespigny (Oral History)," reel 6/7, 15:28–15:34.

215 **kept up their double lives:** Jones, *Clandestine Lives*, 233.

216 **who ran the radio:** See Jones, 233–34; and "Smiley, David de Crespigny (Oral History)," reel 6/7, 15:39–15:48.

216 **Declaring that Roman Catholicism:** Fielding, *One Man in His Time*, 80.

216 **McLean's bride had once:** Vane Ivanović, *LX: Memoirs of a Jugoslav* (New York: Harcourt Brace, 1977), 69.

217 **He was probably not expecting:** Fielding, *One Man in His Time*, 73.

217 **Her twin daughters:** Ivanović, *Memoirs of a Yugoslav*, 69.

217 **Marina remembered nothing:** Author's private conversation with Marina Cobbold, March 1, 2022.

217 **Daška's divorce decree:** Fielding, *One Man in His Time*, 75.

217 **they returned to London:** Fielding, 81.

218 **"gave Philby over drinks":** Macintyre, *A Spy among Friends*, 141.

218 **"that bloody man Philby":** "Smiley, David de Crespigny (Oral History)," reel 6/7, 11:45–11:47.

218 **As one intelligence officer:** Nicholas Bethell, "Rodney Dennys," interview in Bethell, *Albanian Operation*, 60.

219 **"adapt their tactics":** Klugmann and Stewart conversation, 8 August 1945, KV 2/791.

219 **He knew what the senior:** Klugmann and Stewart conversation, 8 August 1945.

219 **Klugmann had been delighted:** Klugmann and Stewart conversation, 8 August 1945.

220 **The MI6 officer signed:** Klugmann and Stewart conversation, 8 August 1945.

221 **This was the secret:** Modin, *My Five Cambridge Friends*, 218–19.

221 **As the onetime Soviet:** Modin, 218.

221 **Amery received a letter:** On Clifford, see "Clifford, Lewis Hugh (Oral History)," interview by Rose Coombs, IWM, catalog no. 4516, audio recording, https://www.iwm.org.uk/collections/item/object/80004476.

221 **Clifford had also deduced:** Letter from Lewis Hugh Clifford to Julian Amery,

n.d. (known to be 1975), AMEJ 2/1/73 (General Correspondence, 1975-03–1975-07), CAC.

221 **on this subject:** "Jack, Archibald Frederick Maclean (Oral History)," interview by Conrad Wood, March 18, 1989, IWM, catalog no. 10640, audio recording, https://www.iwm.org.uk/collections/item/object/80010418.

222 **in the Lords:** *Parliamentary Debates*, Lords, 5th series, vol. 357 (February 26, 1975), col. 891.

222 **The public battles:** Letter from Saul Frampton to David Smiley, 25 November 1996, PPDS.

222 **It was only in private:** Letter from Archie Jack to Lewis Hugh Clifford, n.d. (known to be 1975), AMEJ 2/1/73, CAC.

223 **Opening the door:** Macintyre, *A Spy among Friends*, 196.

223 **"There was no trace":** Macintyre, 194.

223 **Amery promptly asked:** Amery, *Approach March*, 446.

223 **seven years younger:** Bassett, *Last Imperialist*, 144.

223 **"clear and favourable":** Amery, *Approach March*, 446.

223 **Billy McLean stood:** Bassett, *Last Imperialist*, 143–44; and Amery, *Approach March*, 446.

224 **"even his sexuality":** Geoff Andrews, *The Shadow Man: At the Heart of the Cambridge Spy Circle* (New York: I. B. Tauris, 2015), 242.

CHAPTER 14: A SEAT OF MARS

225 **A Seat of Mars:** This title is an allusion to John of Gaunt's soliloquy in Shakespeare's *Richard II*, often more famous for the line that comes just after: "This other Eden, demi-paradise."

225 **Peter Kemp was woken:** Kemp, *Thorns of Memory*, 319.

226 **One of Rákosi's habits:.** The AVO was reorganized and renamed in 1949. The entire agency was abolished by Nagy's government on October 28, 1956. See Peter Kenez, *Before the Uprising: Hungary under Communism, 1949–1956* (Cambridge, UK: Cambridge University Press, 2022), 66–87, https://www.cambridge.org/core/books/abs/before-the-uprising/terror/4787D1CEC6A27EEF-12A666D2556440C7; and "Working Notes from the Session of the CPSU CC Presidium on 30 October 1956," Wilson Center, October 30, 1956, https://digitalarchive.wilsoncenter.org/document/working-notes-session-cpsu-cc-presidium-30-october-1956.

226 **"they have replaced":** Victor Sebestyen, *Twelve Days: The Story of the 1956 Hungarian Revolution* (New York: Pantheon Books, 2006), 94.

227 **"That phrase originated":** Peter Kemp, "Hungarian Tragedy," *Spectator*, October 23, 1976, 9.

227 **"And I did start":** Sebestyen, *Twelve Days*, 151.

228 **As he prepared to leave:** Peter Kemp, "Tanks in Budapest," *Spectator*, November 1, 1986, 15–16.

229 "It'll be a hell": Kemp, *Thorns of Memory*, 319.

229 He was also bringing: Kemp, 320.

229 Kemp had watched: Kemp, 322.

229 "The Russian troops are pulling": Kemp, "Tanks in Budapest," 16; and Kemp, *Thorns of Memory*, 324.

230 Amery was walking: Julian Amery, 1956 typescript diary, July 26 entry, AMEJ 4/1/9, CAC.

230 built by a Frenchman: Donald Neff, *Warriors at Suez: Eisenhower Takes America into the Middle East* (New York: Linden Press, 1981), 16.

230 The agreement indicated: Bassett, *Last Imperialist*, 151. See also *Parliamentary Debates*, Commons, 5th series, vol. 527 (May 17, 1954).

231 "much the best speech": Amery, 1956 typescript diary, March 7 entry, AMEJ 4/1/9.

231 McLean ended the speech: Fielding, *One Man in His Time*, 103; and *Parliamentary Debates*, Commons, 5th series, vol. 549 (March 7, 1956), cols. 2142–47.

231 Eden congratulated McLean: Fielding, *One Man in His Time*, 103.

232 "I don't know whether": Bassett, *Last Imperialist*, 153.

232 "How's the second Bordeaux": Amery, 1956 typescript diary, November 8 entry, AMEJ 4/1/9.

232 "We reckoned with Soviet": Amery, November 8 entry.

232 As one British diplomat later: Kemp, "Hungarian Tragedy," 9.

233 It was unfair . . . to say: Sebestyen, *Twelve Days*, xxv.

233 that although the freedom: Kemp, "Hungarian Tragedy," 9.

233 Stirred this time: Kemp, *Thorns of Memory*, 324.

233 As the Russians crushed: Kemp, 325.

233 The relieved ambassador: Kemp, 325.

233 It was said that in the aftermath: Kemp, "Hungarian Tragedy," 9.

234 He could still recall: Kemp, "Hungarian Tragedy," 9.

234 "I have something": Kemp, *Thorns of Memory*, 326.

235 "Good God!" Kemp exclaimed: Kemp, 326.

235 "Seventeen and sixteen": Kemp, 326.

235 "Time is running out": Kemp, 327.

236 "Oh my God": Kemp, 135.

237 As his body: Kemp, 237.

237 "we felt the full shame": Kemp, 237.

238 "I have a suggestion": Kemp, *Thorns of Memory*, 328.

239 "Angliski journalist": Kemp, 330.

239 When questioned as to: Kemp, 330–31.

240 Sweating as his papers: Kemp, 332.

240 "Thank you very much!": Kemp, 332.

240 "Your pals have arrived": Kemp, 339.

240 "Permission to renew": Kemp, 339.

241 "That's your problem": Kemp, 339.

241 They made it with fifteen: Kemp, 339.

CHAPTER 15: LORD OF THE GREEN MOUNTAIN

243 Uniform soaked straight: Smiley, *Arabian Assignment*, 31.

243 This expanded Smiley's: Smiley, 56.

244 "No oil, no welfare": Bassett, *Last Imperialist*, 161.

244 "their lack of cogent": Allfree, *Warlords of Oman*, 50.

245 in a scathing nod: Bassett, *Last Imperialist*, 167.

245 "spoke an English so faultless": Smiley, *Arabian Assignment*, 54.

246 "I will think about it": Smiley, 56.

246 "You must know": Smiley, 57.

246 Smiley was so appalled: Smiley, 41.

246 He was a proper man: Smiley, 116, 128.

246 Near the British Museum: Allfree, *Warlords of Oman*, 105.

247 "at last we could communicate": Allfree, 105.

247 As Smiley pointed out: Smiley, *Arabian Assignment*, 36.

247 The one instance of what: Smiley, 36.

247 "When I joined this army": Smiley, 36.

248 These passes could: Allfree, *Warlords of Oman*, 72.

248 Temperatures regularly reached: Smiley, *Arabian Assignment*, 79.

248 much to Smiley's chagrin: Smiley, 79.

248 Forty-five of the fifty: Smiley, 79.

248 Shorts were forbidden: Smiley, 79.

248 "if I had been alone": Allfree, *Warlords of Oman*, 40.

248 While he waited: Smiley, *Arabian Assignment*, 59.

249 Only 158 were detonated: David Smiley, "Muscat and Oman," *Journal of the Royal United Service Institution* 105, no. 617 (February 1960): 38.

249 In a letter to Amery: Bassett, *Last Imperialist*, 170.

249 The late 1950s were still: On the anti-Western turn in the UN, see Mark Mazower, *No Enchanted Palace: The End of Empire and the Ideological Origins of the United Nations* (Princeton, NJ: Princeton University Press, 2009); and Mark Mazower, *Governing the World: The History of an Idea, 1815 to the Present* (New York: Penguin, 2012).

249 In response to a friend: Bassett, *Last Imperialist*, 168.

250 Told that regulars: Bassett, 170.

250 "They were the coolest": Allfree, *Warlords of Oman*, 114.

250 Despite the increasing involvement: Smiley, *Arabian Assignment*, 78.

251 It would be a combined: Smiley, 103.

251 "a straight slog": Smiley, 102.

251 "I'm prepared to bet": Smiley, 102.

251 Slog up the mountain: Smiley, "Muscat and Oman," 44.

251 Faced with a cliff: Allfree, *Warlords of Oman*, 124.

251 Enemy resistance collapsed: Smiley, *Arabian Assignment*, 106.

252 Smiley's forces suffered few: Smiley, "Muscat and Oman," 44.

252 was so "criminally careless": Smiley, *Arabian Assignment*, 109.

252 he was still using it: Smiley, 109.

252 "as soldiers—as *your* soldiers!": Smiley, 83.

252 The rebels had stuffed: Smiley, "Muscat and Oman," 37.

253 Smiley's most effective tactic: Smiley, *Arabian Assignment*, 123.

253 In their wake rode: Smiley, 124.

253 simply would not pay: Smiley, 130.

253 "David? How would you": Smiley, 131.

254 No western expedition had: Colin Thubron, introduction to *Arabia Felix: The Danish Expedition of 1761–1767*, by Thorkild Hansen (New York: NYRB Classics, 2017), x.

254 It was ancient even: Hansen, *Arabia Felix*, 212–13.

254 It would also challenge: For a full review of the British situation in Aden and in Yemen more broadly, see Clive Jones, *Britain and the Yemen Civil War, 1962–1965: Ministers, Mercenaries and Mandarins: Foreign Policy and the Limits of Covert Action* (Brighton, UK: Sussex Academic Press, 2010).

255 On this trip: Billy McLean, "Notes on Conversation with King Said, 22 October 1962," AMEJ 1/7/2 (Report on Visit to the Yemen by Neil McLean, 1962-10–1963-04), CAC.

256 The King of Jordan proudly: Billy McLean, Report on Visit to the Yemen, 27–30 October 1962, AMEJ 1/7/2, CAC.

256 "look what you've done": Fielding, *One Man in His Time*, 154–55.

256 "power does not lie": *Parliamentary Debates*, Commons, 5th series, vol. 667 (November 13, 1962), cols. 267–77.

256 The Republicans did hold: McLean, Report on Visit to the Yemen, 27–30 October 1962, AMEJ 1/7/2.

256 Flying them was also moot: McLean, Report on Visit to the Yemen, 27–30 October 1962, AMEJ 1/7/2.

256 These soldiers had been told: McLean, Report on Visit to the Yemen, 27–30 October 1962, AMEJ 1/7/2.

257 In McLean's judgment: McLean, Report on Visit to the Yemen, 27–30 October 1962, AMEJ 1/7/2.

257 But there was still much: Lieutenant Colonel Neil McLean, "The War in the Yemen" (lecture, Royal United Services Institute, London, UK, October 20, 1965).

257 Almost exactly twenty years: Smiley, *Arabian Assignment*, 148.

257 The first person Smiley: David Smiley, diary of first Yemen trip, 1963, 1, PPDS.

257 "there is my old enemy": Smiley, *Arabian Assignment*, 148–49.

258 "You'll do nothing": Smiley, 149.
258 "Colonel Smiley commanded": Smiley, 151.
258 "Colonel Smiley was only": Smiley, 151.
258 It was difficult going: Smiley, diary of first Yemen trip, 24 June 1963 entry, PPDS.
258 "if I had to be": Smiley, 8 July 1963 entry.
259 The Imam's forces were hampered: Smiley, *Arabian Assignment*, 188–89.
259 The same number of heads: Carl von Horn, *Soldiering for Peace* (New York: David McKay Company, 1967), 377.
260 "were reveling in the": von Horn, *Soldiering for Peace*, 307.
260 "then well known for": Bassett, *Last Imperialist*, 180.
260 "a *war* that never was": Bassett, 180.
260 One of the men tasked: Bassett, 181.
260 "Why do you need": Bassett, 181.
260 The bride in question: Bassett, 181.
261 The story at the time: Smiley, *Arabian Assignment*, 193–96. The French mercenaries were formidable; among them was the legendary warrior Roger Faulques.
261 The risk-averse segments: Bassett, *Last Imperialist*, 182.
261 One official sent: Bassett, 182.
262 "President Nasser's idea": McLean, "The War in the Yemen."
262 The Imam retired: "Smiley, David de Crespigny (Oral History)," reel 7/7, 02:40–02:58.

CHAPTER 16: HEIRS THROUGH HOPE

263 Heirs through Hope: This title is an allusion to part of the Anglican Mass said after Communion, which would have been known to all four men: "We are heirs, through hope, of your everlasting kingdom."
263 He had argued that: Fielding, *One Man in His Time*, 161–62.
264 The original crew: Author's private conversation with Simon Courtauld, March 9, 2022.
264 This was a demotion: Author's private conversation with Simon Courtauld, March 9, 2022.
264 "If remarriage is": Kemp, *Thorns of Memory*, 314.
265 The captain briefly considered: Fielding, *One Man in His Time*, 167–68.
265 The boyfriend of the red-haired: Fielding, 168.
265 After the Belgians handed: Kemp, *Thorns of Memory*, 351.
266 Kemp arrived a few months: Kemp, 351.
266 Watching French troops: Fielding, *One Man in His Time*, 91–92.
266 Promising his wife: Fielding, 93.
267 He purported to have: Kemp, *Thorns of Memory*, 341.

267 **After learning about:** Kemp, 345.

267 **This time it took:** Peter Kemp, "Visit to Kingdom of Million Elephants," *Times* (UK), April 3, 1961.

267 **"ferocious artillery and mortar":** Kemp, *Thorns of Memory*, 349.

268 **He boarded a helicopter:** Kemp, 355–56.

268 **"But that wasn't a dangerous":** Kemp, 358.

268 **long had ties to unrecognized:** Fielding, *One Man in His Time*, 158.

268 **a photograph from 1962:** See the photo inserts in Fielding, *One Man in His Time*.

269 **"unpaid undersecretary for":** Fielding, 109.

269 **McLean arrived for lunch:** Author's private conversation with Simon Courtauld, March 9, 2022.

269 **he had difficulty in:** Fielding, *One Man in His Time*, 158.

269 **"Please could you send":** Letter from Billy McLean to Ahmad, 13 December 1967, AMEJ 1/7/10, CAC.

269 **"I am staying":** Author's private conversation with Marina Cobbold, March 1, 2022.

270 **"Splendid!" said McLean:** Fielding, *One Man in His Time*, 157.

271 **Through a series of forty:** Bassett, *Last Imperialist*, 176.

271 **"a superb job":** Bassett, 176.

271 **it was Amery who:** Bassett, 215.

271 **"foiled by the erratic":** "Peter Kemp: Synopsis (Autobiography)," PPPK, IWM, n.d., 8.

271 **"I wouldn't worry about Julian":** Bassett, *Last Imperialist*, 205.

271 **"In life one learns":** "Naim Attallah Talks to Lord Amery," 23.

272 **Amery was subtle:** See Bassett, *Last Imperialist*, 156–57.

272 **"would have ruined us":** Smiley, *Arabian Assignment*, 130.

272 **The second Tara:** Jones, *Clandestine Lives*, 323.

272 **"not very nice":** Author's private conversation with Marina Cobbold, March 1, 2022.

272 **Spearfishing was a pastime:** Smiley, *Arabian Assignment*, 128.

272 **Amery's son, Leo, recalled:** Author's private conversation with Leo Amery, December 28, 2021.

272 **When he was finally:** Ivanović, *LX*, 332.

273 **"What can one think":** "Drawn by the Sound of Guns," *Spectator*, August 17, 1985, 15.

273 **On that journey:** "Peter Kemp: Synopsis (Autobiography)," PPPK, n.d., 8.

273 **McLean entertained Leo:** Fielding, *One Man in His Time*, 181; and author's private conversation with Leo Amery, December 28, 2021.

273 **When McLean's stepdaughter Tessa:** Author's correspondence with Tessa Kennedy, February 8, 2022.

274 **He died on November:** Fielding, *One Man in His Time*, 207.

274 **at St. Margaret's in Westminster:** Fielding, 207.
274 **many more like McLean:** "Billy McLean," eulogy by Julian Amery, AMEJ 8/6/30, CAC.
275 **After one last mission:** "Peter Kemp: Synopsis (Autobiography)," PPPK, n.d., 10.
275 **Kemp inquired of:** Author's private conversation with Simon Courtauld, March 9, 2022.
275 **And while he was:** "Drawn by the Sound of Guns," *Spectator*, 15.
275 **as he pointed out:** Peter Kemp, "Left against Left in Latin America," *Spectator*, April 9, 1977, 6–7.
276 **"the furnaces of Hell!":** "Drawn by the Sound of Guns," *Spectator*, 15.
276 **"Serbs seem to enjoy":** Kemp, "Waiting for a Bloodbath," 14.
276 **"It is dangerous":** Kemp, 14. At one point during this same trip, Kemp, sitting at a café with his experienced journalist escort, was firmly told that it was time to go, as a full-blown riot was being quashed by police not twenty-five meters away. "Can't I finish my beer first?" Kemp asked.
276 **He still looked marvelous:** Photo shared with the author by Richard Bassett.
276 **Ever straight and honest:** Jones, *Last Imperialist*, 327.
276 **Smiley surveyed the:** Nicholas Shakespeare, "Return to the Land of Zog," *Daily Telegraph Weekend*, October 5, 1991.
277 **"Half a century":** Shakespeare, "Return to the Land of Zog."
277 **"This is one of the":** Shakespeare, "Return to the Land of Zog."
277 **"My earliest impression":** Gavin Maxwell, "An Ego and an Id," *New Statesman*, November 29, 1958, PPPK.
278 **Kemp credited her:** Kemp, *Thorns of Memory*, 359.
278 **"let's get married":** Author's private conversation with Ian Kemp, February 15, 2022.
279 **"my closest friend":** Kemp, *Thorns of Memory*, 359. See also the dedication page.
279 **"Eton and Oxford":** Author's private conversation with Charles Moore, March 22, 2022.
279 **"My proudest moment":** "Naim Attallah Talks to Lord Amery," 23.
280 **only one photograph:** Author's private conversation with Leo Amery (Julian Amery's son), December 28, 2021.
280 **Julian Amery died:** Bassett, *Last Imperialist*, 252–53.
280 **the first husband:** On his death, see Retallack, *Welsh Guards*, 141.
281 **But he never woke:** "Lieutenant A. D. Tweedie, Late the Blues and Royals," *Household Cavalry Journal*, no. 11 (2003/2004): 95.
281 **But Smiley was never one:** David Smiley, "Return to Yemen," *British-Yemeni Society Journal* 11 (2003): 19–24, https://britishyemenisociety.org.uk/bysj-2003-vol-11/.
281 **"I'm proud that some":** Jones, *Clandestine Lives*, 337.

EPILOGUE: THIS PENDANT WORLD

283 **This Pendant World:** The title is an allusion to a line from Book II of Milton's *Paradise Lost*. It comes as Satan escapes and wings his way to Earth to contest the souls of humanity: "And fast by hanging in a golden Chain / This pendant world, in bigness as a Starr / Of smallest Magnitude close by the Moon."

285 **in a tribal way:** Tribalism also governed the experience of the men who dropped into the Balkans. How else to explain the otherwise misfit combinations that peppered the place, and that drove history? Think, for example, of the strange partnership between the NKVD spy James Klugmann and the choleric Brigadier Keble: men whose politics could not have been more different but whose shared ambitions led to similar conclusions. Or the remarkably close relationship that the Conservative MP and brigadier Fitzroy Maclean, sent as Churchill's personal representative, shared with the Communist Yugoslav leader Josip "Tito" Broz. After Churchill was warned that support for Tito meant that Yugoslavia would likely turn Communist after the war, Churchill demanded to know if Fitzroy intended to live there himself. No, replied the young brigadier, to which Churchill responded that, in this wartime case, he needed to have short-term considerations. Fitzroy did live in Yugoslavia after the war—Tito temporarily changed the law to allow Fitzroy to buy a house near his own on one of Croatia's resort islands.

285 **As one SOE officer:** Sweet-Escott, *Baker Street Irregular*, 162.

287 **Near the end of his:** "Naim Attallah Talks to Lord Amery," 20.

289 **"only the admiration":** Kemp, "Hungarian Tragedy," 9.

290 **"there will be a harvest":** Amery, *Sons of the Eagle*, viii.

A NOTE ON SOURCES

296 **McLean's own personal archive:** Even certain personal archives have not escaped this distinction. Smiley donated, for copying, a limited portion of his 1943 diary to the official SOE archive at the National Archives in Kew. The National Archives redacted certain information about the Partisans that might have later caused embarrassment. (An unbowdlerized but still limited copy survives at the Imperial War Museums; the full original version rests in private family hands.) The Imperial War Museums also lost the signal book (from the Siam mission) that Smiley donated to its collections. Likewise, Billy McLean's voluminous archive, sadly still uncatalogued, given the Imperial War Museums' limited resources, has apparently seen several files go missing.

296 **"Politicians and staff officers":** O'Brien, *Moonlight War*, 213.

297 **SOE's Cairo and Bari:** Some of the paperwork, such as Keble's signal to Churchill trying to prevent the appointment of Fitzroy Maclean as direct liaison to Tito, was forged. Most of the signal traffic was destroyed or never retained after it was initially deciphered. (What remains from the Concensus II mis-

sion was preserved, tellingly, not by the staff office but by Julian Amery and David Smiley.) Reports filed by pro-Partisan officers were rewarded by staff officers with cover notes warmly recommending them; those filed by men like Tony Simcox, who was arrested by the Partisans and marched to the coast, were judged to be "highly coloured by personal prejudices" and to have conceptions that were "wrong." See, for example, a 1944 report by Captain Victor Smith (HS 5/129, TNA) versus a 1944–1945 report by Major Simcox (HS 5/135, TNA).

The cover sheet to the second Albania report by McLean, Smiley, and Amery contained a staff office rebuttal of no fewer than seven pages, 20 percent of the length of the report itself (HS 5/126, TNA). Those are the ones that survived. Bari was the kind of place where staff officers who had never set foot on the ground in Yugoslavia created maps of areas of Partisan and Chetnik control that bore no relationship to reality; they first gaslit ("you're misinformed") and then banned field officers who had the temerity to point out otherwise. Thus, documents that passed anywhere near the staff office are necessarily suspect.

SELECTED BIBLIOGRAPHY

ARCHIVES AND UNPUBLISHED SOURCES

The National Archives, Kew, UK
Parliamentary Debates, Hansard Archives, UK Parliament
The Papers of Julian Amery, Churchill Archives Centre, Churchill College, Cambridge, UK
Oral Histories, Imperial War Museums, London, UK
Private Papers, Imperial War Museums, London, UK
Political and Secret Department Records, India Office Records, British Library, London, UK
The Private Papers of David Smiley
The Private Papers of Alan Hare

PUBLISHED SOURCES

Aldrich, Richard J. *Intelligence and the War against Japan*. Cambridge, UK: Cambridge University Press, 2000.

Allen, W. E. D. *Guerrilla War in Abyssinia*. New York: Penguin Books, 1943.

Allfree, P. S. *Warlords of Oman*. London: Robert Hale, 1967.

Amery, Julian. *Approach March: A Venture in Autobiography*. London: Hutchinson, 1973.

Amery, Julian. *Sons of the Eagle: A Study in Guerrilla War*. London: Macmillan, 1948.

Anderson, Scott. *Lawrence in Arabia: War, Deceit, Imperial Folly and the Making of the Modern Middle East*. New York: Anchor, 2014.

Andrew, Christopher. *Defend the Realm: The Authorized History of MI5*. New York: Alfred A. Knopf, 2009.

Andrew, Christopher, and Vasili Mitrokhin. *The Mitrokhin Archive: The KGB in Europe and the West*. New York: Penguin, 2000. First published 1999 by Allen Lane (London). Page references are to the 2000 edition.

Andrews, Geoff. *The Shadow Man: At the Heart of the Cambridge Spy Circle*. New York: I. B. Tauris, 2015.

Atkinson, Rick. *An Army at Dawn: The War in North Africa, 1942–1943*. New York: Picador, 2002.

Bailey, Roderick. *The Wildest Province: SOE in the Land of the Eagle*. London: Vintage, 2009. First published 2008 by Jonathan Cape (London). Page references are to the 2009 edition.

Bank, Aaron. *From OSS to Green Berets: The Birth of Special Forces*. Novato, CA: Presidio Press, 1986.

Bassett, Richard. *The Last Imperialist: A Portrait of Julian Amery*. York, UK: Stone Trough Books, 2015.

Beevor, Antony. *Crete 1941: The Battle and the Resistance*. New York: Penguin, 2014.

Beevor, J. G. *SOE: Recollections and Reflections, 1940–1945*. London: Bodley Head, 1981.

Berger, Jean-François, ed. *Dans l'ombre de Tito: Entretiens avec le général Vladimir Velebit*. Geneva: Éditions Slatkine, 2000.

Bethell, Nicholas. *The Great Betrayal: The Untold Story of Kim Philby's Biggest Coup*. London: Hodder and Stoughton, 1984.

Bethell, Nicholas. *The Albanian Operation of the CIA and MI6, 1949–1953: Conversations with Participants in a Venture Betrayed*. Edited by Robert Elsie and Bejtullah Destani. London: McFarland & Company, 2016.

Carton de Wiart, Adrian. *Happy Odyssey: The Memoirs of Lieutenant-General Sir Adrian Carton de Wiart, V.C., K.B.E., C.B., C.M.G., D.S.O.* London: Jonathan Cape, 1950. Reprint, Yorkshire, UK: Pen and Sword, 2020. Page references are to the 2020 edition.

Cooper, Artemis. *Cairo in the War, 1939–1945*. London: John Murray, 2013.

Davidson, Basil. *Special Operations Europe: Scenes from the Anti-Nazi War*. London: Grafton Books, 1987.

Davies, Edmund. *Illyrian Venture: The Story of the British Military Mission to Enemy-Occupied Albania, 1943–44*. London: Bodley Head, 1952.

Daws, Gavan. *Prisoners of the Japanese: POWs of World War II in the Pacific*. New York: William Morrow, 1994.

Djilas, Milovan. *Wartime*. New York: Harcourt Brace Jovanovich, 1977.

Dower, John. *War without Mercy: Race and Power in the Pacific War*. New York: Pantheon Books, 1986.

Dunn, Peter. *The First Vietnam War*. New York: St. Martin's Press, 1985.

Faber, David. *Speaking for England: Leo, Julian and John Amery—The Tragedy of a Political Family*. London: Free Press, 2005. Reprint, New York: Pocket Books, 2007. Page references are to the 2007 edition.

Fevziu, Blendi. *Enver Hoxha: The Iron Fist of Albania*. Edited by Robert Elsie and translated by Majlinda Nishku. London: I. B. Tauris, 2017.

Fielding, Xan. *Hide and Seek: The Story of a Wartime Agent*. London: Secker & Warburg, 1954. Reprint, Philadelphia: Paul Dry Books, 2013. Page references are to the 2013 edition.

Fielding, Xan. *One Man in His Time: The Life of Lieutenant-Colonel NLD ('Billy') McLean, DSO*. London: Macmillan, 1990.

Fleming, Peter. *News from Tartary: A Journey from Peking to Kashmir*. New York: Charles Scribner's Sons, 1936. Reprint, Evanston, IL: Marlboro Press, 1999. Page references are to the 1999 edition.

Foot, M. R. D. *SOE: The Special Operations Executive, 1940–46*. London: Mandarin, 1990. First published 1984 by the British Broadcasting Corporation (London). Page references are to the 1990 edition.

Forbes, Andrew D. W. *Warlords and Muslims in Chinese Central Asia: A Political History of Republican Sinkiang, 1911–1949*. Cambridge, UK: Cambridge University Press, 1986.

Gaddis, John Lewis. *We Now Know: Rethinking Cold War History*. Oxford: Clarendon Press, 1997.

Gati, Charles. *Failed Illusions: Moscow, Washington, Budapest, and the 1956 Hungarian Revolt*. Washington, DC: Woodrow Wilson Center Press, 2006.

Gati, Charles. *Hungary and the Soviet Bloc*. Durham, NC: Duke University Press, 1986.

Glen, Alexander. *Footholds against a Whirlwind*. London: Hutchinson, 1975.

Hansen, Thorkild. *Arabia Felix: The Danish Expedition of 1761–1767*. New York: NYRB Classics, 2017.

Hart-Davis, Duff. *The War That Never Was: The True Story of the Men Who Fought Britain's Most Secret Battle*. London: Century, 2011.

Hastings, Max. *Vietnam: An Epic Tragedy, 1945–1975*. New York: Harper, 2018.

Hedley, John. *Jungle Fighter: Infantry Officer, Chindit & S.O.E. Agent in Burma, 1941–1945*. Brighton, UK: Tom Donovan, 1996.

Hibbert, Reginald. *Albania's National Liberation Struggle: The Bitter Victory*. London: Pinter Publishers, 1991.

Hibbert, Reginald. *Somewhere Near to History: The Wartime Diaries of Reginald Hibbert, SOE Officer in Albania, 1943–1944*. Edited by Jane Nicolov. Oxford: Signal Books, 2020.

Hoxha, Enver. *The Anglo-American Threat to Albania: Memoirs of the National Liberation War*. Tirana, Albania: 8 Nëntori Publishing House, 1982.

Ivanović, Vane. *LX: Memoirs of a Jugoslav*. New York: Harcourt Brace, 1977.

Jeffrey, Keith. *The Secret History of MI6, 1909–1949*. New York: Penguin, 2010.

Jones, Clive. *Britain and the Yemen Civil War, 1962–1965: Ministers, Mercenaries and Mandarins: Foreign Policy and the Limits of Covert Action*. Brighton, UK: Sussex Academic Press, 2010.

Jones, Clive. *The Clandestine Lives of Colonel David Smiley: Code Name 'Grin.'* Edinburgh: Edinburgh University Press, 2020.

Kemp, Ian. *British G.I. in Vietnam*. London: Robert Hale, 1969.

Kemp, Peter. *Mine Were of Trouble*. London: Cassell, 1957. Reprint, Albuquerque: Mystery Grove Publishing Co., 2020. Page references are to the 2020 edition.

Kemp, Peter. *No Colours or Crest*. London: Cassell, 1958. Reprint, Albuquerque: Mystery Grove Publishing Co., 2020. Page references are to the 2020 edition.

Kemp, Peter. *Alms for Oblivion*. London: Cassell, 1961.

Kemp, Peter. *The Thorns of Memory: Memoirs*. London: Sinclair-Stevenson, 1990.

Kröller, Eva-Marie. *Writing the Empire: The McIlwraiths, 1853–1948*. Toronto: University of Toronto Press, 2021.

Lamb, Charles. *To War in a Stringbag*. Rev. ed. 1977. Reprint, London: Bantam Books, 1980. Page references are to the 1980 edition.

Lawrence, T. E. *Seven Pillars of Wisdom*. Hertfordshire, UK: Wordsworth Editions, 1997. First published 1935 by Jonathan Cape (London). Page references are to the 1997 edition.

Leigh Fermor, Patrick. *Abducting a General: The Kreipe Operation in Crete*. New York: NYRB, 2014.

Macartney, Lady. *An English Lady in Chinese Turkestan*. London: Ernest Benn, 1931. Reprint, Oxford: Oxford University Press, 1985. Page references are to the 1985 edition.

Macintyre, Ben. *A Spy among Friends: Kim Philby and the Great Betrayal*. New York: Broadway Books, 2014.

Maclean, Fitzroy. *Eastern Approaches*. London: Jonathan Cape, 1949. Reprint, Chicago: Time-Life Books, 1980. Page references are to the 1980 edition.

Martin, David, ed. *Patriot or Traitor: The Case of General Mihailovich: Proceedings and Report of the Commission of Inquiry of the Committee for a Fair Trial for Draja Mihailovich*. Stanford, CA: Hoover Institution Press, 1978.

Masters, John. *The Road Past Mandalay*. London: Michael Joseph, 1961. Reprint, London: Cassell, 2002. Page references are to the 2002 edition.

Mazower, Mark. *No Enchanted Palace: The End of Empire and the Ideological Origins of the United Nations*. Princeton, NJ: Princeton University Press, 2009.

Mazower, Mark. *Governing the World: The History of an Idea, 1815 to the Present*. New York: Penguin, 2012.

Mitter, Rana. *Forgotten Ally: China's World War II, 1937–1945*. Boston: Mariner Books, 2014.

Modin, Yuri. *My Five Cambridge Friends: Burgess, Maclean, Philby, Blunt, and Cairncross by Their KGB Controller*. New York: Farrar, Straus and Giroux, 1994.

Moss, W. Stanley. *A War of Shadows*. London: T. V. Boardman, 1952. Reprint, Philadelphia: Paul Dry Books, 2014. Page references are to the 2014 edition.

Moss, W. Stanley. *Ill Met by Moonlight: The Classic Story of Wartime Daring*. London: George G. Harrap & Co., 1950. Reprint, London: Weidenfeld & Nicolson, 2014. Page references are to the 2014 edition.

Neff, Donald. *Warriors at Suez: Eisenhower Takes America into the Middle East*. New York: Linden Press, 1981.

Norins, Martin Richard. *Gateway to Asia: Sinkiang, Frontier of the Chinese Far West*. New York: John Day Company, 1944.

O'Brien, Terence. *The Moonlight War: The Story of Clandestine Operations in South-East Asia, 1944–5*. London: William Collins, Sons & Co., 1987. Reprint, London: Arrow Books, 1989. Page references are to the 1989 edition.

Philby, Kim. *My Silent War*. New York: Grove Press, 1968.

Quayle, Anthony. *A Time to Speak*. London: Barrie & Jenkins, 1990.

Retallack, John. *The Welsh Guards*. London: Frederick Warne, 1981.

Schellenberg, Walter. *Invasion 1940: The Nazi Invasion Plan for Britain*. London: St. Ermin's Press, 2000.

Schmidt, Dana Adams. *Yemen: The Unknown War*. New York: Holt, Rinehart and Winston, 1968.

Sebestyen, Victor. *Twelve Days: The Story of the 1956 Hungarian Revolution*. New York: Pantheon Books, 2006.

Smiley, David. *Albanian Assignment*. London: Chatto & Windus, 1984. Reprint, Leeds, UK: Sapere Books, 2020. Page references are to the 2020 edition.

Smiley, David. *Irregular Regular*. Norwich, UK: Michael Russell Publishing, 1994. Reprint, Leeds, UK: Sapere Books, 2020. Page references are to the 2020 edition.

Smiley, David. "Muscat and Oman." *Journal of the Royal United Service Institution* 105, no. 617 (February 1960): 29–47.

Smiley, David, with Peter Kemp. *Arabian Assignment*. London: Leo Cooper, 1975. Reprint, Leeds, UK: Sapere Books, 2020. Page references are to the 2020 edition.

Smith, Richard Harris. *OSS: The Secret History of America's First Central Intelligence Agency*. New York: Dell Publishing Co., 1973.

Starr, S. Frederick. *Xinjiang: China's Muslim Borderland*. Armonk, NY: M. E. Sharpe, 2004.

Strawson, John. *The Battle for North Africa*. New York: Ace Books, 1969.

Stuart, Duncan. "'Of Historical Interest Only': The Origins and Vicissitudes of the SOE Archive." *Intelligence and National Security* 20, no. 1 (2005): 14–26.

Sweet-Escott, Bickham. *Baker Street Irregular*. London: Methuen, 1965.

Tarnowski, Andrew. *The Last Mazurka: A Family's Tale of War, Passion, and Loss*. New York: St. Martin's Press, 2007.

von Horn, Carl. *Soldiering for Peace*. New York: David McKay Company, 1967.

Wilkinson, Peter. *Foreign Fields: The Story of an SOE Operative*. 1997. Reprint, London: I. B. Tauris, 2002. Page references are to the 2002 edition.

Yu, Maochun. *OSS in China: Prelude to Cold War*. Annapolis, MD: Naval Institute Press, 2011.

Zavalani, Tajar. *History of Albania*. Edited by Robert Elsie and Bejtullah Destani. London: Centre for Albanian Studies, 2015.

INDEX

homosexuality, 25–26, 67
Hoover, J. Edgar, 222
Household Cavalry, 121, 153, 280
Hoxha, Enver, 11, 16, 25, 26, 35–37, 41,
   49, 50, 54–55, 58, 75, 77, 81, 82, 91,
   93, 94, 197–100, 103, 104, 106–11,
   201–3, 214, 219, 238, 276, 284, 285,
   288, 290, 316–18n
Hoxha, Mehmet, 77, 84–86
Hudson, Bill, 22, 86–88, 116, 207
Hungary, xxix, 226
   AVO secret police in, 226–28, 234,
      235, 239–40
   Kemp in, 225, 228–29, 232–41
   Revolution in, xxix, 225–29, 232–40
Hunza, 132

Ill Met by Moonlight (Moss), 65
Illustrious, HMS, 38, 238
Imjin River, Battle of, 155
Imperial War Museums, 221, 277
Imphal, 117, 146
India, 19, 37, 68, 104, 117, 120, 123, 128,
   133, 146, 147, 230
   Brindisi, 109, 110, 114
   Calcutta, 128, 149, 151–53, 177,
      182, 184
   Delhi, 122, 130, 132
   Oman and, 244
Indian Army, 37, 101, 117, 146, 183
Indonesia, 193–94, 266–68
   War of Independence in, 194
Iran, 247, 255, 268
Iraq, 121, 122, 230, 255, 268, 280
Iraqi Army, 121
Irene, Princess of Greece, 118
Irish Republican Army (IRA), 6–7
Iron Curtain, 226, 274
Islam, *see* Muslims
Israel, 21, 259
   Jordan and, 271
   in Suez Crisis, 229–32
Istanbul, 207

Italy, 1, 2, 5, 12, 27, 47, 53, 84, 90, 99,
   109–11, 125, 203, 204, 211, 214, 231,
   273, 283
   Albania and, 10, 11, 13, 14, 16, 17, 36,
      44, 45, 47–48, 51, 53, 74, 92
   Bari, 8, 59, 89, 91, 103–4, 109, 110,
      203, 219, 285, 297, 316n, 319n
   Greece and, 214

Jack, Archie, 221, 222
James Bond franchise, xxix, 62, 124
Japan, 6, 117, 123, 148
   armistice and, 170
   atomic bombing of, 156
   China invaded by, 125, 128, 176
   Co-Prosperity Sphere proposal of,
      165, 166
   Dutch East Indies and, 193–97
   French Indochina and, 166, 167,
      169–73, 193–94
   Pearl Harbor attacked by, 38
   POW camps of, xxix, 157–62, 196,
      283–84
   prisoners from, 157
   Soviet Union and, 131
   surrender of, 133–34, 143, 156, 157,
      193–96
   Thailand occupied by, 118, 145, 146,
      150, 151, 156
Java, 194, 198
Jebel Akhdar, 247–52, 257
Jeddah, 257
Jedburgh teams, xxix, 69, 114, 175
Jenkins, George, 91, 95, 96, 101, 105
Jerusalem, 207
Jessore, 125
Jones, C. C., 91, 101
Jordan, 254–57, 259, 268, 274
   Israel and, 271
Joyce, William, 135

Karakoram Hills, 132
Kashgar, 130–35, 268